The Genres and Formulas of the Hebrew Bible: A Glossary

The Contextual Critical Commentary

The Contextual Critical Commentary (CCC) on the Bible offers students, scholars, and clergy an affordable and scholarly resource to inform the reading and interpretation of the books of the Bible. The CCC integrates contextual work that critically explores the historical, literary, and theological context of biblical books in relation to the ancient Near Eastern and Greco-Roman worlds of ancient Israel, Judah, and the early church. The historical context will provide a background for future contextual readings of these texts, their reception, and their interpretation within Judaism and Christianity. Finally, the ancient context and key turning points in reception history will inform the concerns of contemporary readings of biblical texts, suggesting ways that their past contexts can guide both scholarly readers and readers in faith communities today.

The Genres and Formulas of the Hebrew Bible: A Glossary

Volume 2: Narratives, Laws, and Other Prose Genres

TIMOTHY D. FINLAY

CASCADE *Books* • Eugene, Oregon

THE GENRES AND FORMULAS OF THE HEBREW BIBLE: A GLOSSARY
Volume 2: Narratives, Laws, and Other Prose Genres

The Contextual Critical Commentary

Cascade Books
An Imprint of Wipf and Stock Publishers
199 W. 8th Ave., Suite 3
Eugene, OR 97401

www.wipfandstock.com

PAPERBACK ISBN: 979-8-3852-4962-6
HARDCOVER ISBN: 979-8-3852-4963-3
EBOOK ISBN: 979-8-3852-4964-0

Cataloging-in-Publication data:

Names: Finlay, Timothy D., author.

Title: The genres and formulas of the Hebrew Bible : a glossary; volume 2: narratives, laws, and other prose genres / Timothy D. Finlay.

Description: Eugene, OR: Cascade Books, 2026. | The Contextual Critical Commentary. | Includes bibliographical references.

Identifiers: ISBN: 979-8-3852-4962-6 (paperback). | ISBN: 979-8-3852-4963-3 (hardcover). | ISBN: 979-8-3852-4964-0 (ebook).

Subjects: LCSH: Bible.—Old Testament—Criticism, Form.

Classification: BS1182 F56 2026 v. 2 (print). | BS1182 (epub).

Contents

Abbreviations

ABR	*Australian Biblical Review*
ACEBT	*Amsterdamse Cahiers voor Exegese en bijbelse Theologie*
AIL	Ancient Israel and its Literature
AJBA	*Australian Journal of Biblical Archaeology*
AJBI	*Annual of the Japanese Biblical Institute*
AJSL	*American Journal of Semitic Languages and Literatures*
AJSR	*Association for Jewish Studies Review*
AnBib	Analecta Biblica
ANES	*Ancient Near Eastern Studies*
AOAT	Alter Orient und Altes Testament
AUSS	*Andrews University Seminary Studies*
BA	*Biblical Archaeologist*
BARIS	British Archaeological Reports International Series
BASOR	*Bulletin for the American Schools of Oriental Research*
BBB	Bonner biblische Beiträge
BBR	*Bulletin for Biblical Research*
BEATAJ	*Beiträge zur Erforschung des Alten Testaments und des antiken Judentum*
BETL	Bibliotheca Ephemeridum Theologicarum Lovaniensium
BGBE	Beiträge zur Geschichte der biblischen Exegese
BHT	Beiträge zur historischen Theologie
Bib	*Biblica*
BibInt	*Biblical Interpretation*
BibOr	Biblica et Orientalia
BibSem	The Biblical Seminar
BJS	Brown Judaic Studies
BJSUCSD	Biblical and Judaic Studies from the University of California, San Diego

BLS	Bible and Literature Series
BMik	*Beth Mikra*
BN	*Biblische Notizen*
BR	*Biblical Research*
BSac	*Bibliotheca Sacra*
BTB	*Biblical Theological Bulletin*
BWANT	Beiträge zur Wissenschaft vom Alten und Neuen Testament
BZ	*Biblische Zeitschrift*
BZAW	Beihefte zur Zeitschrift für die alttestamentliche Wissenschaft
CahRB	Cahiers de la Revue biblique
CBQ	*Catholic Biblical Quarterly*
ConBOT	Coniectanea Biblica: Old Testament Series
CP	A designation for a cardinal compass point
CurBR	*Currents in Biblical Research*
CurBS	*Currents in Research: Biblical Studies*
DSD	*Dead Sea Discoveries*
EANEC	*Explorations in Ancient Near Eastern Civilizations*
EBib	*Etudes bibliques*
ErIsr	*Eretz-Israel*
EstBib	*Estudios bíblicos*
ETL	*Ephemerides Theologicae Lovanienses*
ETR	*Etudes théologiques et religieuses*
EvQ	*Evangelical Quarterly*
EvT	*Evangelische Theologie*
FAT	Forschungen zum Alten Testament
FOTL	Forms of the Old Testament Literature
FRLANT	Forschungen zur Religion und Literatur des Alten und Neuen Testaments
HAR	*Hebrew Annual Review*
HBT	*Horizons in Biblical Theology*
HDR	Harvard Dissertations in Religion
Hen	*Henoch*
HeyJ	*Heythrop Journal*
HS	*Hebrew Studies*
HSM	Harvard Semitic Monographs
HThKAT	Herders Theolgischer Kommtar zum Alten Testament
HTR	*Harvard Theological Review*

HTS	*HTS Theological Studies*
HUCA	*Hebrew Union College Annual*
IEJ	*Israel Exploration Journal*
Int	*Interpretation*
JAAR	*Journal of the American Academy of Religion*
JANES	*Journal of the Ancient Near Eastern Society*
JAOS	*Journal of the American Oriental Society*
JBL	*Journal of Biblical Literature*
JBQ	*Jewish Biblical Quarterly*
JETS	*Journal of the Evangelical Theological Society*
JHebS	*Journal of Hebrew Scriptures*
JLA	*Jewish Law Annual*
JNES	*Journal of Near Eastern Studies*
JNSL	*Journal of Northwest Semitic Languages*
JQR	*Jewish Quarterly Review*
JR	*Journal of Religion*
JSJ	*Journal for the Study of Judaism in the Persian, Hellenistic and Roman Periods*
JSOT	*Journal for the Study of the Old Testament*
JSOTSup	Journal for the Study of the Old Testament Supplement Series
JSPSup	Journal for the Study of the Pseuedepigrapha Supplement Series
JSS	*Journal of Semitic Studies*
JTS	*Journal of Theological Studies*
LAI	Library of Ancient Israel
LHBOTS	The Library of Hebrew Bible/Old Testament Studies
LOC	A designation for a place
N	A designation for a cardinal number
OBJ	A designation for an object
OBO	Orbis Biblicus et Orientalis
OBS	Osterreichische biblische Studien
OBT	Overtures to Biblical Theology
OLA	Orientalia Lovaniensia Analecta
ORD	A designation for an ordinal number
OTE	*Old Testament Essays*
OTL	Old Testament Library
OTS	Old Testament Studies
OtSt	*Oudtestamentische Studiën*

PN	A personal name
POS	A designation for an official position
ProEccl	*Pro Ecclesia*
RB	*Revue Biblique*
ResQ	*Restoration Quarterly*
RevExp	*Review and Expositor*
RevQ	*Revue de Qumran*
RTR	*Reformed Theological Review*
SANT	Studien zum Alten und Neuen Testaments
SBL	Society of Biblical Literature
SBLDS	Society of Biblical Literature Dissertation Series
SBLMS	Society of Biblical Literature Monograph Series
SBLSP	Society of Biblical Literature Seminar Papers
SBT	Studies in Biblical Theology
ScrHier	*Scripta Hierosolymitana*
SHANE	Studies in the History of the Ancient Near East
SJOT	*Scandinavian Journal of the Old Testament*
StBibLit	*Studies in Biblical Literature*
STDJ	Studies on the Texts of the Desert of Judah
STI	Studies in Theological Interpretation
TA	*Tel Aviv*
TGUOS	Transactions of the Glasgow University Oriental Society
ThSt	Theologische Studiën
TN	A designation for a tribe name
TynBul	*Tyndale Bulletin*
UF	*Ugarit-Forschungen*
VT	*Vetus Testamentum*
VTSup	Supplements to Vetus Testamentum
WMANT	Wissenschaftliche Monographien zum Alten und Neuen Testament
WUNT	Wissenschaftliche Untersuchen zum Neuen Testament
ZABR	*Zeitschrift für die altorientalische und biblische Rechtgeschichte*
ZAH	*Zeitschrift für Althebräistik*
ZAW	*Zeitschrift für die alttestamentliche Wissenschaft*
ZDPV	*Zeitschrift es deutschen Palästina-Vereins*
ZTK	*Zeitschrift für Theologie und Kirche*

1

Genres of Lists

INTRODUCTION

It is not surprising that most people find lists their least favorite type of biblical literature. Biblical passages largely blend the theological/ethical (the good), the informational (the true), and the aesthetic (the beautiful). Lists by their very nature aim to pack the most information into the least space at the cost of the aesthetic. Moreover—with the notable exception of **numerical wisdom lists** and other **wisdom lists** (see wisdom genres chapter) and the ten commandments (see legal genres chapter)—most biblical lists are not concerned with the overtly theological/ethical.

However, the ancient Israelites would have been far more interested than we are in **genealogies** (their ancestors), the **boundary description lists** and the **cities/towns lists** (their tribal inheritances), and the **rosters** (from the names of their legendary musicians to the exploits of their military heroes). The last book of the Hebrew Bible starts with a **table of genealogical information** or complex of lists that sets the stage for the Chronicler's theological interpretation of history (1 Chr 1–9). The New Testament begins with a list in the form of a **linear genealogy** from Abraham through David to Jesus (Matt 1:1–17). Theologians and pastors ignore lists at their peril.

Syntactically, there are three overall categories of lists. The first category is unexplained list such as "Jane, David, Ann, Fred." The only examples in the Hebrew Bible are **unexplained name lists** (1 Chr 1:1–4, 24–27) which we know from other texts (Gen 5, 11) know to be items in a descending **linear genealogy**. The second category is that of syntactically dependent lists, such as "Jane, David, Ann, and Fred went to the shop," where the list is usually a compound subject or a compound direct object. Genesis 14:1–2 lists two groups of kings warring with each other. These sorts of lists do not interrupt the narrative flow and only a sampling of them is given in this chapter, in the first glossary item in the chapter. Rather, this glossary, like most biblical scholarship, concentrates on the syntactically independent lists such as "These are the children of William: Jane, David, Ann, and Fred."

The standard form of the syntactically independent list is a list superscription, a series of records, most of which have the same format, and a list subscription. Many lists omit either a superscription or a subscription. Records can either be simple or contain a number of formulas and other elements. The publishers of modern journals usually keep name and address lists, where the standard record may consist of a name formula, a number and street formula, a city formula, and a state and zip code formula.

The specific genre of a list varies according to the content of the items listed (which is often indicated in either or both of the superscription and subscription), according to the pattern of the records, and according to the principle of categorization underlying the list (assuming that the order of the records is not random). Frequently, a list will have a standard record pattern but occasional records will either omit a formula or add a **note** or an **epithet**. Such changes are marked and call out for interpretation. Where a record consists of many one or two word items, the versification of the MT usually groups these items into sets of three, with the last set being four if necessary. This glossary ignores those groupings.

This chapter first discusses the list subscriptions and superscriptions, then the formulas that either constitute the simpler records or are the building blocks within more complicated, then the more complicated types of records, and finally the lists (and complexes of lists) themselves.

Breuer, "System of Dividing," 184–226; Scolnic, *Theme and Context*.

LIST NOT SYNTACTICALLY INDEPENDENT

There are far too many of these to include them all here. Here is a sampling of the phenomenon. One of the most important categories is the list of Canaanite nations (Gen 15:19–21; Exod 3:8, 17; 13:5; 23:23; 33:2;

34:11; Num 13:29; Deut 7:1; 20:17; Josh 3:10; 9:1; 11:3; 12:8; 24:11; Judg 3:5; 1 Kgs 9:20 [=2 Chr 8:7]; Ezra 9:1; Neh 9:8). There are lists of items in a gift (Gen 32:15; 1 Kgs 10:25; 2 Chr 9:24; Ezra 1:6, 10). There are fauna lists (Exod 9:3; Ps 8:8–9 [NRSV 7–8]; Zech 14:15; Ezra 2:66; Ezek 39:18). There are mineral lists (Ezek 27:12; 28:13; Dan 2:35, 45; 1 Chr 22:16; 2 Chr 2:13). There are agricultural/farming products (Deut 28:51; 32:13–14; 33:13–16; 1 Kgs 5:2–3; Neh 5:11). There are marginalized groups (Deut 24:19, 20, 21; 26:12; 27:19; Jer 7:6; 22:3). There are musical instruments (Isa 5:12; Dan 3:5, 7, 10, 15). There are terms of horror (Jer 24:9; 25:18; 29:18; 44:12; 49:13; related to this is a potential sword, famine, and pestilence formula in Jer 21:7; 24:10; 29:17, 18; 34:17; 38:2; 42:17, 22; 44:13; Ezek 6:11). There are lists within the **hymnic fragments** and related genres in the prophets (Isa 44:24–28; 61:1–3; Jer 10:12–13; Amos 5:8–9; similar lists of divine activities could be produced in the Psalms). And there are many, many more of these.

LIST SUPERSCRIPTIONS AND SUBSCRIPTIONS

Expansion of Subscription

This is a clause or series of clauses which expand the list subscription. Expansions occur after the following categories: **boundary list** (Num 34:13–15; Ezek 47:22–23); **census summary list** (Num 1:45–46; 26:44–45), **exit list** (Ezek 48:35b), **festival calendar list** (Deut 16:16b-17), **gift/ offering list** (Num 7:84–88a), **inventory** (Ezra (1:11b), **muster roll** (1 Chr 12:40–41 [NRSV 39–40]) and **segmented genealogy** (Gen 36:30b; 46:27). Some expansions just give additional information concerning the immediately preceding list, but others connect the individual lists to their larger settings.

Expansion of Superscription

Expansions of superscriptions frequently occur in relation to **rosters**. The pattern is that the expansion of the superscription notifies the reader of the nature of the position, and the superscription itself is a fairly standard one for any **name list**. Examples include "A man from each tribe shall be with you, each man the head of his ancestral house" (Num 1:4), "Solomon had twelve officials over all Israel who provided food for the king and his household; each one had to make provision for one month in the year" (1 Kgs 4:7), "These are the men whom David put in charge of the service of song in the house of the Lord, after the ark came to rest there. They ministered with song before the tabernacle of the tent of meeting, until Solomon had built the house of the Lord in Jerusalem; and they performed their service in due order" (1 Chr 6:16–17 [NRSV 31–32]), and "Now these are the chiefs of David's warriors, who gave him strong support in his kingdom, together with all Israel, to make him king, according to the word of the Lord concerning Israel" (1 Chr 11:10).

There are also expansions of superscriptions to the following genres: **census list** (Ezra 2:1b-2 [= Neh 7:6b-7]), **itinerary** (Num 33:2), and **linear genealogy** (Gen 5:1b-2).

Introduction to List

There are some lists which have an explanation preceding them but not in the syntactic form of a superscription. There are introductions to the **rosters** of David warriors (2 Sam 8:15 [=1 Chr 18:14]; 23:8a), of Solomon's high officials (1 Kgs 4:1) and monthly provision administrators (1 Kgs 4:7).

Various **segmented genealogies** are introduced through mentioning the ancestor's wife or wives (Gen 4:19; 22:20b; 25:1; 36:2–3; 1 Chr 8:29), a standard way of beginning a **birth report**. Other narrative introductions precede a **muster roll** (Num 3:16), a **census list** (Num 10:11–12), and **participants lists** (Neh 12:31a; 1 Chr 8:29).

List Subscription

List subscriptions occur after the list proper and are far more frequent than other type of subscriptions, although not as frequent as list superscriptions. They tend to repeat the information in the superscription, where there is one. For supplements to superscriptions and subscriptions, see **expansion of superscription** and **expansion to subscription** respectively.

Subscriptions occur after **boundary lists** (Num 34:12; Josh 13:23, 28, 32; 18:20b; 19:8b, 16, 23, 31, 39, 48; Ezek 47:21), **census summary lists** (Num 1:44; 26:63; Ezra 2:64–65 [=Neh 7:66–67]), **cities/towns lists** (Josh 21:41–42), **clean/unclean animal lists** (Lev 11:8; Deut 14:8b),

exits lists (Ezek 48:35a), **festival calendar lists** (Exod 23:17; 34:23; Deut 16:16a; Lev 23:44; Num 29:39), **gift/offering lists** (Num 7:88b; 29:39), **inventories** (1 Kgs 7:51a [=2 Chr 5:1a]; Ezra 1:11b), **king lists** (Josh 24:12b), **linear genealogies** (1 Chr 4:2b; 5:41 [NRSV 6:15]), **muster rolls** (Num 3:39, 42–43; 1 Chr 4:38; 5:14, 24c; 7:5, 40; 8:40; 12:38; 2 Chr 17:19), **ordering of camp** (Num 2:32; 10:28), participant list (Neh 12:26; 1 Chr 9:34), **rosters** (2 Sam 23:39b), **rotas** (1 Chr 24:19), **segmented genealogies** (Gen 25:4b; 35:26b; 36:5b, 29b–30a; Exod 6:25b; 1 Chr 1:33b; 2:33b; 7:13c), **son lists** (Gen 25:16; Exod 1:5a; Num 3:3), **tables of directives** (Lev 11:46–47), **tables of genealogical information** (1 Chr 1:9a), and **tribal appointee lists** (Num 1:16; 4:16a).

The subscription found after the second allotment half-list in Ezekiel seems to apply to the whole list, "This is the land that you shall allot as an inheritance among the tribes of Israel, and these are their portions, says the Lord God" (Ezek 48:29).

List Superscription

List superscriptions perform an analogous role to the following list proper as does the **superscription to a psalm** to the following main psalm. They typically describe the nature of the items that follow (sons, names, places, descendants) and frequently add various types of information concerning them. Some list superscriptions are followed by an expansion of superscription.

Superscriptions are found to **allotment half-lists** (Ezek 48:1a, 23a), **blessing/curse lists** (Deut 28:2, 15), **boundary lists** (Num 34:2; Josh 13:15, 24, 29; 18:11; 19:1, 10, 17, 24, 32, 40; Ezek 47:13), **census summary lists** (Num 1:19b; 26:4; Ezra 2:2b; [=Neh 7:7b], **cities/towns lists** (Num 32:33; Josh 21:8; 1 Chr 6:39a [NRSV 54a], **clean/unclean animal** lists (Lev 11:2, 4a, 13, 22a; 14:4a, 7a, 12a), **daughter lists** (Num 26:33b; 27:1b; Josh 17:3; 1 Sam 14:49b), **exit lists** (Ezek 48:30a), **festival calendar lists** (Exod 23:14; 23:2, 4; 29:12), **gentilics lists** (Jer 25:17), **gift/offering lists** (Exod 25:3; 35:5; Num 7:10; 29:12), **inventories** (Num 31:32; 1 Kgs 7:48 [=2 Chr 4:19a]; Ezra 1:9; 2 Chr 4:11), **items to make list** (Exod 28:4; 31:6; 35:10), itineraries (Num 33:1), king lists (Gen 36:31; Josh 12:7–8; 1 Chr 1:43), **linear genealogies** (Gen 25:1; 1 Chr 3:10a; 5:4a; 6:5a, 7a, 10a, 14a, 35a [NRSV 20a, 22a, 25a, 29a, 50a]; see also **toledot formula** which sometimes acts as a superscription to a genealogy), **muster rolls**

(Num 3:34–36; 1 Chr 5:7a, 13a, 24a; 12:23; 2 Chr 7:14a), **name lists** (Neh 10:1 [Check; this seems to be dependent list]; 11:3; 12:1), **orderings of camp** (Num 2:2; 10:12–13), **participant lists** (Neh 12:26; 1 Chr 9:34), **rosters** (2 Sam 23:8; 1 Kgs 4:1–2a, 7–8; 1 Chr 6:18 [NRSV 33]; 11:11; 12:1–2, 8; 15:4, 16; 25:1b; 26:1a, 29a; 27:16a), rotas (1 Chr 24:6; 25:8; 27:1), **segmented genealogies** (Gen 35:22b; 36:20a; 46:8a; Exod 6:16a; see also **birth report introduction** and **son list as superscription**), son lists (too numerous to mention and mainly of the form "[and] the sons of PN"; many of these occur as **son lists as a record in a genealogy**; some extended superscriptions include Gen 25:13a; 35:22b; Exod 1:1; Num 3:2a), **tribal appointee lists** (Num 1:4–5a; 13:4a), and **tribal ritual lists** (Deut 27:12b, 13a). Other examples of this superscription occur in Num 3:1; Ruth 4:18; 1 Chr 1:29; 5:7.

FORMULAS ASSOCIATED WITH LISTS

Age at Death Formula

This formula, "And all the days of PN were X + Y, and he died," where X represents the number in the **age at fatherhood formula** and Y represents the number in the **years after fatherhood formula** is found as the last part of a standard **genealogical record** in Gen 5 but is omitted in Gen 11. Genesis 5:23 contains a shortened form of the formula (missing the "and he died" part) which concerns Enoch who walked with God and who "was no more, because God took him" (Gen 5:24).

Age at Fatherhood Formula

This formula, "When PN1 had lived X years, he begat PN2" (Gen 5:3, 6, 9, 12, 15, 18, 21, 25, 28; 11:10b, 12, 14, 16, 18, 20, 22, 24), occurs as the first part of the **genealogical records** in Gen 5:3–31; 11:10b–25. Variations of the formula where three sons are begotten to Noah (Gen 5:32) and Terah (Gen 10:26) in a shortened final record anticipate the narratives following them. The age at fatherhood formula is a modification of the **begat formula** which enables a linear genealogy to contain more complexity than normal.

Animal and Kind Formula

This formula consists of the direct object marker, the name of the animal and "its kind." It is the standard record in the list of animals in Lev 11:22.

Animal Formula

This formula consists of just the direct object marker and the name of the animal. It is the basic record in the **clean/unclean animal lists**.

Boundary Description Unit

These, together with the **cardinal direction introduction unit** and the **cardinal direction conclusion unit**, are the standard building blocks of the **cardinal direction records** found in the **boundary lists** of Num 34 and Ezek 47. These typically have the form "From LOC1 to LOC2" but either or both of the terms could be expanded by descriptive phrases (Num 34:3b, 4a, 4b, 4c, 5a, 5b, 7b, 8a, 8b, 9a, 11a, 11b, 12a; Josh 15:1b–4a, 5b, 6–11, 12b; Ezek 47:15c, 16a, 16b, 17a, 18b, 19b, 20b).

Begat Formula

This formula typically takes the form PN1 begat PN2. It is found either as the basic record, or as one of several possible basic records, in numerous genealogical lists.

Cardinal Direction Conclusion Formula

"This shall be your CP boundary/side" (Num 34:6b, 9b; Ezek 47:17c, 18c, 19c, 20c). This is the last unit in two of the **cardinal direction records** in Num 34, and of all four in Ezek 47. They are not strictly necessary, as is illustrated by their absence in the other two records, and they therefore reinforce the notion that the extent of the land originally promised by YHWH and that of future Israel is precisely defined. Judah is the only tribe whose **boundary list** includes cardinal direction records, and only the first of these has the cardinal direction conclusion formula: "This shall be your south boundary" (Josh 15:4b) See also **cardinal direction introduction formula**.

Cardinal Direction Introduction Formula

This is the first unit in a **cardinal direction record** and delineates the direction (north, south, east, or west) that the following **boundary description units** apply to. Numbers 34:3a reads, "Your south sector shall extend from the Wilderness of Zin along the side of Edom." Other examples include Num 34:6a, 7a, 10, which bring an orderliness to the **boundary list** of the promised land as a whole that is lacking in the somewhat messier lists of the individual tribal boundaries in Joshua. Judah is the only tribe in Joshua's numerous boundary lists where this formula appears (Josh 15:1a, 5a, 5c, 12a). Judah's uniqueness may be the work of a redactor, or it may represent the interest of the original author if Joshua was composed in the Kingdom of Judah.

Ezekiel's vision of the future boundaries of Israel, however, does include these units in the form "On the north/east/south/west side" (Ezek 47:15b, 18a, 19a, 19b, 19c). See also **cardinal direction conclusion formula**.

Clean Animal Categorization Formula

This formula "Any animal that has attributes X and Y you may eat" (Lev 11:3 [=Deut 14:6]; Lev 11:9; Deut 14:9) provides a criterion for whether an animal is clean or unclean for food. See **clean/unclean animal list** and **table of directives**.

Clean/Unclean Animal Record

This is a general term for a record in a **clean/unclean animal list**. It may consist of the animal and kind formula, or the simple animal formula.

City and Pasture Lands Formula

This formula has the form "CITY with its pasture lands" and occurs in the **cities/towns list** concerning the Levitical inheritances in Josh 21:1–8 and 1 Chr 6:39–66 [NRSV 54–81]. It shows that the Levites were not merely given cities but surrounding agricultural areas to support those cities.

City Formula

The standard record in a **cities list** is simply the name of the city. A common variants is the **city and pasture lands formula**. Syntactically dependent cities lists can become **tribal cities list records** within larger **boundary lists.**

Company of Tribe Formula

This formula, "Over the company of TN was PN1, son of PN2," is found in the **ordering of camp list** in Num 10 and designates the tribes and commanders associated with the standard mentioned in the **standard of camp formula.**

Descendants and Number Formula

This formula, "Sons of PN: N" is the standard record in the **census summary lists** from Ezra 2:3–42, 60 and its parallel in Neh 7:8–45, 62. It shows the number of people descended from an ancestor that returned with Zerubbabel to Judah. See also **people of location and number formula.**

Edomite Succession Formula

The formula "PN1 died and PN2 son of PN3 reigned in his stead" is the most frequent record (Gen 36:33, 34, 35, 36, 37, 38, 39a) in the Edomite **king list**.

From Place to Place Formula

The formula "From LOC1 to LOC2" (Num 21:18b, 19a, 19b, 20) is an alternative to the **set out and camped formula** as a record in an itinerary.

His Son Formula

"PN his son" occurs as a record in a **linear genealogy** that typically has the **son-list superscription** at its head in 1 Chr 3:10b–14

Item and Number Formula

The formula "Item, Number" occurs seven times (Ezra 1:9b–11a) in an **inventory**.

Leader, Patronym and Number Formula

The formula "From the descendants of PN1: PN2 son of PN3 and with him N," occurs in the census summary list (Ezra 8:1–14b) of those who accompanied Ezra in the return from Babylonia.

Name and Building Activity Formula

This formula, "(Next to them), PN built/rebuilt X," where X refers to a part of a city, is standard in the **participants list** of those who rebuilt Jerusalem (Neh 3:1–32). These records would have been a source of pride for any descendants of these workers.

Name and Epithet Record

This is a catch-all term for an expansion of the **name formula**, of which the most common subtypes are **name and father of formula**, **name and gentilic formula**, **name and office formula**, **name and rank formula**, **patronymic formula** and **rank, name and mother formula** but other idiosyncratic epithets exist.

Name and Father Of Formula

This formula, "PN1 father of PN2," is found in the **birth report list** of Maacah (1 Chr 2:49a, 49b), the **son list** of Hur (1 Chr 2:50c, 51a, 51b), and occurs on its own as either the subject or object of a **begat formula**.

Name and Gentilic Formula

The formula "PN the Xite," such as "Helez the Peltite" is an expansion of the **name formula** and is particularly frequent in **rosters** of David's warriors.

Name and Office Formula

This formula, "And PN had POS," is the standard record in the **rosters** in 2 Sam 8:16–18; 20:23–26; and 1 Chr 18:15–17, all of these being lists of David's officers.

Name and Rank Formula

This has the pattern "And PN ORD" and is an extension of the **name formula**. This formula is frequently found in **son lists**. It is also found in **begat lists** (1 Chr 2:13a, 13b, 13c, 14a, 14b, 15a, 15b,). The son list of Josiah (1 Chr 3:15) consists of four such records.

Name Formula

The simple formula "PN" is the standard record in a **name list** (of which the most common type is the **son list**), or in the direct object of a **begat list**. For expansions of this formula, see **name and epithet record**.

Patronymic Formula

The formula "PN, son of PN" is a frequent variant of the **name formula** and is also the first record in a **pedigree**.

People of Location and Number Formula

This formula has two variations that seem to be interchangeable, "Men of LOC N" and "Sons of LOC N." It occurs as the standard record in the second macro-record of the **census summary lists** in Ezra-Nehemiah (Ezra 2:20–35 [=Neh 7:25–38]) and shows how many people of a particular ancestral location returned with Zerubbabel to Judah. See also **descendants and number formula**.

Rank, Name and Mother Formula

"The second, Daniel, by Abigail the Carmelitess." This is the standard record in the **son lists** in 2 Sam 3:2–5 and 1 Chr 3:1–4.

Regimental Encampment Formula

This formula, "The regimental encampment of TN by companies shall be to the CP" (Num 2:3a, 10a, 18a, 25a) is the initial record of an **ordering of camp macro-record**.

Rota of Musicians Formula

The formula "ORD to PN, his sons and his brothers, twelve" in 1 Chr 25:9–31 designates which group of musicians was assigned to each of the twenty-four orders of the priesthood in the **rota**.

Set Out and Camped Formula

This formula, "They set out from LOC1 and camped at LOC2," is the standard record in the **itinerary** of Num 21:10–31 with the **from place to place formula** also occuring. See also **note in itinerary**.

Davies, "Wilderness Itinerary," 46–81; Scolnic, *Theme and Context*, 81–85.

Set Out Order Formula

This formula "They shall set out ORD" (Num 2:9b, 16b, 24b, 31b) is the last element in an **ordering of camp macro-record**.

Slain King Formula

The formula "the king of PN one" is the record for all thirty-one slain Canaanite kings in the **king list** of Josh 12:7–24, followed by the **tally formula** of thirty-one.

Standard of Camp Formula

The **ordering of camp list** in Num 10 discusses the order of four groups of three tribes. This formula, "The standard of the camp of TN set out, company by company" (Num 10:14a, 18a, 22a, 25a), signals which tribe carries the standard for each group. See also **company of tribe formula**.

Tally of Regiment Formula

This formula, "The total enrollment of the camp of TN, by companies is N" (Num 2:9a, 16a, 24a, 31a) gives the tally for the four regional encampments each guarding one direction of the camp in the **ordering of camp macro-records.**

Tribal Leader and Enrollment Formula

This formula, "The leader of TN shall be PN, son of PN2, with a company enrolled of NUMB" (Num 2:3b–4, 5b–6, 7b–8, 10b–11, 12b–13, 14b–15, 18b–19, 20b–21, 22b–23, 25b–26a, 27b–28a, 29b–30a), occurs for each tribe and thus occurs thrice in each **ordering of camp macro-record.**

Tribe and Appointee Formula

This formula, "For the tribe of TN, PN1 son of PN2," is the standard record in the **tribal appointee list.** It occurs in both directives lists concerning who was commanded to assist Moses (Num 1:5b, 6, 7, 8, 9, 10a, 10b, 11, 12, 13, 14, 15) and who would apportion the land (west of the Jordan) for inheritance (Num 34:19b, 20, 21, 22, 23, 24, 25, 26, 27, 28) and in assertives list concerning the scouts sent to explore the promised land (Num 13:4, 5, 6, 7, 8, 9, 10, 11, 12, 13, 14, 15) and the list of Davidic officials (1 Chr 27:16b, 16c; 17a, 17b, 18a, 18b, 19a, 19b, 20a, 21b, 22a).

Tribe Camping Next Formula

This formula, "Camping next to him is TN" (Num 2:5a 7a, 12a, 14a, 18a, 20a, 22a, 27a, 29a), is associated with the two supporting tribes in each regimental encampment and thus occurs twice in each **ordering of camp macro-record.**

Tribe Conclusion and Tally Formula

This formula, "These are the clans of TN: N enrolled" (Num 26:14, 18, 22, 25, 27, 34, 37a, 41, 42c-43, 47, 50) is the typical conclusion to a **census in Num 26 record.** It is missing from the record pertaining to Reuben and there are two such formulas (one pertaining to Manasseh and the other pertaining to Ephraim) in the record concerning Joseph.

Tribe Introduction Formula

This formula begins a **census in Num 26 record**. It has the form "[These are] the descendants of TN by their clans" (Num 26:5a, 12a, 15a, 19a, 23a, 26a, 28a, 38a, 42a, 44a, 48a).

Unclean Food Formula

This formula, "ANIM, though it has attribute X does not have attribute Y; it is unclean for you" (Lev 11:4b, 5, 6; Deut 14:7, 8) occurs in two of the **clean/unclean food lists**. The interchangeable attributes X and Y refer to having cloven hooves and chewing the cud. A variant of the formula concerning sea creatures, "whatever does not have fins and scales is unclean/destable" is found in Lev 11:10–11a and Deut 14:10. See **table of directives**.

Wife's Descendants and Number Formula

"These are the descendants of PN who were born to Jacob, N in all." This formula (Gen 46:15, 18, 22, 25) follows a collection of sons lists all of whom were descended from one of Jacob's wives or concubines and marks the end of a **genealogical macro-record**.

Years after Fatherhood Formula

This formula, "And PN lived after the birth of PN Y years, and he begat other sons and daughters" (Gen 5: 4, 7, 10, 13, 16, 19, 26, 30; 11:11, 13, 15, 17, 19, 21, 23, 25) shows that the ancestor had other sons and daughters in addition to the son mentioned in the **age at fatherhood formula**. A variation of the formula stresses Enoch's special relationship with God: "Enoch walked with God after the birth of Methuselah three hundred years, and he begat other sons and daughters" (Gen 5:22). In the Gen 5 genealogy but not in the Gen 11 genealogy, the years after fatherhood formula is followed by an **age at death formula**.

GENRES OF RECORDS WITHIN LISTS

Allotment Half-List

This is a term used for the two portions of a list of allotments for the Israelite tribes separated by a **list interruption** discussing the portions set aside for certain other groups. This phenomenon occurs in the **boundary and allotments macro-list** in Ezek 47:13—48:29. Both half-lists contain **list superscriptions** and the second one contains a **list subscription** which applies to the entire list of allotments. The **adjoining the territory formula** dominates both half-lists. The first half-list pertains to the allotments of Dan, Asher, Naphtali, Manasseh, Ephraim, Reuben, and Judah, respectively (Ezek 48:1–7) and the second half-list pertains to the territory of Benjamin, Simeon, Issachar, Zebulun, and Gad, respectively (Ezek 48:23–27), followed by a description of the border south of Gad (Ezek 48:28). The two half-lists present a scheme arranging the tribes from north to south in equal latitudinal strips, the distance from north to south being a little over eight miles. Each tribe is depicted as having the same portion of land (Ezek 48:14), and the teleological cause is to create hope for a fair division of Israelite territory in a future age.

Begat List as Genealogical Record

A begat list is a syntactically dependent list that has the form PN1 begat PN2 and PN3 etc. The **linear genealogy** of Adam (Gen 5:1–31) is followed by a begat list of Noah's sons (Gen 5:32). Likewise, the **linear genealogy** of Shem (Gen 11:10–25) is followed by a begat list of Terah's sons (Gen 11:26). After the toledot **formula** concerning Terah (Gen 11:27a) comes another begat list of Terah's sons (Gen 11:27b).

In the **segmented genealogy** of Abraham's descendants by Keturah (Gen 25:1–4), there is a begat list of Jokshan's sons (Gen 25:3). In the **segmented genealogy** of Noah's sons, there are begat lists concerning Cush (1 Chr 1:10a), Egypt (1 Chr 1:11–12), Canaan (1 Chr 1:13–16), and Joktan (1 Chr 1:20–23). In the **table of genealogical information** spanning over seven chapters of First Chronicles, there are begat lists concerning Jesse (1 Chr 2:13–15), Koz (1 Chr 4:18), Heber (1 Chr 7:32), Heglam (1 Chr 8:7), Shaharaim by Hodesh (1 Chr 8:9–10), Shaharaim by Hushim (1 Chr 8:11), Ner (1 Chr 8:33), Jehoaddah (1 Chr 8:36), Ner (1 Chr 9:39), and Jarah (1 Chr 9:42).

Birth Notice

See **birth notice in a genealogy** in chapter on narrative genres.

Blessing/Curse List Record

The list of blessings in Deut 28:3–6 and of curses in Deut 28:16–19 contain the following four records: blessing/curse in the city and field; blessing/curse of fruit of womb, ground, livestock; blessing/curse of basket and kneading bowl; blessing/curse of coming in and going out. The list in Deut 28:16–19 reverses the order of the second and third records.

Boundary Description Record

The **boundary lists** in Joshua, with the notable exception of that pertaining to the tribe of Judah (Josh 15:1–12), do not have the stylized **cardinal direction records** but instead contain **tribal cities records** and boundary description records that vary considerably in form and are often intermingled with **notes**. There are three boundary description records pertaining to Reuben's territory (Josh 13:16–17a, 23a, 23b), two pertaining to Gad's territory (Josh 13:25–26, 27b), one concerning Manasseh's Trans-Jordan territory (Josh 13:30), two concerning Manasseh's Cis-Jordan territory (Josh 17:7, 9), one large record pertaining to Benjamin's territory (Josh 18:12–20a), two pertaining to Asher's territory (Josh 19:26b–27, 29), and one pertaining to Naphtali (Josh 19:32–34).

Cardinal Direction Record

The **boundary list** in which Moses tells the Israelites the boundaries of the promised land consists of four records describing the southern, western, northern and eastern boundaries (Num 34:3–5, 6, 7–9, 10–12a). The standard pattern is a **cardinal direction introduction unit**, a series of **boundary description units**, and a **cardinal direction conclusion formula** (omitted in two cases each of the lists in Num 34 and Josh 15).

The list pertaining to Judah's territory also contains four cardinal direction records (Josh 15:1–4, 5a, 5b–11, 12a). The other **boundary lists** in Joshua of the individual tribes do not employ cardinal direction records but they reappear in Ezekiel's description of the future boundaries of Israel (Ezek 47:15b–17, 18, 19, 20).

Census Record in Ezra/Nehemiah

The form of the basic record is "sons of PN NUMBER." Several of these records are grouped together and preceded by a "number of CATEGORY" formula to form a mini-census-list. These mini-census-lists are the records in the census list as a whole.

Census Summary Record

In Num 1, the record has the format: "The sons of PN, their lineage, in their clans, by their ancestral houses, according to the number of the names, individually, every male from twenty years old and upward, everyone able to go to war: those enrolled of the tribe of PN were NUMBER" and there are records concerning Reuben (Num 1:20–21), Simeon (Num 1:22–23), Gad (Num 1:24–25), Judah (Num 1:26–27), Issachar (Num 1:28–29), Zebulun (Num 1:30–31), Ephraim (Num 1:32–33), Manasseh (Num 1:34–35), Benjamin (Num 1:36–37), Dan (Num 1:38–39), Asher (Num 1:40–41), and Naphtali (Num 1:42–43).

In Num 26, the records are more complicated. The standard record is introduced by a clause mentioning the tribe, followed by various clauses of the format, "For PN the clan of the PNites" followed by a clause giving the number of those enrolled in the clans of that tribe. The records concerning Reuben and Judah also contain **notes**. There are census records pertaining to Reuben (Num 26:5–7), Simeon (Num 26:12–14), Gad (Num 26:15–18), Judah (Num 26:20–22), Issachar (Num 26:23–25), Zebulun (Num 26:26–27), Joseph (Num 26:28–37), Benjamin (Num 26:38–41), Dan (Num 26:42–43), Asher (Num 26:44–47), and Naphtali (Num 26:48–50).

Exit Record in Ezekiel 48

This record is formulaic: "On the CP side, MEASUREMENT, three gates, the gate of PN1 one, the gate of PN2 one, the gate of PN3 one" (Ezek 48:30b–31, 32, 33, 34). The north side contains the gates of Rueben, Judah, and Levi. The east side contains the gates of Joseph, Benjamin, and

Dan. The south side contains the gates of Simeon, Issachar, and Zebulun. The west side contains the gates of Gad, Asher, and Naphtali.

Gatekeeper List Record

The list of gatekeepers in 1 Chr 9:17–18 consists of a one-word superscription and four **name formula** records (1 Chr 9:17a), a **note** (1 Chr 9:17b), and a **gatekeeper list subscription** (1 Chr 9:18b). The entire list is a record in the **roster** of gatekeepers (1 Chr 9:17–26).

Genealogical Record

The standard record in a **linear genealogy** is the simple **begat formula**. However, in Gen 5, the typical record contains an **age at fatherhood formula**, a **years after fatherhood formula** and an **age at death formula**. The records concern Adam (Gen 5:3–5), Seth (Gen 5:6–8), Enosh (Gen 5:9–11), Kenan (Gen 5:12–14), Mahalalel (Gen 5:15–17), Jared (Gen 5:18–20), Enoch (Gen 5:21–24), Methuselah (Gen 5:25–27), and Lamech (Gen 5:28–31), and the records concerning Enoch and Lamech also contain important **notes** about Enoch and Noah, respectively. A shorter but similar patter of record occurs in Gen 11, where the standard record contains an **age at fatherhood formula** and a **years after fatherhood formula**. The records concern Shem (Gen 11:10b–11), Arpachsad (Gen 11:12–13), Shelah (Gen 11:14–15), Eber (Gen 11:16–17), Peleg (Gen 11:18–19), Reu (Gen 11:20–21), Serug (Gen 11:22–23), and Nahor (Gen 11:24–25).

Frequent records in **segmented genealogies** include the **begat formula**, the **begat list as genealogical record, birth reports** and **son lists**. Genesis 46:8–27 organizes the genealogy of Jacob's sons into four collections of **sons lists**, each followed by the **wife's descendants and number formula** (Gen 46:8b–15, 16–18, 19–22, 23–25).

Gentilics Record

There is no standard pattern for records in gentilics lists. In 1 Chr 2, we see clans/families listed from Kiriath-Jearim with a **list subscription** noting that from these descended the Zorathites, and Eshtaolites (1 Chr 2:53) and clans/families listed from the scribes at Jabez with a **subscription** noting that these are the Kenites who came from Hammath (1 Chr 2:55). In Jeremiah 25:18–26a, the records include Jerusalem and surrounding area (Jer 25:18), Pharaoh and his people (Jer 25:19), the "mixed people," the kings of Uz, and the Philistines (Jer 25:20), Edom, Moab, and Ammon (Jer 25:21), Tyre, Sidon, and the coastlands (Jer 25:22), Dedan, Tema, Buz, and all who have shaven temples (Jer 25:23), the kings of Arabia and desert dwellers (Jer 25:24), the kings of Zimri, Elam, and Media (Jer 25:25), and all the kings of the world (Jer 25:26a). Obadiah 19–21 does employ a standard pattern of "Those of PLACE1 shall possess PLACE2."

Hero and Exploit Record

In rosters containing a list of mighty men, some records consist of just the name but others consist of the rank and name of the hero and an exploit by the hero. There are such records regarding Josheb-basshebeth (2 Sam 23:8b [=1 Chr 11:11b]), Eleazar (2 Sam 23:9–10 [=1 Chr 11:12–14]), Shammah (2 Sam 23:11–12), these three as a group (2 Sam 23:13–17 [= 1 Chr 11:15–19]), Abishai (2 Sam 23:18–19 [=1 Chr 11:20–21]), and Benaiah (2 Sam 3:20–23 [=1 Chr 11:22–25]). See **heroic/martial exploit narrative.**

Begg, "Exploits," 139–69; Garsiel, "David's Elite," 1–28.

Job Description Record

This is a record in a **roster** that does not mention the name of the official appointed the task but simply the task itself. Examples include the Levites' duties at the tabernacle (1 Chr 6:33 [NRSV 48]), the Aaronides' duties at the most holy place (1 Chr 6:34 [NRSV 49]); the duties of the gatekeepers (1 Chr 9:23, 24–25, 26–27, 28, 29, 30, 32, 33); and the responsibilities of various Levitical groups to work in the temple, be officers and judges, gatekeepers, and musicians (1 Chr 23:4–5). There is also a speech of David that prescribes the job of the Levites (1 Chr 23:25–32).

Lot Casting Record

Instead of assigning all officers specific responsibilities, sometimes the leader had the officers cast lots for them. The corresponding rosters would have records noting this procedure rather than the **name and**

office formula, say, or the **name/pedigree and task record**. Lot casting records occur in 1 Chr 24:31; 26:13, 14a, 14b, and 15.

Name List as Record

In addition to those discussed in the entry on **son list as record**, **name lists** form **participant group records** in the **participant lists** in Neh 12:1–9, 12–26, 31–43.

Name/Pedigree and Task Record

This is an expanded form of the **name and office formula** and is typically found in **rosters**. It consists of the **name formula**, **patronymic formula**, or **pedigree** of an official and the task assigned to him or the designation of a group and the task assigned to the group (1 Chr 9:19, 20, 21).

Note

Many of the records in various categories of lists have an additional explanatory clause that does not correspond to the standard formula. These can be explanatory, provide additional information on a person or a place, or make connections to other known characters. They are too numerous to list here, but consult the entries on the individual genres of lists—they delineate certain notes that appear in the particular lists. These short notes can repay close study. A note concerning the prayer of Jabez led to a best selling book. See **note in itinerary**.

Note in Itinerary

This typically occurs after the **set out and camped formula** and gives information about the campsite: Ihe-abarim borders Moab toward the sunrise (Num 21:11b), the Arnon is the boundary between Moab and the Amorites (Num 21:13b) and is the subject of an entry in the Book of the Wars of the Lord (Num 21:14–15), Beer is the well that gave rise to an Israelite song (Num 21:16b–18a), Etham is on the edge of the wilderness (Num 33:6b), Rephidim had no water (Num 33:14b), the wilderness of Zin is identified as Kadesh (Num 33:36b), Mount Hor is on the edge of

Edomite territory (Num 33:37b), Iye-abarim is noted to be in Moabite territory (Num 33:44b), Abarim is before Nebo, the camp in the plains of Moab is further described as by the Jordan at Jericho from Beth-jeshimoth as far as Abel-shittim (Num 33:48b–49). After the record camping at Mount Hor, there is an extended note concerning Aaron's death and about the king of Arad hearing about the coming of the Israelties (Num 33:38–40).

On three occasions there is a note between the "set out" clause and the "camped at" clause of the **set out and camped formula**. After setting out from Etham, the Israelites turn back to Pi-hahiroth, which faces Baal-zephon (Num 33:7b); another intermediary note involves the Israelites passing through the sea and going on a three day's journey in the wilderness of Etham (Num 33:8b); and a third one mentions there being twelve springs of water and seventy palm trees at Elim (Num 33:9b), perhaps symbolizing the twelve tribes of Israel and the seventy nations of the world.

Offering Record

The assertive list of offerings made by the tribal chiefs in Num 7 is highly stylized, with twelve records following this precise format: "And on the kth day, PN1 son of PN2, prince of PN3, brought one silver plate, whose weight was a hundred and thirty shekels, according to the shekel of the sanctuary, both of them full of fine flour mixed with oil for a cereal offering; one golden dish of ten shekels, full of incense; one young bull, one ram, one male lamb a year old, for a burnt offering; one male goat for a sin offering; and for the sacrifice of peace offerings, two oxen, five rams,five male goats, and five male lambs a year old. This was the offering of PN1, son of PN2." There is a similarly detailed directive list of offerings to be made on the first seven days of the Feast of Tabernacles, but it is discussed in **quality of item offered** in the chapter of legal genres.

Ordering of Camp Macro-Record

This genre in the **order of camp list** in Num 2 consists of a **regimental encampment formula**, a **tribal leader and enrollment formula**, a **tribe camping next formula**, a **tribal leader and enrollment formula**, a **tribe camping next formula**, a **tribal leader and enrollment formula**, a **tally**

of regiment formula, and a **set out order formula** (Num 2:3–9, 10–16, 18–24, 25–31).

Participant Group Record

This is a subcategory of **name list as record** that occurs in a **participants list**. The lists of two groups of returnees from exile (Neh 12:1–9, 12–26) include participant group records concerning priests (Neh 12:1b–7, 12–21) and Levites (Neh 12:8–9, 22–25). The participant list pertaining to the dedication ceremony led by Nehemiah contains participant group records of those who went right (Neh 12:36b–37) and those who went left (Neh 12:40b–42). The list of post-exilic leaders contains participant group records concerning the people of Judah (1 Chr 9:4–6), people of Benjamin (1 Chr 9:7–9), priests (1 Chr 9:10–13), Levites (1 Chr 9:14–16), and gatekeepers (1 Chr 9:17–21).

Roster of Celebrants/Musicians Record

The **roster** of ark procession celebrants (1 Chr 15:16–24) consists of a **job description record** doubling as a superscription (1 Chr 15:16) and nine records which designate a list of persons and their role (1 Chr 15:17, 18, 19, 20, 21, 22, 23, 24a, 24b). The **name and patronym formula** occurs three times for the singers of the first order (1 Chr 15:17), and the **name formula** is used thirteen times for those of the second order (1 Chr 15:18). The instruments involved are bronze cymbals (1 Chr 15:19), harps (1 Chr 15:20), lyres (1 Chr 15:21), and trumpets (1 Chr 15:24a), with the director of music and gatekeepers discussed in the other records (1 Chr 15:22, 23, 24b). Similarly the **roster** of musicians in 1 Chr 25:1–6 contains records pertaining to Asaph (1 Chr 25:2), Jeduthun (1 Chr 25:3), and Heman (1 Chr 25:4–6a).

Segmented Genealogy Record

This is a record in a **segmented genealogy** which records the children of an ancestor by one woman either implicitly or explicitly. Frequent forms of this record include a **birth report**, a **son list as a genealogical record**, and a **begat formula with a compound object**.

Son List as Geneaological Record

Although a list in its own right, the son list frequently functions as a record within a larger genealogical list.

All the following are in **segmented genealogies** unless stated otherwise, and begin "The sons of PN" or "And the sons of PN." The genealogy of Jacob's sons by different women contains son lists of Leah (Gen 35:23), Rachel (Gen 35:24), Bilhah (Gen 35:25) and Zilpah (Gen 35:26a). The genealogy of Jacob's descendants contains son lists of Reuben (Gen 46:9), Simeon (Gen 46:10), Levi (Gen 46:11), Judah (Gen 46:12a), Perez (Gen 46:12b), Issachar (Gen 46:13), Zebulun (Gen 46:14), Gad (Gen 46:16), Asher (Gen 46:17a), Beriah (Gen 46:17b), Rachel followed by the epithet "Jacob's wife" (Gen 46:19), Benjamin (Gen 46:21), Dan (Gen 46:23), and Naphtali (Gen 46:24). The genealogy in Exod 6:14–25 concerns the descendants of Leah's first three sons: Reuben, Simeon, and Levi. It contains the son lists of Reuben (Exod 6:14b), Simeon (Exod 6:15), Levi (Exod 6:16a), Gershon (Exod 6:17), Kohath (Exod 6:18), Merari (Exod 6:19), Izhar (Exod 6:21), Uzziel (Exod 6:22), and Korah (Exod 6:24).

First Chronicles begins with a complicated genealogy from Adam to Abraham (1 Chr 1:1–27) that is part linear genealogy and part segmented genealogy. Within it are son lists of Japheth (1 Chr 1:5), Gomer (1 Chr 1:6), Javan (1 Chr 1:7), Ham (1 Chr 1:8), Cush (1 Chr 1:9a), Raamah (1 Chr 1:9b), and Shem (1 Chr 1:17). The following genealogy of Abraham contains the son lists of Abraham (1 Chr 1:28), Keturah (1 Chr 1:32a), Jokshan (1 Chr 1:32b), Medan (1 Chr 1:33a), Isaac (1 Chr 1:34b), Esau (1 Chr 1:35), Eliphaz (1 Chr 1:36), Reuel (1 Chr 1:37), Seir (1 Chr 1:38), Lotan (1 Chr 1:39), Shobal (1 Chr 1:40a), Zibeon (1 Chr 1:40b), Anah (1 Chr 1:41a), Dishon (1 Chr 1:41b), Ezer (1 Chr 1:42a), Dishan (1 Chr 1:42b).

The son list of Israel in 1 Chr 2:1–2 functions as a **table superscription** to the entirety of 1 Chr 2–8. Within the following genealogy of Judah are son lists concerning Judah (1 Chr 2:3a), Perez (1 Chr 2:5), Zerah (1 Chr 2:6), Carmi (1 Chr 2:7), Ethan (1 Chr 2:8), Hezron (1 Chr 2:9), Zeruaiah (1 Chr 2:16b), her i.e. Jerioth (1 Chr 2:18b), Jerahmeel, the firstborn of Hezron (1 Chr 1:25), Ram (1 Chr 1:27), Onam (1 Chr 1:28a), Shammai (1 Chr 1:28b), Nadab (1 Chr 1:30a), Appaim (1 Chr 1:31a), Ishi (1 Chr 1:31b), Sheshan (1 Chr 1:31c), Jada, Shammai's brother (1 Chr 1:32a), Jonathan (1 Chr 1:33a), Caleb brother of Jerahmeel (1 Chr 1:42a), Mareshah father of Hebron (1:42b; there is a textual difficulty as no sons are listed), Hebron (1 Chr 1:43), Shammai (1 Chr 1:44a), Jahdai (1 Chr 1:47), Hur the firstborn of Ephrathah (1 Chr 1:50b–51) and Salma (1 Chr 1:54).

The two son lists of David in 1 Chr 3:1–3, 5–8 are tied together by the material in 1 Chr 3:4, 9 as a segmented genealogical unit preceding the linear genealogy of Solomon down to Josiah (1 Chr 3:10–14). The segmented genealogy of Josiah contains the son lists of Josiah (1 Chr 3:15), Jehoiakim (1 Chr 3:16), Jeconiah, the captive (1 Chr 3:17–18), Pedaiah (1 Chr 3:19a), Zerubbabel (1 Chr 3:19b–20), Hananiah (1 Chr 1:21a), Shecaniah (1 Chr 1:22a), Shemaiah (1 Chr 1:22b), Neariah (1 Chr 1:23) and Elioneai (1 Chr 1:24).

The genealogy of Judah in 1 Chr 4:1–23 contains son lists of Judah (1 Chr 4:1), Etam (1 Chr 4:3a), Helah (1 Chr 4:7), Kenaz (1 Chr 4:13a), Othniel (1 Chr 4:13b), Caleb son of Jephunneh (1 Chr 4:15a), Elah (1 Chr 4:15b), Jehallel (1 Chr 4:16), Ezrah (1 Chr 4:17), Shimon (1 Chr 4:20a), Ishi (1 Chr 4:20b), Shelah son of Judah (1 Chr 4:21–22). The largely genealogical material pertaining to Simeon contains son lists of Simeon (1 Chr 4:24) and Mishma (1 Chr 4:26).

The only son list in the genealogy of Reuben is that of Reuben himself (1 Chr 5:3) and the son lists in the genealogy of Gad do not conform to the standard pattern. There are standard son lists in the genealogy of Levi pertaining to Levi (1 Chr 5:27 [NRSV 6:1]), Kohath (1 Chr 5:28, [NRSV 6:2]), Amram (1 Chr 5:29a [NRSV 6:3a]). A second Levite genealogy contains the son lists of Levi (1 Chr 6:1 [NRSV 16]), Gershom (1 Chr 6:2 [NRSV 17], Kohath (1 Chr 6:3 [NRSV 18]), Merari (1 Chr 6:4 [NRSV 19]), Samuel (1 Chr 6:13 [NRSV 28]), and Merari (1 Chr 6:14–15 [NRSV 29–30]).

The genealogy of Issachar contains son lists pertaining to Issachar (1 Chr 7:1), Tola (1 Chr 7:2a), Uzzi (1 Chr7:3a), Izrahiah (1 Chr 7:3b). The genealogy of Benjamin contains son lists of Benjamin (1 Chr 7:6), Bela (1 Chr 7:7a), Becher (1 Chr 7:8a), Jediael (1 Chr 7:10a), and Bilhan (1 Chr 7:10b). The genealogy of Naphtali consists entirely of the son list of Naphtali (1 Chr 7:13). The genealogy of Manasseh contains son lists of Manasseh (1 Chr 7:17), Ulam (1 Chr 7:18), and Shemida (1 Chr 7:19).

Trade List Record

Kings and Chronicles contain references to Solomon trading with various partners but the only full scale **trade list** in the Bible concerns Tyre and each record consists of four elements: the cities or regions trading with Tyre, a word for trade, the items traded, and a vague reference to Tyre's merchandise or goods (Ezek 27:12, 13, 14, 15, 16, 17, 18, 19, 20, 21, 22, 23–24).

Tribal Cities Record

Numbers 32 contains syntactically dependent lists of cities rebuilt by the Gadites (Num 32:34–36) and Ruebenites (Num 32:37–38), each with the form "And the sons of PN built" followed by a list of cities. Then follows a brief **conquest narrative** (Num 32:39–42) involving the cities/regions of Gilead, Havvoth-jair, and Nobah.

As a record in a **boundary list**, tribal cities records occur in lists pertaining to Reuben (Josh 13:23a), Gad (Josh 13:27a), Simeon (Josh 19:2–8a), Zebulun (Josh 19:15), Issachar (Josh 19:18–22), Asher (Josh 19:25–26a, 28, 30), Naphtali (Josh 19:35–38) and Dan (Josh 19:41–46). See also cities/towns lists.

Hess, "Typology," 160–70.

Unclean Animal Record

In addition to records based on the unclean food formula listed above, other records note types of unclean animals. Twenty types of flying creatures are listed as unclean (Lev 11:13–19; Deut 14:12–18), usually with just the animal name but occasionally with the addition of "of any kind." Eight types of swarming unclean creatures are later listed: "the weasel, the mouse, the great lizard according to its kind, the gecko, the land crocodile, the lizard, the sand lizard, and the chameleon" (Lev 11:29–30).

MAIN LISTS

Blessing List

Deut 28:2–6 in a blessings and curses passage.

Boundary Lists

This a subcategory of **onomasticon** which gives instructions demarcating the boundaries of a tribe. In addition to **list superscriptions** and **list subscriptions**, the main constitutents are **boundary description records, cardinal direction records, tribal city records**, and notes. On the surface at least, boundary lists are directive illocutions but the actual examples are more complicated. The boundary lists in Joshua are clearly directives but the presence of **notes** showing the difficulties certain tribes had in dispossessing the Canaanites from the land (Josh 17:12–13, for example) illustrate the different perspectives of the events portrayed and the time of the author/redactor. Similarly, the boundary lists in Num 34 and Ezek 47 function as divine **promises** to Israel and have a commissive aspect.

In Num 34, YHWH commands Moses to proclaim to Israel what their southern, western, northern, and eastern boundaries will be (Num 34:2–12).

There are numerous boundary lists in Joshua, beginning with the Trans-Jordanian tribes of Reuben (Josh 13:15–23), Gad (Josh 13:24–28), and Trans-Jordanian Manasseh (Josh 13:29–31), with an expansion of subscription discussing the Trans-Jordanian tribes and noting that the Levites' inheritance is the Lord God of Israel (Josh 13:32–33).

The Cis-Jordanian tribes are discussed in Josh 15–19, beginning with Judah (Josh 15:1–12) whose prominence is suggested by its use of **cardinal direction records.** The list concerning Cis-Jordan Manasseh (Josh 17:5–13) is preceded by background information (Josh 17:1–4) including a **daughter list** which enables the descendants of the daughters of Zelophehad to inherit. The boundary list concerning Benjamin appears in Josh 18:12–20 and Josh 19 contains no fewer than six boundary lists: Simeon (Josh 19:1–9), Zebulun (Josh 19:10–16), Issachar (Josh 19:17–23), Asher (Josh 19:24–31), Naphtali (Josh 19:32–39), and Dan (Josh 19:40–48).

The two largest sections in the book of Joshua concern the conquest of the land and the apportionment of the land, of which the boundary lists described above and the **cities/towns lists** constitute the major part. They provide specificity regarding YHWH's fulfilment of promises of land made to the patriarchs from Gen 12 onward and confirmed to Moses in Num 34. Israelites living in one of the territories described would be thus enabled to state their historical claims to the land in terms of YHWH's covenant promises.

There is also a boundary list for the future Israelite tribes in Ezek 47:15–20. The boundaries approximate those in Num 34:2–12, excluding the Trans-Jordanian territories of Reuben, Gad, and half of Manasseh, as well as Aramean and Edomite territory that had at times been occupied by conquering Israelites. It corresponds more to the land Israel was originally promised than that occupied at any actual historical period, but with the important addition that resident aliens would be able to inherit land also (Ezek 47:23). Given the nature of the **vision narrative** of Ezek 40–48, underlying the surface of these directives is a divine promise making it, along with Num 34, one of the few commissive lists in the Hebrew Bible. The teleological purpose is likely to provide details regarding the Messianic Age, giving hope to exiles.

Aharoni, "Province List," 225–46; Cross and Wright, "Boundary," 202–26; Hess, "Typology," 160–70; Kallai, "Boundaries," 27–34; Levin, "Numbers 34:2–12," 55–76; Na'aman, *Borders and Districts*; Simons, *Geographical and Topographical.*

Catalogue

A catalogue lists items systematically according to a principle of classification, in which the emphasis is on furthering intellectual knowledge. It is thus different from both a random list and a register (whose categorization is determined by administrative needs). **Wisdom lists**, discussed in the chapter on wisdom genres, would be catalogues as would be the **table of directives** concerning clean and unclean animals. Some **inventories** might have used catalogues as organizing principles.

De Vries, *1 and 2 Chronicles*, 428; Knierim and Coats, *Numbers*, 341–42; Long, *1 Kings*, 245–46.

Census Summary List

Strictly speaking, a census is a list of those registered for military service. The actions depicted in Num 1 and 26, for example, would have required the compilation of actual census lists but what those chapters record is merely the summary information concerning the number of available men from the various tribal sections of the populace.

Exodus 30:11–16, part of the **tabernacle instruction** (see legal genres chapter), contains instructions on how to conduct a census but no actual census. David conducted a census (2 Sam 24 [= 1 Chr 21:1–17]) which resulted in plague (see **divine judgment narrative** in narratives chapter), but the results of the census are not recorded. In the transition of power from David to Solomon, David took a census of the Levites for the purpose of organizing them for temple work according to the main tribal branches (see **roster**). We are given the **tally** of the Levites but not of the tribal branches (1 Chr 23:2–3).

There is a census summary at the beginning of the wilderness period (Num 1) and another one after forty years of wandering in the wilderness (Num 26). See **census record** for the differences in how the two census summaries are described. The tribes in the second census summary follow the same order as in the Num 1 census, but with Manasseh preceding Ephraim reflecting a natural birth order of Joseph's two sons.

A major difficulty is how to interpret what seem like impossibly large numbers which also conflict with other material regarding the Exodus/Conquest. One solution is to interpret the Hebrew word *aleph* here not as "thousand" but as a clan unit of about ten to fifteen people. Another solution is to regard the census lists as hyperbole like numbering Abraham's descendants to the number of the stars (Gen 15:5).

Similar to a census summary is the summary list of the people who returned with Zerubbabel to Jerusalem and Judah after the Babylonian captivity (Ezra 2:1–70 [=Neh 7:6–73]). The main records here are **descendants and number formula** records, **people of location and number formula** records, **name lists, tally formula** records, and **notes.**

The list of people who accompanied Ezra from Babylonia in Ezra 8 is dominated by a series of **leader, pedigree and number formula** records (Ezra 8:3b–14).

Ezra–Nehemiah may be presenting the return to Judah as a second Exodus, in which case the census lists would be more directly related to the census lists in Num 1 and 26, or may construe it as simply restoring pre-exilic institutions. An alternate view regards these census lists, together with the account of the return under Ezra in Ezra 7–8, as having pilgrimage motifs.

Allrik, "Lists of Zerubbabel," 21–27; Galling, "Gola-list," 149–58; Goldstein, "Large Census Numbers," 99–108; Kislev, "Number of Numbers," 189–204; Knierim and Coats, *Numbers*, 342–44; Scolnic, *Theme and Context*, 25–65.

Cities/Towns List

This is a subcategory of **onomasticon** which mainly lists cities and towns allotted to various tribes. In Joshua, we see city lists pertaining to the tribes of Manasseh (Josh 13:31; 17:2–3, 11), Benjamin (Josh 18:21–28), Dan (Josh 19:41–46), Judah (Josh 15:21–62), Simeon (Josh 19:2–7), Issachar (Josh 19:18–21), and Naphtali (Josh 19:35–38). Together with **boundary lists** (see for further discussion), they form a bulk of the apportionment of land section in the book of Joshua. There are also cities of asylum (Josh 20:7–8). Joshua grants the Levites' request for cities (see request narrative), and there is an extensive cities list (Josh 21:9–42). The syntactically dependent city lists that the various Trans-Jordanian tribes rebuild function in much the same manner, allocating cities for Gad (Num 32:34–36), Reuben (Num 32:37–38), and Manasseh (Num 32:39–42).

Nehemiah 11:25–30a lists seventeen towns where the people of Judah lived followed by the note "So they camped from Beer-sheba to the valley of Hinnom" (Neh 11:30b). Then comes a nominal sentence which is clearly intended as a list of fifteen towns where the people of Benjamin lived (Neh 11:31–35), and the section concludes "And certain divisions of the Levites in Judah were joined to Benjamin" (Neh 11:36).

The **table of genealogical information** in 1 Chr 2–8 intersperses its genealogies with some city lists. There is a syntactically dependent list of thirteen cities in which the Simeonites lived (1 Chr 4:28–31) followed by a list of five villages that were their settlements (1 Chr 4:32–34). The list of Levitical cities in 1 Chr 6:39–66 [NRSV 54–81] has a different structure, dominated by **gave group territory formula records, city and pasture lands formula** records, and **to Levitical clan from tribe formula** records. There is also a brief list of Ephraimite cities (1 Chr 7:28–29).

Hess, "Typology," 160–70; Kartveit, *Motive*; Marquis, "Composition," 408–32; Mazar, "Cities," 193–205; Na'aman, "Inheritance," 136–52.

Clan Lists

The **table of genealogical information** about Edom in Gen 36 contains two Edomite chief/clan lists (Gen 36:15–19, 40–43). The first is centered around three **clan list records** concerning Eliphaz (Gen 36:15b–16), Reuel (Gen 36:17), and Oholibamah (Gen 36:18). The second is primarily a **name list** of eleven clans (Gen 36:40b–43a) which is essentially reduplicated in Chronicles (1 Chr 1:51–54). The clan lists in Gen 36 are part of the *toledot* sections (Gen 36:1–8; 36:9–37:1; see overview of Tanak chapter) concerning Esau/Edom. Because of the mainly adversarial role that the Edomites played in Israel's history, the Chronicler ends the preliminary genealogical table of information (1 Chr 1) with this material before starting the larger table (1 Chr 2–8) with the **son list** of Israel.

Clean/Unclean Animal List

All these lists occur in the **table of directives** in Lev 11 and Deut 14 and the purpose of these lists is discussed in the entry on **food law** in the chapter on legal genres. The list of unclean animals in Lev 11:4–8 contains a **list superscription** (11:4a), four **unclean animal records** all of which include a rationale for the animal being unclean (11:4b, 5, 6, 7) and a **list subscription**. The list of unclean flying creatures in Lev 11:13–19 contains a **list superscription** (11:13b) and nine **unclean animal records** (11:13c, 14, 15, 16a, 16b, 17, 18, 19a, 19b). Several of those records contain multiple **animal formulas**, so that twenty unclean creatures are listed.

The list of clean animals in Lev 11:22 contains a list superscription (11:22a) and four records, all of which are the **animal and kind formula** (11:22b, c, d, e).

The list of unclean swarming creatures in Lev 11:29–31a contains a **list superscription** (11:29a), three **unclean animal records** (11:29b, 30a, 30b), and a list subscription (11:31a).

Daughter List

The list of Zelophehad's daughters occurs several times (Num 26:33b; 27:1b; Josh 17:3b) with varying **daughter list superscriptions** but with the same order of daughters in the list proper: Mahlah, Noah, Hoglah, Milcah, and Tirzah. A syntactically dependent form of the list occurs in Num 36:11. There is a note in 1 Chr 7:15 that Zelophehad had daughters but no list of them. Zelophehad's daughters play a key role in changing the **inheritance law** concerning women (see **legal case narrative**), and became revered by the rabbis for having better legal reasoning than Moses.

Immediately after the son list of Saul (1 Sam 14:49a) is a daughter list also (1 Sam 14:49b). Saul's two daughters, Merab and especially Michal, later play a role in various narratives concerning David (see **couple's dispute narrative, crisis narrative, flight narrative, marriage narrative,** and **meeting/visit/reunion narrative**). The extreme scarcity of daughter lists compared to son lists testifies to a society where sons were far more valued than daughters—even as it provides resources, as in the case of Zelophehad's daughters, for improving that society.

Aaron, "Ruse," 1–38; Claasens, "Give Us," 319–337; Clines and Eshkanazi, *Queen Michal's Story*.

Exit List

Ezekiel's vision narrative concludes with a list of the exits of the city. It contains a **list superscription** (Ezek 48:30a), four **exit list records** (Ezek 48:30b–31, 32, 33, 34), a **list subscription** (Ezek 48:35a) and an **expansion of subscription**, "And the name of the city from that time on shall be, The Lord is There" (Ezek 48:35b) which provides a fitting conclusion to this prophecy of eschatological hope.

Kim, "YHWH Shammah," 187–207; Rhyder, "Gates," 752–65.

Festival Calendar List

The festival calendars in Exod 23:14–17; 34:18–23; Lev 23:1–43; Num 28:1–29:40; Deut 16:1–17; and Ezek 45:21–25 are discussed in **cultic calendar law** in the chapter on legal genres.

Genealogy

The term "genealogy" can refer to either a written or oral expression of how a certain person or a group of people are descended from an ancestor or to the propositional content underlying the written or oral expression. These two senses roughly correspond to the material and formal causes of the speech act communicating the genealogy. For an example of the second sense, see **genealogy of Jacob's sons**. Strictly speaking, not all genealogies in the first sense are lists. Although genealogical diagrams, a currently popular form of genealogy, do not occur in the Hebrew Bible, there are some **genealogical narratives** and these are discussed in the narratives chapter rather than this one. If a genealogy starts from the descendant and proceeds to the ancestor, it is called an ascending genealogy or **pedigree**. More frequently, the information flows the other way and this is called a descending genealogy.

The number of generations in a genealogy is the depth of the genealogy. If a genealogy contains only one person in each generation, it is a **linear genealogy**. Otherwise, it is a segmented genealogy and the largest number of persons in any generation is the breadth of a generation. The specific written expressions of genealogies in the Hebrew Bible are covered in the glossary entries on **linear genealogy**, **pedigree**, and **segmented genealogy**. This entry discusses other issues related to genealogies in general.

Uses of genealogies included demonstrating existing relations between Israel and the surrounding nations, linking previously isolated traditions, covering periods not discussed elsewhere in the tradition, legitimizing individuals or providing further information about important characters, and expressing divine providence over history. A further function of some post-exilic genealogies may include constructing genealogies from earlier census lists of no longer existent tribes.

Scholars also compare biblical genealogies with both oral genealogies and the written genealogies of the Ancient Near East. Oral genealogies may not be created for historiographic purposes, and rival groups may promote competing genealogies, but once an oral genealogy achieves general acceptance, it may be cited as historical evidence to support a claim in a current dispute.

Coats, *Genesis*, 318; de Vries, *1 and 2 Chronicles*, 430; Finkelstein, "Historical Reality," 65–83; Finlay, *Birth Report*, 43–84; Glatt-Gilad, "Genealogy Lists," 71–79; Hess, "Genealogies," 241–54; Johnson, *Purpose*; Levin, "Understanding," 11–46; Rendsburg, "Internal Consistency," 185–206; Sasson, "Genealogical Convention," 171–85; Smith, *Role of Mothers*; Sparks, *Chronicler's Genealogies*; Thomas, *Generations*; Wilson, *Genealogy and History*; Zadok, "Reliability," 228–54.

Genealogy of Jacob's Sons

This is a special category for passages which contain genealogical information regarding Jacob's sons, no matter what other genre they may have (Gen 46:8–25; 49:2–28; Exod 1:1–5; 6:14–27; Num 1:5–16, 20–54;

2:2–33; 7:12–83; 10:11–28; 13:4–16; 26:5–51; 34:16–29; Deut 27:11–14; 33:6–29; Josh 13–21; Judg 1:2–36; 5:14–23; Ezek 48:1–29, 30–35; 1 Chr 2:1–2; 2:3–8:40; 2:2–34; 12:1–23, 24–41; 27:16–34). See overview of Tanak chapter for brief discussion of significance.

Smith, *Role of Mothers*.

Gentilics List

This is a list of people groups. The so called "table of nations" in Gen 10 is discussed in **segmented genealogy**. The two gentilics lists that occur in the latter prophets (Jer 25:17–26a; Obad 19–21) occur in the context of **prophecies of judgment against foreign nations**. The two that occur in Chronicles (1 Chr 2:53, 55) are clans that descend from Caleb.

Gottwald, *Tribes*; Kallai, "Twelve-Tribe," 53–90; Schneider, *Mothers of Promise*; Sparks, "Genesis 49," 327–47; Weippert, "Geographische," 76–89.

Gift or Offering List

This can be a **directive** list concerning what people are to give (Exod 25:3–7) or an **assertive** list concerning who gave or offered what (Num 7:12–88). At the beginning of the **tabernacle instruction** (see chapter on legal genres), YHWH commands an offering from the Israelites in a list consisting of an offering superscription (Exod 25:3a) and a series of fifteen **item records** (Exod 25:3b–7), most of which are simply the **item formula**, but some of which include the purpose of the item. These items appear in various sections of the rest of the **tabernacle instruction** section (Exod 25:10–30:38) and in the **construction narrative** concerning the tabernacle (Exod 35:1–40:38).

Following YHWH's command for the Israelites to present offerings, one leader each day, to dedicate the altar, is a **compliance narrative** in the form of twelve highly formulaic **offering macro-records** concerning Nahshon of Judah (Num 7:12–17), Nethanel of Issachar (Num 7:18–23), Eliab of Zebulun (Num 7:24–29), Elizur of Reuben (Num 7:30–35), Shelumiel of Simeon (Num 7:36–41), Eliasaph of Gad (Num 7:42–47), Elishama of Ephraim (Num 7:48–53), Gamaliel of Manasseh (Num 7:54–59), Abidan of Benjamin (Num 7:60–65), Ahiezer of Dan (Num 7:66–71), Pagiel of Asher (Num 7:72–77), and Ahira of Naphtali (Num

7:78–83), followed by an equally formulaic **offering subscription section** (Num 7:84–88). According to Rashi, this offering took place on the day that the tabernacle was set up (Exod 40:17); according to Ramban (Nachmanides), it occurred a week later. Either way, it happened before the **census** in Num 1. Rabbinic tradition sees the courage displayed by Nahshon of Judah in making the first offering, not long after the deaths of Nadab and Abihu, as being connected to Judah's lead role in the **census** of Num 1 and the **ordering of camp** in Num 2.

Knierim and Coats, *Numbers*, 97–104; Milgrom, "Chieftains' Gifts," 221–25.

Inventory

An inventory is simply an assertive list of valuable goods. Standard records include **item formula**, and **item and number formula**. Complicated inventories may include **inventory macro-records**. Inventories are sometimes syntactically dependent.

The **construction narrative** concerning the tabernacle includes an inventory of the gold, silver, and other materials used in the construction (Exod 38:21–31) and an inventory of all that had been constructed (Exod 39:32–43; see **items to construct list**).

The inventory of Moabite booty in Num 31:32–40 forms the bulk of the **compliance narrative** following the **divine command narrative** giving instructions on how to divide the booty (Num 31:25–30). The intent of the passage is to portray the Israelites as duly giving YHWH his portion, but the inclusion of virgin women with this inventory of sheep and goats, oxen, and donkeys, raises troubling ethical issues.

The **construction narrative** concerning the temple includes an inventory of the items that Hiram made (1 Kgs 7:40–50a [= 2 Chr 4:11b—5:1a]). These details look backward as a fulfillment of Nathan's promise that David's son would build YHWH's house (2 Sam 7) and to David's planned inventory for the temple (1 Chr 28:11–18) but ominously look forward to another inventory of the items Nebuchadnezzar would take back to Babylon (2 Kgs 25:13–17 [= Jer 52:17–23]). Ezra also contains an inventory of these temple vessels (Ezra 1:9–11). The inventories in 2 Kgs 25 and Jer 52 are syntactically dependent as is the inventory in Isaiah 3:18–23 of the jewelry items YHWH will take away as part of a **prophecy of punishment**.

De Vries, *1 and 2 Chronicles*, 431; Knierim and Coats, *Numbers*, 294–98; Segal, "Numerical Discrepancies," 122–29.

Items to Construct List

This is a directive list within a **construction narrative** which directs the artisans concerning what they need to construct. Exod 35:10–19 gives YHWH's instructions concerning the tabernacle, the tent and related objects, the ark and the mercy seat, the table, the lampstand, the altars of incense and of burnt offering, the hangings, the pillars, the screen, the pegs, and the vestments. Most of the rest of Exod 35–39 narrates the compliance with YHWH's instructions, i.e. the actual constructing, and the section concludes with an **inventory** of the items built (Exod 39:32–43).

Itinerary

This is a list in which the items are the movements by stages from one place to the next. An itinerary list is the list counterpart of the **journey narrative** (see chapter on narrative genres). It differs from an itinerary in that the latter is a series of more elaborate reports and/or accounts and the arrival and departure formulas simply function as a literary skeleton around which narratives of varying complexity are built.

The itinerary in Num 21 contains five **set out and camped formula** records (Num 21:10, 11, 12, 13–15, 16–18a), including several important **notes in itinerary**, followed by four from **place to place formula** records (Num 21:18b, 19a, 19b, 20). The later itinerary in Num contains an itinerary superscription (Num 33:1), an expansion of superscription (Num 33:2–4), and forty-two **set out and camped formula** records (Num 33:5–49), several of which contain **notes in itinerary**. See also **ordering of camp**.

Coats, "Wilderness Itinerary," 135–52; Coats, *Exodus 1–18*, 164; Davies, "Wilderness Itinerary," 46–81; Knierim and Coats, *Numbers*, 347–48; Miller, "Israelite Journey," 577–99; Scolnic, *Theme and Context*, 67–133.

King List

The list of Edomite kings contains a **list superscription** (Gen 36:31 [= 1 Chr 1:43a]), a record regarding Bela, the first king on the list (Gen 36:32 [= 1 Chr 1:43b]), seven **Edomite succession formula** records (Gen 36:33–39a [= 1 Chr 1:44–50a]), and a note about the wife of Hadar, the last king on the list (Gen 36:39b [= 1 Chr 1:50b]). The Chronicles version has a plus of the death formula of Hadad (1 Chr 1:51a). These lists are a condensed version of the regnal formulas (see narratives chapter) regarding Israelite and Judean kings.

The list of Canaanite kings slain by the Israelites in Josh 12 contains a lengthy **introduction to list** (Josh 12:7–8), thirty-one **slain king formula** records, and a **tally** of thirty-one kings slain. It serves to highlight the success of Joshua's leadership.

The **minor judges narratives** (see chapter on narrative genres) might also be considered a variant of the king list with judges replacing kings.

Bartlett, "Edomite King-List," 301–14; de Vries, *1 and 2 Chronicles*, 430; Knauf, "Alter und Herkunft," 245–53; Malamat, "King Lists," 163–73.

Linear Genealogy

The genealogy of Cain divides into a linear genealogy (Gen 4:17–18) and a **segmented genealogy** (Gen 4:19–22). The linear genealogy contains the **birth report** of Enoch (Gen 4:17a), a **note** concerning Enoch (Gen 4:17b), and four records consisting of the **begat formula** or a passive variant thereof (Gen 4:18), yielding a genealogy with a depth of six generations. There are many similarities between the names in Cain's genealogy and the names in Adam's genealogy through Seth, which has led to much scholarly speculation regarding the derivation of these lists.

The **genealogy** of Adam (Gen 5:1–32) has a standard pattern, with the records consisting of an **age at fatherhood formula**, a **years after fatherhood formula** and an **age at death formula**. The deviation of pattern in the seventh and tenth generations, both of which have **notes**, highlights the significance of Enoch and Noah respectively. Enoch became the subject of apocalyptic literature found in the Pseudepigrapha and the Dead Sea Scrolls, and Noah is the main character in the ensuing **flood narrative**. The New Testament begins with a linear genealogy of Jesus Christ whose superscription is patterned on the LXX of Gen 5:1a.

The genealogy of Shem (Gen 11:10–26) has a standard pattern of **age at fatherhood formula** followed by **years after fatherhood formula**. It has a depth of nine generations and like the genealogy in Gen 5 concludes in a **begat list**, this one concerning Terah's sons, Abram, Nahor, and Haran (Gen 11:26). The similarities between the genealogy of Adam and the genealogy of Shem, in contrast to other genealogies, suggests that they combine to provide a genealogy from Adam to Abram. Versions such as the Septuagint and the Samaritan Pentateuch differ considerably from the Masoretic Text with regard to these genealogies. Most scholars argue, partly on the pattern of other genealogies both biblical and elsewhere in the ancient Near East, that the genealogy from Adam to Abram is a selective genealogy with several generations missing. The exceptionally long ages of the characters in the two genealogies, plus other unusual factors, suggest that some symbolism is involved rather than the characters lived that long.

The genealogy of Perez that forms the epilogue to the book of Ruth begins with a **toledot formula**, and has a depth of ten generations (Ruth 4:18–22) culminating in David.

Amzallag, "Cain Genealogy," 23–50; Bryan, "Reevaluation," 180–88; Steinmann, "Gaps in Genealogies," 141–58.

Muster Roll

Battle narratives sometimes include a section where a military leader musters the army and numbers of troops from different tribes or groups are mentioned (Judg 20:15–17; 1 Sam 11:8; 2 Chr 25:5). A muster roll is a list of fighting men, typically including **tallies** and descriptions of the types of warriors, which would have been used in preparation for battle.

When an army defects from Saulide rule and comes to David in Hebron, a detailed muster roll is given. It contains a **list superscription** (1 Chr 12:24 [NRSV 23]), fourteen **tribe/commander and tally formula records** (1 Chr 12:25–38 [NRSV 24–37]), a **list subscription** (1 Chr 12:39 [NRSV 38]), and an **expansion of subscription** describing the army eating and drinking with David for three days (1 Chr 12:40–41 [NRSV 39–40]).

De Vries, *1 and 2 Chronicles*, 432; Edelman, "Asherite Genealogy," 13–23.

Name list

This is a list of proper names of person, cities or countries, typically organized according to a certain unifying aspect found in the superscription. Subcategories include **chiefs lists**, **daughter lists**, **onomastica**, **participant lists**, **son lists**, and **unexplained name lists**. Other examples include men who had married foreign women (Ezra 10:18–44), and covenant signatories (Neh 10:1–27).

A list of nine names are described as the sons of Beriah (1 Chr 8:14–16); a list of seven names are described as the sons of Elpaal (1 Chr 8:17–18); a list of nine names are described as the sons of Shimei (1 Chr 8:19–21); a list of eleven names are described as the sons of Shashak (1 Chr 8:22–25); and a list of six names are described as the sons of Jeroham (1 Chr 8:26–27). The subscription in 1 Chr 8:28 may apply to this series of name lists or to the entire material in 1 Chr 8:1–27.

Angel, "Literary Significance," 143–52; de Vries, *1 and 2 Chronicles*, 432; Knierim, *Numbers*, 350.

Onomasticon

This is a subcategory of **name list** which lists localities. This genre is found in the Ancient Near Eastern literature of Mari, Ugarit, and Alalakh, associated with military lists of places captured, religious lists of places facing prophetic judgment, and boundary lists. The church historian Eusebius's onomasticon has proved helpful to archeologists in identifying ancient Israelite towns. In the Hebrew Bible, the main subcategories of onomasticon are the **boundary lists** and the **cities/towns lists**, but there is also a **table of trade** in Ezek 27.

Hess, "Typology," 160–70; Knierim and Coats, *Numbers*, 352; Notley and Safrai, *Eusebius*; O'Connor, "Ammonite Onomasticon," 51–64; Zadok, "Notes," 107–17.

Ordering of Camp List

This is a list which either prescribes (Num 2:2–32) or describes (Num 10:12–28) the movements of the Israelite camp. Both lists contain **list superscriptions** and **list subscriptions**, and group the tribes into four sets of three tribes. The first ordering of camp list occurs immediately after the **census summary list** in Num 1 and is part of a **divine command narrative** consisting of a **speech introduction of YHWH formula** (Num 2:1), the ordering of camp list constituting the **divine command** prescribing the camp's movement, and the **compliance section** (Num 2:34). The list itself is dominated by **ordering of camp macro-records** (Num 2:3–9, 10–16, 18–24, 25–31) enveloping a record concerning the tent of meeting (Num 2:17). The second example is set after the sojourn at Sinai (Exod 19:1–Num 10:10) and a dating formula, "In the second year, in the second month, on the twentieth day of the month, the cloud lifted from over the tabernacle of the covenant" (Num 10:11) marks it as the first episode in the Israelite camp's journey from Sinai to Kadesh (Num 10:11–12:16). See the overview of Tanak chapter for how these journey and sojourn sections mark major divisions in Exodus through Numbers. **Standard of camp formulas** and **company of tribe formulas** dominate this list.

Condren, "Organization of Camp," 423–52; Knierim and Coats, *Numbers*, 149–71.

Participant Lists

This is a subcategory of **name list**, in which the people listed participated in some event or activity. Because these activities and events are positive, the lists would be particularly encouraging to the descendants of the people named in them, but would also be encouraging to lay people in general that God takes notice of their works.

The list of people who participated in the building of Jerusalem in Neh 3 is dominated by **name and building activity records**. Nehemiah 12:1–9 is dominated by **participant group records** concerning who participated with Zerubbabel and Jeshua, as is the list of leading priests and Levites in the time of Joiakim (Neh 12:12–26), i.e. the next generation. The teleological cause of the list would be to connect those who participated with Nehemiah and Ezra in the religious reforms of the day to those who participated with Zerubbabel and Jeshua in the return to Jerusalem and building of the second temple.

The list of participants in the dedication ceremony led by Nehemiah (Neh 12:31–43) includes **name lists** of those who went right and those who went left (Neh 12:31b–36a), and **procession records** describing the procession. The list of the leaders in the post-exilic community (1 Chr

9:1–34) contains a series of **participant group records** relating to people of Judah, Benjamin, priests, Levites, and gatekeepers, followed by a **job description record**.

Allrik, "Lists of Zerubbabel," 21–27; Angel, "Literary Significance," 143–52; Burrows, "Nehemiah 3:1–32," 115–40; Galling, "Gōlā-List," 149–58.

Pedigree

A pedigree has the form "PN1, son of PN2, son of PN3, . . ." and is thus an ascending form of **linear genealogy**, having varying depth but a breadth of only one. By its nature, it typically consists of the **patronymic formula** (PN, son of PN) followed by a series of **son of formula** records. This glossary discusses only pedigrees with a depth of at least four generations.

The pedigree of Ezra (Ezra 7:1–6a) has a depth of seventeen generations and is so long that there is a resumptive phrase reminding the reader that Ezra is the subject who went up from Babylonia. The pedigree clearly burnishes the credentials of Ezra, the main protagonist in the book bearing his name. The pedigree of Bela (1 Chr 5:8) has a depth of four generations. The pedigree is set in a **chiefs list** and is followed by two **notes** (1 Chr 5:8b, 9) and functions with them to provide more information on this important Reubenite chief. Abihail's pedigree (1 Chr 5:14) is four generations deep and highlights him in the **muster roll** of Gadites.

The pedigree of Heman the singer (1 Chr 6:18–38) begins with the **name and office formula** followed by twenty-two son of formula records sadly lacking the acrostic pattern which would have prevented this twenty-two item list from being mind-numbingly boring. The **son list** of Heman's fourteen sons (1 Chr 25:4) and their role in the production of ancient Israelite hymns testify to Heman's significance (1 Chr 25:5–6a) but it would have been nice to know also the names of his three daughters or at least the name of his long-suffering wife.

De Vries, *1 and 2 Chronicles*, 433; Kleinig, *Lord's Song*; Kleinig, "Bach, Chronicles," 7–10; Laato, "Levitical Genealogies," 77–99.

Register

A register is an administrative list. It records items for official purposes and its ordering principle is the means by which they are subject to administration by an institution or corporate body. **Boundary lists, census summary lists, inventories, rosters** and **rotas** are all subcategories of register. The *Sitz im Leben* of a register would be the scribal classes responsible for keeping administrative records.

Knierim and Coats, *Numbers*, 357; Long, *1 Kings*, 258–59.

Roster

A roster is a **register** which lists the people within a certain group together with the duties or offices assigned to each. Rosters may stand alone or be part of a larger **table of organization**.

The roster of royal administrators at the beginning of David's Jerusalemite reign contains an introduction to list about David administering justice (2 Sam 8:15) followed by six **name and office formula** records (2 Sam 8:16a, 16b, 17a, 17b, 18a, 18b) naming who did what within that administration. The parallel roster in Chronicles contains an introduction to list (1 Chr 18:14) and six **name and office formula** records (1 Chr 18:15a, 15b, 16a, 16, 17a, 17b). The roster of royal administrators at the end of David's reign omits an introduction and consists solely of seven name and office formula records (2 Sam 20:23a, 23b, 24a, 24b, 25a, 25b, 26). The roster of Solomon's ministers contains an introduction to list (1 Kgs 4:1), a **list superscription** (1 Kgs 4:2a), and nine **name and office formula** records (1 Kgs 4:2b, 3a, 3b, 4a, 4b, 5a, 5b, 6a, 6b). It is followed by a roster of officers responsible for provisions. This contains a **roster introduction** (1 Kgs 4:7), a **list superscription** (1 Kgs 4:8a), and twelve **name and place formula** records (1 Kgs 4:8b, 9, 10, 11, 12, 13, 14, 15, 16, 17, 18, 19a) followed by a **note** (1 Kgs 4:19b).

The roster of David's warriors in 2 Sam 23 and its parallel in 1 Chr 11 contains a **list superscription** (2 Sam 23:8a [=1 Chr 11:10–11a]), six **hero and exploit records** (2 Sam 23:8b, 9–10, 11–12, 13–17, 18–19, 20–23 [= 1 Chr 11:11b, 12–14, omitted, 15–19, 20–21, 22–25]), and a macro-record concerning "the thirty" which is a **name list** of more than thirty warriors (2 Sam 23:24–39 [=1 Chr 11:26–41]). The names and order vary somewhat between the lists of "the thirty" but the most frequent record type is the **name and gentilic formula**, with the **patronymic formula** and **name and epithet records** also represented. There is a **tally** of thirty-seven warriors in the Samuel list that is missing from its Chronicles counterpart. Uriah the Hittite is the last warrior named in the

Samuel list, and this character plays a key role in 2 Sam 11; that episode is missing in Chronicles and Uriah is inconspicuously in the middle of the list in 1 Chr 11.

The roster of warriors that joined with David in 1 Chr 12 has a different pattern: a **list superscription** (1 Chr 12:1), a macro-record concerning Benjaminite warriors (1 Chr 12:2–8 [NRSV 2–7]), a macro-record concerning Gadite warriors (1 Chr 12:9–16 [NRSV 8–15]), a macro-record concerning a group led by Amasai (1 Chr 12:17–19 [NRSV 16–18]), a macro-record concerning deserting Manassites (1 Chr 12:20–22 [NRSV 19–21]), and a **summary statement** (1 Chr 12:23 [NRSN 22]). The macro-records contain a variety of **name and epithet records, name and gentilic formulas, name and rank formulas, name formulas, notes**, and **patronymic formulas**.

The roster of musicians (1 Chr 6:16–34 [NRSV 31–49]) consists of an **expansion of superscription** (1 Chr 6:16–17 [NRSV 31–32]), a **list superscription** (1 Chr 6:18a [NRSV 33a]), three lengthy **name and pedigree formula** records (1 Chr 6:18b–23, 24–28, 29–32 [NRSV 33b–38, 39–43, 44–47]), and two job description records (1 Chr 6:33–34 [NRSV 48–49]).

The roster of gatekeepers contains a **gatekeeper list record** (1 Chr 9:17–18), three **name/pedigree and task records** (1 Chr 9:19, 20, 21), a **tally** (1 Chr 9:22a), a couple of **notes** (1 Chr 9:22bα, 22bβ), and four **job description records** (1 Chr 9:23, 24–25, 26–27, 28).

The roster of Levites contains a **list superscription** (1 Chr 15:4) and six records concerning the Kohathites (1 Chr 15:5), the Merarites (1 Chr 15:6), the Gershonites (1 Chr 15:7), the Elizaphanites (1 Chr 15:8), the Hebronites (1 Chr 15:9), and the Uzzielites (1 Chr 15:10).

The roster of ark procession celebrants contains a **list superscription** (1 Chr 15:16), and nine **roster of celebrants records** concerning the first order of singers (1 Chr 15:17), the second order of singers (1 Chr 15:18), the symbol players (1 Chr 15:19), the harpists (1 Chr 15:20), the lyre players (1 Chr 15:21), the music director (1 Chr 15:22), the gate keepers (1 Chr 15:23), the trumpeters (1 Chr 15:24a), and supplemental gate keepers (1 Chr 15:24b).

The table of organization in 1 Chr 23–27 contains several rosters, including two rosters of Levites. The first roster of Levites (1 Chr 23:2–24) contains a **census list** (1 Chr 23:2–3), a **job description record** (1 Chr 23:4–5), a **segmented genealogy** (1 Chr 23:6–24), and a **job description record** (1 Chr 23:25–32). The second roster begins with a

list superscription which discusses "the rest of the sons of Levi" (1 Chr 24:20a), followed by seven **name list records** (1 Chr 24:20b–21, 22, 23, 24–25, 26–27, 28–29, 30a), a **list subscription** (1 Chr 24:30b), and a **job description record** (1 Chr 24:31). Of the thirty-eight thousand Levites, twenty-four thousand were assigned to work in the temple, six thousand were to be officers and judges, four thousand to be gatekeepers and four thousand to be musicians. These rosters only give us partial information as to which groups did what.

A roster of musicians (1 Chr 25:1–6) consists of a **list superscription** (1 Chr 25:1b) and three **roster of musicians records** concerning Asaph (1 Chr 25:2), Jeduthun (1 Chr 25:3), and Heman (1 Chr 25:4–6a), followed by a **list subscription** that connects Asaph, Jeduthun, and Heman (1 Chr 25:6b).

A roster of gatekeepers (1 Chr 26:1–19) has a **list introduction** (1 Chr 26:1a), a macro record concerning the Kohathites (1 Chr 26:1b-9), a record concerning the Merarites (1 Chr 26:10–11), a macro record consisting of six **job description records** (1 Chr 26:12–13, 14a, 14b, 15, 16, 17–18), and a **list subscription** (1 Chr 26:19).

The roster of Levitical guards (1 Chr 26:20–28) has a **list introduction** placing Ahijah in charge of the treasuries of the house of God and the treasuries of the dedicated gifts (1 Chr 26:20), followed by two **name/pedigree and task records** concerning the treasuries of the house of God (1 Chr 26:21–22, 23–24), and one **name/pedigree and task record** concerning the treasuries of the dedicated gifts (1 Chr 26:25–28). It is followed by a roster of Levitical supervisors outside the temple (1 Chr 26:29–32), consisting of three **name/pedigree and task records** (1 Chr 26:29, 30, 31a), and two **notes** (1 Chr 26:31b, 32).

The table of organization in 1 Chr 23–27 ends with a roster of royal administrators (1 Chr 27:25–34). This has no introduction or subscription. It contains twelve **name/pedigree and task records** (1 Chr 27:25a, 25b, 26, 27a, 27b, 28a, 28b, 29a, 29b, 30a, 30b, 30c), followed by a summarizing **note** (1 Chr 27:31), followed by six more **name/pedigree and task records** (1 Chr 27:32a, 32b, 33a, 33b, 34a, 34b).

Mazar, "Military Elite," 310–20; Mettinger, *Solomonic State Officials*; de Vries, *1 and 2 Chronicles*, 435; Williamson, "We are Yours," 164–76.

Rota

A rota is a **register** involving a fixed order of rotation, usually of officials on duty. The **table of organization** in 1 Chr 23–27 contains a **rota** of priestly divisions (1 Chr 24:1–19), a **rota** of musicians (1 Chr 25:8–31), and a **rota** of officials in charge of the monthly divisions (1 Chr 27:1–15). Because the father of John the Baptist belonged to the course of Abijah (Luke 1:5), New Testament scholars have attempted to use the 1 Chr 24 priestly rota to argue for when John the Baptist was born (Jesus was born six months later), but the issue is very complicated. More positively, the rotas of priests, musicians, and officials in 1 Chr 23–27 function, in harmony with other material in that section, to show David preparing the kingdom for the succession of Solomon.

Steinmann, "Information," 493–504; de Vries, *1 and 2 Chronicles*, 435; Williamson, "Origins," 251–68.

Segmented Genealogy

This is a **genealogy** which contains information on different branches of a family rather than tracing one line of descent. The genealogy of Lamech consists of a **birth report introduction** (Gen 4:19), the **birth reports** of Jabal (Gen 4:20), Jubal (Gen 4:21), Tubal-cain (Gen 4:22a) and a **note** on Naamah, the sister of Tubal-cain (Gen 4:22b). The genealogy is two generations deep and has a breadth of four. When connected to the immediately preceding **linear genealogy** of Cain, the extended genealogy of Cain has a breadth of four.

The genealogy of Nahor is partly in reported speech rather than directly from the narrator. It consists of a speech introduction emphasizing Nahor's wife, Milcah (Gen 22:20a), and a reported speech (Gen 22:20b–22) which consists of a **list superscription** (Gen 22:20b) followed by a **sons list** (Gen 22:21–22), consisting of three **name and epithet** records (Gen 22:21) and five **name formula** records (Gen 22:22). The narrator adds a **note** that one of these sons, Bethuel, begat Rebekah (Gen 22:23a) and follows it with the **list subscription**, again emphasizing Milcah. Finally, there is a birth report concerning the sons of Reumah, Nahor's concubine (Gen 22:24). The genealogy is three generations deep and has a breadth of eleven in the second generation.

The genealogy of Abraham and Keturah in Genesis contains an acquisition of wife element in a **birth report introduction** (Gen 25:1), a **birth report** of Keturah's six sons (Gen 25:2), a **begat list** of Jokshan's two sons (Gen 25:3a), and **sons lists** of Dedan's three sons (Gen 25:3b) and Midian's five sons (Gen 25:4a), and a **list subscription** (Gen 25:4b), yielding a genealogy four generations deep, with a breadth of seven in the third generation.

The **genealogy of Jacob's sons** in Gen 35:22b–26 contains a **list introduction** (35:22b), **sons lists** of Leah's six sons (35:23), Rachel's two sons (35:24), Bilhah's two sons (35:25), and Zilpah's two sons (35:26a), and a **list subscription** (35:26b), yielding a genealogy two generations deep, with a breadth of twelve in the second generation.

The genealogy of Esau begins with the toledot **formula** (Gen 36:1), a **birth report introduction** concerning Esau's wives, Adah, Oholibamah, and Basemath (Gen 36:2–3), the **birth report** of Adah's son, Eliphaz (Gen 36:4a), the **birth report** of Basemath's son, Reuel (Gen 36:4b), and the **birth report** of Oholibamah's sons, Jeush, Jalam and Korah (Gen 36:5a), and the **segmented genealogy subscription** (Gen 36:5b). A second genealogy of Esau consists of the toledot **formula** (Gen 35:9), a **son list** of Esau (Gen 35:10), and three **descendants from wife** records concerning Adah (Gen 36:11–12), Basemath (Gen 36:13) and Oholibamah (Gen 36:14). This genealogy has a depth of three generations with a breadth of ten in the third generation.

The genealogy of Seir the Horite begins with a **list superscription** (Gen 36:20a), a **sons list**of Seir (Gen 36:20b–21a) and a **list subscription** (Gen 36:21b). It then contains **sons lists** of Seir's various sons, Lotan (Gen 36:22a), Shobal (Gen 36:23), Zibeon (Gen 36:24a), Anah (Gen 36:25), Dishon (Gen 36:26), Ezer (Gen 36:27), and Dishan (Gen 36:28), a **list subscription** (Gen 36:29–30a), and an **expansion of subscription** (Gen 36:30b). It has notes in Gen 36:22b, 24b. The genealogy is only three generations deep but has a breadth of eighteen in the third generation.

Exodus 6:14–25 provides information on the descendants of the first three of Israel's sons by Leah: Reuben, Simeon, and Levi. It contains a **list superscription** (Exod 6:14a), followed by two records concerning the sons of Reuben (Exod 6:14b) and Simeon (Exod 6:15), and a full-fledged segmented genealogy of Levi (Exod 6:16–25). This genealogy consists of a **list superscription** (Exod 6:16), a macro-record concerning the descendants of Levi's sons, Gershon, Kohath, and Merari (Exod 6:17–19), a second macro-record concerning the descendants of Kohath (Exod 6:20–22), a third macro-record concerning the next generation but with special attention on Aaron (Exod 6:23–24), a record concerning

Aaron's son, Eleazor (Exod 6:25a), and a **list subscription**. The first two records concerning Reuben and Simeon respectively consist of a **son list superscription** (Exod 6:14bα; 6:15aα), a **son list** proper (Exod 6:14bβ; 6:15aβ), and a **list subscription** (Exod 6:14bγ; 6:15b).

Exodus 6:14–25 is a genealogy seven generations deep from Israel to Phinehas, with a breadth of thirteen in the third generation, eight in the fourth generation, eight in the fifth generation, four in the sixth generation, but only one, Phinehas, in the seventh generation. This fact, plus the fact that the three **birth reports** in this genealogy give information on the female ancestors of Phinehas (Exod 6:20, 23, 25), plus the fact that the **notes** concerning age regarding Levi, Kohath and Amram (Exod 6:16, 18, 20) involved direct ancestors of Phinehas, all suggest that a main function of the genealogy is to provide information on the ancestry of a key character involved in a **covenant establishment narrative** (Num 25:10–18).

The genealogy in 1 Sam 14:49–51 is unusual because it begins by giving information regarding the third and fourth generations before discussing the second generation and then the first generation. It begins with a **son list** of Saul (1 Sam 14:49a) and a **daughter list** of Saul (1 Sam 14:49b). It then has a note about Saul's wife and father-in-law (1 Sam 14:50a), and a **note** about Saul's army commander, Abner who is described as the son of Saul's uncle, Ner (1 Sam 14:50b). Finally, it tells us that Saul's father is Kish (1 Sam 14:51a), and that the father of Ner, and presumably Kish, is Abiel (1 Sam 14:51b). The genealogy is four generations deep and has a breadth of five in the fourth generation.

The genealogy of Adam in 1 Chr 1:1–27 contains an **unexplained name list** going from Adam to Noah's sons, Shem, Ham, and Japheth (1 Chr 1:1–4); macro-records containing multiple **son lists** concerning the descendants of Japheth (1 Chr 1:5–7), Ham (1 Chr 1:8–16), and Shem (1 Chr 1:17–23); and another **unexplained name list** going from Shem to Abraham (1 Chr 1:24–27). This structure of unexplained name lists bracketing explicitly genealogical information parallels the Akkadian King list. The genealogy is twenty generations deep, with thirty-one breadth in the twelfth generation.

The following genealogy of Abraham (1 Chr 1:28–37) contains **sons lists** of Abraham (1:28), Ishmael (1:29–31), Keturah (1:32), Midian (1:33), Isaac (1:34), Esau (1:35), Eliphaz (1:36), and Reuel (1:37), including sundry **list subscriptions**, **list superscriptions** and **begat formulas**.

The genealogy is five generations deep and attains a breadth of eleven in the fifth generation.

The genealogy of Seir (1 Chr 1:38–42) consists of the **son list** of Seir (1 Chr 1:38), followed by the **son lists** of Seir's sons, Lotan (1 Chr 1:39), Shobal (1 Chr 1:40a), Zibeon (1 Chr 1:40b), Anah (1 Chr 1:41a), Dishon (1 Chr 1:41b), Ezer (1 Chr 1:42a), and Dishan (1 Chr 1:42b). The genealogy is only three generations deep but attains a breadth of twenty in the third generation.

The genealogy of Judah has records concerning the sons of Judah (1 Chr 2:3–4), the next generation (1 Chr 2:5–6), and the next generation (1 Chr 2:7–8). The first record contains a **son list** of Judah via Bath-shua (1 Chr 2:3a), a **note** concerning the eldest son, Er (1 Chr 2:3b), a **birth report** of the sons Tamar bore to Judah (1 Chr 2:4a), and a **tally** of Judah's sons (1 Chr 2:4b). The second record consists of a **son list** of Perez (1 Chr 2:5) and a **son list** of Zarah, including a **tally** (1 Chr 2:6).

The genealogy of Hezron begins with a son list (1 Chr 2:9). The macro-record concerning his son Ram (1 Chr 2:10–17) consists of a **linear genealogy** up to Jesse (1 Chr 2:10–12), a **begat list** of Jesse's sons (1 Chr 2:13–15) and a **note** concerning their sisters, Zeruaiah and Abigail (1 Chr 2:16a), a **son list** of Zeruaiah (1 Chr 2:16b), and a **birth report** of Amasa to Abigail and Jether (1 Chr 2:17). The macro-record concerning Caleb (1 Chr 2:18–24) contains a **note** that he had children by Azuba (1 Chr 2:18a), a **son list** by Jerioth (1 Chr 2:18b), a **note** on the death of Azuba (1 Chr 2:19a), a **birth report** of Hur by Ephrath (1 Chr 2:19b), and two **begat formulas** (1 Chr 2:20a, 20b) leading to Hur's grandson, Bezalel. A somewhat difficult intrusion (1 Chr 2:21–23) contains a **birth report** of Segub to the daughter of Machir (1 Chr 2:21), a begat formula leading to Jair (1 Chr 2:22a), a note concerning Jair's towns (1 Chr 2:22b), a note concerning Geshur and Aram (1 Chr 2:23a), and a subscription concerning Machir (1 Chr 2:23b), before Caleb has another son, Ashur, father of Tekoah (1 Chr 2:24), although there are textual difficulties in the verse. The macro-record concerning Jerahmeel (1 Chr 2:25–33) contains four records of successive generations (1 Chr 2:25–26, 27–28a, 28b, 29–30) reaching to Appaim, then a four deep **linear genealogy** leading to Ahlai (1 Chr 2:31), then a leap back to Jada, Jerahmeel's grandson (1 Chr 2:32–33a), and a segmented genealogy subscription (1 Chr 2:33b).

The genealogy of Caleb the brother of Jerahmeel (1 Chr 2:42–50a) is not the easiest to unravel but contains **son lists** (1 Chr 2:42, 43, 45a, 47), the **begat formula** (1 Chr 2:44a, 44b, 46b), **birth reports** (1 Chr 2:46a,

48, 49a), **notes** (1 Chr 2:45b), and a segmented genealogy subscription (1 Chr 2:50a).

The genealogy of Hur contains the **son list** of Hur including Shobal and Salma (1 Chr 2:50b–51), the **son list** of Shobal (1 Chr 2:52–53), the **son list** of Salma (1 Chr 2:54), and **notes** concerning the Jabezites (1 Chr 2:55a) and the Kenites (1 Chr 2:55b). The genealogy has a depth of three generations but the breadth is difficult to assess since the material is partly genealogical and partly gentilic (discussing clans).

First Chronicles 5:1–26 discusses the Trans-Jordanian tribes of Reuben, Gad, and half-Manasseh and contains a genealogical section concerning Reuben (1 Chr 5:1–10), a genealogical section concerning Gad (1 Chr 5:11–17), a short **battle narrative** (1 Chr 5:18–22), a **chiefs list** of half-Manasseh (1 Chr 5:23–24), and a short **exile narrative** that connects the common destiny of Reuben, Gad, and half-Manasseh (1 Chr 5:25–26).

The genealogical section concerning Reuben has a son list of Reuben (1 Chr 5:1–3), a **linear genealogy** of Joel (1 Chr 5:4–6a), a **muster roll** (1 Chr 5:6b–8), and a battle narrative (1 Chr 5:9–10). The genealogical section concerning Gad has a **son list** of Gad (1 Chr 5:11–12), a **muster roll** (1 Chr 5:13–15), a **note** concerning dwelling areas (1 Chr 5:16), and a **note** concerning when they were enrolled (1 Chr 5:17). Difficulties such as the relationship of Joel to other parts of the Reubenite genealogy, and where the Manassite chiefs fit in a genealogy of Manasseh, make it hard to assess the depth and breadth of the implied segmented genealogy in 1 Chr 5:1–26.

The genealogy of Naphtali is a simple two generation genealogy with a breadth of four, consists of a **segmented genealogy superscription** (1 Chr 7:13a), a **son list** proper of four sons (1 Chr 7:13b), and a **segmented genealogy subscription** (1 Chr 7:13c).

The genealogy of Benjamin consists of the **begat formula** (1 Chr 8:1–2) and the **son list** for Benjamin's firstborn, Bela (1 Chr 8:3–5), yielding a three deep generation that has a breadth of nine in the third generation.

The genealogy of Shaharaim consists of a segmented genealogy superscription (1 Chr 8:8), a **son list** via Hodesh (1 Chr 8:9–10), a **son list** via Hushim (1 Chr 8:11), a son list of Hushim's son, Elpal (1 Chr 8:12–13, including notes in 12b and 13b). It has a depth of three generations and a breadth of nine in the second generation.

The genealogy of Jeiel contains an **introduction** (1 Chr 8:29), a **son list** (1 Chr 8:30–31), a **begat formula** presumably, considering the parallel in 1 Chr 9:37, concerning a son accidentally omitted from the son list (1 Chr 8:32a) and a **note** (1 Chr 8:32b). The same pattern occurs in 1 Chr 9:35–38.

The genealogy of Ner contains **begat formulas** (1 Chr 8:33a, 34b, 36a, 36c, 37a), a **begat list** (1 Chr 8:33b, 36b), **son lists** (1 Chr 8:34a, 35, 38, 39), **his son formulas** (1 Chr 8:37b), a **note** concerning the descendants of Ulam (1 Chr 8:40a) and a **list subscription** (1 Chr 8:40b). The genealogy from Kish to Ulam is fifteen generations deep with a breadth of nine in the fifteenth generation. There is a parallel in 1 Chr 9:35–44 that covers the same material as 1 Chr 8:33–38.

The **roster** of Levites appointed by David to work in the temple is organized according to which branch (Gershon, Kohath, or Merari) of Levi's descendants the officials come from, which entails a segmented genealogy of Levi. This genealogy contains **son lists** of Levi (1 Chr 23:6), Gershon (1 Chr 23:7), Ladan (1 Chr 23:8–9, but there are textual problems in verse 9), and Shimei (1 Chr 23:10); two **notes** concerning Shimei's sons (1 Chr 23:11a, 11b); son lists of Kohath (1 Chr 23:12) and Amram (1 Chr 23:13a); **notes** concerning Aaron (1 Chr 23:13b) and Moses (1 Chr 23:14); **son lists** of Moses (1 Chr 23:15), Gershom (1 Chr 23:16), Eliezer (1 Chr 23:17), Izhar (1 Chr 23:18), Hebron (1 Chr 23:19), Uzziel (1 Chr 23:20), Merari (1 Chr 23:21a), and Mahli (1 Chr 23:21b); a **note** concerning Eliezer (1 Chr 23:22); and a **son list** of Mushi (1 Chr 23:23). The genealogy is six generations deep with a breadth of sixteen in the fourth generation.

Son List

This is a subcategory of **name list** in which the names are all sons of the man mentioned in the **son list superscription**. The most common record consists of the **name formula**, but other possibilities are the **name and rank formula** and the **rank, name, and mother formula**. The son list is frequently a record in a **segmented genealogy** and its purpose is to provide genealogical information. Examples are too numerous to include, but **son list as genealogical record** mentions the majority of them.

Tribal Appointee List

This is a subcategory of **name list**, whose organizing principle is the task they have been appointed to carry out. It can develop suspense as to whether the appointees will succeed in their task or not. The list in Num 1:4–16 consists of a **list superscription** (Num 1:4–5a), twelve **tribe and appointee formula** records (Num 1:5b–15) and a **list subscription** (Num 1:16). The appointees then conducted the **census** of their tribes without incident (see bibliography of **census** for articles on Num 1).

The list in Num 13 also contains a **list superscription** (Num 13:4a), twelve **tribe and appointee formula** records (Num 13:4b–15), and a **tribal appointee list subscription** (Num 13:16a). The appointees then explored or spied out the land of Canaan, but (with the exceptions of Caleb from Judah and Hoshea from Ephraim) did not give an adequate report, leading to the Israelites rebelling again and receiving divine judgment of forty years wandering in the wilderness. The two appointees who succeed in their mission are rewarded, and their tribes become the leading tribes in Israelite history.

The list of chief officers in 1 Chr 27:16–22, as part of a **table of organization**, consists of a **list superscription** (1 Chr 27:16a), thirteen **tribe and appointee formula** records (1 Chr 27:16b–22a) and a **list subscription** (1 Chr 27:22b).

Beck, "Geography," 271–80.

Tribal Ritual List

Deut 27:12 divides the tribes into those who bless the people from Mount Gerizim: "Simeon, Levi, Judah, Issachar, Joseph, and Benjamin" and those who curse the people from Mount Ebal: "Reuben, Gad, Asher, Zebulun, Dan, and Naphtali."

Unexplained Name List

This is a **name list** without any explanation of the principle of categorization. The book of Chronicles begins, "Adam, Seth, Enosh; Kenan, Mahalalel, Jared; Enoch, Methuselah, Lamech; Noah, Shem, Ham, Japheth" (1 Chr 1:1–4). In the **linear genealogy** of Gen 5, each name from Seth to Noah is the son of the previous name, but Shem, Ham, and Japheth are the sons of Noah. The same chapter contains another unexplained name list, "Shem, Arpachshad, Shelah; Eber, Peleg, Reu; Serug, Terah, Nahor; Abram, that is, Abraham" (1 Chr 1:24–27) which we know from Gen 11 to be a **linear genealogy**. Both lists are part of the large **segmented genealogy** that opens 1 Chronicles.

Tables

A table is an organized grouping of lists that forms a distinct unit of writing. Like list itself, it does not have to be limited to assertive speech acts, and the food laws in Lev 11 and Deut 14 are tables of directives.

Table of Boundaries and Allotments

The sole example in prophetic literature is in Ezek 47:13–48:29, which is toward the end of the **future temple vision narrative** in Ezek 40–48, and describes the boundaries of the Israelite tribes in the future. It may be patterned on Ancient Near Eastern royal grants, with YHWH granting land to the future loyal vassal Israel. The macro-list consists of a **list superscription** (Ezek 47:13–14), a **boundaries list** (Ezek 37:15–20), a **list subscription** (Ezek 47:21–23), an **allotments half-list** (Ezek 48:1–7), a **list interruption** discussing the portions set aside for the Zadokites, Levites, and the prince (Ezek 48:8–22), a second **allotments half-list** (Ezek 48:23–28) and a **list subscription** (Ezek 47:29).

The boundaries listed in Ezek 47:15–20 approximate those in Num 34:2–12, excluding the Trans-Jordanian territories of Reuben, Gad, and half of Manasseh, as well as Aramean and Edomite territory that had at times been occupied by conquering Israelites. Ezekiel envisions the tribes arranged in parallel with Dan northernmost and then progressing southwards Asher, Naphtali, Manasseh, Ephraim, Reuben, Judah, Benjamin, Simeon, Issachar, Zebulun, and Gad (Ezek 48:1–7, 23–28). Between the allotments for Judah and Benjamin lie the territories assigned to the Zadokites, the Levites, and the prince (Ezek 48:8–22). The six central tribal boundaries are for the first four sons of Leah and the two sons of Rachel, with the sons of the handmaids and Leah's last two sons assigned the outer territories. This continues the theme in Ezek 40–48 of a highly structured hierarchy. As with the rest of Ezek 40–48, this passage's teleological cause is a controversial topic ranging from entirely utopian construct to informing its addressees of the geopolitical realities of the messianic age.

Brodsky, "Utopian Map," 20–26; Greenberg, "Idealism and Practicality," 59–66; Warren, "Tenure and Grant," 323–34.

Table of Directives

This is a complex of lists involving directives—whether they be commands, permissions, or prohibitions—organized around a certain topic. Leviticus 11:1–47 and Deuteronomy 14:3–21 are examples concerning clean and unclean foods (see **food law** in legal genres chapter). The more extensive **festival calendar lists** can also be considered tables of directives and are discussed in **cultic calendar law**.

Table of Genealogical Information

This is a complex of information, much of which is genealogical, about a particular topic. Genesis 36:1–43 is a table of genealogical information about the Edomites which encompasses most of two *toledot* sections (see overview of Tanak chapter). It begins with a **genealogical narrative** concerning Esau (Gen 36:1–9), containing the **toledot formula** (Gen 36:1), a **segmented genealogy** containing **birth reports** (Gen 36:2–5), and a **settlement narrative** (Gen 36:6–8). It is followed by a second **segmented genealogy** of Esau (Gen 36:9–14), also beginning with a toledot **formula** (Gen 36:9). Then comes a genealogically based **chief/clan list** (Gen 36:15–19), the **segmented genealogy** of Seir the Horite (Gen 36:20–30), an Edomite **king list** (Gen 36:31–39), and a second **chief/clan** list (Gen 36:40–43).

First Chronicles 1 contains a **segmented genealogy** of Adam (1 Chr 1:1–27) involving two **unexplained name lists** (1 Chr 1:1–4, 24–27), a **segmented genealogy** of Abraham (1 Chr 1:28–37), a **segmented genealogy** of Seir (1 Chr 1:38–42), an Edomite **king list** (1 Chr 1:43–51a), and an Edomite **chief/clan list** (1 Chr 1:51b–54). The purpose of this table is to set the following table of genealogical information concerning Israel (1 Chr 2–8) in the universal genealogy.

First Chronicles 2–8 is a large table of genealogical information consisting of a **list superscription** (1 Chr 2:1–2), the table of organization proper (1 Chr 2:3–8:40), and a **list subscription** (1 Chr 9:1a). The table proper is divided according to tribe: a complicated section involving Judah (1 Chr 2:3–4:23) and Simeon (1 Chr 4:24–43), an implied **segmented genealogy** involving the Trans-Jordanian tribes (1 Chr 5:1–26), another complicated section involving Levi (1 Chr 5:27–6:66 [NRSV 6:1–81]), a **muster roll** concerning Issachar (1 Chr 7:1–5), a **muster roll** concerning Benjamin (1 Chr 7:6–12), a **name list** concerning Naphtali (1 Chr 7:13), a **segmented genealogy** concerning Manasseh (1 Chr 7:14–19), a brief but complicated section concerning Ephraim (1 Chr 7:20–29), a **muster roll** concerning Asher that contains a **segmented genealogy** and a series of **son lists** (1 Chr 7:30–40), and another complicated section discussing Benjamin again (1 Chr 8:1–40).

The table in 1 Chr 2–8 likely serves several purposes: honoring the pre-exilic heroes, stressing the importance of key lines like David and Aaron, and pointing to Jerusalem and Israel as the theological center of the world populace.

Assis, "Adam to Esau," 287–302; Braun, "1 Chronicles 1–9," 93–105; de Vries, *1 and 2 Chronicles*, 436; Japhet, *Ideology*, 499–504; Kartveit, *Motive*; Levin, "Lists to History," 601–36; Noth, *Chronicler's History*; Oeming, *Wahre Israel*; Sparks, *Chronicler's Genealogies*.

Table of Organization

This is a complex of administrative lists, such as **rosters** and **rotas**, that details portions of the organizational structure of a state. The clearest example is 1 Chr 23:2–27:34 which consists of a **roster** of Levites (1 Chr 23:2–32), a **rota** of priestly divisions (1 Chr 24:1–19), a second **roster** of Levites (1 Chr 24:20–31), a **roster** of musicians (1 Chr 25:1–7), a **rota** of musicians and lots (1 Chr 25:8–31), a **roster** of gatekeepers (1 Chr 26:1–19), a **roster** of Levitical guards (1 Chr 26:20–28), a **roster** of Levitical supervisors outside the temple (1 Chr 26:29–32), a **rota** of officials in charge of the various monthly divisions (1 Chr 27:1–15), a **tribal appointee list** (1 Chr 27:16–24), and a **roster** of royal administrators (1 Chr 27:25–34).

Mettinger, *Solomonic State Officials*; de Vries, *1 and 2 Chronicles*, 188–90.

Trade List

This is a subcategory of **onomasticon** which lists the cities/regions that the thematic city/region traded with and the items traded. Ezek 27:12–24 is the only biblical example. It has no superscription or subscription, but consists of twelve **trade list records** listing Tyre's imports: metals from Tarshish; slaves and bronze from Javan, Tubal, and Meshech; horses from Beth Togarmah; ivory and ebony from Rhodes; jewels and fabrics from Aram/Edom (a text critical issue is involved; the referent is probably Edom because Damascus later in the list is likely a synecdoche for Aram); wheat, honey, and oil from Judah and the land of Israel; wine and wool from Damascus; iron, cinnamon, and spice reed from Uzal; saddlecloths from Dedan; sheep and goats from Arabia and Kedar; and garments and carpets from Haran, Canneh, Eden, Asshur, and Kilmad. This table of trade is part of a **mock dirge** (see prophetic genres) against Tyre (Ezek 27:1–36; Tyre here being portrayed as a ship), and its teleological cause is to portray Tyre's present greatness as a trading ship in contrast to its future calamity.

Goering, "Proleptic Fulfillment," 483–505; Good, "Ezekiel's Ship," 79–103; Liverani, "Trade Network," 65–79; Newsom, "Maker of Metaphors," 151–64; Wilson, "Tyre," 249–62.

2

Legal Genres

INTRODUCTION TO LAW IN THE HEBREW BIBLE

A LAW IS AN authoritative directive illocution that is legally binding upon a community (which can extend to all human beings). With the exception of the laws in the Noahide code, laws in the Hebrew Bible are primarily divine directives addressed to Israelites or subsets thereof. No biblical book is entirely law; rather the laws are elucidated within more than forty legislative speech narratives and legal case narratives. Judaism recognizes 365 positive precepts and 248 negative precepts which constitute the 613 total precepts of Torah. Biblical scholarship identifies certain collections of laws as law codes (the Noahic code in Gen 9, the Decalogue in Exod 20 and Deut 5, the Covenant Code in Exod 21–23, the Exod 34 Code, the Holiness Code in Lev 17–26, the Priestly Code containing the laws in Exodus through Numbers not in the other law codes, and the Deuteronomic Code in Deut 5–26), most of which are discussed in the overview of Tanak chapter. References are often made to these law codes in the glossary entries.

This glossary concerns the legal content of the legislative speech narratives and the legal case narratives in Torah and the legal content of future laws in the book of Ezekiel. It is beyond the scope of this glossary to discuss the extent to which this legal content governed the actual legal practice of ancient Israel and Judah at different periods, a topic on which there is little direct evidence.

Laws regulate human behavior. There are different, overlapping ways of categorizing laws. One categorization method is according to grammatical and syntactical considerations, yielding such categories as **apodictic law, case law, command, order, prohibition** etc.

Another is according to scholastic theological considerations, yielding such categories as eternal law, natural law, divine law, and human law. These categories interest Christian ethicists concerned with which laws in the Hebrew Bible are incumbent upon and hence knowable by all human beings (a thin definition of natural law). Within Judaism, the distinction between natural law and divine law (laws specially revealed in Scripture) is irrelevant to the question of obligations upon Jews. However, the concept of natural law is implicit in Judaism, which considers the Noahic code as incumbent upon all humans, and Jewish theologians have made significant contributions to natural law theory. This glossary does not have entries to these categories (or the related categories of moral law and ceremonial law more common in Protestant circles) but some resources are mentioned in the bibliography below and various entries make reference to natural law. Nor does it analyze which laws are criminal and which are civil; but it does have an entry on civil law, explaining which tractates in Mishnah deal with that topic.

A third categorization method is according to whose behavior is being regulated, yielding such categories as **laws concerning ceremonially unclean persons, laws regulating women, laws regulating priests, laws regulating the king** etc.

Laws may also be categorized according to the severity of the offense and/or punishment inflicted by the law, yielding categories such as **cut off laws, death penalty laws, financial restoration laws** etc. Perhaps the most important method of categorizing is by the content matter of the law, yielding such categories as **cultic calendar instructions, homicide laws, poverty laws, sex laws, slave laws** etc.

Alt, "Origins," 79–132; Barton, *Understanding*; Boecker, *Law and Justice*; Carmichael, *Law and Narrative*; Budziszewski, *Not Know*; Falk, *Hebrew Law*; Feser, *Neo-Scholastic Essays*, 297–356; Fitzpatrick-McKinley, *Transformation of Torah*; Knierim, "Problem," 7–25; Levinson, *Theory and Method*; Matthews, Levinson, and Frymer-Kensky, *Gender and Law*; Novak, *Natural Law*; Patrick, *Old Testament Law*; Rushdoony, *Institutes*; VanDrunen, *Biblical Case*; Watts, *Reading Law*; Weinfeld, *Social Justice*; Westbrook, *Studies*.

LEGAL FORMULAS AND CLAUSE-LEVEL GENRES

Absolute Law

This is a syntactic category and is in opposition to **conditional law**. Its basic subcategories are **command, permission**, and **prohibition**. It does not typically state the penalty for disobedience. An alternative approach regards **apodictic law** as laws that originated in a certain setting and might include **participial construction laws.**

Amen Formula: "And all the people shall say: 'Amen.'"

This formula is a third person directive. It occurs 12 times in a **blessing and cursing passage** in Deut 27:15–26 where it commands the people to affirm the curses pronounced on the disobedient. A variant occurs in Num 5:22, where the accused affirms the **imprecation** invoked if found guilty. More positively, it occurs in a blessing context in the **concluding doxology** of Ps 106:48.

Accusing Question Formula: "Why have you done this thing?" or "What have you done?"

This formula is a **question** at the locutionary level and presupposes an **accusation** at the illocutionary level. It can function as an **expression of disapproval** for the act concerned or as an inquiry to elicit information. In Tanak, it occurs in narratives rather than laws.

"Be Careful Lest" Construction

The Hebrew word translated "be careful" is an imperative, reflecting a command, but is followed by "lest" and a prohibited action and a possible consequence of disregarding the prohibition. The construction is thus parenetic and occurs in the Exod 34 and Deuteronomic law codes (Exod 34:12a; Deut 4:9, 15–18, 23; 6:12; 8:11; 11:16; 12:13–14, 19, 29–30; 15:9).

Benefit of Obedience

This is a subcategory of **parenesis** which focuses on the positive consequences should the addressee keep the law (Exod 13:9, 16; Lev 15:31; 17:5–7a; Num 6:27; 15:39–40 18:5b; Deut 12:25; 14:23b, 29b; 16:3c; 17:13, 19b–20; 24:13b, 19b; 19:10, 13b; 25:15b–16; 30:19c–20; 31:12b–13).

Blessed Are You Formula: "Blessed are you" (Heb: *bārûk 'attâ*)

This formula occurs six times in Deut 28:3–6 concerning blessings for obedience in a **blessings and curses passage**. On other occasions, it can function expressively as a greeting (1 Sam 15:13; 26:25) or, in prayer, as a variant of the **blessed be YHWH formula** (1 Chr 29:10; Ps 119:12). See also **blessing wish formula**.

Gerstenberger, *Psalms 2*, 539; Knierim and Coats, *Numbers*, 363; Salonen, *Hoflichkeitsformeln*, 20–44, 59–60, 72–76, 85–106; Towner, "'Blessed," 386–99.

Blessing Wish Formula: "May YHWH bless you"

This is a **wellwish** using the Hebrew word *bārak*, "bless" and occurs as part of a **greeting** (Ruth 2:4), in a **blessing subunit** of a psalm (Ps 128:5; 134:3; see also Jer 31:23) or as part of a **ritual recitation** (Num 6:24). When preceded in a legal or covenantal context by a conjunction like "so that" it functions as a benefit of obedience (Gen 27:10; Deut 14:29; 15:10; 16:10, 15; 23:21; 24:19). See **blessed are you formula, blessed be YHWH formula**.

Gerstenberger, *Psalms 2*, 539; Knierim and Coats, *Numbers*, 363; Salonen, *Hoflichkeitsformeln*, 20–44, 59–60, 72–76, 85–106; Towner, "Blessed," 386–99.

Blood Restriction Formula: "His blood is upon him."

This formula declares that the guilt typically associated with blood is restricted to the executed and does not affect the executor. It occurs in the Holiness Code (Lev 17:4b; 19:26; 20:11, 12, 13, 16, 27).

Hals, *Ezekiel*, 359; Koch, "Spruch," 396–416; Reventlow, "Sein Blut," 311–27.

Case

This is a syntactical category, namely the protasis (if-clause) in a **case law**, **conditional promise**, or **conditional threat**. It can be either second or third person. For longer procedural laws, see **case for procedure**.

Case Law

This is a syntactic category, a law consisting of a **case** and a **prescription**. The most frequent pattern is for both case and prescription to be third person, but there are consistent second person case laws and mixed person case laws. See also **conditional law**.

Case-Permission Law

This is a variant of **case law**, in which a **permission** replaces the **prescription** (Exod 12:44, 48a; Deut 12:20, 21; 14:24–26; 18:6–8).

Command

A command is a positive authoritative expression to an addressee to perform some action. In speeches within narratives, the standard grammatical form is the imperative and the **command to speak formula** is a good example. In promulgating positive laws, however, imperatives are occasionally used (Exod 13:2; 20:12; Deut 5:16), but the second person imperfect "you shall do X" is far more frequent. An infinitive absolute can also function as an imperative (Exod 20:8; Deut 5:12; on the sabbath the congregations sing a compound form of these infinitive absolutes "keep and remember"). For third person commands (as opposed to prescriptions), the jussive is the usual grammatical form. The opposite of command is **prohibition**. See **absolute law**.

Command to Speak Formula: "Speak to the children of Israel, saying"

This command typically follows the **YHWH Speech Introduction formula** and precedes the legal content of the legislative speech. It is typically addressed to Moses (or Moses and Aaron) and thus highlights Moses as mediator between YHWH and Israel.

Conditional Law

This is a syntactic category, encompassing all laws which prescribe what to do should a certain condition arise. The bulk of conditional laws are **case laws** but **participial construction laws** and **relative pronoun construction laws** also fit this category.

Conditional Promise

This is the legal analogue to the **conditional prophecy of salvation** consisting of a **case** stating the condition, and the **promise** describing the benefits if the condition is met. Its opposite is **conditional threat** and a **branched conditional subunit** combines both. Deuteronomy 11:13–15 contains a **case** in which Israel keeps God's commandments (Deut 11:13), and **promises** concerning fertile agriculture (Deut 11:14–15). Deuteronomy 11:22–25 contains a **case** in which Israel observes God's commandment (Deut 11:22), and a series of promises concerning victory over other nations (Deut 11:23–25). See **blessings and curses passages**.

Conditional Threat

This is the legal analogue to **conditional prophecy of punishment** (see genres of prophetic punishment). It contains a **case** (typically of Israel being disobedient), and YHWH's **threat** (frequently in the form of a curse). The main examples are in the **blessing and curse passages** in Lev 26 and Deut 28. See also **curse list**. A **branched conditional** subunit may combine conditional promise and conditional threat. Its opposite is **conditional promise**.

Cost of Disobedience

This is a subcategory of **parenesis** which emphasizes the negative consequences should the addressee disobey the law (Lev 16:3b; Deut 20:18; 25:3b; 24:15b). Some of the **"be careful lest" constructions** also perform this function. Its opposite is the **benefit of obedience**.

Curse Formula: "Cursed are you when …" or "Cursed is the one who does …"

This formula uses the Hebrew word *'ārûr*, "curse," and occurs in a variety of settings. YHWH uses it as an exercitive upon the serpent, the ground, and Cain (Gen 3:14, 17; 4:11). It can also be part of a **curse list** or a **conditional threat** in a blessings and curses passage (Deut 27:11–26; 28:16–19; Jer 11:3) or as a strong opposite to a beatitude (Jer 17:5; 48:10).

Cut Off Prescription Formula: "That man will be cut off from among his people"

This formula is a subcategory of the **prescription of punishment**. There is a debate about the severity of the punishment involved in this formula. Perhaps it means banishment and loss of inheritance rights or even exclusion from the afterlife. It occurs in Gen 17:14; Exod 12:15, 19; 30:33, 38; 31:14; Lev 7:20, 21, 25, 27; 17:4, 9, 14; 18:29, 19:8; 20:17, 18; 22:3; 23:29; Num 9:13; 15:30, 31; 19:13, 20.

Hartley, *Leviticus*, 272; Milgrom, *Leviticus*, 335; Wold, "Kareth," 1.1–45.

Death Sentence Formula: "He shall surely die/be put to death."

Also known as the *mot yumat* formula from the Hebrew phrase, this is typically used as the apodosis in **death penalty laws**.

Haas, "Surely Die," 67–88; Knierim and Coats, *Numbers*, 364; Schulz, *Todesrecht*.

Holiness Command Formula: "You/he/they shall be holy."

This is a **directive** illocution that can be in 2nd or 3rd person and is typically found in the **Holiness Code** (Lev 19:2; 20:7, 26; 21:6, 7, 8). It directs a person or group in special relationship with YHWH to be holy because YHWH is holy (Lev 19:2).

Hartley, *Leviticus*, 312; Knierim and Coats, *Numbers*, 367.

Identification of Holiness Formula: "It is most holy"

This is typically a nominal clause, such as "it is most holy," identifying an offering as holy or very holy (Lev 2:3b, 10b; 6:10b, 18b, 22b [NRSV 17b, 25b, 29b]; 7:1b, 6b). It is frequently found in proximity to a **disposition of leftovers** section granting the priests the right to eat of the sacrifice.

Make Atonement Formula: "The priest shall make atonement for PN and PN shall be forgiven."

This is a written formula behind which likely lies an oral exercitive formula that the authorized priest would ritually recite and that speech would bring about a new social fact—PN would be forgiven. It can occur in an **offering/sacrifice law** (Lev 4:20b, 26b, 31b, 35b; 5:6b, 10b, 13a, 16b, 18b, 26 [NRSV 6:7]; Num 15:25–26, 28), in a **law concerning ceremonially unclean persons** (Lev 12:7a, 8b; 14:21b, 31), or in the rituals involved on the Day of Atonement (Lev 16:6b, 16; see **Day of Atonement passage**).

Motive Clause

This is a clause, frequently beginning with "because," which provides a rationale for the addressee to keep the particular law. It may be grounded in YHWH's character or past actions on behalf of Israel, or it may be a future oriented **benefit of obedience** or **cost of disobedience**.

Barton, *Ethics*, 137–44; Sonsino, *Motive Clauses*.

Manner of Death Clause

This occurs in relation to a **death sentence law** and decrees how the execution is performed. Syntactically, the clause may be a command or a prescription. The most frequent manner of death is stoning (Exod 21:29; Lev 20:2, 27; 24:14, 16; Num 15:35 Deut 13:10; 17:5; 21:21; 22:21, 24). Hanging is mentioned in Deut 21:22 but may refer to hanging as a warning to others after the actual execution. The avenger of blood (**asylum law**) would obviously have used a method other than stoning.

One Law Formula: "You shall have one law/statute for the stranger and for the native."

This formula expresses the validity of the law for all classes of society (Exod 12:49; Lev 24:16, 22; Num 9:14; 15:15, 16, 29). YHWH desires resident aliens to be treated equally as native Israelites for many laws. In scholastic terms, it exhibits the principle of impartiality (see **prohibition of partiality** which disallows judges from showing favoritism to the poor or to the rich [Exod 23:3; Deut 1:17]) because, while certain classes such as priests may have special obligations and privileges in narrowly-defined situations, there was the expectation that the basic laws applied evenly to all people.

Hartley, *Leviticus*, 410–11; Knierim and Coats, *Numbers*, 366.

Order

Although "order" can be used as a general term of which **command** and **prohibition** are subcategories, this glossary reserves it for laws which juxtapose **command** and **prohibition** (in either order) concerning the same topic. The second element may be for clarification or for emphasis (Lev 19:15; 23:7, 8b, 22; 25:43; Num 5:2; 18:17; 35:31–32; Deut 7:26; 12:2–4, 16, 17–18, 23–24; 13:5–6a, 9–11, 16–17a; 15:23; 16:3a, 5–6, 8b, 16b–17; 17:11; 19:15; 22:19b; 24:1, 3, 4, 10–11, 12–13a, 14–15a; 25:12, 19; Ezek 44:2b, 20, 22; 45:8b; 46:18).

Knierim and Coats, *Numbers*, 353.

Participial Construction Laws

This is a syntactical category in which the protasis is a participle and the apodosis is a third person imperfect. Examples include **death penalty laws** (Exod 21:12); **cut off laws** (Lev 7:25), **declarations of uncleanness** (Lev 14:46), **prescriptions of washing** (Lev 14:47) etc. It is a subcategory of **conditional law**.

Permission

This is midway between a **command** and a **prohibition** in that the action/activity it regulates is neither obligatory nor prohibited. Most examples of permissions occur in contexts where they are contrasted with **prohibitions** (Lev 11:2b–3, 9, 21; 21:1b–5, 11–12, 22; 22:11, 13a; 25:3, 6–7, 12c, 31a, 32, 45–46a); Num 18:30b–31a; Deut 12:15, 22, 27b; 14:6, 9, 11, 20, 21b; 15:22; 16:7b; 17:14–15; 18:1b, 3–4; 23:9, 17a, 21a, 24, 25a, 26a [NRSV 8, 16a, 20a, 23, 24a, 25a]; Ezek 44:2c, 29). See also **case-permission laws.**

Prescription

This is a general term for the authoritative pronouncement of actions, usually in the third person, that are to be taken in a specific situation. A frequent subcategory, **prescription of punishment**, appears as the apodosis in a **case-prescription** law. In **procedural laws**, such as **offering laws** and **laws concerning ceremonially unclean persons**, the **ritual procedure** subunit functions as a prescription.

Prescription of Capital Punishment

This is a subcategory of **prescription of punishment** used in laws that mandate the death penalty. It can be the general **death sentence formula** or be a more specific **manner of death clause.**

Prescription of Punishment

This is a subcategory of prescription which involves punishing the criminal. Capital punishment was prescribed in Ancient Israel on occasion for violating certain **apostasy laws**, **blasphemy laws**, **homicide laws**, **sabbath laws**, and **sex laws** (not every subcategory of these types laws carried the death penalty). Disobedient sons could also be put to death (Deut 21:21), and Achan was executed for violating the holy ban against Jericho and stealing plunder (see **sentencing narrative**). Another punishment was being "cut off" from the community (see **cut off prescription formula**). Corporal punishment was restricted to forty strokes (Deut 22:18). Mutilation was permitted in proportion to the damage that the victim suffered in the **lex talionis laws**. Most common in practice was financial remuneration. This is clearly prescribed in certain laws in Tanak, but replaced mutilation and corporal punishment in later Judaism with the victim being able to claim remuneration for the damage or loss of a bodily organ, the physical pain inflicted, loss of wages during a recovery period, the medical costs, and any humiliation experienced by the victim. Capital punishment has increasingly come under fire in Jewish and Christian circles, yet traditional believers in both communities have to acknowledge its legitimacy in principle at least (that it is not inherently unjust) because YHWH commanded it on some occasions.

Bessette and Feser, *By Man*; Novak, *Jewish Justice*, 29–41.

Proclamation of Holiness Formula: "It shall be holy to you."

This formula is a **directive** illocution whose efficient cause is YHWH. Its perlocutionary intent varies according to setting.

Knierim and Coats, *Numbers*, 367.

Prohibition

This is a negatively formed authoritative directive, forbidding the addressee from a certain action or activity. Its opposite is command. The most common grammatical construction is *'al* followed by a jussive verb but *lo'* followed by an imperfect verb also occurs, most notably in the Decalogue (this may be an emphatic form).

Purge the Evil Formula: "So you shall purge the evil from your midst."

This is a subcategory of benefit of obedience which only occurs in the Deuteronomic law code and usually in the context of a death penalty law (Deut 13:5b; 17:7b, 12; 19:13a, 19b; 22:21b, 22b, 24b). It communicates that according to Israelite law, certain sins so affect the community that the death penalty, when justly applied, has a purgative effect.

Relative Pronoun Law

This is a syntactical category in which the protasis is introduced by a relative pronoun and the apodosis is usually a third person imperfect (Lev 20:12) but can be second person (Lev 20:16) or even first person (Lev 17:10). It is a subcategory of **conditional law**.

Self-Revelation of YHWH Formula: "I am YHWH (your God)"

This formula is an **assertive** illocution whose **efficient cause** is YHWH. It can occur in a **vision report** to a patriarch (Gen 15:1, 7; 26:24; 28:13; 46:3), or the related genres of **dream report** to a patriarch (Gen 28:13) or **theophany report** (Gen 35:11; Exod 3:6; 6:2), where its purpose is straightforwardly for the addressee to recognize the identity of the speaker. Within a legal context, an expanded form of the formula mentioning YHWH's saving act in the Exodus is used to introduce the **Decalogue** (Exod 20:2; Deut 5:6), and either a short or an expanded form is used after various **commands**, **prohibitions** and **instructions** in the **Holiness Code** (Lev 18:2, 4, 5, 6, 21, 30; 19:3, 4, 10, 12, 14, 16, 18, 25, 28, 30, 31, 32, 34, 36, 37; 20:7, 8, 24; 21:12, 15, 23; 22:2, 3, 8, 9, 16, 30, 31, 32, 33; 23:22, 43; 24:22; 25:17, 38, 55; 26:1, 2, 13, 44, 45), and in the **Priestly Code** (Lev 11:44, 45; Num 3:13, 41, 45; 10:10; 15:41). Here the purpose likely is to highlight the divine, and thus supremely authoritative, nature of the lawgiver. See also **recognition formula** in the prophetic genres chapter.

Hals, *Ezekiel*, 362–63; Knierim and Coats, *Numbers*, 367; Zimmerli, *I am YHWH*.

Statutory Law Formula: "This is/will be a (perpetual) statute ..."

This formula is found in the Priestly Code and is an **exercitive** illocution by which YHWH establishes that a certain statute by its foundational nature will be perpetual. It can occur at the beginning, middle, or ending of a law (Exod 12:14, 17, 24; 27:21; 28:43; 29:9, 28; 30:21; 31:16; Lev 3:17; Num 10:8; 15:15; 18:23; 19:10, 21).

Knierim and Coats, *Numbers*, 367.

Threat

This is a first person commissive where the speaker commits to an action X antithetical to the audience's interest. In Israelite law, following a case in which Israel disobeys, YHWH threatens Israel with series of curses in the **blessing and curses passages** in Lev 26 and Deut 28.

SUBUNIT LEVEL GENRES

This level, the subunits which are the basic constituents of the longer laws, is frequently overlooked in analysis of legal genres. Marking the various subunits of a law in different colors (either on paper or electronically in Bible software) is a very effective tool to understanding the larger laws better.

Alternative Ritual Procedure

A subcategory of **ritual procedure**, it prescribes what should be done in special circumstances which make the previously given standard procedure difficult or impossible to perform. In an offering law, alternate procedures (Lev 5:8–10a, 12a) follow **cases of financial difficulty**. The same is true in certain **laws concerning ceremonially unclean persons** (Lev 12:8b; 14:21b–31a). Financial ability mattered in Israelite procedural law. The three **case for procedures** in Lev 1:3a, 10a, 17a reflect this principle also.

Branched Conditional

This is a subunit which prescribes, promises, or threatens different outcomes depending upon whether the addressee is obedient or disobedient to the law. Examples include Num 19:12 and Deut 11:26–28; 30:15–19a.

Calendrical Designation

This is a divine exercitive which designates a particular day/year as having a special significance (Exod 12:2, 14a, 16; 13:6b; Lev 16:31a; 23:5, 6a, 34a, 35a; 25:4a, 5b, 10b, 11a, 12a; Num 28:16–17a, 18a 25a; 29:12a). It usually occurs in a **cultic calendar law**.

Case of Financial Difficulty

This is a subcategory of **case for procedure** in which the participant is unable to afford the standard procedure. There are examples in offering/sacrifice laws (Lev 5:7a, 11a), laws concerning ceremonially unclean persons (Lev 12:8a: 14:21a), and there is a **case-prescription law** in Lev

25:35 concerning a relative in financial difficulty. See **alternate ritual procedure** for a discussion of the remedies.

Case of Possible Impurity

This is a subcategory of **case for procedure** in a **law concerning ceremonially unclean persons**, occurring frequently in Lev 11, 12, 13, 14, and 15. It covers situations where the person might be unclean (and thus usually followed by an **examination procedure**) or is known to be unclean (and is typically followed by a **declaration of impurity**, a **prescription of washing** or a more elaborate **ritual purification procedure**). Examples include contact with unclean swarming creatures (Lev 11: 31, 33, 34, 35, 36, 37, 38, 39, 49), a woman bearing a male child (Lev 12:2b) or female child (Lev 12:5a), numerous situations with skin diseases (Lev 13, 14), a man having a discharge of semen (Lev 15:2b, 16a), such a man spitting on a clean person (Lev 15:8a) or lying with a woman (Lev 15:18a), a woman having a discharge of blood (Lev 15:9a, 25a), or such a woman lying with a man (Lev 15:24a).

Case for Procedure

This is the subunit in procedural law which is analogous to **case** in the case-prescription laws. The most important subcategories are case of offering in offering law, and case of possible uncleanness in **law concerning ceremonially unclean persons**. Another subcategory is the **case of financial difficulty** (which is standardly followed by an **alternate ritual procedure** or perhaps a different **quality of item offered**). The **marriage and family law** concerning the jealous husband also begins with a case for procedure (Num 5:12b–14).

Case for Offering/Sacrifice

This is the standard subcategory of case for procedure in **offering/sacrifice laws**, which are often subdivided into several specific cases. The burnt offering law includes cases where the sacrificial animal is from the herd, flock, or turtledoves/pigeons (Lev 1:3a, 10a, 14a); the grain offering law divides into a general case and three specific cases (Lev 2:1a, 4a, 7a, 14a); the peace or wellbeing offering law divides into four cases (Lev 3:1a,

6a, 7a, 12); the sin offering law first divides into cases involving different agents who sin: a priest, the whole congregation, a ruler, an ordinary person (Lev 4:3a, 13–14a, 22–23a, 27–28a), and then discusses the animals offered: the standard case of a sheep, and two progressive **cases of financial difficulty** (Lev 4:32a; 5:7a, 11a); the guilt offering law has two cases also (Lev 5:15a, 17a) but the second one may be iterative in nature rather than indicating a different situation; the restitution offering has only one case for procedure but it is exceptionally detailed (Lev 5:21–24a [NRSV 6:2–5a]); and further instructions on the peace or wellbeing offering divide into cases where it is offered for thanksgiving and offered as a freewill offering (Lev 7:12a, 16a) and then a case for any wellbeing sacrifice (Lev 7:29b) is followed by further details.

The **offering law** in Deut 26:1–11 (perhaps a **Feast of Weeks passage**) begins with a **case for procedure** (Deut 26:1–2).

Declaration of Cleanness

This is the opposite of the more common **declaration of impurity** and and calls for the official (priest) to pronounce an exercitive declaring the person clean. Examples include Lev 11:36b; 13: 6b, 8c, 13c, 17c, 23b, 28b, 34c, 37b, 39c, 40b, 41b, all in **laws concerning ceremonially unclean persons**.

Declaration of Impurity

A subcategory of **verdict of guilt/uncleanness**, this occurs in a **law concerning ceremonially unclean persons** and calls for the official (priest) to pronounce an exercitive declaring the person unclean. It can take two forms: the apodosis to a case of possible impurity or a syntactically independent **relative pronoun law** or **participial construction law** such as "All who do X shall be unclean." It is frequently followed by a **prescription of washing**. Its opposite is **declaration of cleanness**. Examples include Lev 13:3c, 11a, 14b–15, 20c, 22d, 25c, 27c, 30c, 36c, 44, 51c, 55c, 57b; and Num 19:11, 14b–16, 21b–22.

Determination of Clean/Unclean Procedure

This is a subcategory of **ritual procedure** which follows a **situation requiring examination** in a **law concerning ceremonially unclean persons**. It prescribes that the priest shall examine the skin condition of the afflicted person and notes the condition that would entail that person being declared ceremonially unclean. It implies that if the person is found clean by the procedure, nothing further is required. It is instructional in nature, detailing how to discern whether a particular person is clean or unclean. Examples include Lev 13:2b–3, 4b–8, 9b–11, 13–15, 16b–17, 19b–23, 25–28, 30, 31b–37a, 39, 43–46.

Disposition of Leftovers

This occurs in some **offering/sacrifice laws** and prescribes how the sacrificial remains are to be treated, whether given to priests (Lev 2:3a, 10a; 5:13b; 6:9–10a, 11 [NRSV 16–17a, 18, 26, 29a]; 7:6a, 7–10), burned in a clean place outside the camp (Lev 4:11–12, 21), or simply wholly burned and not eaten (Lev 6:16 [NRSV 23]). When the sacrifice is to be eaten by the priest, it is often accompanied by an **identification of holiness**.

Divine Exercitive Num 8:1b, 7; 18:8b–15a, 18–19

This is an exercitive speech by YHWH which brings into existence a new legal situation. The designation of the Levites as consecrated for special purposes (Num 3:13–15; 18:8b–15a, 18–19) and Phinehas and his descendants similarly (Num 25:10–12) are examples (see **covenant establishment narrative**).

Examination Procedure

This is a subcategory of **ritual procedure** in which a medic examines a patient to determine the situation. It typically occurs in a **law concerning ceremonially unclean persons** (13:2b–3a, 4b–6a, 7b–8a, 9b–10a, 13a, 16b–17a, 19b–20a, 21b, 25a, 26b–27a, 30a, 31b–32a, 33–34a, 36a, 39a, 43a, 49b–51a, 54–55; 14:2b–3) and followed either by a **declaration of impurity** or a **declaration of cleanness**.

Historical Reminder

This is an assertive genre (YHWH asserts things about the past) but its teleological cause is not to give information but rather to remind them of YHWH's covenant faithfulness as part of **parenesis**, encouraging them to obey laws. It is particularly prominent in Deuteronomy (Deut 1:6–3:29; 4:3–4, 10–14, 20–22, 34–38; 5:1b, 22–30; 8:2–4; 9:7–10:11; 11:2–7; 29:1b–7 [NRSV 2b–8]). See also the section on Deuteronomy in the overview of Tanak chapter.

I Am YHWH

Leviticus 19 contains fourteen subunits ending in the **self-revelation of YHWH formula**, "I am YHWH (your God)" (Lev 19:2b, 3, 4, 5–10, 11–12, 13–14, 15–16, 17–18, 19–25, 26–28, 29–30, 31, 32, 33–34, 35–36, 37). Many of the laws in these subunits are **loving neighbor laws**.

Identification of Offering/Sacrifice

This is a clause or phrase, such as "it is a burnt offering, an offering by fire of pleasing odor to the Lord" (Lev 1:13b) which reiterates what type of offering in an **offering law** is under consideration. It may consist of a nominal clause containing the far demonstrative pronoun (Hebrew: *hû'* or *hî'*), usually translated as "it" in this context; or it may lack the demonstrative pronoun and function more as a nominal phrase in apposition such as "an offering by fire of pleasing odor to the Lord" (Lev 2:2b). Many offering laws have divisions which begin with a **case for procedure** and end with an **identification of offering/sacrifice**. Examples of this division ending function include Lev 1:9b, 13b, 17b; Lev 2:6b, 16b; 3:5b, 11b; 4:21b. Examples where the identification of offering/sacrifice is followed by other material include Lev 2:2b, 9b, 15b; 3:14b; 4:24b; 5:7c, 11c, 12b, 15c, 18b, 19a; 7:5b.

Law Subscription

A law subscription is a portion of text written immediately after a law and referring to it such as "this is the law concerning X." Examples include Lev 7:37–38; 12:7b; 13:59; 14:32, 54–57; 15:32–33; 16:29–34a; 22:15–16a;

23:37–38; 26:46; 27:34; Num 29:39; 36:13; and Deut 5:22. Five of the major divisions of Leviticus end with such subscriptions (see overview of Tanak chapter; Lev 8–10 contains narratives rather than laws), as does Numbers.

Parenesis

In a legal context, parenesis is persuasion to keep the laws—it exhorts rather than commands, it admonishes, rather than prohibits, it shows the **benefits of obedience** and the **cost of disobedience**. Especially in Deuteronomy, YHWH does not simply decree laws but encourages obedience to them. Parenesis subunits occur at the beginning of passages (Lev 18:3–4a, 5a; Deut 27:1b), in the middle (Exod 13:4–5; Lev 25:17–19; Deut 7:9–11; 15:4–6; 30:11–14), and at the end (Lev 11:44–45; 18:24–30a; Num 35:33–34; Deut 11:31–32; 12:28; 13:17b–18; 16:12; 24:22; 28:13b–14; 29:28).

Prescription of Washing

A subcategory of **ritual purification procedure** in which involves washing as part of the cleansing process. It primarily occurs after an **event leading to uncleanness** in a **law concerning ceremonially unclean persons** (Lev 14:47; 15:5–7, 8b, 10–11, 21–23, 27; 17:15; Deut 23:11) but also occurs in the instructions to the high priest in one of the **Day of Atonement passages** (Lev 16:4b, 24a, 26, 28; see **cultic calendar instruction**) and in the ritual instruction on red heifer (Num 19:7–10a).

Qualification of Item Offered

This is a section in an **offering/sacrifice law** which specifies certain qualities that the item offered must satisfy such as age or sex of the animal, unblemished animal, grain of fine flour or unleavened or mixed with oil etc. It usually follows the **case for procedure** and precedes a **ritual sacrificial procedure**.

The burnt offering from the herd is to be a male without blemish (Lev 1:3b) as is the one from the flock (Lev 1:10b), the burnt offering from the birds is to be of turtledoves or pigeons (Lev 1:14b); depending on specific **case for procedures**, the grain offering is to be of choice flour

(Lev 2:1a), of unleavened cakes or wafers mixed with oil (Lev 2:4b), of unleavened choice flour mixed with oil (Lev 2:5b), of choice flour in oil (Lev 2:7b), or coarse new grain from fresh ears parched with fire (Lev 2:14b); the peace or wellbeing offering whether from the herd or the flock is to be a male or female without blemish (Lev 3:1b, 6b); the sin offering varies according to who the agent is—it can be a bull without blemish (Lev 4:3b), a bull of the herd (Lev 4:14b), a male goat without blemish (Lev 4:23b), a female goat without blemish (Lev 4:28b), a female sheep without blemish (Lev 4:32b), or for those too poor to afford anything else it can be two turtledoves/pigeons (Lev 5:7) or a tenth of an ephah of choice flour without oil or frankincense (Lev 5:11b; see **alternative ritual procedure**); a restitution offering is a ram without blemish from the flock or the equivalent (Lev 5:15b, 18a, 25 [NRSV 6:6]); the offering when a priest is anointed is one tenth of an ephah of choice flour (Lev 6:13b [NRSV 20b]).

In the **cultic calendar law** of Num 28–29, the qualification of item offered for the daily sacrifice consists of two male lambs without blemish a year old, and an ephah of choice flour mixed with a fourth of a hin of beaten oil for each lamb (Num 28:3b, 5); that for the sabbath consists of an additional offering of the same (Num 28:9); that for a new moon consists of two young bulls, one ram, seven male lambs without blemish a year old, with three tenths of an ephah of flour for each bull, two tenths of an ephah for each ram, and one tenth of an ephah for each of the seven lambs, plus a male goat for a sin offering (Num 28:11b–14, 15a); that on the first day of Unleavened Bread, like the monthly offering, is to be two young bulls, one ram, seven male lambs without blemish a year old with three tenths of an ephah of flour for each bull, two tenths of an ephah for each ram, and one tenth for each of the seven lambs, and a male goat for a sin offering (Num 28:19b–22; this is to be repeated for the other days of Unleavened Bread); the same for the Festival of Weeks (Num 28:27b–30); the same for the first day of the seventh month (Num 29:2b–5); the same for the tenth day of the seventh month (Num 29:8b–10); that for the fifteenth day of the seventh month, the first day of the Feast of Tabernacles, is to be thirteen young bulls, two rams, fourteen male lambs without blemish a year old, three tenths of an ephah of oil for each bull, two tenths of an ephah of oil for each ram, one tenth for each lamb, and a male goat for a sin offering (Num 29:13b–16a); that for the second day of the Feast is twelve bulls but otherwise the same (Num 29:17b–19a); that for the third day of the Feast is eleven bulls but otherwise the same

(Num 29:20b–22a); that for the fourth day is ten bulls but otherwise the same (Num 29:23b–25a); that for the fifth day is nine bulls but otherwise the same (Num 29:26b–28a); that for the sixth day is eight bulls but otherwise the same (Num 29:29b–31a); that for the seventh day is seven bulls but otherwise the same (Num 29:32b–34a); but that for the eighth day (see **Eighth Day of Tabernacles passage**) is quite different indicating it is not a simple continuation of the Feast of Tabernacles: one bull, one ram, seven male lambs without blemish a year old, accompanying grain and drink offerings, and a male goat for a sin offering (Num 29:36b–38a).

Reason for Law

This is a subunit analogue to **motive clause**.

Ritual Recitation

This typically consists of a **command to speak formula** and the content of an exercitive speech that a participant would recite at the appropriate point in the ritual. Numbers 6:24–26 is the famous "Priestly Benediction": "The Lord bless you and keep you; the Lord make his face to shine upon you, and be gracious to you; the Lord lift up his countenance upon you, and give you peace." In a blessings and curses passage, the Levites pronounce ritual curses on twelve categories of evil doers (Deut 27:15a, 16a, … 26a). Some recitations were performed by parents to explain ritual actions to their children (Exod 12:25–27a; 13:8, 14b–15; Deut 6:20–25; see **Passover/Unleavened Bread passage**). Others were performed in connection with **offering laws** (Deut 26:5b–9) or **tithe laws** (Deut 26:13–15). There were even recitations for military leaders in a war law (Deut 20:2–4, 5–7, 8).

Ritual Purification Procedure

A subcategory of **ritual procedure** which effects the ritual cleansing of a person. It may simply involve a **prescription of washing**. Other examples include dipping in water articles made unclean by contact with unclean foods (Lev 11:32), circumcising a male child (Lev 12:3), abstaining from entering the sanctuary or touching holy things during the time of ritual impurity (Lev 12:4), bringing a sacrifice or series of sacrifices after fulfilling a time of ritual impurity (Lev 12:6), lengthy rituals involving exercitives/declaratives performed by the priest pronouncing the individual clean (Lev 14:2b–20a, 21b–31a), combinations of prescriptions of washings and offering sacrifices (Lev 15:13b–15a, 28b–30), and even taking ashes of the red heifer, adding running water, and then sprinkling (Num 19:17–19).

Ritual Sacrificial Procedure

This is a subcategory of **ritual procedure** which is the central element in an **offering/sacrifice law**. It contains a series of directives which give instructions on how the official is to conduct an offering/sacrifice. The basic ritual for the whole burnt offering in Lev 1 is laying a hand on the animal, slaughtering it, manipulation of the blood, cutting of the animal, washing of the innards and legs, and turning of the whole into smoke. The basic ritual for the grain offering in Lev 2 is preparing the offering, presenting the offering, pinching off or offering up the offering, and then burning the offering. The basic ritual of the wellbeing offering in Lev 3 and of the offering for inadvertent sin in Lev 4:1—5:13 is laying a hand on the animal's head, slaughtering the animal, manipulation of blood, removal of the fat, and burning of the fat. The basic ritual in Lev 5:14–26 (NRSV 5:14–6:7) is to make restitution and add one fifth to the item. Additional ritual instructions concerning these sacrifices are contained in Lev 6:1—7:38 (NRSV 6:8—7:38). For the details of the ritual sacrificial procedure in Lev 16, see **Day of Atonement passage**. The basic ritual in the offering law of Deut 26:1–11 is to place the fruit offering at the place YHWH will choose and make a creedal recitation of what YHWH has done for Israel.

Summary Subscription

This comes after the main law and summarizes the cases that the above law covers. It typically begins a phrase like "This is the law/ritual" or "Thus it shall be done." Examples occur in different law codes (Lev 11:46–47; 12:7b; 13:59; 14:54–57; 15:11–14, 32–33; 16:29–34a; 17:8b–9, 12, 14b; 22:9, 15–16a; 23:37–38; Num 5:29–31; 6:21, 27; 8:26b; 15:11–14; Deut 20:19–20; Ezek 45:17).

Superscription Classification

Although most procedural laws contain an **identification of offering/sacrifice subunit** (or analogous subunit in other types of procedural law) in the body of the text or at the conclusion of a division in the text, a few have the classification as a superscription to the main body of the law. Examples include "This is the torah of the burnt offering" (Lev 6:2b [NRSV 9b]; see also Lev 6:7a, 13a, 18b [NRSV 14a, 20a, 25b]; 7:1a, 11) in an **offering/sacrifice law** and "This shall be the torah for the leper at the time of his cleansing" (Lev 14:2a) in a **law concerning ceremonially unclean persons**. The general principle "Every seventh year you shall grant a remission of debts" (Deut 15:1) acts as a superscription to the following **sabbatical year/jubilee passage** which spells out the details. "These are the ordinances that you shall set before them" (Exod 21:1) acts as a superscription to the entire **covenant code**.

Verdict of Guilt/Uncleanness

This is a section which predicates an undesirable social state (usually guilt or uncleanness) to persons having committed certain actions or had certain events befall them. The most frequently occurring of these is the **declaration of impurity** found in several **laws concerning ceremonially unclean persons**. Verdicts of guilt also occur in **offering laws** (Lev 5:1b, 2b, 3b, 4b, 17b, 19b). A verdict can also function as (part of) the apodosis in an individual case law, either with a **prescription of punishment** (Lev 20:17b, 20b) or without the punishment specified (Lev 20:19). It is likely that in Israelite society, an authority figure would have pronounced an exercitive speech something like "You have been found guilty."

LEGAL GENRES CATEGORIZED ACCORDING TO WHOSE BEHAVIOR IT CONCERNS

Law Concerning Ceremonially Unclean Persons

This is a law that gives ritual instructions for how a person who has become ceremonially unclean can be restored to the community. Ceremonial uncleanness does not imply moral fault; people were going to become unclean through bodily emissions, contact with unclean items, childbirth, having a skin condition, or certain other reasons. The teleological cause of the law is to enable the ceremonially unclean become clean and rejoin the camp/community. Standard subunits of the law include **case of possible impurity** (a broad category of protasis which includes cases requiring examination to see if there is impurity but also actions/events leading to known impurity), **examination procedure**, **declaration of cleanness** or conversely **declaration of impurity**, **ritual purification procedure**, and **prescription of washing**. Just as **offering laws** dominate the book section Lev 1–7, so laws concerning ceremonially unclean persons dominate the book section Lev 11–15. When a sacrifice is required before the unclean person is restored to the camp, elements such as **qualification of item offered**, **ritual sacrificial procedure**, and **make atonement formula** may occur.

Leviticus 11:31b–40 discusses ritual impurity caused by contact with unclean swarming creatures (see **food law** in same chapter). It contains **cases of possible impurity** (11:31b, 33a, 34a, 34c, 35a, 36a, 37a, 38a, 39a, 40a, 40c), **declarations of impurity** (11:31c, 33b, 34b, 34d, 35b, 35d, 37b, 38b, 39b), a **ritual purification procedure** (11:32), **prescriptions** of destruction of object (11:33c, 35c), a **declaration of cleanness** (11:36b), and **prescriptions of washing** (11:40b, 40d).

Leviticus 12 discusses purification after childbirth. It contains **cases of possible impurity** (12:2b, 5a), **declarations of impurity** (12:2c, 5b), a **ritual purification procedures** (12:3–4), a **ritual sacrificial procedure** (12:6), a **make atonement formulas** (12:7a, 8b), a **law subscription** (12:7b), a **case of financial difficulty** (12:8a), and an **alternative ritual procedure** (12:8b). Birth-giving itself is celebrated but it is the flow of blood accompanying it that causes uncleanness. For a male child, the length of time for ceremonial uncleanness is seven days and the total period of purification is forty days (seven plus thirty-three), both frequent biblical numbers. Why these numbers are double for a female child is unclear; the sacrifices are the same for a daughter as for a son (Lev 12:6–7). Importantly, there was not female circumcision in ancient Israel. The **law subscription** in Lev 12:7b suggests that this concluded an earlier redaction of the law, with the law being amended later to help the poor (although no versional evidence reflects an earlier text). Genesis 21:1–7, part of an **annunciation narrative**, portrays Isaac being circumcised on the eighth day and thus more Torah-observant than Ishamel (circumcision narrative). Luke 2:22–24 portrays Mary and Joseph making this alternative ritual offering for Jesus.

Leviticus 13 and 14 are both concerned with skin diseases. Leviticus 13 contains **cases of possible impurity** (13:2a, 3b, 4a, 7a, 8b, 9a, 10b, 12, 13b, 14a, 16a, 17b, 18–19a, 20b, 21a, 22a, 23a, 24, 25b, 26a, 27b, 28a, 29, 30b, 31a, 32b, 34b, 35, 36b, 37a, 38, 39b, 40a, 41a, 42, 43b, 47–49a, 51b, 53, 55b, 56a, 57a, 58a), **examination procedures** (13:2b–3a, 4b–6a, 7b–8a, 9b–10a, 13a, 16b–17a, 19b–20a, 21b, , 25a, 26b–27a, 30a, 31b–32a, 33–34a, 36a, 39a, 43a, 49b–51a, 54–55a), **declaration of impurity** (13:3c, 11a, 14b–15, 20c, 22d, 25c, 27c, 30c, 36c, 44, 51c, 55c, 57b), **declaration of cleanness** (13:6b, 8c, 13c, 17c, 23b, 28b, 34c, 37b, 39c, 40b, 41b), **prescriptions of washing** (13:6c), **ritual prohibition** (13:11b), **prescription for unclean person/item** (13:45–46, 52a, 55d, 56b, 57c), and a **law subscription** (13:59).

Leviticus 14:1–32 contains a **superscription classification** (14:2a), an **examination procedure** (14:2b–3a), a **case of possible impurity** (14:3b), **ritual purification procedures** (14:4–7, 8b–9a), **prescriptions of washing** (14:8a, 9b), **qualifications of item offered** (14:10, 21b–22; fewer animals following the **case of financial difficulty**), **ritual sacrificial procedures** (14:11–13a, 14–18a, 19b–20a, 23–31a), an **identification of holiness formula** (14:13b), **make atonement formulas** (14:18b–19a, 20b, 31b), a **case of financial difficulty** (14:21a), an **alternate ritual procedure** (14:23–31a) and a **law subscription** (14:32). Leviticus 14:34–52 contains **cases of possible impurity** (14:34, 37b, 39b, 43, 44b, 46b, 48a), **examination procedures** (14:35–37a, 38–39a, 44a), a **ritual purification procedure** (14:40–42), a **prescription for unclean person/item** (14:45), a **prescription of washing** (14:47), a **ritual sacrificial procedure** (14:50–53a), a **make atonement formula** (14:53b), and a **law subscription** (14:54–57).

Leviticus 15:1–33 deals with impurity due to bodily emission. It contains **cases of possible impurity** (15:2b, 8a, 13a, 16a, 18a, 19a, 24a, 25a, 28a), **declarations of impurity** (15:2c-4, 9, 19b–20, 24), **prescriptions of washing** (15:5–7, 8b, 10–12, 13b, 16b–17, 18b, 21–23, 27b), **qualifications of item offered** (15:14, 29), **ritual sacrificial procedures** (15:15a, 30a), **make atonement formulas** (15:15b, 30b), a **ritual purification procedure** (15:28b), a **benefit of obedience** (15:31), and a **law subscription** (15:32–33). Deuteronomy 23:11–15 [NRSV 10–14] deals with this subject briefly and contains **case-prescription laws** concerning nocturnal emissions and excreting (23:11, 14b [10, 13b]), a **prescription of washing** (23:12 [NRSV 11]), **commands** to have a designated area outside the camp for excrement, and a trowel amongst utensils (23:13, 14a [NRSV 12, 13a]), and a **motive clause** (23:15 [NRSV 14]).

The **legislative speech narrative** in Num 5:1–4 contains a **YHWH speech introduction formula** (5:1), a **command** to put the ceremonially impure outside the camp (5:2), an **order** that men and women be put outside and not defile the camp where YHWH dwells (5:3), and a **compliance subunit** (5:4). This reinforces the attitude to ceremonial impurity exhibited in Lev 12–15 whose laws detail procedures for the ceremonially unclean to rejoin the camp.

Deuteronomy 24:8–9 contains commands to guard against skin disease outbreaks, to observe what the priests command, and to remember what YHWH did to Miriam (afflicted her with skin-disease in the **revolt/rebellion narrative** in Num 12).

Tractate Qinnim discusses the offering of birds in order to become ritually clean. The final and longest Mishnaic order is Ṭohorot ("purities") which unsurprisingly deals extensively with the topic of ceremonial uncleanness. Tractate 'Ohalot discusses defilement through contact with a corpse; Negaʿim concerns skin diseases; Ṭeharot covers miscellaneous purity laws; Miqwa'ot discusses ritual baths; Niddah deals with uncleanness due to a woman's menstrual cycle; Makširin discusses liquids that can lead to uncleanness; Zabim deals with uncleanness due to a man's ejaculation of semen; Ṭebul Yom concerns what a person who has had a *miqwah* cleansing must avoid during the period before complete ritual cleanliness; Yadayim discusses Rabbinic impurities related to the hands; and ʿUqṣim has no Torah citations at all but represents further implications drawn by the Rabbis from other laws concerning uncleanness. The fact that one of the six Mishnaic orders is devoted to this subject shows the importance of these laws in Judaism. Christianity largely regards these as ceremonial laws pertaining to Israel and thus not obligatory for Christians (but with some universal principles of cleanliness).

Baden and Moss, "Origin and Interpretation," 643–662; Douglas, *Purity and Danger*; Kazen, "Explaining Discrepancies," 348–71; Kiuchi, *Purification Offering*; Thiessen, "Legislation," 297–319; Whitekettle, "Leviticus 12," 393–408; Wright, *Disposal of Impurity*.

Law Concerning Judges/Elders

The **meeting/visit/reunion narrative** between Moses and Jethro in Exod 18 established the need for judges besides Moses to adjudicate basic legal cases. A few chapters later, the covenant code contains several important principles for judges, mainly in the form of prohibitions (Exod 23:1–3, 6–9). These include prohibitions against abusing the authority to support wickedness (23:1), not to give in to peer pressure by siding with a majority in the wrong (23:2), not showing partiality to the wrong simply because they are poor (23:3), not perverting the justice to which the poor are entitled (23:6), not killing those in the right (23:7), not accepting bribes (23:8), and not oppressing resident aliens (23:9). There are important motive clauses in Exod 23:7, 8, 9. All of these used to be uncontroversial ethically (though frequently flouted by corrupt officials). However, critical social justice theory is arguably opposed to the prohibition against partiality to the poor in a lawsuit, also found in the **holiness code** in an **order** not to be partial to the poor or to the great but to judge righteously (Lev 19:15).

Deuteronomy 16:18–20 begins with **commands** to appoint judges and for those judges to render just decisions (Deut 16:18), followed by similar **prohibitions** found in Exod 21, flavored with the standard Deuteronomic flourish concerning the towns/land "that the Lord your God is giving you" (Deut 16:18, 20). Deuteronomy 17:8–13 centers on the **ritual procedure** when a **case** is too hard for a local judge and updates the advice Jethro gave Moses (Exod 18:21–22). It has standard Deuteronomic style: the place that YHWH will choose (Deut 18:8, 10; see **central sanctuary law**), an **order** (Deut 17:11), a **purge the evil formula** (Deut 17:12), and a **benefit of obedience** (Deut 17:13). For the judicial procedure in Deut 21:1–9, see **homicide law**.

Deuteronomy 25:1–3 contains a **case** in which the guilty party deserves to be flogged (Deut 25:1–2a), a **prescription of corporal punishment** in the presence of the judge with the number of lashes proportionate to the offense (Deut 25:2b), a **prohibition** against giving more than forty lashes (Deut 25:3a), and a **cost of disobedience** (Deut 25:3b). The principle of proportionality of punishment explicit in this law is foundational to the traditional retribution theory of justice.

Willis, *Elders*.

Law Concerning Kings

Deuteronomy 17:14–20 contains a **permission** to have an Israelite, but not a foreigner, as king (Deut 17:14–15), followed by **prohibitions** of the king multiplying horses for himself, returning the people to Egypt, multiplying wives for himself, and gaining great wealth (Deut 17:16–17), a **command** for the king to read a copy of this law daily (Deut 17:18–19a), and a **benefit of obedience** (Deut 17:19b–20). See the **dispute narrative** in which Samuel does not wish to give Israel a king despite YHWH telling him to give the people what they want (1 Sam 8:4–22), the testament/farewell narrative in which Samuel warns the people what a king will do (1 Sam 12:1–25), and the **regnal narrative** of Solomon who multiplies wives, horses, and wealth for himself on a colossal scale (1 Kgs 10–11).

Block, "Burden," 259–78; Day, *King*; Knoppers, "Deuteronomist," 329–46; Nihan, "Rewriting Kingship," 315–50.

Law Concerning Levites/Priests/High Priest

Leviticus 21:1–15 contains a **prohibition** on the priest defiling himself by mourning relatives with **permissions** for certain close relatives and stricter prohibitions against mourning for the high priest (Lev 21:1b–5, 11–12), **marriage laws** stricter for the priest than for regular Israelites and stricter still for the high priest (Lev 21:6–8, 13–15), a **death penalty law** if a priest's daughter prostitutes herself (Lev 21:9), and a clothing/personal appearance law concerning the high priest (Lev 21:10). Leviticus 21:16–23 contains **prohibitions** of a priest with a blemish from offering the bread of presence and approaching the altar, but a **permission** of the blemished priest to eat from the offering.

Leviticus 22:1–16 contains a **cut off prescription formula** for a ceremonially unclean priest approaching the donation (Lev 22:3), a **prohibition** against such a priest eating of the donation until evening after he has washed his body in water (Lev 22:4–7), a **prohibition** against a priest eating an animal that died of natural causes or was torn by wild animals (Lev 22:8), **prohibitions** and **permissions** concerning who else may eat the donation (Lev 22:10–13), a case-prescription law on how to rectify eating the donation unintentionally (Lev 22:14), and **summary subscriptions** (Lev 22:9, 15–16a). The **holiness command formula** (Lev 21:6, 7, 8) and the **YHWH self-revelation formula** (Lev 21:8, 12, 15, 23; 22:2, 3, 8, 9, 16) appear frequently.

Numbers 6:22–27 contains **commands** to bless the Israelites and give a **ritual recitation** (Num 6:23b–26) known as the priestly benediction, "The Lord bless you and keep you; the Lord make his face to shine upon you, and be gracious to you; the Lord lift up his countenance upon you, and give you peace" (Num 6:24–26), and a **benefit of obedience** (Num 6:27). The blessing well-wishes in the priestly benediction resonate with the **blessing subunits** in Psalms. Numbers 8:23–26 combines the genres of **command** and **prohibition** to set the age of active priestly service between twenty-five years and fifty years, and to set the limits of their service. The law begins with a **superscription** and ends with a **summary subscription** (Num 8:24a, 26b).

Numbers 18:1–7 contains **divine exercitives** appointing Aaron's family to the priesthood (Num 8:1b, 7) and for Levites to serve at the tent of meeting (Num 8:6), **commands** for Aaron's family to perform duties at the sanctuary and altar (Num 8:5) and the Levites to perform other duties (Num 18:2, 3a, 4a, 5a), **prohibitions** against the Levites approaching the sanctuary utensils or outsiders approaching at all (Num 18:3b, 4b), and a **benefit of obedience** (Num 18:5b). Numbers 35:1–8 contains **commands** for the Israelites to give the Levites towns and pasture lands from their tribal inheritance, six cities of refuge and forty-two other towns making forty-eight towns in total (Num 35:2–3, 6–8), and a **ritual procedure** to measure the extent of the pasture land (Num 35:4–5). Numbers 18:8–19 contains **divine exercitives** reserving to Aaron and his sons obligations and privileges associated with gifts and offerings as a perpetual covenant (Num 18:8b–15a, 18–19), a **command** to redeem human firstborn (Num 18:15b–16), and an **order** not to redeem the firstborn of cows, sheep, or goats, but to offer them (Num 18:17). A separate speech contains a **prohibition** against Aaron's descendants having an allotment in the land (Num 19:8b).

Deuteronomy 18:1–8 partly balances **prohibitions** against Levi having an allotment like the other tribes with **permissions** for the Levites to eat the donation and portions of sacrifices, again connecting the legislation to the **central sanctuary law**.

Tractate Terumot discusses the donation given to priests; *Middot* discusses the priestly workshifts and the architecture of the Second Temple.

Hartley, *Leviticus*, 341–57; Levine, *Leviticus*, 142–50; Meyer, "Ritual Innovation," 133–47.

Law Concerning Poor and Marginalized Persons

Many laws not treated in this entry reflect concern for the less well off, such as different **quality of item offered** subunits in the **offering laws,** material in the **laws concerning judges**, and some of the **motive clauses** portray YHWH as defending the marginalized. Leviticus 23:22 contains an **order** prohibiting harvesting the corners of the land and commanding them to be left for the poor. It is followed by the **YHWH self-identification formula**, suggesting that YHWH identifies as protector of the poor. It also follows a **feast of weeks passage** and thus would be particularly relevant at that time when the Israelites would harvest the wheat. The larger setting in Lev 23 is that of a **calendrical calendar law**, and in Deut 16 there is another calendrical calendar law which commands the Israelites to include the marginalized as they celebrate the feast of weeks (Deut 16:11) and the feast of tabernacles (Deut 16:13).

Deuteronomy 23:25–26 [NRSV 24–25] enables poor people to go scrumping and contains a **permission** to eat grapes from a neighbor's vineyard (Deut 23:25a [NRSV 24a]), a **prohibition** against putting grapes in a container to take away (Deut 23:25b [NRSV 24b]), a **permission** to pluck ears from a neighbor's standing grain (Deut 23:26a [NRSV 25a]), and a **prohibition** against putting a sickle to a neighbor's grain (Deut 23:26b [NRSV 25b]).

Deuteronomy 24:10–22 contains **orders** for a creditor not to enter someone's house to take a pledge but wait until it is returned, not to sleep in the pledge of the poor person but to return it before sunset, not to withhold wages of the need but pay them promptly (Deut 24:10–11, 12–13a, 14–15a), **benefits of obedience** (Deut 24:13b, 19b), a **cost of disobedience** (Deut 24:15b), a **death sentence law** limiting capital punishment to the guilty party not their families (Deut 24:16), **prohibitions** against depriving resident aliens or orphans of justice or taking a widow's garment in pledge (Deut 24:17), **parenesis** (Deut 24:18), **case-laws** ensuring the needy have opportunities for gleaning and scrumping (Deut 24:19–21), and **parenesis** (Deut 24:22).

Baker, *Tight Fists*; Wiele, "Justice for Orphans," 69–83; Wright, *Old Testament Ethics*.

Law Concerning Resident Aliens

Not all of the laws authoritative upon Israelites were authoritative on non-Israelites who lived in the promised land.

Law Concerning Slave Owners and Slaves

See **slavery law**.

Law Concerning Witnesses

The **prohibition** against giving false testimony is in the Decalogue (Exod 20:16; Deut 5:20) and is repeated in the covenant code (Exod 23:1). Witnesses must not simply go along with the majority but provide truthful testimony (Exod 23:2). For capital crimes, the testimony of a single witness is insufficient for conviction (Num 35:30; Deut 19:15); nor shall a murderer be put to death before a trial (Num 35:12).

Law Concerning Women

With the exception of the laws pertaining to the Levites/priests/high priest (and even some of these involved whom the priest could marry), many of the laws were incumbent on women and men alike. Laws particularly affecting women are discussed in **inheritance laws**, **marriage and family laws**, **sex laws**, **laws concerning ceremonially unclean persons**, etc., the type of legislation discussed in the Mishnaic order on women. The brief bibliography below represents a small portion of reflection upon some of these thorny issues, including scholarly comparison of differences between how the law codes, especially the covenant code and the deuteronomic code, treat certain topics.

Edenburg, "Ideology," 43–60; Matthews, Levinson, and Frymer-Kensky, *Gender and Law*; Pressler, *View of Women*; Rofé, "Family," 131–59.

LEGAL GENRES ACCORDING TO CONTENT OF LAW

Admissions to YHWH's Assembly Law

Deuteronomy 23:2–9 [NRSV 1–8] contains **prohibitions** against admittance to YHWH's assembly for eunuchs, those born of an illicit union, Ammonites and Moabites (Deut 23:2–4 [NRSV 1–3]), a **reason for law** regarding the Moabites (Deut 23:5–7 [NRSV 4–6]; see also **prophecy of punishment against Moab** in chapter on prophetic genres), and a prohibition against promoting their welfare (Deut 23:7 [NRSV 6]). By contrast there are prohibitions with **motive clauses** against abhorring Edomites and Egyptians (Deut 23:8a, b [NRSV 7a, b]) and a permission for the children of the third generation of them to be admitted (Deut 23:9 [NRSV 8]). Isaiah 56:1–8 (see **call to justice** in genres of prophetic literature) envisions a time when these admittance laws will no longer apply to eunuchs or to gentiles who keep the Sabbath (see **Sabbath passage**).

Orian, "Numbers 20:14–21," 109–16.

Agricultural/Environmental Law

These include the **prohibitions** against reaping to the very edge of the field and stripping vineyards bare, thus permitting the poor to glean (Lev 19:9–10), returning for a forgotten sheaf (Deut 24:19), sowing with two types of grain or mating animals from different species (Lev 19:19), preventing a working animal from eating the produce of the land in which it is working (Deut 25:4), taking a mother nesting bird with her young (Deut 22:6–7), against sowing grain in a vineyard (Deut 22:9), and against ploughing with two different species of animals yoked together (Deut 22:10). Several of these are parenetic in nature, containing either a benefit of obedience or a cost of disobedience.

Deuteronomy 23:25–26 [NRSV 24–25] allows scrumping and contains **permissions** to eat grapes or pluck ears of grain from a neighbor's property (Deut 23:25a, 26a [NRSV 24a, 25a]), but **prohibitions** against larger scale pillaging (Deut 23:25b, 26b [NRSV 24b, 25b]). Deuteronomy 25:4 is a **prohibition** against muzzling an ox while it is treading out the grain. See also **Sabbatical Year/Jubilee law**.

Mishnaic tractate Bekorot discusses the redemption of firstborn animals. Much of the order Zeraʿim in the Mishnah deals with agricultural laws. Tractate Pe'ah discusses laws involving gleaning and scrumping which help the poor; Kil'ayim discusses the "forbidden mixtures" of species in animal breeding and in agriculture; 'Orlah discusses the requirements regarding fruit trees; and *Bikkurim* discusses first-fruit offerings.

Altar Law

Exodus 20:24–26 shortly follows the Decalogue and prescribes an altar of earth for sacrifices but permits an altar of stone providing that it is not of hewn stones nor contains steps. Exodus 27:1–8 is part of the **tabernacle instructions narrative** and prescribes an altar of burnt offering to be made of acacia wood, five cubits square and three cubits high, with a bronze grating and four bronze rings at the corners through which go poles of acacia wood to transport the altar. Its construction is narrated in Exod 38:1–8. Similarly, Exod 30:1–5 prescribes the details for the altar of incense which Exod 37:25–28 narrates the construction of.

Deuteronomy 27:1–8 contains **parenesis** (Deut 27:1b), and **commands** to set up large stones and laster them, write words of this law on them, set them on Mt. Ebal, build an altar of unhewn stones there and offer sacrifices there, rejoicing (Deut 27:2–7), followed by a repeated **command** to write on the stones the words of this law (Deut 26:8).

Heger, *Biblical Altar Laws.*

Apostasy Law

This law warns Israelites against apostasy or turning from YHWH into idolatry, a major theme in Deuteronomy through Kings (see apostasy narrative). In the specific laws section of Deut 12–26, this law comes second after the **central sanctuary law** which is unique to Deuteronomy. Deuteronomy 13 has three parts with cases (Deut 13:2–4, 8–9, 13–14 [NRSV 1–3, 7–8, 12–13]) respectively concerning a prophet leading the people into apostasy, idolatry instigated by a relative, or an entire town committing idolatry. The parenetic nature of the law is indicated by **motive clauses** or **benefits of obedience** (Deut 13:4b, 6b, 18b–19 [NRSV 3b, 5b, 17b–18]), orders (Deut 13:5–6a, 9–11, 16–17a), and the purge the evil formula (Deut 13:5b).

Deuteronomy 17:2–7 contains an established **case** after inquiry of someone worshiping other gods (Deut 17:2–4), and a **prescription of capital punishment** by stoning provided it is based on the evidence of more than one witness (Deut 17:5–6), a **prescription** for the witnesses to be the first to carry out the execution (Deut 17:7a), and a **purge the evil formula** (Deut 17:7b). That Deut 13 and 17 invoke **death penalty laws** as the punishment indicates the severity of the offence. Israel disobeyed this law frequently, providing justification with the Primary History for YHWH's exiling of Israel (2 Kgs 17)and then Judah (2 Kgs 25).

Halpern and Hobson, *Law and Ideology*; Weijola, "Wahrheit," 287–314.

Blasphemy Law

The prohibition against taking YHWH's name in vain is in the Decalogue (Exod 20:7; Deut 5:11), profaning the divine name is forbidden in the holiness code (Lev 19:12; 22:32), and a **legal case narrative** establishes that committing blasphemy violates a **death penalty law** (Lev 24:16).

Blessing and Curse Passage

Leviticus 26:14–39 contains a **case** in which Israel disobeys YHWH and breaks the covenant (Lev 26:14–15), and a series of **threats** (Lev 26: 16–17, 19–20, 22, 25–26, 29–32) concerning plagues, defeat by enemies, drought wild animals, war, pestilence, famine, desolation of land, exile, and even cannibalism of one's own children, punctuated by four **prescriptions of punishment** emphasizing sevenfold severity (Lev 26:18, 21, 23–24, 27–28), and concluding with a lengthy **reason for law** (Lev 26:34–39).

In the final part of the general laws (before the specific laws), Deut 11:26–32 contains a **branched conditional subunit** with blessings for obedience and curses for disobedience (Deut 11:26–28), a **command** to perform a ceremony involving blessing on Mount Gerizim and curse on Mount Ebal (Deut 11:29–30; see Deut 27:11–13), and **parenesis** (Deut 11:31–32). Deuteronomy 27:11–26 contains **tribe lists** of those commanded to stand on Mount Gerizim and those on Mount Ebal (Deut 27:12, 13), a command for the Levites to speak (Deut 27:14), **ritual recitation subunits** against idolaters, disobedient children, those who remove boundary markers, oppressors of the marginalized, those who commit bestiality and various types of incest, the violent, the corrupt who facilitate violence, and those who disobey Torah (Deut 27:15a, 16a,

17a, 18a, 19a, 20a, 21a, 22a, 23a, 24a, 25a, 26a), each followed by the congregation responding with an **amen formula** (Deut 27:15b, 16b etc).

Deuteronomy 28:1–14 contains a **conditional promise** of blessing (Deut 28:1), a **blessing list** (Deut 28:2–6), and a series of **promises** (Deut 28:7–13a), and **parenesis** (Deut 28:13b–14). Deuteronomy 28:15–68 contains a conditional threat of curses (Deut 28:15a), a **curse list** (Deut 28:15b–19), and a longer series of **threats** (Deut 28:20–68).

Deuteronomy 30 contains a **case** of Israel in exile calling to mind the blessings and the curses set before them and returning to YHWH (Deut 30:1–2), followed by **promises** of restoration, YHWH circumcising their heart and punishing their enemies (Deut 30:3–10), **parenesis** that YHWH's commandment is near to them for them to observe (Deut 30:11–14), a **branched conditional subunit** (Deut 30:15–19a), a **command** to choose life (Deut 30:19b), and a **benefit of obedience** (Deut 30:19c-20).

Blood Law

The **holiness code** begins with a legislative speech narrative which concerns issues related to blood (Lev 17:1–16). After the introductory formulas, the first main section contains a **case** of someone slaughtering a clean animal without bringing it to the tent of meeting (Lev 17:3–4a), a **blood restriction formula** (Lev 17:4b), a **cut off prescription formula** (Lev 17:4c), a **benefit of obedience** (Lev 17:5–7a), and a **statutory law formula** (Lev 17:7b), a **commissioning formula** (Lev 17:8a), and a **summary subscription** (Lev 17:8b–9). The second main section contains a **case** concerning an Israelite or a resident alien eating blood (Lev 17:10a), a **cut off prescription formula** (Lev 17:10b), a **motive clause** (Lev 17:11), and a **summary subscription** (Lev 17:12). The third main section contains a **command** to pour out the blood of a clean creature before eating it (Lev 17:13), a **motive clause** that connects the life of every creature to its blood (Lev 17:14a), and a **summary subscription** (Lev 17:14b). The fourth main section contains a **prescription of washing** for any "who eat what dies of itself or what has been torn by wild animals" (Lev 17:15), and a **result of disobedience** (Lev 17:16).

Fuad, "Leviticus 17," 20–33; Gilders, *Blood Ritual*; Hanson, "Blood and Purity," 215–30; Olyan and Anderson, *Priesthood and Cult*; Whitekettle, "Study in Scarlet," 685–704.

Central Sanctuary Law

Deuteronomy 12 emphasizes that worship is to be conducted only at the central sanctuary that YHWH will choose, which for Israel became Jerusalem after David captured it in 2 Sam 5 (the Samaritan Pentateuch reads "the place that YHWH has chosen" throughout Deutronomy and the Samaritans regard Mount Gerizim as that place). Laws in Deuteronomy that presuppose the central sanctuary include **tithing laws** (Deut 14:22–26), **homicide laws** (Deut 19:1–9), and **cultic calendar laws** (Deut 16:1–17). **Permission** to slaughter (clean) animals for food and not for cultic purposes is granted in Deut 12:15, 20–22. The theological evaluation in the **regnal accounts of Judean monarch** often includes whether the monarch obeyed this law or allowed worship at other "high places."

After an **order** against idolatry (Deut 12:2–4), Moses gives positive **commands** to go and sacrifice, rejoice, tithe at "the place that the Lord your God will choose" (Deut 12:5–7, 10–12, 26–27a), **prohibition** against acting "as we are acting here today" (Deut 12:8–9), **be careful lest constructions** against offering sacrifices except at the central sanctuary but ensuring that Levites are taken care of (Deut 12:13–14, 19), **permissions** and **case-permissions** to slaughter animals to eat elsewhere (Deut 12:15, 20–22, 27b), **orders** against eating blood at all and against eating tithes other than at the place God will choose (Deut 12:16, 17–18, 23–24), a **benefit of obedience** (Deut 12:25), and **parenesis** (Deut 12:28).

Arnold, "Deuteronomy 12," 236–48; Greenspahn, "Deuteronomy and Centralization," 227–35; Milgrom, "Does H Advocate," 59–76.

Clothing/Personal Appearance law

Clothing and appearance historically have been strong indicators of religious affiliation (they still are in Jerusalem). Leviticus 19:27–28 contains the **prohibitions**, "You shall not round off the hair on your temples or mar the edges of your beard. You shall not make any gashes in your flesh for the dead or tattoo any marks upon you" (Lev 19:27–28). Numbers 15:37–41 contains **commands** to make fringes with blue corners on the corners of their garments (Num 15:38; see also Deut 22:12), a **benefit of obedience** (Num 15:39–40), an **exodus formula** (Num 15:41a), and a **self-revelation formula** (Num 15:41b). This is recited daily in the *Shema'* prayer. Deuteronomy 14:1–2 contains **prohibitions** against self-laceration and shaving forelocks for the dead (Deut 14:1), and an expanded

holy to YHWH formula (Deut 14:2). There are further **prohibitions** against crossdressing (Deut 22:5), and wearing clothes made of wool and linen (Deut 22:11). Tractate *Kil'ayim* discusses the forbidden mixing of species in clothing.

Garroway, Palmer, and Erisman, *Essays on Dress.*

Cultic Calendar Instruction

This is a **legal instruction** concerning when and how festivals and holy days are to be observed. Specific commands, prohibitions etc. regarding the individual festivals are discussed in glossary entries pertaining to those festivals (**Passover/Unleavened Bread passage, Day of Atonement passage** etc). Those entries employ intertextual methods to analyze not only the legal genres associated with the festivals but also the narrative genres and the prophetic genres associated with the festivals. The **Decalogue** does not contain legislation pertaining to the annual festivals but it does contain two **Sabbath day passages** (Exod 20:8–11; Deut 5:12–15). The legal content portion of the **legislative speech narrative** in Exod 31:12–17 consists entirely of a **Sabbath day passage** (Exod 31:12b–17).

The **covenant code** contains legislation about the three pilgrimage festivals: a **command** to hold a festival three times in the year (Exod 23:14), a **Passover or Unleavened Bread passage** (Exod 23:15), a **Feast of Weeks passage** (Exod 23:16a), a **Feast of Tabernacles passage** (Exod 23:16b), and a **command** for all males to appear before YHWH on these three occasions (Exod 23:17). The legislative speech narrative in Exod 34:10–26 contains a **Feast of Unleavened Bread passage** (Exod 34:18), a **Sabbath passage** (Exod 34:21), a **Feast of Weeks passage** (Exod 34:22a), a **Feast of Tabernacles passage** (Exod 34:22b), and a **command** for all males to appear before YHWH at the three pilgrimage festivals (Exod 34:23).

The calendars in Lev 23 and Num 28–29, which details the sacrifices to be offered on these days, also include the weekly Sabbath and other annual holy days such as the Day of Trumpeting and the Day of Atonement; and Lev 16 gives further detailed instruction as to how the Day of Atonement is to be observed. Ezekiel 45:21–25 is an example of a **future law** (see prophetic genres chapter) that deals with the topic of which festivals will be observed.

The legal content portion of the **legislation speech narrative** in Lev 16 is a **Day of Atonement passage** which contains a **ritual prohibition** against the high priest entering the Holy of Holies at just any time (Lev 16:2b), a **ritual sacrificial procedure** (Lev 16:3–28), and a **summary subscription** (Lev 16:29–34a). The following **obedience formula** (Lev 16:34b) may have marked the conclusion of the major portion of the **priestly code.**

Leviticus 23 contains five **legislative speech narratives** (Lev 23:1–8, 9–22, 23–25, 26–32, 33–44). These narratives are linked together by the **law introduction formulas** (Lev 23:2b, 4), the **summary subscription** (Lev 23:37–38), and the conclusion after the final legislative speech, "Thus Moses declared to the people of Israel the appointed festivals of the Lord" (Lev 23:44; see **compliance narrative** in chapter on narrative genres). The legal content portion of the first narrative consists of a **law introduction formula** pertaining to all the appointed festivals (Lev 23:2b), a **Sabbath law** (Lev 23:3), a **law introduction formula** to the annual festivals (Lev 23:4), and a **Passover/Unleavened Bread passage** (Lev 23:5–8). The legal content of the second narrative consists of an **offering/sacrifice law** regarding the wave sheaf (Lev 23:10b–14a), a **statutory law formula** (Lev 23:14b), a **Feast of Weeks passage** (Lev 23:15–21a), and a **statutory law formula** (Lev 23:21b). The legal content in the third narrative consists of a **Day of Trumpeting passage** (Lev 23:24b–25). The legal content in the fourth narrative consists of a **Day of Atonement passage** (Lev 23:27–32). The legal content in the fifth narrative consists of a **Feast of Tabernacles passage** (Lev 23:34b–36a), an **Eighth Day of Tabernacles passage** (Lev 23:36b), a **summary subscription** (Lev 23:37–38), a **Feast of Tabernacles passage** (Lev 23:39a), an **Eighth Day of Tabernacles passage** (Lev 23:39b), a **Feast of Tabernacles passage** (Lev 23:40–43a), and a **YHWH self-revelation formula** (Lev 23:43b).

The legal content portion of the **legislative speech narrative** in Num 28:1—30:1 [NRSV 28:1—29:40] is discussed in the entry on **offering law** but various sections of it are also discussed in the entries on **Sabbath day passage** (Num 29:9–10), **new moon passage** (Num 29:11–15), **Passover/Unleavened Bread passage** (Num 29:16–25), **Feast of Weeks passage** (Num 29:26–31), **Day of Trumpeting passage** (Num 29:1–6), **Day of Atonement passage** (Num 29:7–11), **Feast of Tabernacles passage** (Num 29:12–34), and **Eighth Day of Tabernacles passage** (Num 29:35–38).

Deuteronomy 16:1–17 contains a **Passover/Unleavened Bread Passage** (Deut 16:1–8), a **Feast of Weeks passage** (Deut 16:9–12), a **Feast of Tabernacles passage** (Deut 16:13–15), a **command** for all males to appear before the Lord "at the place that he will choose" during the three pilgrimage festivals (Deut 16:16a; see central sanctuary law), and an **order** for the males not to be empty-handed but to give an offering (Deut 16:16b–17).

The teleological cause of this genre is for the Israelites to celebrate YHWH's annual festivals properly. These instructions are a paradigmatic example of **divine law** that is not part of **natural law** as these festivals commemorate various historical aspects of YHWH's special covenant relationship with Israel, such as the exodus from Egypt (Feast of Passover/ Unleavened Bread), the giving of the law on Mt. Sinai (Feast of Weeks), and the dwelling in booths for forty years in the wilderness (Feast of Booths/Tabernacles). For the importance of these festivals in Israel's history, see **festival observance narrative** in the chapter on narrative genres.

In the Mishnah, the order Mo'ed deals with the various appointed times. The tractate Ḥagiga deals with the three pilgrim feasts (Passover, Weeks, and Tabernacles) and Beṣah deals with individual holy days. Pesaḥim deals with the high days of Passover, Sukkah deals with the high days of Tabernacles, and *Mo'ed Qaṭan* deals with the intermediate days of Passover and Tabernacles. Roš Haššanah deals with the Day of Trumpeting (Rosh Hashanah), Yoma deals with the Day of Atonement (Yom Kippur). Post-Torah calendrical observances are discussed in Ta'anit (other fast-days) and Megillah (Purim, when the Scroll of Esther is read).

Beckwith, *Calendar and Chronology*; Beckwith, *Calendar and Worship*; Cohen, *Cultic Calendars*; Goldstein and Cooper, "Festivals of Israel," 19–31; Knierim and Coats, *Numbers*, 344; Talmon, "Gezer Calendar," 177–87; Vanderkam, *Calendars*; Vaux, *Ancient Israel*, 408–506; Wagenaar, *Origin*; Wellhausen, *Prolegomena*; Weyde, *Appointed Festivals*.

Cut Off Law

This is a **contingent law** whose apodosis is the **cut off prescription formula**.

Day of Atonement Passage

The legal content portion of the **legislation speech narrative** in Leviticus 16 is a **Day of Atonement passage** which contains a **ritual prohibition** against the high priest entering the Holy of Holies at just any time (Lev 16:2b), a **motive clause** (Lev 16:2c) a **ritual sacrificial procedure** (Lev 16:3–28), and a **summary subscription** (Lev 16:29–34b). The following **obedience formula** (Lev 16:34c) may have marked the conclusion of the major portion of the **priestly code**.

The ritual sacrificial procedure contains ritual **commands** for Aaron to wear specific vestments, make certain offerings at certain points in the procedure, put incense on the fire, sprinkling blood, loosening the Azazel goat in the wilderness etc. (Lev 16:3, 4a, 4c–10a, 11a, 11c–13a, 14–15, 18–21, 22b–23, 24b, 25, 27, 28b, 31b, 32), **prescriptions of washing** (Lev 16:4b, 24a, 26, 28), **reasons for law** (Lev 16:10b, 11b, 22a, 24c), a **cost of disobedience** (Lev 16:13b), a **make atonement formula**, (Lev 16:16, 30, 33, 34b), **prohibitions** pertaining to the Day of Atonement (Lev 16:17, 29c), **statutory law formulas** (Lev 16:29a, 31c, 34a), and a **calendrical designation** of the day as a sabbath of complete rest (Lev 16:31a).

It was on the Day of Atonement in the fiftieth year that a trumpet sounded loud and jubilee was proclaimed (see **Sabbatical Year/Jubilee passage**), so that later documents such as 11QMelchizedek in the Dead Sea Scrolls and Hebrews in the New Testament combine motifs and passages associated with *Yom Kippur* or jubilee.

Isaiah 58 is a **call to justice** (see chapter on prophetic genres for analysis of subunits) and has several motifs associated with the Day of Atonement: the sound of a trumpet, announcing to people their sins, fasting, afflicting oneself, and the jubilee theme of freeing the oppressed and breaking every yoke. It is read in synagogues on the morning service of Yom Kippur. In the afternoon service, the book of Jonah is read (see confrontation narrative). The **fast narrative** in Jonah 3:5 has the people of Nineveh believing God proclaiming a fast and everyone afflicting themselves. Then the king of Nineveh, Israel's arch-enemy, proclaims: "No human being or animal, no herd or flock, shall taste anything. They shall not feed, nor shall they drink water. Human beings and animals shall be covered with sackcloth, and they shall cry mightily to God. All shall turn from their evil ways and from the violence that is in their hands" (Jonah 3:7b–8). God then does not carry out (Jonah 3:10) the threat contained in the prior **prophecy of punishment against Assyria** (Jonah 3:1–4), demonstrating God's mercy and the efficacy of fasting accompanied by repentance.

Grabbe, "Scapegoat," 152–67; Helm, "Azazel," 217–26;. Pinker, "Goat," 1–25; Rendtorff, "Leviticus 16," 252–58; Sklar, *Sin, Impurity*; Wiley and Eberhardt, *Sacrifice, Cult*.

Day of Trumpeting Passage

This is a passage concerning the first day of the seventh month in the sacred calendar or New Year's Day in the civil calendar (Rosh Hashanah; see tractate in Mishnah of same name). A shofar or ram's horn is blown. The clearest examples include the portions of the **cultic calendar laws** concerning that day (Lev 23:23–25; Num 29:1–6). In Judaism, this day begins ten days of awe/repentance culminating in the Day of Atonement, and the prayer Avinu Malkenu is sung on these days.

Day of Trumpeting Passage

This is a passage concerning the first day of the seventh month in the sacred calendar or New Year's Day in the civil calendar (*Rosh Hashanah*; see tractate in Mishnah of same name). A shofar or ram's horn is blown. The clearest examples include the portions of the **cultic calendar laws** concerning that day (Lev 23:23–25; Num 29:1–6). In Judaism, this day begins ten days of awe/repentance culminating in the Day of Atonement, and the prayer *Avinu Malkenu* is sung on these days.

Death Penalty Law

This is a category of **law** categorized by the penalty for breaking it, namely death. It typically involves either the **death sentence formula** or some other **prescription of capital punishment**. The means by which the death sentence was carried out varied: stoning, burning or impaling/hanging. Even a criminal who was hanged/impaled had to be buried the same day (Deut 21:22–23).

Good, "Capital Punishment," 947–77; McKeating, "Development," 46–68; Schulz, *Todesrecht*.

Divination/Sorcery/Witchcraft Law

There is a prohibition against letting a sorceress live (Exod 22:18), there are **prohibitions** against mediums and wizards (Lev 19:31), and against any who "practices divination, or is a soothsayer, or an augur, or a sorcer, or one who casts spells, or who consults ghosts or spirits, or who seeks oracles from the dead" (Deut 18:10–11).

Deuteronomy 18:9–14 contains **prohibitions** against learning Canaanite practices, against making one's child pass through fire, against divination, soothsaying, augury, sorcery, casting spells, consulting spirits, or seeking oracles from the dead (Deut 18:9–11), a **motive clause** (Deut 18:12), a **command** to be completely loyal to YHWH (Deut 18:13), and a **prohibition** against heeding soothsayers and diviners (Deut 18:14).

Eighth Day of Tabernacles Passage

Although the Feast of Booths/Tabernacles strictly lasts only seven days, Lev 23:36 prescribes that on the eighth day there shall be a holy convocation and that occupational work is prohibited (see also Lev 23:39). Numbers 29:35–36 prescribe a different **quality of item offered** than for the preceding seven days of Tabernacles in the offering law. There are **festival observance narratives** which mention keeping the eighth day (Neh 8:18; 2 Chr 7:8–10). John 7:37–39 may refer to the Eighth Day or to the water ceremony on the previous day, *Hoshannah Rabbah*. In the Mishnah, tractate Sukkah gives information on the Eighth Day. Other important references are Tosefta 3:17 and Pisqa 28 of Pesiqta de Rab Kahana.

False Prophet/Future Prophet Law

Deuteronomy 13:1–5 is a **prohibition** against heeding a prophet who makes true predictions but advocates idolatry (**apostasy law**). Deuteronomy 18:15–22 contains a **prophecy** that "The Lord your God will raise up for you a prophet like me from among your own people" (Deut 18:15a; see chapter on prophetic genres), a **command** to heed that prophet (Deut 18:15b), a **reason for law** grounded in a previous request to YHWH by the Israelites (Deut 18:16–18), a **case** of a person not heeding the words of the future prophet like Moses (Deut 18:19a), a **threat** of being accountable to YHWH (Deut 18:19b), a **case** of a prophet false claiming to speak in YHWH's name (Deut 18:20a), a **death penalty prescription** (Deut 18:20b), a **hypothetical question** regarding how to recognize a false prophet (Deut 18:21), and a **response** that if the prophet's prediction fails then that prophet was false (Deut 18:22a), and a **prohibition** against being disturbed by such a prophecy (Deut 18:22b).

Leuchter, "Royal Background," 364–83.

False Witness Law

The **Decalogue** contains a **prohibition** against giving false witness (Exod 20:16; Deut 5:20). The **order** against conviction of a crime on the testimony of a single witness but only on the testimony of two or more witnesses (Deut 19:15) prevents a conviction on the testimony of a single malicious witness. Deuteronomy 19:16–20 is a **procedural law** containing a **case** of a malicious witness making an accusation (Deut 19:16), a **command** for the disputants to appear before the officiating priests and judges (Deut 19:17), a **command** for the judges to make a thorough inquiry (Deut 19:18a), a **case** of the witness having provided false testimony (Deut 19:18b), a **prescription of punishment** proportionate to the charge brought by the false witness (Deut 19:19a), a **purge the evil formula** (Deut 19:19b), and a **reason for law** (Deut 19:20).

Feast of Booths/Tabernacles Passage

This entry begins with an analysis of the legal passages concerning the Feast of Taberncacles and then more briefly discusses other passages that have connections with the Feast of Tabernacles. In the **covenant code** and **Exodus 34 code**, there are commands to observe the autumn festival, called here the Feast of Ingathering in Exod 23;16b and Exod 34:22c, respectively.

In the **holiness code**, the fifth **legislative speech narrative** contains a mixture of Feast of Tabernacles passages and **Eighth Day of Tabernacles passages** (see **cultic calendar instruction** for details). The material pertaining to the Feast of Tabernacles contains **calendrical designations** of the fifteenth day of the seventh month as a holy convocation with no arduous/occupational work and as the first of seven days of the Feast of Tabernacles (Lev 23:34a, 35a), **commands** to offer sacrifices for seven days at that pilgrim festival for seven days from the fifteenth of the seventh month "when you have gathered in the produce of the land" (Lev 23:39a), a **command** on the first day to take four species: "the fruit of majestic trees, branches of palm trees, boughs of leafy trees, and willows of the brook" (Lev 23:40a), a **command** to rejoice before YHWH for seven days (Lev 23:40b), a **command** to celebrate this pilgrim festival to YHWH for seven days (Lev 23:41a), a **statute formula** (Lev 23:41b), a **command** to live in tabernacles/booths for seven days (Lev 23:42a), a **command** for all native Israelites to live in booths (Lev 23:42b), and a **reason for law** "so that your generations may know that I made the people of Israel live in booths when I brought them out of the land of Egypt" (Lev 23:43a). The summary subscription in Lev 23:37–38 likely indicates the conclusion to an earlier form of the legislation. The reason "so that your generations may know that I made the people of Israel live in booths when I brought them out of the land of Egypt."

Numbers 29:12–34 is the part of a larger offering law which discusses the Feast of Tabernacles. It contains a **calendrical designation** of the fifteenth day of the seventh month as a holy convocation (Num 29:12a), a **prohibition** of arduous/occupational work (Num 29:12b), a **command** to celebrate a pilgrim festival for seven days (Num 29:12c). The sacrifices themselves are detailed in the entry on **offering law**. What is of note here is that a total of seventy bulls are offered during the Feast of Tabernacles. In Jewish thinking, seventy represents the number of nations of the world and the Mishnaic tractate *Sukkah* connects the seventy bulls offered at Tabernacles/*Sukkot* with the seventy nations of the world. As discussed below, Zechariah 14 also associates the Feast of Tabernacles with the nations of the world.

Deuteronomy 16:13–15 contains **commands** to keep the Feast of Tabernacles at ingathering time, to rejoice with various groups of marginalized persons (Deut 16:14; see **law concerning marginalized persons**), a **command** to keep the festival at the place that YHWH would choose (Deut 16:13–15a; see law concerning marginalized persons, **central sanctuary law**), and a **motive clause** (Deut 16:15b). The legal content portion of the **legislative speech narrative** in Deut 31:10–13 contains a command to read "this law" during the Feast of Tabernacles in the sabbatical year (Deut 31:10b–11; see sabbatical year/jubilee law), a **command** for the Israelites to assemble (Hebrew *qāhal*) the people including resident aliens (Deut 31:12a), and a **benefit of obedience** (Deut 31:12b–13).

There are **festival observance narratives** relative to the Feast of Booths observed by King Solomon (1 Kgs 8:11–66 [= 2 Chr 6:1—7:10]), and by Ezra and Nehemiah (Ezra 3:1–7; 6:19–22; Neh 8:1–18). Isaiah 25:6–8 connects the end of death and tears with the feast of well-aged wines, the Feast of Booths, and Zechariah 14 envisions all nations keeping the Feast of Booths in the Messianic Age. The **YHWH-Kingship Psalms** have many thematic connections with Zech 14, 1 Kgs 8, and other passages associated with the Feast of Booths. In the New Testament, John 7 shows Jesus at the Feast of Booths and the themes of living water and light of the world in John 7–9 resonate with Zech 14. The account of the Triumphal Entry in John 12 contains palm-waving and other themes associated with Booths. The transfiguration of Jesus in Matt 17:1–8 and parallels specifically mention booths (for Moses, Elijah, and Jesus) and has the themes of clouds and shade found in tractate Sukkah, plus the white clothing. Revelation 7:9–17 and Rev 21–22 are positively drenched in Sukkot symbolism.

Ayali-Darshan, "Seventy Bulls," 9–19; Daniélou, "Symbolism eschatologique," 19–40; Draper, "Heavenly Feast," 133–47. Mowinckel, *Psalm Studies 1*, 175–491; Mowinckel, *Israel's Worship I*; Reynolds, "Feast of Tabernacles," 245–68; Rubenstein, *History of Sukkot*; Schaefer, "Ending," 165–238; Spaulding and Keith, *Commemorative Identities*; Ulfgard, *Setting, Shaping*; Weyde, *Appointed Festivals*, 163–236.

Feast of Weeks Passage

In the covenant code, Exod 23:16a is the command to observe "the festival of harvest, of the first fruits of your labor, of what you sow in the field." In the Exod 34 code, Exod 34:22a is the command to observe "the festival of weeks, the first fruits of wheat harvest."

It is in the holiness code that one learns why the wheat harvest festival in late Spring is known as the Feast of Weeks. Leviticus 23:15–22 contains **commands** to count seven weeks from the day of the wave sheaf offering, the day after the Sabbath, until the day after the seventh Sabbath, fifty days ("Pentecost" comes from the Greek of counting fifty), to offer two loaves of new grain as an elevation offering (Lev 23:15–17a), a **qualification of item offered** (Lev 23:17b), a **classification/purpose of sacrifice** (Lev 23:17c), a **command** to bring seven lambs (Lev 23:18a), a **qualification of item presented** (Lev 23:18b), a continuation of the

command to include a young bull and two rams (Lev 23:18c), and a **classification/purpose of sacrifice** (Lev 23:18d), a **command** to offer a male goat as a sin offering (Lev 23:19a), a continuation of the **command** to offer two male lambs a year old as a peace offering (Lev 23:19b), a **ritual sacrificial procedure** (Lev 23:20), a **command** to have a holy convocation (Lev 23:21a), **prohibitions** of arduous/occupational work, of preventing gleaning (Lev 23:21b, 22a), a **statutory law formula** (Lev 23:21c), a **command** to leave them for the poor and for the resident alien (Lev 23:22c; see **laws concerning poor and marginalized persons**), and a **self-revelation of YHWH formula** (Lev 23:22d).

For analysis of Num 28:26–31, see **offering law**. The offering consisted of two young bulls, one ram, seven male lambs a year old, a grain offering, and a male goat to make atonement, all in addition to the regular burnt offering and its grain offering.

Deuteronomy 16:9–12 contains **commands** to count seven weeks from the time the sickle is put to the standing grain, to keep the Feast of Weeks and make a freewill offering to YHWH, to rejoice before YHWH with various categories of marginalized persons at the central sanctuary (Deut 16:9–11; see **law concerning marginalized persons, central sanctuary law**), and **parenesis** (Deut 16:12).

There is a **festival observance narrative** connected with a **covenant renewal narrative** in 2 Chr 15:8–15 when Asa and the people observe the Feast of Weeks. Psalm 50 is a **divine speech hymn** which may also be connected to Sinai and Weeks. It is curiously absent from the **future law** concerning the festivals in Ezek 45. The most important passage in the New Testament is Acts 2, the Day of Pentecost on which the Church began, which has a theophany reminiscent of Exod 19.

De Vries, "Festival Observance," 104–24; Gerhards and Leonard, *Jewish Liturgy*; Park, *Pentecost and Sinai*; Weinfeld, "Pentecost," 7–18; Weinfeld, "Uniqueness of Decalogue," 21–27.

Financial/Property Law

The Decalogue contains a **prohibition** against stealing (Exod 20:15; Deut 5:19). Three passages deal with the issue of charging interest. Exodus 22:25 contains **prohibitions** against dealing in a usury manner with the poor. Leviticus 25:35–37, part of a sabbatical year/jubilee law, contains commands to support Israelites in financial difficulty (Lev 25:35), and

prohibition against taking interest in advance or profiting from them (Lev 25:36a, 37), an **exhortation** to fear YHWH (Lev 25:36b), a **command** to let them live with you (Lev 25:36c), Deut 23:20–21 [NRSV 19–20] contains a **prohibition** against charging interest on anything lent to another Israelite (Deut 23:20, 21b [NRSV 19, 20b]), and a **permission** to charge interest to foreigners (Deut 23:21a [NRSV 20a]). Options for understanding the relationships between these passages include the Deuteronomy passage overriding an earlier law which permitted charging interest to non-poor Israelites so that now only non-Israelites may be charged interest, that the Deuteronomy passage does not override the earlier covenant code law but distinguishes between commercial loans to travelling merchants where paying interest is common practice and loans made of solidarity with a poor Israelite brother which should be done without interest, or that charging interest is ethically wrong in all circumstances.

Mishnaic tractate Baba Meṣiʿa discusses this law and related material in the Babylonian Talmud permitted loans among Israelites for mortgages and certain other commercial purposes. Christian understanding of the law changed during the late medieval period to distinguish between interest and usury (excessive interest), with the former being permitted on commercial loans in proportion to inflation, business risk, and reasonable payment to merchant for time and effort involved in processing the loan. This topic remains controversial.

Deuteronomy 19:14 is a **prohibition** against moving a neighbor's boundary marker. Deuteronomy 24:6 contains a **prohibition** against taking a mill or an upper millstone in pledge. Deuteronomy 25:13–16 contains **prohibitions** against having two kinds of weights or two kinds of measures (Deut 25:13–14), **commands** to have honest weight and honest measures (Deut 25:15a), and a **benefit of obedience** (Deut 25:15b–16).

Issler, "Lending and Interest," 761–89; Neufeld, "Prohibition against Loans," 355–412.

Firstborn Redemption Law

The first such law occurs prior to the Sinai covenant, where YHWH commands, "Consecrate to me all the firstborn; whatever is the first to open the womb among the Israelites, of human beings and animals, is mine" (Exod 13:2). Exodus 13:11–16 contains an **enter land formula** (Exod

13:11), **commands** to set apart firstborn males and to redeem a firstborn donkey with a sheep (Exod 13:12–13a), a **case-prescription law** for not redeeming a donkey (Exod 13:13b), a **question and answer subunit** including a ritual recitation (Exod 13:14–15) and a **benefit of obedience** (Exod 13:16).

In the **covenant code**, Exodus 22:28–29 [NRSV 29–30] specifies the eighth day as when the firstborn offering takes place. In the **Exodus 34 code**, Exod 34:19–20a contains the basic obligation (Exod 34:19), followed by a ritual procedure for how to redeem the firstborn: "The firstborn of a donkey you shall redeem with a lamb, or if you will not redeem it, you shall break its neck. All the firstborn of your sons you shall redeem" (Exod 34:20). The firstborn laws in Exod 13 and 22 are traditionally interpreted in accord with the **human sacrifice prohibitions** as a requirement to redeem firstborn sons with a lamb sacrifice as the Exod 34 passage makes explicit. Deuteronomy 15:19a commands that Israelites consecrate the firstlings of herd and flock.

Deuteronomy 15:19b–23 contains a **prohibition** against working with a firstling ox (Deut 15:19b), a **prohibition** against shearing a firstling from the flock (Deut 15:19c), an implied **command** to sacrifice the animal at one of the pilgrim festivals (Deut 15:20; see **cultic calendar instruction**), a **prohibition** against sacrificing an animal with a blemish (Deut 15:21), a **permission** to eat a blemished animal (Deut 15:22; see food law), and an **order** not to eat the blood but to pour it on the ground (Deut 15:23; see food law).

Finsterbusch, "First-born," 87–108; Yaakov, "Ransoming," 305–19.

Food Law

Leviticus 11:1–47 and Deut 14:3–21 are both **tables of directives** (see list genres chapter). The genre details of the **clean/unclean animals lists** in Lev 11:4–7, 13–19, 22, 29–31a; Deut 14:4–5, 12–18 are discussed in the lists chapter. In addition to these lists, Lev 11 contains **permissions** to eat animals that part the hoof and chew the cud (Lev 11:2b–3a), to eat fish that have fins and scales (Lev 11:9), to eat winged insects with jointed legs above their feet (Lev 11:21), and **prohibitions** against eating fish that do not have both fins and scales (Lev 11:10–12), against eating winged insects that walk upon all fours (Lev 11:20, 23), and against eating creatures that swarm upon the earth (Lev 11:41–43), **laws concerning**

ceremonially unclean persons (Lev 11:24–28, 31b–40), **parenesis** (Lev 11:44–45), and a **summary subscription** (Lev 11:46–47). In addition to the lists, Deut 14:3–21 contains a **prohibitions** against eating any abhorrent thing (Deut 14:3), fish that do not have fins and scales (Deut 14:9), winged insects (Deut 14:19), and creatures that die naturally (Deut 14:21a), **permissions** to eat animals that part the hoof and chew the cud (Deut 14:6), to eat fish that have fins and scales (Deut 14:9), to eat clean birds (Deut 14:11), to eat clean winged creatures (Deut 14:20), and to give creatures that die naturally to a resident alien or sell it to a foreigner (Deut 14:21b). The legislation concludes with an **identification of holiness formula** (Deut 14:21c), and a **prohibition** against boiling a kid in its mother's milk (Deut 14:21d).

The **clean food lists** and the **unclean food lists** are paradigmatic rather than exhaustive. Permission is given to eat any ruminant ungulate (animal that chews the cud and parts the hoof) not merely the species that are listed in Deut 14:4–5. The lists in Lev 11:4–8 and Deut 14:7–8 contain partial and paradigmatic lists of hard cases concerning animals which have one but not both characteristics of clean animals, so that, *a fortiori*, animals which neither chew the cud nor part the hoof are unclean without this needing to be specified. The material concerning clean and unclean aquatic creatures is entirely by explicit paradigm: clean aquatic creatures have fins and scales, and aquatic creatures lacking either feature are unclean. Laws such as the permission to eat any clean bird (Deut 14:11) presuppose significant knowledge by the addressees of the categories of clean and unclean. In their larger canonical setting, the laws are embedded in a narrative where the antediluvian Noah had knowledge of the categories of clean and unclean animals. Underlying the lists of unclean winged creatures may be paradigmatic principles such as prohibiting birds of prey (also prohibited in Vedic India and certain other ancient Eastern societies), birds which eat fish, birds without craws, and flying creatures which are not birds (such as bats). If the "all" in "All winged insects that walk upon all fours are detestable to you" (Lev 11:20), then there would be a contradiction with the next two verses. A more charitable interpretation would see Lev 11:20 as a general principle and the following two verses as an exception which permitted Israelites to eat locusts.

The teleological cause of the various food laws is disputed. If it is for the general health of human beings (ruminant ungulates and locusts are known to be excellent sources of concentrated protein), then it is part of natural law; if it is for the particular holiness of Israel, it is solely divine law. It is possible that some food laws but not others are part of the natural law.

Burnside, "Wisdom's Table," 223–45; Douglas, *Purity and Danger*; Firmage, "Dietary Laws," 177–208; Houston, *Purity and Monotheism*; Milgrom, "Ethics and Ritual," 159–91; Mindiola, "Reception History," 39–60; Moskala, "Categorization," 5–41; Wright, "Observations," 193–98.

Goring Ox Law

In the covenant code, Exod 21:28–36 considers various scenarios involving an ox goring a man or a woman to death. The standard pattern is case (Exod 21:28a, 29a, 30a, 31a, 32a, 33, 35a, 36a), followed by **prescription** (Exod 21:28b, 29b, 30b, 31b, 32b, 34, 35b, 36b). The law distinguishes between accidental death and manslaughter (by negligent behavior) but, like its ANE counterparts, fails to value the life of slaves the same as free Israelites (adults or children).

Finkelstein, *The Ox That Gored*; Hallo, *COS* 2, 350.

Homicide Law

This is a **law** categorized according to content, namely a law pertaining to the death of a human being. This category includes laws regarding premeditated murder, accidental manslaughter, self-defense, homicides in warfare, executions etc. While the deliberate killing of an innocent human being is murder and a **death penalty law**, certain other forms of homicide are either permitted or carry a lesser penalty.

The Torah envisions cities of asylum/refuge to where someone who committed accidental homicide might flee as early as Exod 21:12–14. Numbers 35:9–34 expands on this and contains **commands** to set aside cities of refuge where someone who committed accidental homicide might flee to, three each side of the Jordan (Num 35:10b–11a, 13–14), **reasons for law** (Num 35:11b–12, 15), môt yûmāt **laws** concerning deliberate violent deaths (Num 35:16, 17, 18, 20–21a), **prescriptions** for the avenger of blood to carry out the execution (Num 35:19, 21b), and **case-prescription laws** of unintentional death or the avenger killing the slayer outside the bounds of the city (Num 35:22–25, 26–27), a **motive clause** (Num 35:28), a **statutory law formula** (Num 35:29), **prescription**

of capital punishment for a murder established by multiple witnesses (Num 35:30a), a **prohibition** of capital punishment if there is only one witness (Num 35:30b), an **order** against accepting ransom instead of capital punishment (Num 35:31–32), and **parenesis** (Num 35:33–34).

Deuteronomy 19:1–13 contains a **command** to set aside three cities of refuge in the promised land (Deut 19:1–3, 7), a **law introduction** (Deut 19:4), **case-prescription laws** concerning accidental homicide (Deut 19:5–6), YHWH enlarging the territory (Deut 19:8–9), and deliberate murder (Deut 19:11–12), a **purge the evil formula** (Deut 19:13a), and **benefits of obedience** (Deut 19:10, 13b). Deuteronomy 21:1–9 contains a **case** where a corpse is found and the killer is unknown (Deut 21:1), a **ritual procedure** for a town to absolve itself of the guilt (Deut 21:2–8), and a **purge the evil formula** (Deut 21:9). Joshua 20:1–9 names the cities of refuge as Kedesh, Shechem, Hebron, Bezer, Ramoth, and Golan.

Altman, "Basic Concepts," 323–42; Burnside, "Exodus and Asylum," 243–66; Haas, "Surely Die," 67–88; Hadad, "Unintentionally," 155–73; McKeating, "Development," 46–68; Sulzberger, *Ancient*.

Human Sacrifice Prohibition

Genesis 22, a **crisis narrative** in which YHWH at the last moment prevents an obedient Abraham from sacrificing Isaac, is likely a pre-Word to the human sacrifice prohibitions in Leviticus (and Christians also see it as a pre-Word to the sacrifice of Christ). The prohibition against sacrificing offspring to Molech (Lev 18:21a) takes the more emphatic syntactical form. Leviticus 20:2b–6 contains a **case-prescription law** against those sacrificing offspring to Molech (20:2b; **death penalty law**) followed by YHWH's **conditional threat** to cut them and their followers off from the people if the people fail to put them to death (20:3–5). The **battle narrative** in 2 Kgs 3 where the Moabite king sacrifices his son and the **vow narrative** in Judg 12 where Jephthah presumably sacrifices his daughter should be read against this background.

Idolatry Law

Jacob and his family destroying idols in a divine command narrative (Gen 35:1–7) is a pre-Word to the idolatry laws in Torah. There are prohibitions against idolatry in the Decalogue (Exod 20:4–5; Deut 5:8–9), the covenant code (Exod 23:13, 33), the Exod 34 code (Exod 34:17), the Holiness code (Lev 19:4) and the Deuteronomic Code (Deut 7:1–26; 13:6–9). These prohibitions included the setting up of sacred poles or stone pillars (Lev 26:1; Deut 16:21–22). The laws concerning the Canaanite genocide are seen against the threat of idolatry in Deut 7.

Following the expanded **self-revelation of YHWH formula** (Exod 20:2; Deut 5:6), the first actual directives in the Decalogue concern idolatry and, along with the **Sabbath passage**, are more detailed than other laws in the Decalogue. There is a **prohibition** against other gods before YHWH (Exod 20:3; Deut 5:7), a **prohibition** against making an idol "whether in the form of anything that is in heaven above, or that is in earth beneath, or that is in the water under the earth" (Exod 20:4; Deut 5:8), a **prohibition** against bowing down to them (Exod 20:5a; Deut 5:9a), a **prohibition** against worshiping them (Exod 20:5b; Deut 5:9b), and a **motive clause** (Exod 20:5c–6; Deut 5:9c–10).

The covenant code continues this theme of emphatically rejecting idolatry (Exod 20:23; 22:19 [NRSV 20]; 23:13, 32–33). The Exod 34 law code connects idolatry to the Canaanites. It contains a **be careful lest construction** against covenants with Canaanites (Exod 34:12), **commands** to tear down their altars, pillars, and sacred groves (Exod 34:13), and **prohibitions** against idolatry (Exod 34:14, 17), and making covenants with Canaanites (Exod 34:15–16). The background to the **war law** in Deut 7 is to avoid Israelites worshiping Canaanite gods (Deut 7:5, 25).

One **I am YHWH subunit** in the **holiness code** consists of a **prohibition** against turning to idols (Lev 19:4a), a **prohibition** against making cast metal gods (Lev 19:4b), and a **self-revelation of YHWH formula** (Lev 19:4c).

Prohibitions and **be careful lest constructions** against idolatry include Deut 4:23; 11:16; 12:29–32; and 16:21–22. There is also a **conditional threat of punishment** for idolatry (Deut 8:19–20) and a curse on idolaters in a **ritual recitation subunit** (Deut 27:16).

Keel and Uehlinger, *Gods, Goddesses*; Tigay, *No other Gods*; Toorn, *Image.*

Improper Intervention Law

This is a **law** categorized by content, namely an improper intervention in a fight. Deuteronomy 25:11–12 contains a **case** of two men fighting and the wife of one seizing the genitals of her husband's opponent (Deut 25:11), and an **order** to cut off the woman's hand and not show pity (Deut 25:12).

Inheritance Law

There had been an expectation that only sons would inherit, but the legal case narratives (see narratives chapter) concerning Zelophehad's daughters changed that. Daughters could inherit but had to marry within the tribe so that their father's inheritance would remain within the tribe (Num 27:1–11; 36:1–12). Deuteronomy 21:15–17 forbids a man with two wives from preferring the son of his loved wife but to give the firstborn son a double portion of the inheritance.

Kidnapping Law

Deuteronomy 24:7 contains a **case** in which an Israelite kidnaps a fellow Israelite (Deut 24:7a), a **prescription of capital punishment** (Deut 24:7b), and a **reason for law** (Deut 24:7c).

Law in Legal Case Narrative

See entry in chapter on narrative genres. The legal precedents established in the cases concern violations of **blasphemy law** (Lev 24:10–23), **Sabbath law** (Num 15:32–36), and **inheritance law** (Num 27:1–11; 36:1–12).

Burnside, "Sabbath-Gatherer," 45–62; Fuad, "Curious Case," 51–70; Knierim and Coats, *Numbers*, 275, 329–30; Leuchter, "Ambiguous Details," 431–50; Trevaskis, *Holiness, Ethics*.

Lex Talionis

This is the standard name for the laws of retributive justice prescribing a punishment of mutilation (or even death) proportionate to the crime itself. The covenant code contains a case of a violent fight causing a woman either to miscarry or to bear prematurely a healthy child (Exod 21:22a), a prescription of financial restitution (Exod 21:22b), a case of further harm following (Exod 21:23a, contrary to the case in Exod 21:22a), and the prescription of retributive justice, "Then you shall give life for life, eye for eye, tooth for tooth, hand for hand, foot for foot, burn for burn, wound for wound, stripe for stripe" (Exod 21:23b–25). The different sides of the abortion issue hotly dispute the interpretation of this passage which does have a number of exegetical cruxes.

The holiness code version contains a case of one person maiming another (Lev 24:19a), and a prescription of punishment proportionate to that inflicted (Lev 24:19b–20), with an emphasis on the principle of proportionality (Lev 24:19b, 20b), already implicit in the môt yûmāt **law** for the murderer (Lev 24:17). One teleological cause for the law is to prohibit retribution beyond the initial harm inflicted. However, that the *lex talionis* is not simply a restriction showing the maximum punishment is demonstrated in the prohibition against pity in its Deuteronomic code formulation: "Show no pity: life for life, eye for eye, tooth for tooth, hand for hand, foot for foot" (Deut 19:21).

Jackson, "Ius Talionis," 273–304; Sprinkle, "Interpretation," 233–53.

Loving YHWH Law

There are requirements to believe in YHWH (Exod 20:2; Deut 5:6), affirm YHWH's oneness (Deut 6:4), love YHWH (Deut 6:5), fear YHWH (Deut 6:13), cleave to YHWH (Deut (10:20; 11:22), swear only in YHWH's name (Deut 6:13; 10:20), walk in YHWH's ways (Deut 10:12; 28:9), sanctify YHWH's name (Lev 22:32), read the Shema (Deut 6:7), and study the Torah (Num 15:39; Deut 31:12). To remind one of YHWH, there are requirements to put phylacteries containing the Shema on the forehead and arm (Exod 13:9, 16; Deut 6:8; 11:18), put fringes on the corners of garments to remember YHWH's commandments (Deut 15:38–39), and put a mezuzah on the doorposts (Deut 6:9; 11:20). Every seven years, the people were to read the Torah at the Feast of Tabernacles (Deut 31:10–12), the king was to write out the Torah (Deut 17:18), the Torah was to be a song for the Israelites (Deut 31:19), and the people were to bless YHWH after meals (Deut 8:10). All of these concern loving YHWH with one's whole being, central to Judaism and Christianity alike.

Loving Neighbor Law

Most of the laws that are not specifically loving God laws could be categorized as loving neighbor laws which are expansions of "You shall love your neighbor as yourself" (Lev 19:18). The Hebrew Bible affirms the principle that one is obligated to all people at a basic level and the principle that one has additional obligations to one's kin (kin here is primarily family, but occasionally extends to tribe, nation, or some other association). In the **Decalogue** (Exod 20:2–17; Deut 5:6–21), the **command** to honor one's father and one's mother exemplifies the latter and the **prohibitions** against murder, stealing, bearing false witness, and coveting a neighbor's property exemplify the former. Adultery violates the general obligations to one's neighbor and the specific obligations to one's spouse and so the **prohibition** against adultery exemplifies both principles. Both principles are exemplified in other law codes of the Ancient Near East that precede Moses, and underlie natural law. Marxism and libertarianism typically deny the principle that one has special obligations to one's family. Consequently, they respectively replace the family with the state or with the individual as the primary social unit.

Many of the specific loving neighbor laws are contained in the fourteen **I am YHWH subunits** in Lev 19. These include honoring one's father and one's mother (Lev 19:3); **agricultural laws** designed to help the poor (Lev 19:9–10a); **prohibitions** against stealing, dealing falsely, and lying (Lev 19:11), against swearing falsely (Lev 19:12), against oppressing neighbors, robbery, and wage suppression (Lev 19:13), against oppressing the deaf/blind (Lev 19:14), against slandering or endangering the life of a neighbor (Lev 19:16), against hating one's brother (Lev 19:17), against taking private vengeance or grudge bearing (Lev 19:18a); and the famous **command** "You shall love your neighbor as yourself" (Lev 19:18b), a favorite of Hillel and Jesus. Leviticus 19 further contains principles pertaining to the elderly and resident aliens (Lev 19:32–34), and **financial laws** concerning honesty with one's neighbors (Lev 19:35–36).

Deuteronomy 22:1–4 contains **orders** (Deut 24:1, 3, 4) and a **case-law** (Deut 24:2) regarding care of a neighbor's animals. Deuteronomy 22:8 contains a **command** to build a parapet on the roof of a new house to prevent a neighbor from falling.

Marriage and Family Law

This is a **law** whose content concerns marriages and/or relatives. In addition to the sex laws prohibiting sexual relations with various close relatives (Lev 18, 20), this would include allowing daughters to inherit when there are no sons but restricting them to marry within the tribe to preserve tribal inheritances (Num 27:6–11; 36:1–9), **prohibitions** against Israelites marrying women from the seven Canaanite nations (Deut 7), laws concerning marrying women captured in war (Deut 21:10–14), rights of firstborn sons in polygamous marriages (Deut 21:15–17), the punishment of insubordinate sons (Deut 21:18–21), divorce laws (Deut 24:1–4), and levirate marriage laws where a childless widow marries her brother-in-law (Deut 25:5–10), divorce laws (Deut 24:1–4).

Also Num 5:11–31 concerns a man suspecting that his wife committed adultery and contains a **case for procedure** (Num 5:12b–14), the **ritual procedure** (Num 5:15–26), a **branched conditional** (Num 5:27–28), and a **summary subscription** (Num 5:29–31). Deuteronomy 21:15–17 forbids a man with two wives from preferring the son of his loved wife but to give the firstborn son a double portion of the inheritance. Both the midrash Sifrei Devarim and the Talmudic tractate Baba Batra interpret this so that if there were five sons, the eldest would receive two sixths of the inheritance and the other sons one sixth each.

The teleological cause of the law permitting capital punishment for rebellious sons is to emphasize the importance of filial obedience while also limiting the *patria potestas*, which in other societies permitted a father to kill his children without any accountability. Rabbinic interpretation of the law developed this second aspect with further restrictions that made it almost impossible to carry out this law.

Divorce laws have always been controversial. Simplifying things, Jesus interpreted divorce laws more strictly than Shammai (although Protestants recently have become way more lax than Christians have historically), and Shammai interpreted them more strictly than Hillel.

The levirate marriage law in Deut 25:5–10 is relevant to understanding passages like Gen 38 and Ruth 3–4, not to mention the beginnings of the Church of England.

Not surprisingly, several tractates in the Mishnaic order *Našim* (Women) deal heavily with marriage and family law. Yebamot concerns Levirate marriage; Ketubbot concerns prenuptial agreements and the marital obligations of husband and wife; Soṭah discusses the trial by ordeal of the woman suspected of adultery; Giṭṭin deals with divorce; and Qiddušin deals with betrothal, permitted marriages, and legitimacy of children.

Belkin, "Levirate," 275–329; Davies, "Inheritance Rights," 138–44, 257–68; Epstein, *Marriage Laws*; Leggett, *Levirate and Goel*; Yaron, "Divorce," 117–28; Zakovitch, "Woman's Rights," 28–46.

Non-Food Items that Become Unclean

Leviticus 14:47–58 discusses items that have become unclean because of contact with someone who is ceremonially unclean due to a skin condition. The passage contains **prescriptions of washing** (Lev 14:47), a **case for procedure** (Lev 14:48a), a **determination of clean/unclean procedure** (Lev 14:48b–53), and a **summary subscription** (Lev 14:54–58).

Offering Law

This is a subcategory of **legal instruction** in which the contents are those of offering sacrifices in a ritual ceremony. The main subunits are the **case for offering/sacrifice**, the **qualification of item offered**, the **ritual sacrificial procedure**, and the **identification of offering/sacrifice**. At one level, the teleological cause is for the Israelites to adhere to the instructions given when performing the various sacrifices. At another level, it exhibits an ethos that God's people should find ways to put God first in their lives. With the Roman destruction of the second temple, prayer has replaced animal offerings in Judaism (at least until a third temple is built).

The largest block of offering law is in Lev 1–7 which contains instructions for the whole offering (1:3–17), the grain offering (2:1–16), the well-being/peace offering (3:1–17), the purification offering for unintentional sin (4:1–5:13), the reparation offering (5:14–26) and further instructions regarding the various sacrifices (6:1—7:38).

The main subunits in this block are as follows: **case for offering/sacrifice** (Lev 1:3a, 10a, 14a; 2:1a, 4a, 7a, 14a; 3:1a, 6a, 7a, 12; 4:3a, 13–14a, 22–23a, 27–28a, 32a; 5:15a, 17a, 21–24a [NRSV 6:2–5a]; 7:12a, 16a, 29b), **qualification of item offered** (Lev 1:3b, 10b, 14b; 2:1a, 4b, 5b, 7b, 14b; 3:1b, 6b; 4:3b, 14b, 23b, 28b, 32b; 5:7, 11b, 15b, 18a, 25 [NRSV 6:6]; 6:14b [NRSV 20b]), **ritual sacrificial procedure** (Lev 1:3c–9a, 11–13a, 15–17a; 2:1c–2a, 6a, 8–9a, 11–13, 15a, 16a; 3:2–5a, 7b–11a, 12b–16a; 4:4–10,

15–20a, 24a, 25–26a, 29–31a, 33–35a; 5:5b–6a, 8–10a, 12a, 16a, 24b–25a [NRSV 6:5b–6a]; 6:2c–6, 7b–8, 14–15, 18c, 20–21 [NRSV 9c–13, 14b–15, 21–22, 25c, 27–28]; 7:2–5a, 12b–15, 16b–18, 29c–34), and **identification of offering/sacrifice** (Lev 1:9b, 13b, 17b; 2:2b, 6b, 9b, 15b, 16b; 3:5b, 11b, 14b; 4:21b, 24b; 5:7c, 11c, 12b, 15c, 18b, 19a; 7:5b).

The whole offering presupposes different wealth levels within Israelite society: the wealthy offer a male bull (Lev 1:3–9), the average offer a sheep or goat (Lev 1:10–13), the poor offer turtledoves or pigeons (Lev 1:14–17). The grain offering is of choice flour, unleavened cakes mixed with frankincense, and the law provides for **disposition of leftovers** (Lev 2:3, 10). The well-being/peace offering can be a male or female animal and separate instructions concern whether it is from the herd (Lev 3:1–5), the flock (Lev 3:6–11), or a goat (Lev 3:12–16). A **statutory law formula** emphasizes the prohibition against eating fat or blood (Lev 3:17).

The purification offering is subdivided according to whether the sinner is the anointed priest (Lev 4:3–12), the congregation (Lev 4:13–21), a ruler (Lev 4:22–26), or ordinary person (Lev 4:27–31). Further instructions are given in Lev 4:32–5:13 depending on whether the sinner can afford to offer a lamb, or two turtledoves, or only a flour offering. Of particular note is the **make atonement formula** (Lev 4:20, 26, 31, 35; 5:6, 10, 13) which connects this offering to the Day of Atonement law in Lev 16. Leviticus 5:1–4 lists various categories of offense followed by **prescriptive verdicts of guilt**. The restoration offering involves offering a ram without blemish, making restitution and adding one fifth to the amount; the **make atonement formula** is expanded with "and you shall be forgiven" (Lev 5:16, 18), demonstrating the law's efficacy; and the **case of financial difficulty** (Lev 5:7a, 11a) followed by **alternative ritual procedures** (Lev 5:8–10a, 12a) make explicit the principle that offering is according to means.

There are further legislative speech narratives expanding on the above categories of offering law in Lev 5:20–26 [NRSV 6:1–7]; 6:1–11, 12–16 [NRSV 8–18, 19–23]; 6:17—7:21 [NRSV 6:24—7:21]; 7:22–27, 28–38. Of note in this section of law are some **superscription classifications** (Lev 6:2, 7, 13, 18 [NRSV 9, 14, 20, 25]; 7:1, 11), the **identification of holiness formula** (Lev 6:18 [NRSV 25]), and a lengthy **law subscription** (Lev 7:37–38), marking the end of a major division within Leviticus.

Two legislative speech narratives in the Holiness Code cover offering law. Leviticus 22:17–25 focuses on the **qualification of item offered** for offerings in general and the well-being offering in particular.

Leviticus 22:26–33 prohibits offering an animal younger than eight days old, and offering an animal and its young on the same day. The law ends in parenesis, with the **YHWH self-revelation formula** prominent (Lev 22:30, 31, 32, 33).

Numbers 15:1–16 focuses on the **ritual sacrificial procedure** if the offering is a lamb (Num 15:4–5), a ram (Num 15:6–7), or a bull (Num 15:8–10), followed by a **summary subscription** (Num 15:11–14). The **one law formula** (Num 15:15a, 15c–16; 15b is a **statutory law formula**), shows that these procedures apply to native Israelites and resident aliens alike. Numbers 15:17–31 begins with legislation concerning offering the first batch of dough (Num 15:18–21). Then comes legislation rectifying unintentional sin by the congregation (Num 15:22–26) and unintentional sin by an individual (Num 15:27–29), both of which include a make atonement formula (Num 15:25, 28). The law concludes with a cut off law for anyone—Israelite or resident alien—who sins intentionally (Num 15:30–31). Numbers 15 emphasizes solidarity between Israelites and law-abiding resident aliens, makes provision for unintentional sin and strongly warns against intentional sin.

Numbers 28:1—30:1 [NRSV 28:1—29:40] contains material related to **cultic calendar instruction** as well as that of offering law. There are two **command to speak formulas** (Num 28:2a, 3a) enveloping a **superscription** to the cultic calendar laws (Num 28:2b), after which comes the legal content portion of the individual offering laws. First comes the daily offering (Num 28:3–8), followed by the offerings in addition on the sabbath (Num 28:9–10), and new moon (Num 28:11–15), the daily offering focusing on the **ritual sacrificial procedure** but the rest of the material in Num 28–29 focusing on the **qualification of item offered.**

The sections for the individual annual Holy Days begin with a calendrical designation (Num 28:16, 26; 29:1, 12, 35) followed largely by qualification of item offered. For further information on their particular festivals, see **Passover/Unleavened Bread passage** (Num 28:16–25), **Feast of Weeks passage** (Num 28:26–31), Day of Trumpeting passage (Num 29:1–6), Day of Atonement passage (Num 29:7–11), **Feast of Booths passage** (Num 29:12–34), and **Eighth Day of Tabernacles passage** (Num 29:35–38). There is a subscription noting that the sacrifices for the annual Holy Days are in addition to the other offerings that may apply on that day (Num 29:39).

Deuteronomy 17:1 contains a **prohibition** against sacrificing an animal with a serious defect (Deut 17:1a), and a **motive clause** (Deut

17:1b). This law is specifically exemplified in many of the **qualification of item offered** parts of the previous offering laws. Deuteronomy 26:1–11, which is probably a **Feast of Weeks passage**, contains a **case for procedure** involving first fruits (Deut 26:1–2), a **ritual sacrificial procedure** (Deut 26:3–10), which involves a **ritual recitation** concerning what YHWH has done for Israel (Deut 26:5b–9), and a **command** to celebrate with the bounty that YHWH has provided (Deut 26:11).

Two Mishnaic tractates in order Zera'im discuss offerings: Ḥallah discusses the dough offering and Bikkurim discusses first-fruit offerings. Several tractates in the Mishnaic order Qodašim are relevant. Tractate Zebaḥim expands on the laws for animal and bird offerings; Menaḥot discusses grain and drink offerings; Temurah discusses the circumstances permitting one sacrificial animal to be substituted for another; *Tamid* discusses the morning and evening sacrifices performed daily; Me'ilah discusses restitution offerings needed for misuse of holy objects; and Qinnim discusses the offerings of birds in specific circumstances.

Anderson, *Sacrifices and Offerings*; Eberhart, *Studien*; Gorman, *Ideology of Ritual*; Haran, "Complex," 272–301; Knierim, *Hauptbegriffe*; Knierim, *Text and Concept*; Knohl, *Sanctuary of Silence*; Marx, *Theology of Sacrifice*; Watts, *Ritual and Rhetoric*.

Parenetic Passage

In addition to the **subunits of parenesis** that many individual laws contain, there are some lengthy passages in Deuteronomy that are exhortations to obey YHWH with reminders of what YHWH has done for them and promises of what YHWH will do for them.

Deuteronomy 1:6–4:40 contains a **historical reminder subunit** (Deut 1:6—3:29), various **exhortations to obey** (Deut 4:1–2, 5–6, 39–40a), some shorter **historical reminder subunits** (Deut 4:3–4, 10–14, 20–22, 34–38), series of **rhetorical questions** (Deut 4:7–8, 32–33), **be careful lest constructions** (Deut 4:9, 15–18, 23), a **prohibition** against apostasy and idolatry (Deut 4:19), a **motive clause** (Deut 4:24), a conditional **prophecy of punishment and restoration** (Deut 4:25–31), and a concluding **motive clause** "so that you may long remain in the land that the Lord your God is giving you for all time" (Deut 4:40b).

Deuteronomy 5:1b–5 functions as a preface to the Decalogue and contains a **call to attention formula** (Deut 5:1b), an **exhortation to obey**

(Deut 5:1c), and an **historical reminder subunit** (Deut 5:2–5). Immediately after the Decalogue, Deut 5:22—6:25 contains a **historical reminder subunit** (Deut 5:22–30), **exhortations to obey** (Deut 5:31–33; 6:1–2, 3), a **loving God law** known by Jews as the Shema and by Christians as the great commandment (Deut 6:4–9), a **be careful lest construction** not to forget YHWH when you enter the land (Deut 6:10–12), compound parenetic constructions (Deut 6:13–15, 16–19), and a **Passover/Unleavened Bread passage** which is a **ritual recitation** that combines reciting how YHWH delivered Israel from slavery in Egypt with a commitment to keep the commandments (Deut 6:20–25; see also Exod 12:24–27a).

Deuteronomy 8 contains **exhortations** to obey (Deut 8:1a, 5–6, 18a), **motive clauses** (Deut 8:1b, 7–10, 18b), a **historical reminder subunit** (Deut 8:2–4), a **be careful lest construction** not to forget YHWH (Deut 8:11), **admonitions** (Deut 8:12–14a, 17), a **motive clause** focusing on YHWH's deliverance and providence (Deut 8:14b–16), and a **conditional threat** of punishment for idolatry (Deut 8:19–20).

Deuteronomy 9:1—10:22 contains an abbreviated **call to attention formula** (Deut 9:1a; see prophetic genres), a **promise** of victory over the Anakim (Deut 9:1b–3), an admonition against boasting (Deut 9:4a), a **reason for admonition** (Deut 9:4b–6), a lengthy **historical reminder subunit** focusing on Israel's rebelliousness (Deut 9:7–10:11), a **rhetorical question** (Deut 10:12a), an **exhortations** (Deut 10:12b–13, 16, 19a, 20–21a), and **reasons for exhortation** (Deut 10:14–15, 17–18, 19b, 21b–22). The theme of circumcising their hearts (Deut 10:16) will reappear in Deut 30:6 and Jer 4:4.

Deuteronomy 11:1–32 contains **exhortations to obey** (Deut 11:1, 8a 18–20, 31–32), a **historical reminder subunit** (Deut 11:2–7), **reasons for exhortation** (Deut 11:8b–12, 21), **conditional promises** for obedience (Deut 11:13–15, 22–25), a **be careful lest construction** against idolatry (Deut 11:16–17), and a parenetic **blessing and curse passage** (Deut 11:26–30).

Deuteronomy 29:1b–28 [NRSV 2b–29] contains a **historical reminder subunit** (Deut 29:1b–7 [NRSV 2b–8]), an **exhortation to obey** (Deut 29:8 [NRSV 9]), an **exposition of addressee** (Deut 29:9–16 [NRSV 10–17]), a **conditional prophecy of punishment** for apostasy (Deut 29:17–23 [NRSV 18–24]), a **basis for punishment** (Deut 29:24–27 [NRSV 25–28]), and **parenesis** almost in the form of a wisdom saying, "The secret things belong to the Lord our God, but the revealed things belong to us and to our children forever, to observe all the words of this law" (Deut 29:28 [NRSV 29]).

Passover/Unleavened Bread Passage

The basis for keeping Passover/Unleavened Bread occurs earlier canonically than the giving of the law on Mount Sinai. Exodus 12:1–20 is an **offering law** which contains **calendrical designations** for the first month, for Passover, and for the first and last days of Unleavened Bread (Exod 12:2, 14a, 16), **qualification of item offered** as a one year old unblemished male lamb or goat (Exod 12:3–5), a **ritual sacrificial procedure** involving putting blood of the slain lamb on the doorposts and lintel of the houses in which they eat it (Exod 12:6–7), a **ritual procedure** on how to eat the lamb (Exod 12:8–11a), a **classification/purpose** of sacrifice (Exod 12:11b), a **reason for law** (Exod 12:12–13) including a **YHWH self-revelation formula** (Exod 12:12b), **statutory law formulas** (Exod 12:14b, 17b), **commands** to eat unleavened bread for seven days and keep the feast (Exod 12:15a, 17a, 18, 20b), **cut off laws** for any who eat leaven during the seven days (Exod 12:15b, 19b), and **prohibitions** of leaven in the houses for seven days (Exod 12:19a, 20a).

Exodus 12:21–28 contains a **ritual sacrificial procedure** (Exod 12:21b–22), a **reason for law** (Exod 12:23), a **statutory law formula** (Exod 12:24), and a **ritual recitation** (Exod 12:25–27a) which is a pre-Word to the Passover event for which Deut 6:20–24 is a post-Word ritual recitation. This is followed by a brief **compliance narrative** (Exod 12:27b–28), and a **divine judgment narrative** in which YHWH strikes the firstborn of Egypt, the Israelites plunder the Egyptians, and journey from Rameses to Succoth while eating unleavened bread (Exod 12:29–42), events commemorated by the holy convocation on the first day of Unleavened Bread.

Exodus 12:43–51 contains a **superscription** (Exod 12:43b), **prohibitions** (Exod 12:43c, 45, 48b), a **command** (Exod 12:46), and **case-permission laws** (Exod 12:44, 48a) concerning who may eat the Passover meal, a **ritual procedure** regarding the Passover sacrifice and meal (Exod 12:46), and a **one law formula** (Exod 12:49). It is followed by the Event of deliverance: "That very day the Lord brought the Israelites out of the land of Egypt, company by company" (Exod 12:51).

Exodus 13:1–2 is a **firstborn law**, which is connected to Passover because YHWH slew Egypt's firstborn at the Passover. Exodus 13:3–10 contains **commands** to remember this day, to eat unleavened bread for seven days (Exod 13:3b, 6a, 7a), **prohibitions** against eating leavened bread or possessing it (Exod 13:3c, 7b), **parenesis** (Exod 13:4–5), a **calendrical designation** of the seventh day (Exod 13:6b), a **command** to make a **ritual recitation** (Exod 13:8), a **benefit of obedience** (Exod 13:9), and a **summary subscription** (Exod 13:10).

The **divine judgment narrative** in Exodus 13:17–14:31 tells how YHWH parted the Reed Sea and delivered the Israelites from the Egyptians, and this is what the seventh day of Unleavened Bread celebrates. Exodus 15:1–21 contains a **song of thanksgiving** (see genres of Psalms) by Moses and Miriam and the Israelites about YHWH hurling Pharaoh's army and chariots into the sea. It is against all this background—and the background of passages such as the **wife-sister narrative** in Gen 12:10–20 and the **covenant narrative** in Gen 15 which foreshadow the events recorded in Exodus—that the material in the covenant code and canonically later codes should be read.

The covenant code contains a **command** to keep the Festival of Unleavened Bread (Exod 23:15a), a **command** to eat unleavened bread for seven days at the appointed time in the month of Abib, the Canaanite name for the first month (Exod 23:15b), a **motive clause** (Exod 23:15c), and a **prohibition** against appearing empty-handed (Exod 23:15d).

The Exodus 34 code contains **commands** to keep the Festival of Unleavened Bread for seven days in the month of Abib (Exod 34:18), and **prohibitions** against eating leaven and against leaving the Passover sacrifice until morning (Exod 34:25).

In the holiness code, Lev 23:5–8 contains **calendrical designations** of the fourteenth day of the first month between the evenings as the Passover sacrifice to YHWH and the fifteenth day as the Festival of Unleavened Bread (Lev 23:6a), **commands** to eat unleavened bread seven days and present offering those days (Lev 23:6b, 8a) and **orders** to have holy convocations on the first day and seventh days in which there is no occupational work (Lev 23:7, 8b).

Numbers 9:1–5 is set as approaching the first anniversary of the Exodus and contains **commands** for the Israelites to keep the Passover on the fourteenth day of this month at twilight according to all its regulations (Num 9:2–3), and a **compliance narrative** (Num 9:4–5). In Num 9:6–8 those unable to observe the Passover because of ceremonial uncleanness ask Moses what to do. Numbers 9:10–14 is the legislative reply: After a **case-prescription** law saying that such people can still keep Passover (Num 9:10b), there are **commands** to keep Passover one month later with unleavened bread and bitter herbs (Num 9:11), **prohibitions** against leaving the Passover until morning or breaking the bones of the Passover sacrifice (Num 9:12b), a **command** to keep the entire statute for the Passover (Num 9:12c), a **cut off law** for those who deliberately refrain from keeping the Passover but not doing so (Num 9:13), a **case-law** permitting a resident alien desiring to keep this second Passover (Num 9:14a), and a **one law formula** (Num 9:14b).

The section of the **cultic calendar law** (also **offering law**) in Num 28:1—29:40 dealing with Passover and Unleavened Bread contains **calendrical designations** of the fourteenth day of the first month as Passover and the fifteenth day of the month as a pilgrim festival (Num 28:16–17a, 18a, 25a), a **command** that for seven days unleavened bread be eaten and an offering by fire made (Num 28:17b, 19a), **prohibitions** of arduous/occupational work (Num 28:18b, 25b), and a qualification of item offered subunit (Num 28:19b–24).

Similarly, the cultic calendar law in Deut 16 contains **commands** to observe the month of Abib by keeping the Passover at the central sanctuary, to eat unleavened bread for seven days (Deut 16:1a, 2, 7a, 8a), **motive clauses** (Deut 16:1b, 3b), **orders** not to eat leaven but to eat unleavened bread for seven days, not to observe Passover at just any place but at the central sanctuary in the evening, and to have a holy convocation on the seventh day but not work (Deut 16:3a, 5–6, 8b), a **benefit of obedience** (Deut 16:3c), **prohibitions** of leaven for seven days and of the meat remaining until morning (Deut 16:4), and a **permission** to go back to one's tent the next morning (Deut 16:7b).

Shortly after the Israelites cross the Jordan, they are circumcised (Josh 5:1–9) and then observe the Passover on the fourteenth of the month, and the next day eat unleavened products from the produce of the promised land, as the manna ceases (Josh 5:10–12; see **festival observance narrative**). The passage fits with the Mosaic prohibition of uncircumcised men eating the Passover. Hezekiah observes the so-called Second Passover as part of a revival of Israel's covenant relationship to YHWH (2 Chr 30:1–27; see **festival observance narrative** and **restoration narrative**) which has its legal background in Num 9:9–14 discussed above. Josiah observes the standard Passover (2 Kgs 23:21–23; 2 Chr

35:1–19; see **festival observance narrative** and **restoration narrative**) as part of a whole-scale revival based on Deuteronomic law.

Song of Songs is the festival scroll read at Passover/Unleavened Bread and the chapter on genres in Song of Songs discusses its connection with the festival. In the New Testament, the passion narratives in the Gospels take place against the background of Passover/Unleavened Bread and Paul proclaims, "Clean out the old yeast so that you may be a new batch, as you really are unleavened. For our paschal lamb, Christ, has been sacrificed. Therefore, let us celebrate the festival, not with the old yeast, the yeast of malice and evil, but with the unleavened bread of sincerity and truth" (1 Cor 5:7–8). Connections between most Christians and Passover/Unleavened Bread are less tight since the Quartodeciman controversy. In the Mishnah, Pesaḥim deals with the high days of Passover, and Mo'ed QaṬan deals with the intermediate days of Passover and Tabernacles.

Prosic, *Development*; Segal, *Hebrew Passover*; Wagenaar, "Passover," 250–68.

Ritual Instruction on Red Heifer

Numbers 19:1–22 contains a **qualification of item offered** concerning a red heifer (Num 19:2b), **ritual sacrificial procedure** (Num 19:3–6), a series of **prescriptions of washing** (Num 19:7–10a), **statutory law formula** (Num 19:10b), a **declaration of impurity** for those touching a human corpse (Num 19:11), a **branched conditional subunit** (Num 19:12), a **cut off law** for those who do not purify themselves (Num 19:13), a **law introduction formula** (Num 19:14a), a series of **declaration of impurity formulas** (Num 19:14b–16), a **ritual procedure** leading to purification (Num 19:17–19), a **cut off law** concerning those who do not perform the purification procedure (Num 19:20), a **statutory law formula** (Num 19:21a), and a series of **declarations** of impurity (Num 19:21b–22).

Baumgarten, "Paradox," 442–51.

Sabbath Law

Genesis 2:1–3 is a pre-Word to the sabbath law, which is made explicit as the rationale for Israel keeping the sabbath in Exod 31:16–17. The sabbath law in the Decalogue contains a **command** to remember (Exod

20:8) or to keep the sabbath (Deut 5:12), a command (or permission) to work for six days (Exod 20:9; Deut 5:13), a **calendrical designation** (Exod 20:10a, Deut 5:14a), a **prohibition** against working on the seventh day (Exod 20:10b; Deut 5:14b), and a **motive clause** which either looks back to creation (Exod 20:11; 31:17) or to the exodus (Deut 5:15). There is a **death penalty prescription formula** for profaning the sabbath (Exod 31:14) and for working on the sabbath or kindling a fire on the sabbath (Exod 35:2–3). There are general commands to "keep my sabbaths" (Lev 19:3, 30; 23:38). In Num 15:32–36, there is a **legal case narrative** of a man who violated the prohibition against kindling a fire on the sabbath and is executed (**execution narratives**). There is a **ritual instruction** regarding the sabbath offerings in Num 28:9–10 and a corresponding eschatological instruction regarding the Sabbath and new moon in Ezek 46:1–5.

What is permissible or not on the Sabbath is discussed in the Mishnaic tractates *Šabbat* and *'Erubin*. Christians hold differing views: some do not observe it; some observe it on the first day; and some observe it on the seventh day but not adhering to Talmudic standards. Whether or not it is obligatory, reserving one day in seven for rest and worship yields benefits in physical health and in spiritual relationship with God.

Andreasen, *Old Testament Sabbath*; Heschel, *The Sabbath*; Knohl, "Priestly Torah," 65–117.

Sabbatical Year/Jubilee Passage

This entry covers not only passages that cover the legal obligations pertaining to the sabbatical year and/or jubilee, but also to narratives or prophetic passages where this concept is present (see also **Day of Atonement passage**). In the **covenant code**, there is a **command** to let the land lie fallow in the seventh year (Exod 23:11). In the holiness code, Lev 25:2b–7 concerns the sabbatical year and contains a **command** for the land to observe a Sabbath (Lev 25:2c), **calendrical designations** (Lev 25:4a, 5b), **permissions** to do regular farming for six years and eat what the land yields in the seventh year (Lev 25:3, 6–7), and prohibitions against sowing fields, pruning vineyards, and reaping in the seventh year (Lev 25:4b–5a).

Leviticus 25:8–55 concerns the Jubilee and contains **commands** for counting forty-nine years, blasting trumpets on the Day of Atonement, proclaiming liberty throughout the land, returning to one's property, calculating years until jubilee, providing for the redemption of the land, for houses in unwalled villages and for property sold by Levites to be returned in the jubilee, to return financially dependent kin to their property (Lev 25:8–10a, 10c, 13, 15–16a, 31b, 33a, 41), **calendrical designations** of jubilee (Lev 25:10b, 11a, 12a), **prohibitions** against sowing and reaping during jubilee, against cheating a neighbor when buying or selling, against selling the land in perpetuity, against selling land around Levitical cities, against profiteering from financially dependent kin or making them slaves (Lev 25:11b, 14, 23a, 34a, 36–37, 39–40, 46b), a **proclamation of holiness formula** (Lev 25:12b), **permissions** to eat what the field itself produces and only that, for houses in unwalled villages to be redeemed beyond a year, for Levites to redeem houses in Levitical cities, to acquire slaves from surrounding nations (Lev 25:12c, 31a, 32, 45–46a), **motive clauses** (Lev 25:16b, 23b, 33b, 34b, 42, 55a), **parenesis** (Lev 25:17–19), a **question and answer subunit** (Lev 25:21–22), **case-prescription laws** regarding next of kin redeeming land, selling a house in a walled city, of kin becoming financially dependent, of kin selling themselves to a resident alien (Lev 25:25–30, 35, 47–54) **YHWH self-revelation formulas** (Lev 25:38, 55b), and an **order** not to rule financial dependents harshly but to fear God (Lev 25:43).

Deuteronomy 15:1–18 contains **commands** to remit debts in the seventh year (Deut 15:1–2a, 3b, 10a, 11), **motive clauses** (Deut 15:2b, 10b), a **permission** to exact a debt from a foreigner (Deut 15:3a), **parenesis** (Deut 15:4–6), a **case-prescription law** of a community member in need (Deut 15:7–8), a **be careful lest construction** against viewing a needy neighbor hostilely (Deut 15:9), and a **law pertaining to slaves/slave owners** (Deut 15:12–18).

The book of Deuteronomy was also to be read at the Feast of Tabernacles during the sabbatical year (Deut 31:9–13). Eschatological passages such as Isaiah 35; 58:6–12 and 61:1–3 are associated with Jubilee as is 11QMelchizedek in the Dead Sea Scrolls and Luke 4:16–21 in the New Testament.

Chrichigno, *Debt-Slavery*; Hamilton, *Social Justice*; Kaplan, "Credibility," 183–203; Weinfeld, "Sabbatical Year," 39–62.

Sanctuary Law

Leviticus 24:1–9 contains a **command** to have a continually burning lamp in the tent of meeting (Lev 24:2–3a), a **statutory law formula** (Lev 24:3b), a **command** to set up the lamp on the lampstand (Lev 24:4b), a **command** concerning the bread of presence on the table of pure gold (Lev 24:5–8), and a **motive clause** (Lev 24:9).

Sexual Relations Law

This is a **law** categorized according to the content of the law, namely the subject of sexual relations. The biblical norm is for sexual relations to be between a man and a woman within the confines of marriage, a norm which is traditionally understood to be part of the natural law. Hence, there are specific **prohibitions** or **death penalty case laws** against adultery (Exod 20:14; Lev 18:20; 20:10; Deut 5:18; 22:22), various types of incest (Lev 18:6–18; 20:11–12, 14), homosexual acts (Lev 18:22; 20:13) and bestiality (Exod 22:19; Lev 18:23; 20:15–16). There were **procedural laws** for investigating charges of a woman suspected of adultery ('Num 5:11–31) or sex during the betrothal period (Deut 22:13–21). There are **case laws** for dealing with seducing an unbetrothed virgin (Exod 22:15–16 [16–17]) or raping an unbetrothed virgin (Deut 22:28–29). Sex with a menstruant was also prohibited (Lev 15:19–24; 18:19; 20:18). See also **marriage and family laws.**

Leviticus 18 is traditionally read on Yom Kippur (see **Day of Atonement passage**) and the legal content portion of the legislative speech narrative contains **self-revelation of YHWH formula** (Lev 18:2b, 4b, 5b, 6b, 21b, 30b), **parenesis** (Lev 18:3–4a, 5a), **prohibitions** against incest and specific subcategories of incest (Lev 18:6a, 7, 8, 9, 10, 11, 12, 13, 14, 15, 16, 17, 18), further **prohibitions** against sexual relations with a menstruating woman (Lev 18:19), against adultery with a neighbor's wife (Lev 18:20), human sacrifice (Lev 18:21a), homosexual relations (Lev 18:22), against bestiality (Lev 18:23a), and **parenesis** (Lev 18:24–30a). With the exception of the **human sacrifice prohibition** (Lev 18:21a), all these are **sex laws.**

Leviticus 20:10–21 contains **case-prescription laws** with the **death penalty formula** applying to both partners in the union) against a man committing adultery with his neighbor's wife, or his father's wife, or his daughter-in-law, or for having sex with another man or with his mother-in-law, of for either a man or a woman to have sex with an animal (Lev 20:10, 11a, 12a, 13a, 14, 15, 16a), often with **blood restriction formulas** (Lev 20:11b, 12b, 13b, 16b), followed by **cut off laws** for both partners against a man having sex with his sister, or a menstruating woman (Lev 20:17, 18, 19), but strangely the cases of a man lying with his uncle's wife or taking his brother's wife (Lev 20:20a, 21) bring the threat of childlessness.

Deuteronomy 22:13–21 contains a **case for procedure** of a man's false charge against his wife's virginity (Deut 22:13–14), a **ritual procedure** for the woman's father to produce evidence (Deut 22:15–17), a **prescription of financial penalty** on the false accuser (Deut 22:18–19a), an **order** that she remain his wife and that he not divorce (Deut 22:19b), a **case** where the man's testimony was true (Deut 22:20), a **prescription of capital punishment** by stoning for the wife (Deut 22:21a), and a **purge the evil formula** (Deut 22:21b).

Deuteronomy 22:22–29 has four **case-prescription laws** of a man committing adultery, having sex in town with an engaged woman, seizing an engaged woman in the open country, and seizing an unengaged virgin in the country (Deut 22:22a, 23–24a, 25–27, 28–29), the first two with **purge the evil formula** (Deut 22:22b, 24b). Deuteronomy 23:1 [NRSV 22:30] is a **prohibition** against a man marrying his father's wife.

Deuteronomy 23:18–19 [NRSV 17–18] contains **prohibitions** against Israelite women or men being "sacred prostitute [or "holy woman/man]" (Deut 23:18 [NRSV 17]), and against using prostitute's [or "dog's"] wages to pay vows (Deut 23:19a [NRSV 18a]), and a **motive clause** (Deut 23:19b [NRSV 18b]). Whether sacred prostitution existed in Israel is disputed.

Bigger, "Family Laws," 187–203; Budin, *Myth*; Destro, *Law of Jealousy*; Epstein, *Marriage Laws*; Hoffner, "Incest, Sodomy," 81–90; Neufeld, *Ancient Hebrew Marriage*; Novak, *Jewish Justice*, 81–123.

Silver Trumpet Law

Numbers 10:1–10 contains **commands** to make two silver trumpets for summoning the congregation and breaking camp, for blowing when they set out, that the priests blow the trumpets, at appointed festivals and new moons (Num 10:2, 6b, 8a, 10a), **case-prescription laws** for when both trumpets are blown, when just one trumpet is blown, when a first alarm is blown, when a second alarm is blown, when the assembly is to be gathered (Num 10:3, 4, 5, 6a, 7), a **statutory law formula** (Num 10:8b), **case-command laws** of going to war in the promised land and rejoicing/sacrificing at appointed festivals (Num 10:9a, 10a), **motive clauses** (Num 10:9b, 10b), and a **YHWH self-revelation formula** (Num 10:10d). The silver trumpets signify YHWH's leadership through wilderness wanderings and conquest of promised land.

Knierim and Coats, *Numbers*, 129–34.

Slavery Law

This is a **law** categorized according to content, namely the treatment of slaves and indentured servants. In the covenant code, the law in Exod 21:2–11 concerns Hebrew indentured servants. There are case-prescription laws that limit servitude to six years, and which further describe what happens to the wife of the servant (Exod 21:2–4). The parallel in the Deuteronomic law code includes a command to provide liberally for the servant (Deut 15:12–15). A servant had a choice not to go free in the seventh year and become a slave for life (Exod 21:5–6; Deut 15:16–17). If a woman was sold by her father into servitude, she had fewer rights (Exod 21:7–11). If a slaveowner, struck the eye of a slave or knocked out a tooth, the slave would be set free. A slaveowner striking a slave who died immediately would be punished, but if the slave survived a couple of days before dying would not be punished "for the slave is the owner's property" (Exod 21:21b). This cuts against the principle from Gen 1 that all human beings are made in the image of God. Christians have used the Bible to justify slavery but also to advocate for the abolishment of slavery. More generally, a legal permission to do something does not imply a moral right. The Tanak permits polygamy, but Jewish and Christian societies prohibit the practice. See also **sabbatical year/jubilee passage** which are relevant slave laws also.

Carmichael, "Three Laws," 509–25; Chirichigno, *Debt-Slavery*, 296–314; Mendelsohn, *Slavery*; Seters, "Hebrew Slave," 534–46.

Tabernacle Instruction

Following an **offering command** (Exod 25:2–9) intended to generate the materials necessary for the construction of a tabernacle and the sacred objects in it, YHWH gives **instruction** to Moses regarding the construction and maintenance of a tabernacle and various sacred objects (Exod 25:10–30:38). Subsections of this material include instructions regarding the ark (25:10–22), instructions regarding the table (25:23–30), instructions regarding the lampstand (25:31–40), instructions regarding the tabernacle (26:1–37), instructions regarding the altar (27:1–8), instructions regarding the tabernacle court (27:9–19), instructions concerning keeping the light (27:20–21), instructions concerning the priests' vestments (28:1–43), instructions concerning the priests' ordination (29:1–46), instructions concerning the altar of incense (30:1–10), instructions concerning the half-shekel atonement (30:11–16), instructions concerning the laver of washing (30:17–21), and instructions for the anointing oil and the incense (30:22–38). The efficient cause of the tabernacle instruction is YHWH, the addressee is Moses, the source setting is the Priestly material, it is a **directive** illocution and its perlocutionary intent is for the Israelites to construct the tabernacle and related objects according to the instructions given. The realization of much of this is related in the **tabernacle construction account** in Exod 35:1—40:38.

Mishnaic tractates Me'ilah and Middot draw on what is said about the tabernacle to discuss laws pertaining to the second temple.

Cross, "Priestly Tabernacle," 84–95; Hendrix, "Structural Overview," 123–38; Koch, *Priesterschrift*; Levine, "Tabernacle Texts," 307–18.

Tithing Law

Tithing is giving a tenth of one's income to a designated party, or setting it aside for a particular purpose, ultimately out of a religious obligation. Genesis narrates both Abraham and Jacob paying tithes (Gen 14:20; 28:22). Numbers 18:20–24 contains **prohibitions** against the Levites having a tribal allotment and against Israelites approaching the tent of meeting (Num 18:20b, 22, 23c, 24b), divine exercitives designating the Levites as receiving tithes (Num 18:21, 24a), a **command** for the Levites to perform the service of the tent of meeting (Num 18:23a), and a **statutory law formula** (Num 18:23b).

Numbers 18:25–32 contains a **command** for the Levites to give "a tithe of the tithe," to the Aaronic priesthood (Num 18:26b–29), a **permission** for the Levites to eat the rest of the tithe (Num 18:30b–31a), a **motive clause** (Num 18:31b–32a), and a **prohibition** against profaning the tithe

(Num 18:32b). See also Neh 10:37–38. Mishnaic tractate Ma'aśerot is the main tractate on the tithe and tractate Demai deals with cases where it is doubtful that tithes of produce have been set apart for the priests.

Deuteronomy 14:22–29 contains **commands** for the Israelites to tithe on their produce, eat it at the central sanctuary (**central sanctuary law**), and give Levites and marginalized a tithe every third year (Deut 14:22, 23a, 28–29a) **benefits of obedience** (Deut 14:23b, 29b), a **case-permission law** where transporting the tithe is difficult (Deut 14:24–26), a **prohibition** against neglecting the Levites (Deut 14:27a), and a **motive clause** (Deut 14:27b). Deuteronomy 26:12–15 is a **case-command law** involving a **ritual recitation** of having performed the third year tithe (Deut 26:13b–15) analogous to an **affirmation of innocence** (see Psalms genres). The Mishnaic tractate Ma'aser Sheni is devoted to these passages on the second and possibly third tithe.

In Josephus (*Antiquities* 4.68, 240) and Tobit 1:5–8, these laws combine to give three tithes, but in the Mishnah the tithe every three years in Deut 14:28–29 is instead of the tithe in Deut 14:22–27. There is a pre-Word to the basic tithing law in the lives of Abram (Gen 14:18–20) and Jacob (Gen 28:22). Christian denominations typically give considerably less than a tithe but some give a full tithe plus further offerings.

Jagersma, "Tithes," 116–28.

Vow Law

Leviticus 27:2b–13 concerns votive offerings and is similar to the practice of **firstborn laws** redeeming humans and animals for a fixed price. It contains a series of **case-prescription laws** concerning men, women, children, very young children, old people, and situations where the vow maker is poor (Lev 27:2b–3, 4, 5, 6, 7, 8). It also has case-prescription laws pertaining to votive offerings of clean animals (Lev 27:9, 10) and unclean animals (Lev 27:11–12, 13).

Numbers 6:1–21 concerns Nazirite vows and contains a **case** for making the vow (Num 6:2b), **prohibitions** against alcohol, grape products, cutting head-hair, and contact with corpses (Num 6:3–7), a **proclamation of holiness formula** (Num 6:8), **cases for procedure** concerning broken nazirite vows and completing the vow (Num 6:9a, 13a), **ritual procedures** for renewal and completing the vow (Num 6:9b–12, 13b–20), and a **summary subscription** (Num 6:21).

Numbers 30:2–17 [NRSV 1–16] consists entirely of **case laws** with the following results: a man making a vow must keep it, as must a woman who makes a vow which her father or husband does not disapprove, as must a divorced or widowed woman (Num 30:3, 4–5, 7–8, 10, 11–12 [NRSV 2, 3–4, 6–7, 9, 10–11]); a father or husband may disallow his daughter's vow immediately on hearing about it but not afterwards (Num 30:6, 9, 13–16 [NRSV 5, 8, 12–15]). A **law introduction** and **subscription** (Num 30:2a, 17 [NRSV 1a, 16]) bracket the law.

Deuteronomy 23:22–24 [NRSV 21–23] contains a **case-prohibition law** (Deut 23:22 [NRSV 21]) and a **command** (Deut 23:24 [NRSV 23]) affirming the principle of keeping vows, but also an implied **permission** to refrain from vowing (Deut 23:23 [NRSV 22]).

The main Mishnaic tractates on vows are Nedarim ("vows") and Šebuot ("oaths") but Nazirite vows are discussed in Nazir and 'Arakin deals with how much must be paid to fulfill a vow.

Eichler, "Sin is Borne," 317–28; Lemardelé, *Cheveux du Nazir*; Olyan, "Shaving Rites," 611–22; Schiffman, "Law of Vows," 199–214.

War Law

Deuteronomy 7:1–26 contains an **enter land formula** expanded by YHWH handing over the Canaanite nations to Israel (Deut 7:1–2a), **commands** to utterly destroy them, break down their altars and sacred poles, burn their idols (Deut 7:2b, 5b, 25a), **prohibitions** against making covenants with or intermarrying the Canaanites with them, or coveting the gold and silver on their idols (Deut 7:2b–3), **motive clauses** (Deut 7:4, 6–8), **parenesis** (Deut 7:9–11), a **conditional promise** of blessing (Deut 7:12–16), a **reassurance subunit** (Deut 7:18–24; see prophetic genres), a **command** to burn the images of their gods (Deut 7:25a), and an **order** not to bring an abhorrent thing into one's house but to utterly detest it (Deut 7:26).

Deuteronomy 20:1–20 contains **prohibition** against fearing larger enemy armies (Deut 20:1a), a **motive clause** (Deut 20:1b), **commands** for **ritual recitations** encouraging the troops but permitting certain groups not to fight (Deut 20:2–4, 5–7, 8), **commands** for the military commanders to take charge, to offer a town terms of peace (Deut 20:10), **case-prescription laws** concerning towns accepting peace and those making war, and use of trees in warfare (Deut 20:11, 12–14, 19–20), a

summary subscription which indicates that the above legislation applied to far towns (Deut 20:15), a **command** to annihilate the Canaanite tribes (Deut 20:16–17), and a **cost of disobedience** (Deut 20:18).

Deuteronomy 21:10–14 has two parts: a **case-permission law** where a soldier wants to marry a captive (Deut 21:10–13) containing a **ritual procedure** the soldier must follow (Deut 21:12b–13a); and a **case law** where the soldier who later becomes dissatisfied with his captive wife must not sell her for money but either free her or stay married (Deut 21:14). See also **law concerning women**, **marriage and family law**. Deuteronomy 25:17–19 contains a **command** to remember how Amalek attacked Israel (Deut 25:17–18), and an **order** that Israel "blot out the remembrance of Amalek from under heaven" and not forget (Deut 25:19). See **battle narrative**.

Crouch, *War and Ethics*; Lohfink, *Krieg und Staat*; Malamat, "Conquest," 68–96; Niditch, *War*; Quick, "Averting Curses," 209–23; Rofé, "Laws of Warfare," 23–44.

SOME OVERARCHING LEGAL CATEGORIES

Apodictic Law

Apodictic law consists mainly of (usually 2nd person) **commands** and **prohibitions** with no explicit mention of penalties for failure to obey these commands and prohibitions. This genre occurs frequently in the Old Testament but rarely in other ancient Near Eastern law codes. For the formal similarities of apodictic law to **parenesis**, see the discussion of parenesis in the section on wisdom genres. Apodictic law is a **directive** illocution and its perlocutionary intent is for the community to abide by the norms prescribed in the apodictic law. The efficient cause of the law is typically YHWH speaking through an intermediary. Some scholars include as apodictic law those laws that have the **death penalty formula** and even the **list of curses** in Deut 27:15–26.

Alt, "Origins," 79–132; Boecker, *Law*, 190–207; Bright, "Apodictic Prohibition," 185–204; Hutton, *Declaratory Formulae*; Knierim, "Problem Prescriptive," 7–25.

Case Law

This term, or "casuistic law," was used in early form criticism as one of the two syntactic categories, along with apodictic law. This glossary prefers the term **contingent law**.

Alt, "Origins," 101–71; Boecker, *Law*, 150–71; Brin, *Studies*, 52–73; Gilmer, *If–You Form*; Knierim and Coats, *Numbers*, 340–41.

Civil Law

The Hebrew Bible does not clearly distinguish between the categories of civil law and criminal law which are important in most societies today. However, the three tractates that begin Mishnaic order Neziqin—Baba Qamma, Baba Meṣi'a, and Baba Batra—all deal with civil law. These tractates mean "the first gate," "the middle gate," and "the last gate" as subdivisions of an original tractate dealing with damages. Baba Qamma discusses both damages caused without criminality (hence part of civil law) and criminally caused damages. Baba Meṣi'a discusses lost property, paid trustees, borrowers, hirers and usury. Baba Batra discusses multiply held property, duties and rights of ownership, purchase, inheritance, and documents.

Buss, "Distinction," 51–62; Cocco, *Torah*; Daube, "Civil Law," 351–407.

Future Law

YHWH instructs Ezekiel concerning future laws for the offerings at the dedication of the altar (Ezek 43:18–27), the shutting and entering of the outer gate of the sanctuary (Ezek 44:1–3), admission to the temple (Ezek 44:4–14), the Levitical priests (Ezek 44:15–31), the holy district (Ezek 45:1–9), weights and measures (Ezek 45:10–12), offerings (Ezek 45:13–17), festivals (Ezek 45:18–25), Sabbath and new moons (Ezek 46:1–7), the prince (Ezek 46:8–18), and places for priests and kitchen servants (Ezek 46:19–20, 21–24).

These laws are presented in **legislative speech narratives** in which either an angelic guide speaks to Ezekiel as a divine representative (the **messenger of YHWH formula** in Ezek 43:18b; 45:18a; 46:1a and the **utterance of YHWH formula** appearing as a syntactic isolate in Ezek

43:19, 27; see chapter on prophetic genres) or YHWH speaks directly to Ezekiel (the **speech introduction formulas** in Ezek 44:2a, 5a).

The future **offering law** in Ezek 40–48 contains a **law introduction** (Ezek 43:18c), **cases** concerning the day(s) the offering takes place (Ezek 43:18d, 22a, 25a, 27a), **qualifications of item offered** (Ezek 43:19, 22b–23, 25b, 27b), **reason for law** (Ezek 43:20b, 22c, 26, 27c), and **ritual sacrificial procedures** (Ezek 43:20–21, 24).

Ezekiel 44:1–3 contains an order for the gate to remain shut and not be opened (Ezek 44:2b), a **motive clause** (Ezek 44:2c), a **permission** for the prince to sit in it to eat food before YHWH (Ezek 44:3a), and a **command** for the prince to enter and go out by way of the gate's vestibule (Ezek 44:3b).

The admittance to YHWH's assembly law contains messenger of YHWH formulas (Ezek 44:6b, 9a), **commands** to stop admitting foreigners and for Levites to minister and offer sacrifices in the temple (Ezek 44:6c–7a, 11), **accusations** of breaking YHWH's covenant and neglecting to keep charge of the sacred offerings (Ezek 44:7b–8), **prohibitions** against foreigners entering the sanctuary and against Levites who strayed from serving as priests (Ezek 44:9b, 13a), **verdicts of guilt** for the Levites who went astray (Ezek 44:10, 13b), a **reason and consequences subunit** (Ezek 44:12), and a **divine exercitive** relegating those Levites to do temple chores (Ezek 44:14).

Analogous to **law concerning Levites/priests/high priest**, Ezek 44:15–31 promotes the Zadokite priesthood. It contains **commands** for the faithful Zadokites to minister to YHWH, offer fat and blood, keep YHWH's charge at the sanctuary, wear linen vestments, exchange garments when returning to the outer court, to differentiate between holy and common, to act by YHWH's statutes when judging, to keep the appointed festivals and sabbaths, to wait seven days after becoming clean before returning to duties and offering a sin offering then, and to give priests the first of first fruits (Ezek 44:15–16, 17a, 18a, 19, 23–24, 26–27, 30), **prohibitions** against woolen vestments and things that cause sweat, against drinking wine when ministering, against priests mourning the dead (with exceptions), against tribal inheritances for priests, and against priests eating anything that died by itself or was torn by animals (Ezek 44:17b, 18b, 21, 25, 31), **orders** not to shave their heads or let locks grow long but to trim beards, and not to marry a widow or a divorced woman but only a virgin Israelite or a priest's widow (Ezek 44:20, 22), and a **permission** for priests to eat various offerings (Ezek 44:29).

Ezekiel 45:1–8 contains **commands** to set aside a holy district for YHWH, a plot within it for the sanctuary, a broader sacred area, another district for the Levites, another district for the house of Israel, land for the prince (Ezek 45:1a, 2, 3, 4b, 5, 6, 7–8a), **proclamation of holiness formulas** (Ezek 45:1b, 4a), and an **order** for the prince not to oppress but to let Israel have their tribal boundaries (Ezek 45:8b).

Ezekiel 45:10–12 is a **financial law** and contains **commands** to have honest balances, an honest ephah and an honest bath which are to be of the same measure (Ezek 45:10–11a), and **divine exercitive** designations of the bath as one-tenth of a homer, the ephah as one-tenth of a homer, the homer as the standard measure, the shekel as twenty gerahs and a total of sixty shekels as a mina (Ezek 45:11b–12).

Ezekiel 45:13–17 is an **offering law** and contains a **law introduction** (Ezek 45:13a), a **qualification of item offered** (Ezek 45:13b–15a), a **classification/purpose of sacrifice** (Ezek 45:15b), a **command** for the people to join with the prince in making the offering (Ezek 45:16), and a **summary subscription** (Ezek 45:17).

Ezekiel 45:18–25 is an example of **cultic calendar instruction** and contains a **messenger of YHWH formula** (Ezek 45:18a), **cases** pertaining to the day of the calendar (Ezek 45:18b, 21a, 22a, 23a, 25a), **quality of item offered** (Ezek 45:18c, 22b, 23b–24, 25b), a **ritual sacrificial procedure** (Ezek 45:19), and a **make atonement formula.** The ceremonies on the first and seventh days of the first month as having a similar purpose to the Day of Atonement in Torah, the omission of the feast of weeks, and the differences in offering law at the Feast of Tabernacles all mark a considerable break with the **cultic calendar instruction** in Torah.

Ezekiel 46:1–15 contains a **messenger of YHWH formula** (46:1a), **third person instructions** concerning the inner court gate (46:1b), the prince (46:2a, 2c, 8, 10, 12), the priests (46:2b), the people (46:3, 9), **qualifications of item offered** on the Sabbath, the new moon, the pilgrim festivals, and by the prince (Ezek 46:4–5, 6–7, 11, 13–16).

Ezekiel 46:16–18 contains a **messenger of YHWH formula** (46:16a), **case-prescription laws** concerning the prince's inheritance (46:16b, 17), and an **order** not to give any inheritance from the people's holding but only his own (46:18).

There are discrepancies between the laws in Ezekiel and those in Torah. One approach says that laws in the Messianic Age will be different. Another regards the Ezekiel laws as applying to extenuating circumstances. Some of the sacrifice laws can be regarded as inaugural sacrifices or in addition to Torah. Tractate Menaḥot in the Babylonian Talmud discusses some of this as does the Midrashic commentary Sifrei. In Christianity, views regarding the Messianic Age (Millennium) vary widely.

Boyle, "Holiness," 1–21; Hullinger, "Divine Presence," 405–22; Kasher, "Anthropomorphism," 192–208; Kilchör, "Ezekiel 44,6–14," 191–207; Kim, "YHWH Shammah," 187–207; Klein, "Reconciling Sacrifices," 211–22; Levenson, *Program of Restoration*; Tuell, *Law of Temple*.

3

Biblical Narratives

INTRODUCTION

NARRATIVES ARE MORE FREQUENT than any other genre in the Hebrew Bible. The basic structure of narrative is that of third person prose writing in the past tense. Some categories of narrative found in the Hebrew Bible, such as fables and parables, do not intend to inform the audience directly about characters and events in the real world. But most biblical narratives do so intend, whether they are biographical, historical or quasi-historical (until the books of Kings and Chronicles, most narratives do not discuss the sort of details historians are interested in, such as the names of the Pharaohs concerned or synchronous dating of events). All biblical narratives are theologically laden and have a teleology that goes beyond informing readers of the past.

In recent decades, scholars have increasingly compared the narrative techniques displayed in the Hebrew Bible with those found in other narratives, whether fiction or non-fiction, yielding numerous insights. Among the most important topics are plot, characters and characterization, dialogue, and the narrator.

The plot is the sequence of events (which are causally linked together in at least a loose fashion) described by the narrative. Narratives frequently begin with a relatively stable state of affairs, which may be described with a simple introductory clause or via an expositional passage. They then progress through a process of some tension or tensions (perhaps the tension between a divine promise and the present reality, or the tension between the protagonist's goal or desire and the formidable obstacles to that goal or desire) until some sort of resolution is achieved. In biblical narratives, one tension may be resolved but another may be ongoing or a new one created, so that in a large narrative complex like Genesis or Samuel, there are often overlapping story arcs.

Unlike painting, narrative is linear in nature—the reader reads one clause after another, and the standard pattern is for the sequence of clauses in the narrative to follow the chronological order in the storyline. However, the narrator may include an analeptic comment (flashback) to describe an earlier event that has relevance to the present plot or a proleptic comment to foreshadow something that will happen in the future.

Hierarchical Levels of Narrative

This glossary does not have entries for clausal levels and below but briefly discusses the more important clausal genres here. Although clauses can be analyzed via phrase-structure grammar into smaller units, and these units in turn are comprised of lexemes, which are comprised of graphemes (the written equivalent of phonemes), these smaller units seldom concern us. In Gen 26:26, "Then Abimelech went to him from Gerar, with Ahuzzath his adviser and Phicol the commander of his army," the second part of the verse is an "accompaniment." In theory, an accompaniment could be several verses long. So could the addressee, which is a syntactic isolate, be several verses long. The glossary does not analyze these subclausal genres.

The most important clausal element of biblical narrative is the action (see **main actions subunit**), a third-person prose clause relating a past action performed by a character, e.g. "Then Jacob kissed Rachel" (Gen 29:11a). Most biblical narrative is third-person, but Ezra-Nehemiah and some narratives within the prophetic books are first-person. This introduction will focus on third-person constructions. Narratives are primarily about characters intentionally performing actions, with one action leading to another. Grammatically, this is most frequently achieved through a clause beginning with an active *wayyiqtol* verb. One particularly important subcategory is that of speech action which typically consists of a **speech introduction** such as "And PN1 said to PN2" followed by the **speech proper**. Some speeches proper can be very lengthy indeed, and the genres of speeches and their components are dealt with in a separate chapter. Speeches contribute a great deal to characterization because they reveal how characters feel about themselves, about other characters including YHWH, and about events.

Related to action is experience (see **experiences subunit**), which is a clause depicting what a character saw/heard/smelled/tasted/felt. Biblical narratives are not stream-of-consciousness, and experiences are secondary to actions in terms of plot development. Like actions, experiences also frequently begin with an active *wayyiqtol* verb, but with a verb of cognition. Alternatively, experiences can be conveyed through passive verbs so that the subject of the clause experiences being acted on by another party. A third element of biblical narrative is that of event (see **event subunit**) such as "there was a famine in the land" or "so-and-so died." Events focus on what happened rather on what someone did. All three of these elements serve to drive the plot of a narrative, but only action contributes significantly to characterization.

Biblical narrative is plot-centered and tends not to have lengthy character descriptions such as one finds in Dickens. However, the biblical narrator will frequently intersperse the action with an exposition, a clause that gives information regarding a character's age, lineage, location, name, occupation, possessions, or virtue (see **exposition subunit**). Exposition typically occurs through clauses whose finite verb is "to be" or which lack a finite verb entirely. An exposition contributes to characterization rather than plot. Related to exposition is past activity, which employs either a *yiqtol* verb or a *weqatal* verb in its frequentative sense to convey what a character habitually did. This element also contributes more to characterization than to plot.

There are also a variety of clausal genres where the narrator gives the audience information either not available to the characters or not directly relevant to the immediate narrative. These can include aside "His father and mother did not know that this was from YHWH" (Judg 14:4a), etiological comment showing the origin of marriage (Gen 2:24), explanatory comment such as discussing how prophets used to be called seers (1 Sam 9:9), proleptic comment "Samuel did not see Saul again until the day of his death" (1 Sam 15:35a), or theological evaluation "And the thing which David did was bad in the eyes of YHWH" (2 Sam 11:27b). What is remarkable is that all such editorial remarks are assertives—there are no directives for the reader not to worry nor expressives rhapsodizing about the providence of YHWH. The only exception comes in the autobiographical remarks of Nehemiah who petitions YHWH to remember him (Neh 13:14, 22, 29, 31).

The next level up would be the narrative subunits (main actions, dialogue, commands or requests, compliance or non-compliance, reactions, results, summaries, narratorial asides) which are the constituent units of the individual narratives. Many of these are standard in all narratives; one important distinguishing feature in biblical narratives is when God is acting or speaking. This glossary includes entries on the narrative subunits, but space is lacking to delineate the narrative subunits for each narrative the way we have done for legal subunits in laws, records in lists, psalms subunits in psalms, and prophetic subunits in prophetic speech.

The primary attention in this glossary is on narrative passages (pericopes) conveying the same type of information whether it be of a marriage, a battle, a reign, a crisis, or a confrontation. It does contain entries for standard form-critical categories such as account, legend, story, etc., but it does not list which passages belong to those categories (the boundaries between report, account, and story are quite fuzzy; and the categories of legend, saga, myth, and tale are somewhat problematic). Beyond the pericope level are complexes such as cycles (judges cycle, patriarchal cycle), phase of the monarchy etc., and these are discussed in canonical order in the overview of Tanak. One area which could be considerably expanded is the use of ANE parallels. There are conceptual parallels in many legends and myths from Mesopotamia, Egypt, and Ugarit to **annunciation narratives, negotiations narratives** etc. beyond what this glossary lists.

Alter, *The Art of Biblical Narrative*; Alter and Kermode, *Literary Guide*; Auerbach, *Mimesis*; Bal, *Narratology*; Bar-Efrat, *Narrative Art*; Berlin, *Poetics*; Fokkelmann, *Reading Biblical Narrative*; Frei, *Eclipse*; Gunkel, *Legends of Genesis*; Gunn and Fewell, *Narrative*; Hallo, *COS*; Johnson, *Making Sense*; Kermode, *Genesis of Secrecy*; Lord, *Singer of Tales*; Miller, *Representation of Speech*; Muilenburg, "Beyond Form Criticism," 1–18; Niditch, *Folklore*; Niditch, *Oral World*; Parker, *Pre-Biblical Narrative*; Parker, *Ugaritic Narrative Poetry*; Propp, *Morphology*; Sternberg, *Poetics*; Wolde, *Narrative Syntax*.

NARRATIVE FORMULAS

Accession Age Formula: "RN was X years old when he began to reign."

This is a specification of the **age formula** and is only used with kings of Judah (or of united monarchy) and is typically part of the **introductory regnal resumé** in a **regnal narrative** (1 Sam 13:1; 2 Sam 2:10; 5:4; 1 Kgs 14:21 [= 2 Chr 12:13]; 22:42 [= 2 Chr 20:31]; 2 Kgs 8:17, 26 [= 2 Chr 21:5, 20]; 12:1 [= 2 Chr 24:1]; 14:2 [= 2 Chr 25:1]; 15:2 [= 2 Chr 26:3], 33 [= 2 Chr 27:1, 8]; 16:2 [= 2 Chr 28:1]; 18:2 [= 2 Chr 29:1]; 21:1 [= 2 Chr 33:1], 19 [= 2 Chr 33:21]; 22:1 [= 2 Chr 34:1]; 23:31 [= 2 Chr 36:2], 36 [= 2 Chr 36:5]; 24:8 [= 2 Chr 36:9], 18 [= 2 Chr 36:11]; Jer 52:1; 2 Chr 22:2).

Campbell, *1 Samuel*, 340; de Vries, *1 and 2 Chronicles*, 437; Long, *1 Kings*, 264; Long, *2 Kings*, 318.

Age Formula: "And PN was X years old when . . ."

This is an exposition clause which establishes the age of the protagonist at an important life event. For example, it can occur as the **accession age formula** or the concluding statement in an **annunciation narrative**.

Coats, *Exodus 1–18*, 175; Coats, *Genesis*, 320; Finlay, *Birth Report Genre*, 91.

And It Was So Formula: "And it was so."

This formula occurs in Gen 1 to show the efficacy of God's **exercitive** speeches regarding creation. On the first **day of creation section**, after God's speech "Let there be light," the narrator states "And there was light" (Gen 1:3) and the formula does not appear. However, the formula does appear on the second day (Gen 1:7), twice on the third day (Gen 1:9, 11), on the fourth day (Gen 1:15), and twice on the sixth day (Gen 1:24, 30). On the fifth day, God gives an exercitive speech calling into existence sea creatures and flying creatures (Gen 1:20) which is followed not by the and it was so formula but by "And God created the great sea monsters and every living creature that moves, of every kind, with which the waters swarm, and every winged bird of every kind" (Gen 1:21). The specification here may be to emphasize that the sea creatures—considered divine chaos gods in other creation stories in the Near East—are created by

God and thus on a much lower ontological level than God. See Creation Passage.

Middleton, *Liberating Image*, 278–87.

Arrival/Itinerary Formula: "And encamped at GN"

This formula notes the point of arrival in a journey and is typically found in an itinerary or an itinerary list (Gen 12:8; 13:1, 3, 18; 20:1; 26:17, 22, 23; 28:10; 33:18; 35:16, 21; 46:1, 5, 6, 7; 12:37; 13:20; 15:22, 27; 16:1; 17:1; 19:2; Num 11:35; 12:16; 20:1, 22; 21:4, 10, 11, 12, 13, 16, 18, 19, 20; 21:1; and throughout 33:1—35:34).

Knierim and Coats, *Numbers*, 365.

As Written in Torah Formula: "As written in the Torah of Moses/YHWH" or "As written in the book of the Torah."

Similar to the authorization formula, this demonstrates the obedience of the character who performs an action according to Torah (Josh 8:34; 1 Kgs 2:3; 2 Kgs 14:6 [=2 Chr 25:4]; 23:21; Ezra 3:2; 6:18; Neh 10:35, 37 [NRSV 34, 36]; 1 Chr 16:40; 2 Chr 23:18; 31:3; 35:12).

De Vries, "Moses and David," 619–39.

Authorization Formula: "As PN had spoken/written/ commanded."

This formula attests that the previously mentioned action was performed with proper authorization and is a standard element in the **compliance narrative** when YHWH is the commander. With Moses commanding (Josh 8:31, 33; 1 Chr 6:34 [NRSV 49]; 15:15; 2 Chr 8:13); with David commanding (Neh 12:24, 45; 2 Chr 29:25; 35:15), with the king, either Hezekiah of Josiah commanding (2 Chr 29:15; 30:6, 12; 35:10, 16). Davidic authorization in 1 Chr 6:16–17; 9:22 is achieved without the authorization formula.

De Vries, "Moses and David," 619–39; Wright, "Legacy of David," 229–42.

Casualty Report Formula: "PN slew X enemies."

This formula typically has its literary setting in a **heroic exploit narrative** (Judg 3:31) or in a **summary subunit** of a **battle narrative**.

De Vries, *1 and 2 Chronicles*, 437–38.

Citation Formula: "And the rest of the acts of RN + and all he did + are they not written in the chronicles of the kings of Judah/ Israel?"

This formula refers the reader to other sources of information about a particular king's reign. It typically occurs as part of the **concluding regnal resumé** (1 Kgs 11:41; 14:19, 29; 15:7, 31; 16:5, 14, 20, 27; 22:39, 45; 2 Kgs 1:18; 8:23; 10:34; 12:19; 13:8, 12; 14:15, 18, 28; 15:6, 15, 21, 26, 31, 36; 16:19; 20:20; 21:17, 25; 23:28; 24:5; 2 Chr 9:29; 12:15; 13:22; 16:11; 20:34; 24:27; 25:26; 26:22; 27:7; 28:26; 32:32; 33:18–19; 35:26–27; 36:8). The middle part of the formula, which is an epitomizing allusion to the reign, exhibits great variety of form.

De Vries, *1 and 2 Chronicles*, 438; Long, *2 Kings*, 320.

Conception and Birth Formula: "And PN conceived and bore a son."

This formula combines the conception element and the birth element in the birth report section of a **birth narrative**. Many birth reports employ a conception and birth formula; other birth reports have more developed forms for either the conception element or the birth element or else there is intervening material between the conception element and the birth element.

Finlay, *Birth Report Genre*, 23–42

Conveyance Formula: "YHWH gave/sold Israel into the hands of X."

This formula typically follows the **did evil formula** at the beginning of a **judges cycle**, which establishes the standard that when YHWH punished Israel, the punishment was merited (Judg 3:8; 4:2; 6:1; 10:7; 13:1). In the Ehud cycle, the element is there (Judg 3:12) but the wording is different.

The enemy (X) can be an individual or a nation. The formula also occurs in Judg 2:14, 20, as part of a **Deuteronomistic history summary**.

Frolov, *Judges*, 17; Frolov and Stetckevitch, "Repentance in Judges," 129–39; Greenspahn, "Theology," 385–96; Long, *2 Kings*, 320.

Dating Formula: "In the pth day of the qth month of the rth year."

This formula is used to give a relative dating for the events that are recorded immediately after. In the books of Exodus through Deuteronomy, the reference point is the date of Israel's departure from Egypt. See overview of Tanak chapter for its use as the structuring device in Ezekiel.

Knierim and Coats, *Numbers*, 364; Mayfield, *Literary Structure*.

Day of Creation Formula: "And there was evening and there was morning, day N / ORD."

This formula is used to conclude each of the first six **day of creation sections** in Gen 1. On the first day, the number is the cardinal number "one" (Gen 1:5). On the second through sixth days, ordinal numbers are used: "second" (Gen 1:8, 13, 19, 23, 31).

Middleton, *Liberating Image*, 278–87; Pelt, "Exegetical Evidence," 199–216.

Death and Burial Formula: "PN lay with his fathers and was buried" or "PN was gathered to his fathers and was buried."

This formula is a miniature version of the **death and burial narrative**. It occurs most frequently as part of the **concluding regnal resumé** (1 Kgs 2:10; 14:31), where it may contain only the death element or only the burial element.

Bin-Nun, "Formulas," 414–32; Dubovsky, "Usual," 321–39; Green, "Regnal Formulas," 167–80; Halpern and Vanderhooft, "Editions," 179–244; Hom, "Use," 3–12; Long, *2 Kings*, 318; Meyers, "Theological Implications," 95–119; Na'aman, "Death Formulae," 245–54.

Departure Formula: "PN set out from so-and-so."

This formula notes the point of departure in a journey and is typically found in an **itinerary list**.

Did Evil Formula: "And the children of Israel did evil in the eyes of YHWH."

This formula usually begins a **judge cycle** in the book of Judges (Judg 3:7, 12; 4:1; 6:1; 10:6; 13:1) and is typically followed by the **conveyance formula**.

Frolov, *Judges*, 16; Frolov and Stetckevitch, "Repentance in Judges," 129–39.

Homage Formula: "And PN1 came/kneeled and bowed to the ground before PN2."

This combination of a verb of motion, the verb "bow," and the phrase "toward the ground" occurs frequently (Gen 18:2; 19:1; 33:3; 42:6; 43:26; Ruth 2:10; 1 Sam 24:9 [NRSV 8]); 25:23, 41; 2 Sam 1:2; 14:4, 22, 33; 24:20 [=1 Chr 29:20]; 1 Kgs 1:23; 2 Kgs 2:15; 4:37; Job 1:20; Neh 8:6). Shortened versions occur when the initial verb is missing (Gen 24:52; 48:12; Exod 34:8; 1 Sam 28:14) or when the phrase "toward the ground" is lacking (Gen 23:7; 33:6, 7; 1 Kgs 1:16; 2:19). It occurs in a variety of narrative types.

Long, *2 Kings*, 321.

Instructions Executed Formula: "And PN did so" or "And PN1 did as PN2 commanded."

This formula states the execution of an instruction or an order (Gen 7:9, 16; 21:4; 47:11; 50:12; Exod 7:6, 10, 20; 12:28, 50; 16:34; 23:15; 34:4, 18; 39:1, 5, 7, 21, 26, 29, 31, 43; 40:19, 21, 23, 25, 27, 29, 32; Lev 8:4, 9, 13, 17, 29; 9:10, 21; 16:34; 24:33; Num 1:19; 2:33; 3:16, 42, 51; 4:49; 8:3, 22; 15:36; 16:47; 17:11; 20:9, 27; 27:22, 23; 31:7, 31, 41, 47; Deut 34:9; Josh 4:8; 8:29, 31, 33; 10:40; 11:12, 15, 20; 14:5; 21:8; 1 Sam 17:20; 2 Sam 5:25; 7:11; 13:29; 24:19; Job 42:9; 1 Chr 14:16; 15:15; 24:19; 2 Chr 7:17). It is an abbreviated form of a compliance subunit and frequently occurs as the last element in a divine command narrative.

Intimidation Formula: "And the fear of YHWH came upon . . ."

This formula frequently occurs in battle narratives involving holy war. It portrays YHWH as the primary cause of victory, though Israelite soldiers/officers may be secondary causes.

Introduction Formula: "And it came to pass (in those days)."

This formula is the most common beginning of an **introductory subunit**.

Invasion Formula: "X came up against Y"

This formula occurs in a battle narrative, often in an introductory subunit. Either a person or a nation attacks, besieges, plunders, or threatens another nation (often Israel/Judah).

Israel Servitude Formula: "The Israelites served X for Y years."

This formula follows the **did evil formula** and the **conveyance formula** in the Othniel and Ehud cycles (Judg 3:8, 14). After that, there are various ways in which the length of Israel's servitude is mentioned (Judg 4:3; 6:1; 10:8). This element may play a role in a chronological scheme. The fact that the servitude period is typically less than the rest in the **land rest formula** highlights YHWH's graciousness to Israel.

Frolov and Stetckevitch, "Repentance in Judges," 129–39.

Land Rest Formula: "And the land had rest for X years."

This formula concludes the account of a judge's leadership in the Othniel, Ehud, Deborah/Barak, and Gideon cycles (Judg 3:11, 30; 5:31; 8:28). The formula shows the value of YHWH-inspired leadership and, when compared with the **Israel servitude formula**, highlights YHWH's graciousness. The fact that it does not occur in the Jepthah and Samson cycles indicates the extent to which the cycles are becoming a downward spiral, as Israel moves ever farther from YHWH.

Frolov, *Judges*, 17.

Length of Reign Formula: "RN reigned X years in Y."

This formula is part of the **introductory regnal resumé** and is used to narrate the length of a particular king's reign (1 Kgs 15:2). It frequently adds the name of the capital city.

Green, "Regnal Formulas," 167–80.

Murmuring Formula: "PN1 murmured against PN2."

This formula is typically used to introduce a report of a murmuring/rebellion against YHWH or YHWH's representatives. It is mainly found in the Exodus and Wilderness Wanderings traditions.

Naming Formula: "And PN1 called his/her name PN2."

This is the standard way of naming a person or place in the Hebrew Bible. Many **naming subunits** consist solely of this formula but others give an explanation of the name.

No King in Israel Formula: "In those days, there was no king in Israel."

This formula occurs in the **epilogue** of Judges and is an example of a **narratorial aside/evaluation subunit**. It can occur at the end of an episode (Judg 17:6a; 21:25a) or at the beginning of one (Judg 18:1a; 19:1a); it is twice supplemented by a note that everyone did what was right in their own eyes, to emphasize the negative evaluation. A variant occurs discussing no king in Edom (1 Kgs 22:47) which the king list in Gen 36 shows was unusual.

Boling, "In Those Days," 33–48.

Obedience Formula

See **Instructions Executed Formula**

Prophetic Conveyance Formula: "I will give X into your hand."

This formula is a variant of the **conveyance formula** but is a future tense **assertive** (1 Kgs 20:13) rather than a past tense one. It is because the formula speaks of God's future activity that the formula is primarily an assertive rather than a **commissive.** The prophetic conveyance formula is a **prophecy**, whereas the notice of conveyance fomula is a **divine action.** Because the giving of a person or group into the addressee's hand is positive from the addressee's viewpoint, the prophetic conveyance formula is typically part of a **prophecy of salvation** which is also a **message from YHWH.** Thus the **efficient cause** of the prophetic conveyance formula is typically YHWH and its **perlocutionary intent** is to assure the addressee of the coming salvation.

Long, *2 Kings*, 320.

Prophetic Fulfillment Formula: "According to the word of YHWH which PN spoke."

This formula is part of an assertive that an event happened because it was prophesied by YHWH, usually through a particular prophet (1 Kgs 16:34). It occurs in a **fulfillment subunit**. The efficient cause is the narrator/editor of the historical work and the teleological cause is to demonstrate that events happen according to the divine plan spoken by the prophets. This formula occurs frequently in the **Deuteronomistic History**, tying together prophecies and their fulfillments throughout the books of Joshua through Kings.

Long, *1 Kings*, 265; von Rad, *Studies in Deuteronomy*, 74–91.

Queen Mother Formula: "His mother's name was RN"

This typically occurs in the **introductory regnal resumé** of a king of Judah. Its teleological cause is both to provide information concerning the king and to highlight the important role played in Judah by the queen mother (1 Kgs 11:26; 14:21, 31; 15:2, 10, 13; 22:42; 2 Kgs 8:26; 12:1; 14:2;

15:2, 33; 18:2; 21:1, 19; 22:1; 23:31, 36; 24:8, 18; 2 Chr 12:13; 13:2; 20:31; 22:2; 24:1; 25:1; 26:3; 27:1; 29:1). That Asa removed his mother from being queen mother because of her idolatry (1 Kgs 15:13 [=2 Chr 15:16]) demonstrates the importance of the role for good or bad. The **walked after predecessor formula** occasionally mentions the mother also.

Ackerman, "Queen Mother," 385–401; Glatt-Gilad, "Regnal Formulae," 184–209; Green, "Regnal Formulas," 167–80; Halpern and Vanderhooft, "Editions of Kings," 179–244.

Raising a Deliverer Formula: "And YHWH raised up a deliverer for them."

This formula occurs after the captivity element in the judge cycle. This formula only occurs in the **Deuteronomistic history summary** near the beginning of Judges and in the **judge cycles** of Othniel and Ehud (Judg 2:16, 18; 3:9; 15). In the Gideon cycle, the basic element is present in the angel of YHWH's command for Gideon to deliver Israel (Judg 6:14). In the Samson cycle, it is partly present in the destiny element of the **annunciation scene**, which proclaims that Samson would begin to deliver Israel from the Philistines. In the Deborah/Barak cycle the roles of judge and deliverer are split, with the emphasis on the former, "At that time Deborah, a prophetess, wife of Lappidoth, was judging Israel" (Judg 4:4). This sentence is overloaded with grammatically feminine words, perhaps foreshadowing that the enemy ruler will be killed by a woman, Jael. In the Jephthah cycle, the people turn for leadership to a man whom they had driven away.

Repentance Formula: "And the children of Israel cried out to YHWH."

This formula usually occurs after the **did evil formula**, the **conveyance formula**, and the **Israelite servitude formula** in the beginning of a **judge cycle** (Judg 3:9, 15; 4:3; 6:6; 10:10). Its absence from the Samson cycle is significant in a couple of ways.

Boda, *Return*, 51–52; Frolov and Stetckevitch, "Repentance in Judges," 129–39; Hoyt, "Reassessing Repentance," 143–57; Lambert, *Repentance*, 43.

Saw That It Was Good Formula: "And God saw that it was good."

This formula occurs in all but the second of the first six **day of creation sections** and occurs twice on the third and sixth days (Gen 1:4, 10, 12, 18, 21, 25, 31). This positive divine evaluation of creation as good is contrary to Platonic thought and even more so to Gnostic ideology, which regarded creation as evil. The variation of "very good" in Gen 1:31 is one of several factors that highlight the sixth day—with humans being created in the image of God, then being blessed by God and given dominion over other living things on earth—as the climax of the creation account.

Middleton, *Liberating Image*, 278–87.

Speech Introduction Formula: "And he/she/PN said," "And he/she/PN1 spoke to PN2 saying" etc.

This formula has a quotation as its object in the narration of direct discourse and is extremely common throughout the Hebrew Bible.

Statement of Judging Formula: "And PN judged Israel X years."

This formula is usually used in Judges either for non-deliverer judges or for deliverers where there is no statement that the land had rest.

Subdued Formula: "And X was subdued by the hand of (the children of) Israel."

This occurs after the major military victory in a **judge cycle** (Judg 3:30; 4:23 [with significant variation]; 8:28; 11:33). In the Othniel cycle, the element has a different formulation which emphasizes YHWH's guidance over Othniel personally: "YHWH gave King Cushan-rishataim of Aram into his hand" (Judg 3:10). The glory of killing Sisera does not go to Barak, the glory of killing Oreb and Zeeb does not go to Gideon, it does not say who killed Sihon in the Jephthah cycle and the names of the enemy rulers are not even mentioned in the Samson cycle. This element suggests that Othniel and Ehud are more successful than the other judges. The omission of the subdued formula in the Samson cycle ties in with the **annunciation scene**, where Samson is prophesied only to begin the deliverance from the Philistines.

Frolov, *Judges*, 17.

Succession Formula: "And RN reigned in his stead."

This formula identifies the person succeeding to the throne (1 Kgs 14:31) and is part of the concluding regnal resumé. Often, information indicating the relation of the successor to his predecessor is contained in the formula also.

Synchronistic Accession Formula: "In the nth year of RN1, king of Israel, RN2 King of Judah began to reign."

This formula synchronizes the accession date of the king of Judah/Israel with his counterpart in Israel/Judah (1 Kgs 15:9, 25). The precise form of the formula varies significantly. This formula is part of the introductory regnal resumé. This formula is characteristic of history.

Testimony Formula: "Until this day."

This formula occurs in a **narratorial aside/evaluation subunit** and testifies to the continuing effects of a past event into the writer's time (Josh 7:26; 15:63; 1 Kgs 12:19).

Theological Evaluation Formula: "And RN did what was right/wrong in the eyes of YHWH."

This is the quintessential element of a **theological evaluation subunit** in a regnal narrative. The monarch is not evaluated according to success in battle or building projects but in obedience to YHWH.

Walked after Predecessor Formula: "And RN1 walked in the way of RN2/his father"

This occurs in a **theological evaluation subunit** of a regnal narrative and whether it is positive or negative depends upon whether RN obeyed

YHWH or not. When not compared to their father, Judean kings are frequently compared to David who was a good king; Israelite kings are frequently compared to Jeroboam who was a bad king.

NARRATIVE SUBUNITS

Blessing Subunit

This is either an action clause employing the verb "bless" or a subunit in which the main thrust of a character's speech is either to express devotion to God through a **blessing of YHWH formula** or to pronounce a blessing upon another character through a **blessing well-wish** (see **blessing subunit** in the chapter on psalms for further details). Within the narratives, the blessing well-wish arguably is an exercitive speech act as well as being an expressive one, i.e. in circumstances such as Isaac blessing Jacob, the pronouncement has real world effects. It is the starring subunit of a **blessing narrative** but also plays a role in certain other narratives. Its counterpart is **curse subunit**.

Character's Report Subunit

This is a subcategory of **character's speech subunit** in which a character gives an assertive speech concerning past events and actions which is not part of a dialogue subunit. The addressee then typically acts upon this information. When the biblical narrator has expounded on the events mentioned in the character's report, the reader is offered insight by comparing the two versions.

Character's Speech Subunit

This is a catch-all term for a subunit consisting of a **speech introduction formula** followed by the speech of a character in the narrative. Important subcategories include **cohortative subunit**, **command subunit**, **request subunit**, and various divine speech subunits.

Cohortative Subunit

This is a subcategory of **character's speech subunit**, in which the speech which proposes a joint action, typically by using the cohortative construction in Hebrew. Such speeches combine the qualities of commissive and directive speech acts because they concern what both speaker and addressee will do in the future. Most cohortative speeches occur in **dialogue subunits**. Those that do not are typically followed by a **compliance subunit** which may focus on the speaker, addressee, or both.

Command and Compliance Subunit

Often a verse, or even part of a verse, contains both a command subunit and a compliance subunit. It is often desirable to refer to the command and compliance together.

Command Subunit

This typically consists of a **speech introduction formula** followed by a speech in which one human character gives authoritative directives (whether commands or prohibitions) to one or more other human characters regarding a specific situation. For when God gives the authoritative directives, see **divine command subunit**. For non-authoritative directives, see **request subunit**. A command subunit is typically followed by either a **compliance subunit** or a **non-compliance subunit**. The authority figure issuing the directives may be a ruler, court official, judge, or parent.

Compliance Subunit

This is a subunit which indicates that the agent has obeyed the directives issued in a preceding **command subunit**, **dialogue subunit**, **divine command subunit**, or **request subunit**. It may vary in complexity from a simple **instructions executed formula** (obedience formula) to a series of action clauses in which the addressee performs the required directives (see also **compliance narrative**).

Concluding Subunit

A **concluding subunit** is not merely the last subunit within a pericope but is one in which the narrator clearly concludes a story arc within the larger narrative; its counterpart is **introductory subunit**. Not all biblical narratives have a concluding subunit; many simply end. The standard pattern in **divine command narratives** and **legislative speech narratives**, for example, terminate with the end of the speech or with a brief **compliance subunit**. Many other narratives end with a speech or otherwise lack a clear narrative conclusion. In certain circumstances, ending a passage with a dialogue without resolution may heighten the dramatic tension. Examples include Gen 34 and Jonah 4.

Biblical narratives can conclude in a variety of ways: a **narratorial aside subunit** (Gen 2:24–25; 11:9); a **divine actions subunit** (Gen 3:23–24; 20:17b–18); an **event subunit** such as a character's death (Gen 9:28–29; 35:28–29; 50:26); a **summary subunit** which recapitulates aspects of the preceding narrative (Gen 17:26–27; 19:29; 49:28; 50:12–13, 21b) and no doubt others.

Covenant Speech Subunit

This is a subcategory of divine exercitive subunit in which God explicitly establishes a covenant with another party. It is normally found in **covenant establishment narratives** or **legislative speech narratives**.

Curse Subunit

The counterpart to **blessing subunit**, a curse subunit contains a speech introduction formula and a speech pronouncing a malediction or curse upon someone. It is the key element in a **curse narrative**.

Dialogue Subunit

Along with main actions subunit, this is the most frequent of narrative subunits. It consists primarily of a series of **character's speech subunits** by two characters or parties addressed to each other which form an organic whole within the larger passage. The parties can be terrestrial or celestial beings, including God. Occasionally one of the characters/

parties will perform an action and then give a speech. Dialogue subunits contribute greatly to both plot and characterization. Speeches frequently reveal how the characters perceive themselves, their dialogue partners, other human characters, and God. They also illustrate the speaker's virtues and vices. They often contain expressives which make the passage more vivid. Dialogue subunits are far more prevalent in Samuel than in the parallel passages in Chronicles; more sermons are based on the Samuel passages. They are the major element in interrogation narratives.

Miller, "Pragmatics," 165–91; Miller, *Representation of Speech.*

Divine Actions Subunit

Like **main actions subunit**, it consists of a series of action clauses but in which the agent, X, acting is not human but the supreme being, God. God may be referred to by name or title, pronoun, or simply as the implied subject of a third masculine singular verb. God is usually understood by believers to be the ultimate author of everything, including the Bible; God is the metaphysically ultimate Being upon whom all other beings depend for their existence. God is likewise understood to be greater than the biblical portrayal of God, including the portrayal of the character God in the divine actions subunits. From divine actions subunits that refer to God's body parts, for example, one should not infer that God actually has body parts (which would imply real limitations). Like main actions subunit, it is a major driver of the plot—especially so because it frequently illustrates the sovereignty of God, such that human plans cannot succeed unless God wills it. Divine actions subunits also often create irony, enabling the reader to know something that the human characters in the narrative do not.

Divine Blessing Subunit

This is a subcategory of **divine exercitive subunit** in which God pronounces blessings upon the man and the woman at creation (Gen 1:28; 5:2), the seventh day (Gen 2:3), Noah (Gen 9:1), Abraham (Gen 24:1), Isaac (Gen 25:8), Jacob (Gen 35:9; see also Gen 32:30), Joseph (Gen 39:5), Obed-edom (2 Sam 6:11=1 Chr 13:14). Several **divine promise** subunits include a promise of blessing.

Divine Command Subunit

This is a subcategory of **character speech subunit** in which YHWH gives authoritative directives (commands, permissions, prohibitions) to a human addressee concerning a particular situation rather than having ongoing legal implications such as **legislative speech narratives** contain. It is the main element in a **divine command narrative** but also occurs in other narratives where God interacts with humans.

Divine Exercitives Subunit

This is a subunit in which God brings about a new reality (whether social reality or brute reality) through speech. The divine fiats in Gen 1 beginning with "Let there be light" (Gen 1:3) are exercitives as are the blessings God pronounced (see blessing subunit). For legal exercitives, see entry in legal genres.

Divine Judgment Subunit

This typically consists of an introductory speech formula in which the agent is God, followed by a speech containing commissives in which God threatens punishment or assertives which prophesy punishment or a combination thereof. Because of God's presumed omnipotence and omniscience, the semantic difference between the commissive threat of punishment and the assertive prophesy of punishment almost vanishes when God is the speaker.

Divine Promise Subunit

This consists of an introductory speech formula followed by a commissive speech in which the agent, God, promises some form of wellbeing to the addressee. The theme of divine promise is particularly important in Gen 12–50 (see overview of Tanak chapter).

Divine Promise/Command Subunit

This is a **character speech subunit** in which YHWH issues directives as well as promises. If it is followed by a compliance subunit, the narrative may be classified as a divine command narrative.

Divine Reactions Subunit

This is analogous to a **reactions subunit** but in which the agent reacting is the character God.

Divine Response to Complaint Subunit

This is a subunit, **following a complaint subunit**, which contains a speech by God responding to the complaint. It is a standard element in a **murmuring narrative**.

Dream/Vision Subunit

This is a subunit which narrates that a man had a dream or vision and then what the contents of his dream/vision were (there are no examples in the Hebrew Bible reporting a woman experiencing a dream). This genre is important in **court narratives**, **dream epiphany/theophany narratives**, **dream interpretation narratives**, **reports of prophetic symbolic visions**, and **vision narratives**, the latter two being discussed in the prophetic narratives chapter.

Event Subunit

This is a subunit describing something that happens within the narrative time-frame but which is not an action or experience of a character. This can include characters dying, natural disasters, etc. The event subunit is frequently limited to a single event clause, but it could be expanded by one or more exposition clauses or consist of multiple event clauses.

Exercitives Subunit

Exercitives, also known as declaratives, are the least frequent category of speech act in the Hebrew Bible. The social life of Ancient Israel likely included exercitives in weddings, appointment of officials, coronations and other ceremonies but the Hebrew Bible usually narrates these without including the exercitive speeches. When it does occur, an exercitive subunit typically consists of an introductory speech formula and a speech consisting of one or more exercitive speech acts.

Experiences Subunit

This is a subunit dominated by **experience clauses** such as occur when the agent sees something, hears something (or is told via the passive "he was told" construction as opposed to character's report subunit), or otherwise experiences something rather than making an action (looking and listening are acting; seeing and hearing are experiencing). It is typically followed by a **reactions subunit** where the agent reacts to the experience. In the prophetic narratives chapter, further subcategories are discussed, such as auditory experience, behold experience, tactile experience, and visual experience. See also the discussion of various subcategories of sensual image in the chapter on Song of Songs.

Exposition Subunit

This is a subunit dominated by exposition clauses (and thus by either nominal clauses or clauses whose finite verb is "to be") providing the reader with information concerning a character, place, or thing in the narrative. It may also include activity clauses, thus informing the reader about a person or group's routines. Compared to other works such as Dickens' novels or Homer's epics, the Hebrew Bible contains little exposition. Conversely, there is a higher expectation that details given in the exposition will play a role in the narrative.

Fulfillment Subunit

This subunit consists of material that could be labeled as **main actions subunit** or **event subunit** but which also fulfills what had been said in a previous speech (such as contained in **divine judgment subunits, divine promise subunits, interpretation** etc.) concerning then future events. The mentions of seven plenteous years and seven years of famine (Gen 41:53–54, 57) conform to what Joseph had said when interpreting Pharaoh's dreams (Gen 41:26–32).

Von Rad, *Studies in Deuteronomy*, 74–91.

Hardening Heart Subunit

This narrates how Pharaoh's heart was hardened, typically after a plague on Egypt ceases and is frequently the final element in the **sign narratives** in Exodus (Exod 7:13, 22b; 8:11, 15b, 28 [NRSV 15, 19b, 32]; 9:7b, 12, 34–35; 10:20, 27; 11:10; 14:8). The agent in this subunit may be God, Pharaoh, or left ambiguous; and there are differences between the Masoretic text and the Septuagint regarding the agent in some subunits.

Introductory Subunit

This is the counterpart to **concluding subunit**. Some narratives do not have an introductory subunit but begin abruptly such as 1 Kgs 17:1, where a new character Elijah gives a speech to Ahab. Introductory subunits can give a time setting, introduce a new character or make other formal indications that a new narrative is beginning.

Journey Subunit

This is a subcategory of **main actions subunit** which narrates the journey of a person or group. The patriarchs and matriarchs lived semi-nomadic lives which involved moving frequently, and the Israelites wandered in the wilderness during a forty-year period so there are several of these type subunits in the Torah (see **journey narrative** for further details).

Legislative Speech Subunit

This is the primary narrative unit within which the Torah's legal material is contained. It typically consists of an **introductory speech formula** in which the agent is Moses and a speech containing directives which have ongoing legal significance, or a **speech introduction of YHWH formula**, followed by a **command to speak formula** and the doubly embedded legal content of the speech. It frequently comprises the entirety of a **legislative speech narrative** (although following compliance subunits can occur) but may also appear in a **legal case narrative**.

List/Poem Subunit

Analogous to legislative speech subunit, this is a catch-all category for the sometimes lengthy non-narrative genres embedded within a narrative; the details of such units are discussed in the chapters on lists and psalms respectively.

Main Actions Subunit

This is the workhorse subunit in narratives. It typically consists of a series of *wayyiqtol* (preterite) clauses performed by the human protagonist(s), antagonist(s), or both, i.e. it narrates what actions the characters initiate within the main plot of the narrative. A speech introduction formula could be considered a short, specialized form of a main actions subunit.

Naming Subunit

This is a subunit in which a human agent gives a name to a person or place. Frequent elements in this subunit are a naming action, an introductory speech formula, and an etiological speech which gives the reason for the name. This subunit is a standard element in birth narratives and etiological narratives.

Narratorial Aside/Evaluation Subunit

This is when the narrator interrupts the story flow to address the audience directly. It can give the audience future information about a character (1 Sam 15:35b), explain a custom or term (1 Sam 9:9), explain the divine purpose behind the events unfolding (Judg 14:4), evaluate a character's actions (2 Sam 11:27b). The until this day formula is a narratorial aside also.

Noncompliance Subunit

This is the opposite of the more common **compliance subunit**, and narrates how a character refused to comply with a directive given in a preceding **command subunit**, **dialogue subunit**, or **request subunit**. Because it derives from conflicting positions between certain characters, it contributes strongly to both plot and characterization.

Preparations Subunit

This is a subcategory of main actions subunit in which the actions taken are preparatory to some other actions. Battle narratives and journey narratives often contain this subunit.

Prayer Subunit

This typically consisting of an introductory speech formula and then a speech (prayer) addressed to God, excluding situations where God is physically manifest in the scene or where the speech is in response to a speech from God. It is the central element in a **prayer narrative** but occurs in several other types of narratives also.

Question and Answer Subunit

This is a subcategory of dialogue subunit which typically consists of a speech introduction formula followed by an inquiry and a second speech introduction formula followed by an answer or at least a response. Because an inquiry is a directive illocution, requesting that the addressee give the speaker information, and an answer implicitly complies with that directive, this subunit is actually a subcategory also of a **command and compliance subunit**.

Reactions Subunit

This is a subunit which narrates how one or several parties react to an event, action, or something else that has just happened in the narrative. It may consist solely of actions, or a speech in response to the event etc., or a combination thereof. Sometimes it contains the differing reactions of two parties.

Request Subunit

This is similar to a **command subunit**, but the directives are not from an authority figure so the addressee is not obliged to heed them. It is typically followed either by a compliance subunit or a non-compliance subunit.

Results Subunit

This is a subunit which discusses the consequences or results of the previous **actions subunit** or **divine action subunit**. Because it often narrates ongoing significance of something, this subunit lends itself to being a **concluding subunit** but it does not have to be. They are particularly prominent in the primeval cycle of Gen 1–11.

Summary Subunit

This subunit summarizes what happened in that narrative, for example an offering narrative concludes, "All the Israelite men and women whose hearts made them willing to bring anything for the work that the Lord had commanded by Moses to be done, brought it as a freewill offering to the Lord" (Exod 35:29).

Theological Evaluation Subunit

This subunit is a standard subunit in the regnal narratives, where it typically follows the **introductory regnal resumé**. Its central element is the **theological evaluation formula** but it may be expanded in a variety of ways: intensifying, modifying, or detailing the initial evaluation.

Vow Subunit

This is a subcategory of character speech subunit in which a character makes a vow (a strong commissive illocution) to God if a certain condition is fulfilled. See **vow narrative**.

STANDARD NARRATIVE FORM-CRITICAL TERMS

Account

This term has been used by form critics to designate a narrative that is longer and more complex than a **report**, and which may involve some level of explanation for the events it depicts. An account may be similar in complexity and length to a **story**. However, it is typically less concerned than a story with entertaining the audience through arousing tension and resolving it through the unfolding of a plot than it is in conveying pertinent information. Many **regnal narratives** in Kings and Chronicles are good examples of accounts; their purpose is to convey what the narrator considers the most significant events of a monarch's reign to the audience.

Campbell, *1 Samuel*, 341; Campbell, *2 Samuel*, 224; de Vries, *Chronicles*, 226–27; Frolov, *Judges*, 363; Knierim and Coats, *Numbers*, 337; Long, *1 Kings*, 243; Long, *2 Kings*, 291; Sweeney, *Isaiah 1–39*, 512; Sweeney, *Isaiah 40–46*, 386.

Anecdote

An anecdote is a short narrative of an amusing or memorable incident. Examples include Pharaoh's daughter hiring Moses's biological mother to be his wet-nurse (Exod 2:7–9) or Michal deceiving her father Saul by pretending an idol covered in clothes was David sick in bed (1 Sam 19:11–17).

Campbell, *1 Samuel*, 341; Campbell, *2 Samuel*, 224; Frolov, *Judges*, 363; Knierim and Coats, *Numbers*, 338; Long, *1 Kings*, 243; Long, *2 Kings*, 291.

Autobiography

This is a first-person analogue to **biography**. While there is no full autobiography of a person's major life events in the Hebrew Bible, short first-person accounts of certain events occur in Nehemiah and in the so-called Isaianic memoir (Isaiah 6:1–9:6 [NRSV 7]). The book of Ecclesiastes also contains some first-person reflections.

Koh, *Royal Autobiography*; Sweeney, *Isaiah 1–39*; 515; Smith and Watson, *Reading Autobiography*; Sturrock, *Language of Autobiography*.

Biography

This is a subcategory of history, whose topic is the significant events in an individual's life. The Hebrew Bible does give a lot of information about certain individuals, but it is usually as they are connected to the larger salvation-historical story of YHWH's covenant relationship to the elect. When we meet Abram, later Abraham, he is already seventy-five years old (Gen 12:1–4); one chapter (Exod 2) covers the first eighty years of Moses's life, before the **vocation account** at the burning bush that will utterly change his life; Samuel's birth and boyhood is discussed but almost nothing about his activities as a judge; David is first introduced to us when Samuel anoints him king (1 Sam 16:1–13). The narratives about Jacob in Gen 25–50 and Jeremiah in Jeremiah 26–45 perhaps come closest to biography but even here the material is largely didactic than merely informational and the genre of the book as a whole definitely is not that of biography.

Coats, *Genesis*; 317; Long, *1 Kings*, 245; Long, *2 Kings*, 294.

Chiastic Structure

This is a structure whose first and last elements match each other in some respect, whose second and second to last elements match, and so on until either the middle two elements match or there is a central unmatched element. Chiastic structures range in size from part of a verse to complexes of several chapters. Chiastic structures complement other ways of categorizing texts. The overview of Tanak chapter gives some examples.

Assis, "Chiasmus," 273–304; Berman, "Criteria," 57–69; Boda, "Chiasmus," 55–70; Bovell, "Symmetry, Ruth," 175–91; Brouwer, "Understanding

Chiasm," 99–127; Cassuto, "Function of Chiasmus," 1–40; Shea, "Chiastic Structure," 378–96; Webster, "Pattern," 73–93; Willis, "Juxtaposition," 465–80.

Chronistic Report

This is a subcategory of **report** occurring in the historical books that is explicitly dated by regnal year. In the Ancient Near East, there were annals consisting of series of chronistic reports, and the works of Kings and Chronicles may have used some of these annals as sources. Within Kings and Chronicles themselves, the chronistic report is typically an element of a **regnal narrative**.

Long, *1 Kings*, 246; Long, *2 Kings*, 295.

Comedy

The term "comedy" can be used to refer to a work, typically a play or drama, with a happy ending, or to a work which is intended to be humorous. Perhaps the best examples of humorous stories in the Hebrew Bible are those of Balaam's donkey speaking to him (Num 22:13–35) and when Haman's conceit contributes to his downfall and the elevation of his mortal enemy Mordecai (Est 6:1–13). The book of Esther could also be considered a comedy in the sense of a literary work with a happy ending, as could Ruth. The closest book to a drama in the Bible is the poetic portion of Job (Job 3:1–42:6), which is largely a debate involving long dramatic speeches, with the narrator limited to brief **speech introductions**. The prose epilogue (Job 42:7–17) restores Job's health, fortune and family so the work as a whole could also be categorized as a comedy, but Job is much more than that.

Craig, *Reading Esther*; Wilkens, *Funny*.

Contemporizing Summary

This is a subcategory of **narratorial aside/evaluation subunit** which affirms the continuing effect of an event into the narrator's own time, e.g. "So Israel has been in rebellion against the house of David to this day" (1 Kgs 12:19). Other ancient historians, such as Herodotus, used contemporizing summaries in support of their historical claims and to connect the present to the past for cultural or national reasons. The biblical narrators do likewise, emphasizing the theological significance of the events.

Childs, "Study," 279–92; Long, *2 Kings*, 297.

Fable

See entry in the chapter on prophetic speech.

Historical Story

This genre is a subcategory of **story**, in terms of literary sophistication and of intention to entertain the audience through creating suspense and tensions but then resolving them as the plot unfolds. However, it participates in the genre of **history**, in that it is interested in portraying the causes of an historical event.

Campbell, *1 Samuel*, 342; Campbell, *2 Samuel*, 225; de Vries, *1 and 2 Chronicles*, 431; Long, *1 Kings*, 6–7; Long, *2 Kings*, 301; Sweeney, *Isaiah 1–39*, 521.

History

This is a large-scale narrative concerned with chronology, named historical persons, and cause-effect relationships typically devoted to a particular period of a nation's existence. Because a narrative is not historical, does not make it fiction. Much of Genesis through Judges and into Samuel might be described as quasi-history. A difference between quasi-history and history can be seen by comparing the narratives pertaining to Joseph and Moses—which do not mention the name of the Pharaohs involved—with narratives in Kings which name the Pharaohs involved and often designate which year in their reigns the narrated events take place.

The books of Kings and Chronicles are clearly history with a strong interest in chronology. Ezekiel, Haggai, and Zechariah are examples of prophetic history.

Coats, *Genesis*, 9–10; Galil, *Chronology*; Japhet, "Historical Reliability," 83–107; Johnson, *Making Sense*, 34–53; Kitchen, *Reliability Old Testament*; Long, *1 Kings*, 7–8; Long, *2 Kings*, 301–2; Pehike, "Observations,"

65–85; Provan, Long, and Longman, *Biblical History*; Smelik, *Converting the Past*; Thiele, *Mysterious Numbers.*

Legend

In form criticism, this term was taken from the German word *Legende*, which referred at one time to the story of a Christian saint (usually performing a miracle) that would be read on that saint's day. Legend thus frequently referred to narratives concerning miracles whose purpose was edification rather than entertainment. There is a considerable overlap between such stories of saints and many of the episodes involving Elijah and Elisha, both of whom performed numerous miracles.

Other uses of the term legend include origin stories concerning places of worship, ancient epic poetry which deals with human heroes (the epic poetry dealing with the gods would be "myth"), or materials which scholars regard as non-historical but which scholars argue that the original readers would have regarded as historical. Gunkel applied the term "legend" to almost every narrative in Genesis, at which point it is of limited usefulness. This glossary contains entries such as **hieros logos narrative**, **prophetic miracle narrative**, and **sign narrative**, most examples of which might be considered legend, depending upon definition.

Coats, *Genesis*, 8–9; Coats, *Saga, Legend*; Gunkel, *Legends of Genesis*; Knierim and Coats, *Numbers*, 348; de Vries, *1 and 2 Chronicles*, 432; Long, *1 Kings*, 252; Long, *2 Kings*, 304; Sweeney, *Isaiah 1–39*, 523–24.

Myth

In contemporary society, the term "myth" is often merely a synonym for "something which is false." In literary analysis, "myth" can be used for foundational origin story (**etiological narrative** in this glossary) but more often refers to works in which deities battle or outwit each other or in which deities and humans interact, have sexual relations, and bring forth demi-gods. [Other uses of the term "myth" include a narrative recited when performing a ritual, or as attempts to deal with the most foundational level of reality via symbolic narratives rather than through metaphysics/ontology.] Although the ancient Near East is replete with myths, they are scarce in the Hebrew Bible. The **creation narrative** in Gen 1 has thematic parallels with Enuma Elish and similar mythologies, but is anti-mythological, not even naming the sun and moon (which were the names of pagan deities) but designating them as mere lights. There is no struggle between the gods or birth of the gods in Gen 1.

Although it obviously does not use philosophical terms, Gen 1 works as a stylized presentation of God being metaphysically ultimate. Likewise—in contrast to other nations, where people can gain power over the deities through tapping into a primordial or meta-divine level from which the gods sprang—Israel fails spectacularly in their attempts to manipulate YHWH through taking the ark into battle (1 Sam 4–6) and Jeremiah admonishes similarly with regard to the temple (Jer 7).

Nevertheless, biblical poetry does employ mythical imagery to portray God. God uses might to break the head of dragons and crush the sea monster Leviathan both of old at creation (Ps 74:13–14) and in eschatological victory (Isa 27:1). A similar motif occurs with another mythical sea monster, Rahab (Isa 51:9; Ps 89:11; Job 9:13; 26:12). Another term for sea-monster, *tannin*, occurs in parallel to either Leviathan (Isa 27:1) or Rahab (Isa 51:9) or the sea, Yam (Ps 74:13). These images of conflict are in tension with Gen 1:21, where God creates the great sea monsters (*tanninim*) and sees that they are good. One could resolve this tension by arguing that earlier Israelites believed that YHWH had to battle against other deities, much as Marduk had to battle Tiamat in the Babylonian creation epic *Enuma Elish*, but that they eventually grew to a fuller understanding of God, as represented in Gen 1. Or one could argue that the Israelite poets knew (perhaps by insight granted mystically) that God was metaphysically ultimate but used mythic motifs to express God's sovereignty in dramatic form.

There are certainly difficulties. Psalm 82 declares, "God has taken his place in the divine council; in the midst of the gods he holds judgment" (Ps 82:1). That Tanak proclaims that entities which it calls "gods" exist cannot plausibly be denied. What classical theists claim is that these "gods" depend on YHWH for their very existence; they are not close to the same ontological level. Genesis 6:1–4 does look like a mythic fragment in which "sons of God" have sexual relations with human women and produce Nephilim (possibly giants) as a result, and 1 Enoch interprets it so. Targum Onqelos, the authoritative targum for Jews, precludes this interpretation; for Christians also, the mythic interpretation conflicts with Jesus's teaching on angels (Matt 22:30).

Childs, *Myth and Reality*; Coats, *Genesis*, 10, 318–19; Collins, *Daniel*, 113; Day, *God's Conflict*; Hallo, *COS*, 1:1–37, 147–56, 239–83,

381–416, 509–26; Hasel, "Polemical Nature," 81–102; Heiser, *Unseen Realm*; Heiser, *Supernatural*; Kramer, *Mythologies*; Walton, *Lost World*.

Narrator's Prayer Directive

This is the exception to the rule that everything in biblical narrative outside of speeches by the characters is an assertive. The narrator Nehemiah appeals directly to God. On the negative side, Nehemiah requests God to remember how Tobiah, Sanballat and Noadiah had opposed him (Neh 6:14) and those who had defiled the priesthood (Neh 13:29). Contrasting this is Nehemiah's request that God remember him for his good (Neh 5:19; 13:14, 22, 31).

Schnittjer, "Bad Ending," 32–56.

Notice

Form-critics used this term for the most basic clause-level genre of narrative. It would include clause-level genres such as action, event, and experience (see the introduction section in the narratives chapter).

Campbell, *1 Samuel*, 344; Campbell, *2 Samuel*, 277; Frolov, *Judges*, 365; Long, *1 Kings*, 253.

Novella

This term designated a long narrative produced by a literary artist more as an aesthetic creation than for historiographic purposes. Novellas may include elements of the miraculous, usually focus on one or two main characters, and one main plot line. A rise in status for the major character by displaying steadfastness is another frequent theme. Ruth, Esther, Jonah, Daniel 1–6, and the Joseph story (Gen 37–50) have been categorized as novellas by certain scholars, as has the lengthy **marriage narrative** in Gen 24.

Coats, *Genesis*, 319; Coats, *Saga, Legend*; Collins, *Daniel*, 114–15; Meinhold, "Gattung I," 306–24; Meinhold, "Gattung II," 72–93.

Report

This term arose from a report by a messenger (see **messenger narrative**) but was used to categorize a brief narrative whose purpose was informational rather than to develop plot or characterization. A report is usually considered more complex than a **notice**, but less complex than an **account**. Thus, a report would typically contain several notices unified in a simple narrative. One FOTL volume listed eight types of reports (adoption, battle, birth, blessing, death, dream, theophany, and marriage) but there were not separate entries for each. Most of the **divine command narratives** and **legislative speech narratives** would be reports at the narrative level, for example, no matter the length and complexity of the speeches contained within them.

Campbell, *1 Samuel*, 345; Campbell, *2 Samuel*, 228; Coats, *Genesis*, 10, 319; de Vries, *1 and 2 Chronicles*, 434; Knierim and Coats, *Numbers*, 357; Long, *1 Kings*, 259; Long, *2 Kings*, 312; Sweeney, *Isaiah 1–39*, 536.

Saga

The term "saga" was used by some form critics for larger scale narratives containing numerous episodes within the hypothetical sources underlying the Pentateuch, especially Genesis. Although accepting that earlier sources do lie behind portions of the Hebrew Bible, this glossary prefers to analyze the units of the canonical text. See the Genesis section of the overview of Tanak chapter.

Coats, *Genesis*, 5–7, 319; Coats, *Saga, Legend*; Knierim and Coats, *Numbers*, 358–59; de Vries, *1 and 2 Chronicles*, 435; Long, *1 Kings*, 260; Long, *2 Kings*, 313–14.

Story

This is a narrative with a significant aesthetic value but typically not as long as a **novella**. It is considerably more complex than report. Many of the narratives in Gen 12–50 and the books of Samuel are stories, and individual examples of story occur in Exodus, Numbers, Joshua, Judges, Kings, to take just the Primary History. Often, a narrative which occurs in both Samuel and Chronicles will be a story in Samuel and an account in Chronicles. The briefer regnal narratives in Kings are reports or accounts, but some of the longer ones could be categorized as stories, or contain a mixture of stories and accounts within them.

Campbell, *1 Samuel* 346–48; Campbell, *2 Samuel*, 228–230; de Vries, *Chronicles*, 435; Frolov, *Judges*, 367; Long, *1 Kings*, 261–62; Long, *2 Kings*, 315.

Tale

This term derives from a comparison of small single scene units of biblical narrative to oral folktales such as those collected by the Grimm brothers in Germany. Many of the subcategories of folktale analyzed by Vladimir Propp, and others who focus on actants, are exemplified in biblical narratives and such analysis complements rather than replaces the entries in this glossary on narratives categorized according to content.

Gunkel, *Folktale*; Long, *1 Kings*, 262; Long, *2 Kings*, 316; Propp, *Morphology of Folktale*.

NARRATIVES CATEGORIZED ACCORDING TO CONTENT

Adversary Narrative

Other genres of narrative discuss people doing bad things (**anti-hero cycles**, **monarch behaving badly narratives**, and **regnal narrative**) but this entry deals with narratives concerning the antagonist in the main story arc.

The narratives concerning Haman—the adversary to Esther and Mordecai in the book of Esther—are quintessential adversary narratives and in the liturgical reading of Esther at Purim, children boo and shake their rattles at every mention of Haman's name. Haman's hatred of Mordecai is so great that it leads him to seek the annihilation of the Jews (Est 3:1–15). Not satisfied with this, Haman builds a gallows on which to hang Mordecai (Est 5:9–14). His demise is foreshadowed in Est 6:1–14, where the reward he seeks for himself is given to Mordecai, and he ends up hanged on the gallows he built for Mordecai (Est 7:10).

In Daniel, the protagonists are Daniel and his three friends. Several narratives focus on the actions of their adversaries, high level officials (Dan 3:8–13; 6:5–15 [NRSV 4–13]; see also **test narrative**). God delivers

Daniel's three friends from the fiery furnace and then Daniel from the lion's den. Opposition to the rebuilding of Jerusalem is a main theme in Ezra-Nehemiah, with the opponents writing to Ahasuerus, at first getting a favorable response in reply, but then when the Jews write to the Persian king, he adjudicates in their favor (Ezra 4:1–7:26; see also **written document narrative**). The activities of Nehemiah's opponents are described in Neh 2:19–20; 4:1–15; and 6:1–13; but this opposition is also overcome. The adversary narratives, in addition to their historiographical function, would serve as encouragement to readers who face opposition for their trust in YHWH.

A different purpose underlies 1 Kgs 11:14–22, 23–25, two narratives in which YHWH raises up an adversary against Solomon (see **prophetic dismissal of monarchy narrative** for more details).

Agricultural/Pastoral Activities Narrative

Although there are numerous **laws** concerning agricultural activities, there are relatively few narratives dominated by them. Abram and Lot have too many flocks for the land (Gen 13:5–7); Jacob and shepherds discuss watering times for the flock (Gen 29:2–10); Jacob increases the number of sheep and goats that are speckled and spotted (Gen 30:25–43); and Ruth goes to glean during the harvest and then awaits Boaz on the threshing floor after he has finished winnowing barley (Ruth 2:1–23; 3:1–18). The examples concerning Jacob and Ruth are part of a **marriage narrative**.

Borowski, *Agriculture*.

Annunciation Narrative

The full pattern of the annunciation narrative is as follows: 1) depiction of the woman's barrenness (Gen 11:30; 16:1; 25:21; Judg 13:2; 1 Sam 1:2–8; 2 Kgs 4:14); 2) prayer element (Gen 20:17–18; 25:21; 1 Sam 1:9–16; and in certain parallels such as the Ugaritic poems Keret and Aqhat, the Egyptian Tale of the Doomed Prince, and the Hurrian Tale of Appu); 3) annunciation from an angel or prophet that the woman will bear a child (Gen 16:7–12; 17:1–8; 18:1–15; 25:22–23; Judg 13:3–5, 9–14; 1 Sam 1:17; 2 Kgs 4:16; the annunciation might contain a "fear not" formula, a conception element, a birth element, a naming element, an etymological element and a destiny element); 4) the birth report (Gen 16:15; 21:1–4, 6–7; 25:24–26a; Judg 13:24a; 1 Sam 1:19–20; 2 Kgs 4:17; for more information, see **birth narrative**); and 5) a concluding statement (Gen 16:16; 21:5, 8a; 25:26b–28; Judg 13:24b–25; 1 Sam 2:21; either about the child growing up or the age of the father). Many of these narratives are esthetic **stories** and contribute greatly to the characterization of Hagar, Sarah, Rebekah, the wife of Manoah, Hannah, and the woman of Shunem. Even though two of these women are not named, they are the most vivid characters in the narratives.

Genesis 16 begins with Sarai's barrenness; instead of either Sarai or Abram praying about the situation, Sarai gives Hagar to Abram to have children and Hagar conceives; the annunciation by an angel to Hagar who has fled from Sarai tells of her son Ishmael's destiny; obeying the angel, Hagar returns and gives birth to Ishmael; and Abram's age at the birth of Ishmael is given (Gen 16:1–16). There are two annunciation scenes regarding Sarah's giving birth to Isaac (Gen 17:15–22; 18:1–15) which befits other elements of the larger narrative: there are two depictions of Sarai's barrenness (Gen 11:29; 16:1); the birth report contains two divine aid formulations and two etiological speeches (Gen 21:1–7); and there are statements about both Abram's age at Isaac's birth (Gen 21:5) and of the lad growing (Gen 21:8a). The annunciation scene also sets a pattern concerning the importance of the promise going through the right wife in Genesis. The prayer element occurs when Abram intercedes on behalf of the barren women in Gen 20, the barren women including his own wife Sarah.

In Gen 25:19–28, the narrator portrays Isaac's love for Rebekah by telling us of his entreaty to YHWH on her behalf before we even know that she is barren. Rebekah has a difficult pregnancy and inquires why (see oracular inquiry narrative), and receives the annunciation that two nations are in her womb, with the elder predestined to serve the younger. The birth reports reveal characteristics of Esau and Jacob that will play a role in the later cycle, and both Isaac's age and a statement that the boys grew up conclude the narrative.

In Judg 13:2–24, Manoah's wife is barren and the lack of prayer parallels Israel's failure to cry out to God in that particular judges cycle. Twice an angel appears to Manoah's wife and the annunciation includes that Samson would only begin to deliver Israel from the Philistines. The birth report is brief but the concluding statement anticipates the way YHWH would use Samson in the coming cycle. In 1 Sam 1:1–2:21,

Hannah's barrenness is expounded in moving detail, Hannah herself not only prays for God to heal her but vows to dedicate her son as a Nazirite (see vow narrative), and Eli asks that her petition be granted, and Hannah gives birth to Samuel. Hannah keeps her vow, and eventually is rewarded with three further sons and two daughters; only then do we read of Samuel growing up. In 2 Kgs 4:8–17, Elisha hears that a Shunammite woman who has helped him is barren, and he announces to her that she will have a son at the same time the following year (recalling the same motif regarding Sarah). The birth report is comparatively brief.

The term "annunciation" is taken from New Testament iconography and many aspects of the same pattern can be found in Matthew 1:18–25 and especially in the interlocking annunciation narratives concerning John the Baptist and Jesus in Luke 1–2.

Alter, "Convention," 115–30; Ashmon, *Birth Annunciations*; Brenner, "Female Social Behavior," 257–73; Brown, *Birth of Messiah*; Finlay, *Birth Report Genre*, 85–161; Grohmann, *Fruchtbarkeit und Geburt*; Neff, *Announcement*; Parker, *Pre-Biblical Narrative Tradition*, 104–6; Schneider, *Sarah*, 8–23, 56–74, 90–93.

Anti-Hero Cycle

An anti-hero cycle is a series of episodes concerning a villain. The Balaam Cycle has seven episodes (Num 22:7–14, 15–20, 21–40a; 22:40b–23:12; 23:13–24; 23:25–24:9; 24:10–25) and is an ironic **blessing narrative** in which the anti-hero, Balaam, has been hired by Balak of Moab to curse the Israelites, but is instead used by YHWH to bless them. For the prophetic oracles contained within this cycle, see **Balaamite Psalm** in the chapter on Psalms.

The Abimelech Cycle has four episodes (Judg 9:1–6, 7–21, 22–49, 50–57) and concerns a son of Gideon (from the tribe of Manasseh) who murders seventy of his half-brothers to become in effect the king of Greater Shechem and ends up known as the man who died when a woman threw a millstone on his head (Judg 9:50–57; 2 Sam 11:21). The **epilogue** in Judges begins with an anti-hero cycle involving Micah and Jonathan that has three episodes (Judg 17:1–6, 7–13; 18:1–31) involving an Ephraimite who makes his own shrine and idols, hires his own priests, and portrays the Danites negatively also. In the context of Judges, these anti-hero episodes serve to disqualify the tribes of Manasseh, Ephraim and Dan from monarchic leadership.

Hull, "Finding the Center," 145–58; Moore, *Balaam Traditions*; Mueller, *Micah Story*; Sasson, "Book," 283–309.

Apology for Hero/Leader

There are three main elements: 1) the ruler tries to murder the hero (Exod 1:22; 1 Sam 18:10–16; 19:9–11; 2 Kgs 11:1; Est 3:8–15); 2) someone within the royal household saves the hero (Exod 2:5–10; 1 Sam 19:12–17; 2 Kgs 11:2; Est 7:1–6); and 3) the hero replaces the ruler (who dies violently) as the leader of the people (Exod 5–14; 2 Sam 5:1–5; 2 Kgs 11:13–21; Est 7:7–10; 10:2–3). The purpose of the genre is to justify the accession of a hero (Moses, David, Joash, Mordecai) from any charges of regicide. Postmodern readers who employ the hermeneutics of suspicion interpret these passages diametrically opposite to readers who accept a reliable biblical narrator.

McCarter, "Apology of David," 489–504.

Apostasy Narrative

This narrates either a people or an individual turning away from God religiously, rather than merely acting badly (see **monarch behaving badly**). Apart from the examples of **apostasy formula** in a **judges cycle**, most examples occur within **regnal narratives**. Many of these occur in the book of Kings: Solomon's apostasy (1 Kgs 11:1–13) is followed by Jereboam's revolt and the division of the kingdom; Jeroboam himself commits apostasy (1 Kgs 14:22–24) and Ahijah announces the end of his dynasty in a **prophetic dismissal narrative**; 2 Kgs 16:2–4, 10–18 [= 2 Chr 28:1b–4, 22–25] concerns the apostasy of Ahaz; 2 Kgs 21:2–16 [=2 Chr 33:2–10] concerns the apostasy of Manasseh which Kings presents as the point at which Judah was irrevocably doomed to exile; and 2 Kgs 21:20–22 [= 2 Chr 33:22–23] concerns the apostasy of Amon. Others occur, at least in detail, just in Chronicles: the apostasy of Joash (2 Chr 24:17–22); the apostasy of Amaziah (2 Chr 25:14–16); and the apostasy of Uzziah (2 Chr 26:16–21). The narratives serve to justify the divine punishment upon individual leaders and upon the nations of Israel and Judah described in the histories.

Gileadi, *Israel's Apostasy*; Halpern, "Manasseh Blamed," 473–514.

Apostolic Prophecy Narrative

These are a subcategory of **divine command narratives** with two basic parts: 1) YHWH sends/commissions the prophet to go and prophesy to a person or people; and 2) the prophet complies (Exod 6:1–9, 10–13; 7:1–7; 1 Sam 2:27–36; 2 Sam 7:1–17; 12:1–15a; 1 Kgs 13:1–6; 14:1–18; 16:1–4, 7; 2 Kgs 1:3–4, 15–16; 2 Chr 15:1–7; 16:7–10). Israel and Mari were the two main places in the ancient world evidencing apostolic prophecy. By contrast, see **oracular prophecy narrative** and **revelatory prophecy narrative**. Examples in the latter prophets are discussed in the **prophetic genres** chapter. The examples in Exodus 6 and 7 concern prophesies of salvation for Israel and 2 Chr 15 contains a conditional prophecy of salvation for Judah. There are prophesies of punishment in 1 Sam 2, 2 Sam 12, 1 Kgs 13, 14, 16, 2 Kgs 1 and 2 Chr 16. Nathan's prophecy in 2 Sam 7 is part of a covenant establishment narrative and promises David a dynasty.

Appointment/Ordination Narrative

There are numerous narratives in which a king or leader appoints a person or group of people to a particular position. On some occasions, the emphasis of the larger narrative is upon the appointees (who sometimes fail and sometimes succeed) and on others it is upon the leaders who appointed them. Elements can include a **command subunit** or a **divine command section** to appoint or ordain the party, the names and attributes of the people chosen, a **compliance subunit** or an **exercitive speech section** effecting the ordination, and a statement of success or failure by the party ordained (Gen 41:37–46; Exod 35:30–35; Lev 8:1–9:24; 10:4–7; Num 13:1–16; 18:1–7; 25:10–13; 27:12–13; 34:16–29; Deut 4:41–43; 31:14–23; Judg 17:7–13; 1 Sam 16:14–23; 1 Kgs 1:1–4; 2:35; Est 2:1–20; Dan 1:1–7, 17–21; 6:1–4 [NRSV 5:31—6:3]; Ezra 8:24–30; 1 Chr 24:1–6; 2 Chr 19:4–11). These narratives primarily serve to further the plot by describing a significant event in the life of the person ordained.

Fleming, "Biblical Tradition," 401–14; Niditch and Doran, "Success Story," 179–93.

Assassination Narrative

These narratives range, in the biblical narrator's perspective, from a hero assassinating a villain (Judg 3:18–25; 4:16–21), through one villain/rival eliminating another (2 Sam 3:22–39; 4:1–8; 13:23–29; 20:4–10; 2 Kgs 8:13–15), to a villain assassinating a hero (Jer 40:7—41:8), and even a failed assassination thwarted by a hero (Est 2:21–23).

Means include surprise frontal stabbing (Judg 3:18–25; 2 Sam 3:22–39; 20:4–10), putting to sleep and smashing a tent-peg through the skull (Judg 4:16–21), using two people to kill someone lying on a bed (2 Sam 4:1–8), ordering minions to kill a drunk half-brother (2 Sam 13:23–29), and suffocating the victim in his sleep (2 Kgs 8:13–15). Some narratives show the resourcefulness of the hero eliminating an enemy leader (Ehud killing Eglon, Jael killing Sisera), others depict vengeance (Joab and Abishai killing Abner and avenging their brother Asahel in 2 Sam 3:22–39; Absalom killing Amnon and avenging his sister Tamar in 2 Sam 13:23–29; see **rape narrative**; this partially fulfills Nathan's prophecy in 2 Sam 12:10 also), others portray David as innocent of several deaths which advantage him (2 Sam 4:1–8; 20:4–10; and possibly 3:22–39; see **apology for hero narrative**).

Several incidents in which one Israelite king is killed in a conspiracy involving his successor (2 Kgs 15:10, 14, 25, 30) exemplify the chaos of the northern kingdom shortly before the exile. And Ishmael's assassination of Gedaliah in Jeremiah 41 tragically ends hope of Judah's recovery after the Babylonian conquest. See also **opportunity for regicide narrative** for two passages in which David refuses to assassinate Saul.

Alter, *Art of Biblical Narrative*, 43–47; Birnbaum, "Political Assassination," 191–99; Campbell, *2 Samuel*, 30–52, 125–37, 167–72; Chisholm, "Ehud," 274–82; Frolov, *Judges*, 105–54; Ritzema, "After Zedekiah," 73–91; Sternberg, *Poetics*, 264–83; Yee, "Hand of Woman," 99–132.

Banquet Narrative

In these narratives, the banquet typically provides a setting for an ominous event or action. In Gen 21:8–13, at Abraham's banquet for the weaning of Isaac, Ishmael "sports" with Isaac, perhaps sexually. This leads to Sarah demanding the expulsion of Hagar and Ishmael (see **separation narrative**). In Gen 29:22–27, Laban gives Jacob a good marriage feast before switching Leah for Rachel as Jacob's bride. In Pharaoh's banquet

(Gen 40:20–23), Pharaoh restores the butler to his former position but hangs the baker as Joseph had foretold in the immediately preceding **dream narrative** (Gen 40:1–19). Genesis 43:15–34 is less ominous but builds tension by highlighting Joseph's knowledge at the expense of his nervous brothers.

The seven-day banquet at Samson's marriage to a Philistine woman (Judg 14:10–18) ends with Samson killing thirty Philistines (Judg 14:19; **heroic exploit narrative**). Nabal holds a banquet, gets very drunk, and dies about ten days later (1 Sam 25:36–37), allowing David to marry Nabal's widow, Abigail. It is likely at a banquet that Absalom deliberately gets Amnon drunk before having his men kill him (2 Sam 13:23–33; **assassination narrative**). Belshazzar's banquet (Dan 5:1–4) is the setting of the infamous "hand-writing on the wall," which in the following **wisdom narrative** signals Belshazzar's doom. Belshazzar is duly slain that night.

Banquets play a major role in Esther, which is referred to as "The Megillah" (festival scroll) and which Jews read at Purim with much merriment and with permission to drink more than usual. Esther opens with a banquet in which Vashti refuses to be paraded before King Ahaseurus "in her crown" (Est 1:1–12) and this leads to Vashti's banishment (Est 1:13–22; **sentencing narrative**). There are other banquets (Est 2:18–20; 5:1–8; 7:1–9), at the last of which Esther reveals Haman's plans against the Jews, and King Ahaseurus orders that Haman be hanged on his own gallows (**sentencing narrative**). The pattern continues in the New Testament with John the Baptist getting executed because of what happened at Herod's banquet.

Altmann, *Festive Meals*; Gordis, "Studies in Esther," 43–58; Pracht, "Tragic Death," 241–56.

Battle Narrative

The history of most nations is replete with military conflicts and Israel is no different. Scholars sometimes distinguish battles in which Israel/Judah invokes YHWH's help (or in which YHWH has commanded them to go to war) from regular battles. In the first category, known as holy war, phrases such as "YHWH's army" or "YHWH's enemy" may appear, and elements can include blowing a trumpet, sanctification of the army, consulting YHWH, offering a sacrifice, YHWH promising victory, YHWH indicating who leads the battle or giving other instructions, etc. But many battle narratives do not fit into the category of holy war. Some battle narratives are **notice** or **report** level brief mentions, but longer ones tend to include things such as the cause of the conflict (perhaps in an **introductory subunit**), and **preparations subunits** and **summary subunits** occur more frequently here than in most other narratives.

Battle narratives in the Torah include Gen 14:1–16; Exod 17:8–16; Num 21:21–31, 31–35; and 31:1–40. For the battles in Josh 6:15–27; 7:2–5; 8:3–29; 10:1–27; 11:1–11; and Judg 1:1–8, 9–13, see **campaign to conquer Canaan narrative**. Within the rest of Judges, there are battles against the Moabites (Judg 3:26–30), the Canaanites (Judg 4:12–15), the Midianites (Judg 7:15–25), as well as battles in two civil war narratives (Judg 9:22–49; 11:29–33). There are many battle narratives in the books of Samuel, Kings, and Chronicles (1 Sam 4:1b–11; 11:27b—12:11; 13:15b—14:23; 31:1–3; 2 Sam 2:12–32; 5:17–25 [=1 Chr 14:10–17]; 10:1–19 [=1 Chr 19:1–19]; 12:26–31 [=1 Chr 20:1–3]; 17:24–18:18; 1 Kgs 12:21–24 [=2 Chr 11:1–4]; 15:16–22 [=2 Chr 16:1–6]; 16:11–19; 2 Kgs 3:4–27; 8:28–29 [=2 Chr 22:5–6]; 13:3–7; 14:7 [=2 Chr 25:5–13]; 14:8–14 [=2 Chr 25:17–24]; 16:5–6 [=2 Chr 28:5–15]; 20:22–34; 22:29–38 [=2 Chr 18:28–34]; 2 Chr 13:2–20; 14:9–15; 22:22–30; 24:22–23; 26:6–8). Esther 9:1–19 records the Jews successfully defending themselves from Haman's attempt to exterminate them.

See also **civil war narrative, heroic exploits narrative**, and **siege narrative**.

Craigie, *Problem of War*; Hobbs, *Time for War*; Niditch, *War*; von Rad, *Holy War*; Stern, *Biblical Ḥerem*.

Birth Narrative

A short birth narrative contains an introductory setting (with one or more of the following elements: acquisition of wife; divine action to overcome barrenness; and intercourse) and birth report proper (with typically four elements: conception; birth; naming; and etymology). In most cases, either the biological mother or the adopting mother gives a speech naming the child unless God has given a pre-word of the child's name. Another frequent pattern is an introductory setting followed by a series of birth reports proper by the same mother.

These birth reports contribute greatly to the larger narratives in which they are set. See especially **annunciation narrative** for the births of Ishmael, Isaac, Esau and Jacob, Samson, Samuel, and the son born to the Shunammite woman (and John the Baptist and Jesus in the New Testament). See **genealogical narrative** for the births of Jacob's first eleven children. See the entry on **prophetic symbolic action narratives** in the chapter on prophetic genres for the births of Maher Shalal Hash Baz, Jezreel, Lo-Ruhama, and Lo-Ammi. See **birth notice in a genealogy** for the abbreviated form of the genre set within a genealogical list.

Some of the remaining birth narratives concern tribal identities. Lot's daughters get their father drunk and mate with him, which results in the births of Moab and Ben Ammi (Gen 19:30–38). The repeated phrase "he is the ancestor of the Moabites/Ammonites to this day" (Gen 19:37, 38), an ill omen for relations between Israel and these nations. The series of birth reports concerning Judah's sons Er, Onan, and Shelah (Gen 38:3, 4, 5) are followed by YHWH slaying Er and Onan. The plot culminates not with Shelah having children but by Judah having two more children through Tamar, Perez and Zerah (Gen 38:27–30), in a manner that clearly makes out Perez as the more significant figure. These very different lines are brought together in the book of Ruth where Boaz the descendant of Perez marries Ruth the descendant of Moab (Ruth 4). Their son, Obed, becomes an ancestor of David.

The story of Moses' birth (Exod 2:1–10) does have parallels with the Sargon Legend, in which the mother puts the baby boy into a carefully constructed ark sealed with bitumen. However, Sargon's mother tried to get rid of him as soon as she could while Moses' mother keeps him as long as possible, and ironically is paid to wet nurse him later by the adopting mother. Further, Moses eventually identifies with his own people rather than those who adopt him. Exodus 1 and 2 highlights the role of female heroes beginning with the midwives Shiphrah and Puah. Moses' birth story fits perfectly into this setting, with Moses's mother, sister, and his adopting mother (Pharaoh's daughter, who is the subject of the naming and etiological elements) defying Pharaoh's commands. The birth of Moses' own son (Exod 2:22) is almost an addendum to the **marriage narrative** of Moses and Zipporah.

Bathsheba is the only woman in the Bible to say "I am pregnant" (2 Sam 11:5), and it is an unwanted pregnancy which drives the narrative arc: Uriah, Bathsheba's husband, does not cover up the affair, David has Uriah eliminated in battle, David marries Bathsheba and she bears their son. The circumstances of their second son's birth (2 Sam 12:24–25) are very different and this son's two names (Solomon and Jedidiah) contrast with no name being mentioned for their first son.

Finally, two brief but poignant narratives portray women dying while giving birth to a son: Rachel names her second son "Benoni" ("son of my sorrow") but Jacob renames him "Benjamin" (Gen 35:18). And when the wife of Phinehas hears that her husband has died and the ark captured, she dies naming her son Ichabod (1 Sam 4:19–22), a fitting name for the glory departing Israel.

Ashmon, *Birth Annunciations*; Brenner, "Female Social Behaviour," 257–73; Fewell and Gunn, "Son Is Born," 99–108; Finlay, *Birth Report*; Grohmann, *Fruchtbarkeit und Geburt*; Prewitt, "Kinship Structures," 87–98.

Birth Notice in a Genealogy

This is an extremely abbreviated form of birth narrative, which has the standard formulation of "And PN1 bore PN2," where PN1 is the mother and PN2 is the child. Most genealogical lists are not interested in the mother who bore the child, so when birth notices do occur it is usually for one of the following reasons: a man has children by more than one wife (Gen 4:19–22; 36:2–5; 1 Chr 2:2–4, 18–24; 4:5–7; 2 Chr 11:18–20); in addition to his more legitimate children, a man has children by a concubine (Gen 22:24; 36:12; 1 Chr 1:32; 1 Chr 2:46–49; 7:14); a sister of a male descendant bears important children of her own (1 Chr 2:16–17; 7:14–19); a daughter carries on the inheritance of a man with no sons (1 Chr 2:34–35); or to give information about the mother of an important figure (Gen 41:50–52; 46:19–22; Exod 6:16–25).

There are also fuller birth reports than mere notices in the Gen 4 genealogy concerning Cain and Abel (vv. 1–2), Enoch (v. 17), and Seth (v. 25); as well as of Beriah (1 Chr 7:23); see also the **genealogical narrative** in Gen 29:30–30:24.

Finlay, *Birth Report*, 43–84; Kartveit, *Motive*; Prewitt, "Kinship Structures," 87–98.

Blessing Narrative

This is a narrative where a **blessing subunit** is significant. In Gen 14:17–24, Melchizedek blesses Abram—a significant passage in Christianity because of the Christology in Hebrews 5:5–7:28 which comments at length on this passage and on the only other reference to Melchizedek in Psalm 110:4. The Dead Sea Scroll, 11QMelchizedek, shows the interest of the Qumran community in this enigmatic figure.

In Gen 27:1–40, Rebekah instructs Jacob on how to displace his older brother Esau and obtain the blessing from Isaac. Jacob pretends to be Esau and his blind father Isaac is eventually convinced to bless him, upon which Esau returns and is devastated to find that Jacob has stolen his blessing. This episode fits the *toledot* section concerning Jacob in many ways: it fulfills the **oracular inquiry** in which Rebekah is told that the younger brother will supplant the older brother (Gen 25:23), it illustrates Jacob's "heel-grabbing" nature reflected in the etiological element of his **birth narrative** (Gen 25:26), it illustrates Rebekah's preference for Jacob and Isaac's preference for Esau (Gen 25:28), it is fitting in that Esau had despised his birthright by selling it to Jacob for a bowl of red pottage (Gen 25:29–34), it motivates Esau's desire to kill Jacob which results in Jacob's flight to Paddan Aram (Gen 27:41–45), and Jacob himself will be deceived via a sibling switch by his uncle Laban (Gen 29:21–25).

In Gen 27:46, the sagacious Rebekah uses the fact that Esau has married Canaanite wives to persuade Isaac to send Jacob to Aram to find a wife. In the **commission to find wife narrative** (Gen 28:1–5), Isaac pronounces a blessing upon Jacob. In Gen 48:1–22, Jacob blesses and adopts Joseph's sons Manasseh and Ephraim, but gives the greater blessing to the younger son Ephraim, continuing a theme in Genesis that the younger son supplants the elder. This theme continues in the blessings upon Jacob's sons (Gen 49:1–28) which is a **testament narrative**. Reuben the firstborn has lost his pre-eminence (vv. 3–4) and instead Judah (vv. 8–12) and Joseph (vv. 22–26) receive the greater blessings.

Similarly to Jacob, Moses pronounces blessings on the tribes of Israel in a **testament narrative** (Deut 33:1–29) that immediately precedes his **death and burial narrative**. The Balaam **anti-hero cycle** is also a blessing narrative in which Balaam, against his desire to be rewarded by Balak for cursing Israel, is forced by YHWH to pronounce blessings on Israel (Num 22:2–24:25). Related to the blessing narrative genre is the **blessing subunit** of a psalm and the famous instructions on how to bless, the priestly benediction (Num 6:24–26).

Mitchell, *Meaning of BRK*; Steymans, "Blessings," 71–89.

Boundary List Narrative

The second half of Joshua concerns the apportionment of the land to the various tribes and thus contains several **boundary lists** within a narrative framework (Josh 13:8–14, 15–23, 24–28, 29–33; 16:1–10; 17:1–18; 18:1–19:51).

Hess, "Book of Joshua," 493–506.

Building Restoration Narrative

Related to construction narrative, this genre focuses on repair/restoration activities rather than initial building. In 2 Kgs 12:5–17 [NRSV 4–16] and 2 Chr 24:4–14, Jehoash does restoration work on the temple; as does Hezekiah later (2 Chr 29:3–19). Manasseh, after his repentance, also repairs the temple (2 Chr 33:14–16). The account in Kings does not record Manasseh's repentance nor his repair of the temple and it is Manasseh's wickedness that is the reason for the exile in the Deuteronomistic History, so the treatment of Manasseh's reign is one of the major differences between the books of Kings and Chronicles. The temple restoration of Josiah (2 Kgs 22:3–7 [=2 Chr 34:8–13]) is just the first part of a larger covenant renewal movement in his reign. Haggai, Zechariah, and Ezra-Nehemiah narrate the building/restoration of the Second Temple (Ezra 5:1–5). The participants list in Neh 3:1–32 concerns those participating in restoration of the Second Temple, and this work continues in Neh 4:1–23.

Cogan, "Raising the Walls," 84–95; Na'aman, "Temple Restorations," 640–51.

Campaign to Conquer Canaan Narrative

The conquest of Canaan in Joshua partially completes a story arc begun with the divine promises to Abraham in Gen 12, leading to the term Hexateuch for the books of Genesis through Joshua. The narratives concerning the conquest of different portions of the land vary considerably. The scouting narrative in Josh 2 functions as a preparation narrative for the conquest but the campaigns proper begin in Josh 6 with Jericho as the first target. This campaign involves marching around the city once a day for six days, then seven times on the seventh day, after which the priests blow seven trumpets and YHWH causes the walls of Jericho to fall down

(Josh 6:15–27). There is a strange NT parallel in Revelation in that there are seven seals, and the seventh seal consists of seven trumpet blasts, and after the blast of the seventh trumpet, seven bowls of wrath are poured out, culminating in the sudden fall of the archetypal city of opposition, Babylon (Rev 6:1–17; 11:15–19; 16:1–19).

The campaign against Ai and Bethel (Josh 7:2–5; 8:3–29) is interrupted by dealing with the sin of Achan (see **execution narrative**), and Joshua's military strategy is discussed in some detail. The battle at Gibeon against a coalition of Canaanite kings that had attacked the Gibeonites (now Israel's vassals) includes the famous "sun standing still" incident (Josh 10:1–27).

In Judg 1, the successful campaigns of Judah (Judg 1:1–8, 9–13, 17–20) and the house of Joseph (Judg 1:22–26) are contrasted to the failures of the other tribes (see **failure to conquer narratives**). Given that the failures (Judg 1:27–36) include both Manasseh and Ephraim, it rather undermines the success of the house of Joseph in Judg 1:22–26 and thus argues that eventual kingship should come from Judah.

There are huge debates about archeological/chronological issues concerning the cities mentioned above, the manner of the occupation (conquest, peaceful infiltration, peasant revolt etc.), and ethical issues regarding the "Canaanite genocide."

Aharoni, *Land of Bible*, 184–227; Albertz, *Israelite Religion*, 1:67–78; Bright, *History of Israel*, 127–39; Copan and Flannagan, *Command Genocide?*; Finkelstein and Silberman, *Bible Unearthed*, 72–96; Jagersma, *History*, 59–75; Kaiser, *History*, 129–172; Kelle and Ames, *Writing*; Moore and Kelle, *Biblical History*, 77–144; Provan, Long, and Longman, *Biblical History*, 190–258; Rainey and Notley, *Carta Bible Atlas*, 41–48; Younger, *Ancient Conquest Accounts*.

Circumcision Narrative

There is no set pattern to the narratives in which a person or group of people are circumcised. Gen 17:23–27 follows a **covenant narrative** (Gen 17:1–22) in which God the males in Abraham's household to be circumcised; thus, the narrative functions as a **compliance narrative**, highlighting Abraham's obedience. The circumcising of Isaac in Gen 21:4 is the only example of circumcision in a **birth narrative** and, remarkably, the only actual example of circumcision on the eighth day in the Hebrew

Bible; thus, it serves as one of several features in the larger annunciation narrative to establish Isaac rather than Ishmael as the Torah-observant son (Lev 12:3). In Luke 1–2, the annunciation narratives of John the Baptist and Jesus both include circumcision narratives (Luke 1:59–80; 2:21).

The circumcision of Hamor and the Shechemites (Gen 34:13–24) is set in a **rape narrative** (Gen 34) and serves as a means by which Simeon and Levi murder them to enact their revenge for the rape of their sister, Dinah (similarly, Absalom avenges the rape of his sister, Tamar. by killing her rapist in 2 Sam 13; see assassination narrative). The circumcision by Zipporah of Moses's son in Exod 4:24–26 by contrast is a means to life in the rescue element of a **crisis narrative**. Finally, the mass circumcision in Josh 5:1–9 precedes the observance of the Passover at Gilgal (Josh 5:10–12; see **festival observance narrative**) in accordance with the Passover instruction in Exodus 12, thus functioning as a **preparation narrative**.

Fox, "Sign of Covenant," 557–96; Goldingay, "Significance," 3–18; Propp, "Bloody Bridegroom," 495–518; Winslow, *Early Jewish*.

Civil War Narrative

While most battle narratives oppose Israel/Judah against another nation, several involve civil war. The full pattern contains three elements: the grievances which occasioned the war; the war itself (or its avoidance thereof); and the aftermath. Gideon prudently avoids a civil war with Ephraimites upset by not being part of his force by praising their accomplishment (Judg 8:1–3), but rash Jephthah exercises no such restraint and engages in a bloody civil war with Ephraim, which Ephraim loses (Judg 12:1–7). The downward spiral in Judges culminates in the civil war between the tribe of Benjamin and the rest of Israel in which Benjamin is almost annihilated (Judg 19–21). This ignominious section begins and ends with rape narratives (Judg 19:1–30; 21:1–25), with the central section comprising a failed **negotiations narrative** (Judg 20:1–13) and three **battle narratives** (Judg 20:14–21, 22–25, 26–48).

David initially reigned only over Judah and had to win a civil war with Saul's son, Ishbosheth, for rule of all Israel (2 Sam 2:1—5:5). David later had to fight a civil war against Absalom (2 Sam 15–18), whose putative grievances are listed in 2 Sam 15:1–6 but who is unwittingly fulfilling Nathan's pre-Word in 2 Sam 12:10–12. The aftermath includes David's grief, "O my son Absalom, my son, my son Absalom! Would I had died instead of you, O Absalom, my son, my son!" (2 Sam 18:33).

Campbell, *2 Samuel*, 30–52, 138–66; Eversmann, "Gottesbefragung und Bruderkrieg," 17–30; Frolov, *Judges*, 203–29, 301–29; Mann, *Run, David Run!*; Trible, *Texts of Terror*, 65–91.

Combat Narrative

In contrast to **battle narrative**, this genre primarily concerns not armies but individuals in combat to the death (1 Sam 17:8–58; 2 Sam 2:12–16, 19–23). Examples may portray a character's virtue (David's courage and faith) or vice (Joab's bloodthirsty nature).

Vaux, "Single Combat," 122–35.

Commission to Get Wife Narrative

Abraham commands his servant to find a wife for Isaac (Gen 24:1–9) and Isaac commands Jacob to find a wife for himself (Gen 27:41—28:5). These preludes to **marriage narratives** provide the reason for travel to the foreign country (other cases involve the protagonist fleeing trouble, such as Moses in Exodus 2:11–15a and Jacob's other motivation in Gen 27:41–45, or accompanying somebody else, such as Ruth in Ruth 1). See also **journey narrative**.

Martin, "Betrothal Journey Narratives," 505–23.

Compliance Narrative

A standard element of the **divine command narrative** is the compliance subunit, which often consists of the simple **instructions executed formula**. The genre of compliance narrative is reserved for lengthier accounts recording the protagonist's actions according to God's instructions (whether or not obedience is made explicit). These narratives illustrate divine sovereignty and commend the obedient protagonists (Noah, Abraham, Jacob, Moses, Joshua) as worth emulating. (Gen 7:5–9; 12:4–9; 17:23–27; 22:3–10; 35:2–4; Exod 12:21–28, 40; Num 1:17–20, 54; 2:32–34; 3:16–39, 42–43, 49–51; 4:34–49; 5:4; 7:1–89 [see also **offering/sacrifice narrative**], 17:6–13; 26:3–51; 34:13–15; Josh 1:10–18; 6:6–21; 7:16–26; 8:3–17, 18b; 20:7–9).

Concluding Regnal Resumé

This is the part of the regnal resumé that occurs at the end of a **regnal narrative.** It typically consists of a **citation formula**, a **death and burial of king formula**, and a **succession formula.** Some regnal narratives omit the concluding resumé.

Halpern and Vanderhooft, "Editions of Kings," 179–244; Provan, *Hezekiah and Kings*; Sweeney, *King Josiah*.

Confrontation Narrative

These are narratives in which a servant of YHWH confronts an ideologically opposed authority. Many of these narratives contain **opposition subunits** and **prophecies of punishment**. We see Moses against Pharaoh (Exod 5–14; see **sign narratives**); Elijah against the prophets of Baal (1 Kgs 18:17–40; **prophetic miracle narrative**); an unnamed prophet against Ahab (1 Kgs 20:35–43; **prophecy of punishment against individual**); Isaiah against Ahaz (Isa 7:1–25; **prophetic symbolic action narrative**, **prophecy of sign**); Amos against Amaziah (Amos 7:10–17; **vocation narrative**; **written document narrative**); and Jonah, eventually, against Nineveh (Jonah 3; **fast narrative**). Nehemiah against Eliashib, the Sabbath breakers, and Jews who married foreign wives (Neh 13:4–13, 15–22a, 23–31a) has a different power dynamic. Many of the opposing authorities either come to a sticky end or are prophesied to do so, but others repent (1 Kgs 21:17–29; 2 Chr 25:5–10; Jonah 3:3–10; see **call to repentance** in prophetic speech chapter). See prophetic narratives chapter for further examples.

Bronner, *Stories*; Hoffmeier, "Arm of God," 378–87; Irvine, *Isaiah, Ahaz*; Sweeney, *Isaiah 1–39*, 143–64.

Construction Narrative

This narrates the building or manufacture of official/cult edifices or objects. There are frequent mentions of materials, dimensions, and decorations. Exodus 35:30—39:43 corresponds to the lengthy **tabernacle instructions narrative** (Exod 25:10—31:18), detailing how the work was carried out: authorization of Bezalel and Aholiab (Exod 35:30—36:1); freewill offering to pay for the construction (Exod 36:2–7); construction of the tabernacle (Exod 36:8–38); construction of the ark of the covenant (Exod 37:1–9); construction of the table for the showbread (Exod 37:10–16); construction of the gold lampstand (Exod 37:17–24); construction of the altar of incense along with the oil and incense (Exod 37:25–29); construction of the altar of burnt offering (Exod 38:1–7); construction of the bronze laver (Exod 38:8); construction of the court of the tabernacle (Exod 38:9–20); inventory of the tabernacle (Exod 38:21—39:1); construction of the ephod (Exod 39:2–7); construction of the breastplate (Exod 39:8–21); construction of the other priestly garments (Exod 39:22–31); bringing the completed work to Moses for inspection (39:32–43).

The main narrative of Solomon's temple construction (1 Kgs 5:27—7:51 [NRSV 5:13—7:51=2 Chr 3:1—4:22]) discusses first the dimensions of the main structures, and then describes the furnishings. There are also narratives discussing Solomon's fortifications (1 Kgs 9:15–28 [=2 Chr 8:1–11]), Rehoboam's fortifications (2 Chr 11:5–12), Asa's fortifications (2 Chr 14:6–8), Omri's building project of his new capital Samaria (1 Kgs 16:24), Uzziah's fortifications (2 Chr 26:9–15) and Jotham's building of the upper gate of the temple (2 Kgs 15:35 [=2 Chr 27:3–4]).

The rebuilding of Jerusalem and the temple is also a major theme in Ezra-Nehemiah and considerable attention is paid to which group of artisans did each task (Neh 3:1–32; 6:15–7:4). There is a certain continuity in many of these construction narratives: the building of the tabernacle was done according to the detailed instructions previously given, Solomon's temple was patterned after the tabernacle, and the second temple was patterned after Solomon's temple. Many of the Judean kings follow their predecessors in making military preparations by fortifying certain cities. At another level, the narratives naming and emphasizing the artisans have served as an inspiration to other artisans down through the centuries that their work also has significance to God.

Assis, "Build," 514–27; Cross, "Priestly Tabernacle," 84–95; Floyd, *Minor Prophets* 2, 266–77; Hendrix, "Structural Overview," 123–38; Kitchen, "Tabernacle," 119–29; Long, *1 Kings*, 76–93, 247; Morgenstern, "Ark, Ephod," 153–265.

Coronation Narrative

On three occasions, Saul is designated, anointed, or proclaimed king (1 Sam 9:1—10:16; 10:17–27; 11:12–15), interspersed with speeches by

Samuel denouncing the institution of monarchy, raising the possibility of a **composite narrative**. Three episodes involving David's coronation have a plausible development: David is privately anointed king by Samuel while Saul still reigns (1 Sam 16:1–13); after Saul's death, David is acclaimed king by Judah, while the rest of Israel support Ishbaal (2 Sam 2:1–4a, 8–11); after Ishbaal's death, David is recognized as king by all Israel (2 Sam 5:1–5 [=1 Chr 11:1–3]). The coronation of Solomon (1 Kgs 1:32–53 [=1 Chr 29:20–25]) takes place while Adonijah is claiming the throne and the only other coronation narrated is that of Jehu (2 Kgs 9:1–13) who, with prophetic backing from Elisha, overthrows the entire Omride dynasty. This suggests that the **perlocutionary intent** of coronation narratives is to legitimize the reign of the monarch at a time of turmoil.

Campbell, *Prophets and Kings*; Campbell, *1 Samuel*, 85–133, 161–65; Campbell, *2 Samuel*, 15–29, 53–63; de Vries, *1 and 2 Chronicles*, 117–26; Long, *1 Kings*, 33–43; Moore, "Jehu's Coronation," 97–114.

Couple's Dispute Narrative

These narratives highlight emotional disputes between husband and wife: Abram and Sarai (Gen 16:5–6), Jacob and Rachel (Gen 30:1–3), Samson and his wife (Judg 14:16–17), Samson and Delilah (Judg 16:6–17), David and Michal (2 Sam 6:20–23). Most contribute as much or more to characterization than to plot development and show the heroes as flawed.

Alter, *Art of Biblical Narrative*, 143–58; Bal, *Lethal Love*; Clines and Eshkanazi, *Queen Michal's Story*; Greenstein, "Riddle of Samson," 237–60; Schneider, *Sarah*, 46–53.

Court Narrative

This term is used for narratives about Joseph and Daniel (along with the Tale of Aḥiqar and many other folk tales) which have the following structure: someone of high status poses a difficult problem than none of the courtiers can solve (Gen 41:1–8; Dan 2:1–11; 4:1–7 [NRSV 4–10]; 5:1–9); a person of low status is brought before the court (Gen 41:9–14; Dan 2:12–16; 4:8–18 [NRSV 11–21]; 5:10–16) and solves the problem (Gen 41:15–36; Dan 2:17–45; 4:19–27 [NRSV 22–30]; 5:17–28); and the person of low status is rewarded (Gen 41:37–45; Dan 2:46–49; 5:29–31;

no parallel in Daniel 4). See also **dream interpretation narrative**. There is a slight inversion of the genre when an angel interprets a vision by the hero in Dan 7:15–27; 8:15–27, a theme that occurs outside the Hebrew Bible in certain apocalyptic literature.

Nebuchadnezzar's dream in Dan 2 has a parallel in the bookend of the Aramaic section of Daniel when Daniel's dream of four beasts is interpreted by an angel to mean four successive empires also (Dan 7:1–28). The traditional understanding of these empires is that they refer to the Babylonian, Persian (including Medes), Hellenistic, and Roman empires; but the current critical view is that they refer to the Assyrian-Babylonian, Medes, Persians, and Hellenistic (including Seleucid) Empires. The Dan 4 narrative has similarities to the historical experience of Nabonidus's ten-year desert sojourn in Tema. The Dead Sea Scroll "The Prayer of Nabonidus" (4Q242) describes Nabonidus as having been afflicted by God with madness for seven years in Teman and supports the hypothesis that Dan 4 reflects Nabonidus's experience. The scope of Daniel's dreams goes beyond that of Joseph to encompass world empires, which fits the genre of apocalyptic.

Collins, "Court-Tales in Daniel," 218–34; Collins, *Daniel*, 46–53, 59–70; Fewell, *Circle of Sovereignty*; Fidler, *Dreams*; Husser, *Dreams*; Niditch and Doran, "Success Story," 179–93; Patterson, "Joseph," 148–64; Wills, *Jew in Court*.

Covenant Affirmation/Renewal

Joshua is the model leader in terms of following Moses/Torah. He reinstitutes the Passover (Josh 5; see **festival observation narrative**), he builds an altar to offer sacrifices to YHWH (Josh 8:30–35, see **construction narrative**), and he renews the covenant (Josh 24:1–28) in an elaborate ceremony that has creedal resonances with Deut 6:20–25; 26:1–11. In Solomon's reign, we see the construction of the temple (which thereafter becomes the central sanctuary as designated in Deut 12), but we also see illegitimate high places cropping up. The reforming kings after Solomon need to tear down the high places as well as renew the covenant. We do see this with respect to Jehoash (2 Kgs 11:17–20 [=2 Chr 23:16–21]); and especially with regard to Hezekiah (2 Kgs 18:3–7 [=2 Chr 31:1–21]; 2 Chr 29:3–36) and Josiah (23:1–3 [=2 Chr 34:29–33] 2 Chr 15:1–16).

In the cases of both Hezekiah and Josiah, there are significant **festival observance narratives** also.

In Ezra–Nehemiah, we see the rebuilding of the temple, the observance of the Feast of Tabernacles, and finally a covenant renewal also (Neh 7:72—10:40).

Duggan, *Covenant Renewal*; Eynickel, *Reform of Josiah*; Hahn, "Covenant," 263–92; Lowery, *Reforming Kings*; Mendenhall, "Covenant Forms," 50–76; Provan, *Hezekiah and Kings*; von Rad, *Problem of Hexateuch*; Rendtorff, *Covenant Formula*; Sweeney, *King Josiah*.

Covenant Establishment Narrative

The Hebrew word ברית (*berith*) can mean a treaty between human beings (see **treaty narratives**), or it can refer to a covenant between YHWH and a human party. The latter contain various promises by YHWH and various obligations upon humans. The covenant after the flood with Noah, his family, and the animals contains laws considered incumbent upon all human beings (Gen 9:1–17; see Noahic **law code** in chapter on legal genres); Jewish tradition says that these laws were implicit in Eden. They form a core part of what Christians call natural law, that part of the eternal law which humans can know even without the special revelation in scripture, simply by using their rationality to consider what obligations follow from how things are—from the nature or essence of things. The Noachic laws provide for the establishment of law courts including the prerogative of execution for murderers, permission to eat meat, and prohibitions against murder, idolatry, blasphemy, various forbidden sexual unions, theft and eating from a living animal.

There are three covenant narratives involving YHWH and Abraham and Sarah (Gen 12:1–3; 15:1–21; 17:1–22 [see **circumcision narrative**]) and these involve primarily YHWH's promises concerning name, descendants, and land. (Interpretational cruxes in the Hebrew of Gen 12:1–3 include whether Abram is obligated to act in a blessing-worthy way, and whether the nations will be blessed, bless themselves, or, without specifying agency, find blessing through Abram). The tension between YHWH's promises of multiple descendants and the present reality of Sarai's womb drives the plot of the Abraham cycle, with Sarah's role becoming more prominent as the narrative progresses. YHWH reconfirms his covenant with Isaac (Gen 26:1–5) and Jacob (Gen 35:9–15), but it becomes increasingly obvious that having descendants by the right wife is very important (see **annunciation narrative** and **genealogical narrative**).

By Exodus, the Israelites are already numerous and Exodus through Josh largely concerns how YHWH will give them the land of Canaan and what Israelites must do to stay in the land. On Mt. Sinai, YHWH makes an initial covenant with Israel including the ten commandments/words (Exod 19–24; the Decalogue and Covenant Codes are the relevant **law codes**), and then reissues another after the golden calf episode (Exod 34:10–35; another distinct **law code**). The **journeying/sojourn division** of Torah covering the sojourn at Mt. Sinai (Exodus 19—Numbers 10) also contains the Holiness Law Code (Lev 17–26) and much of the Priestly Law Code. Also the entire book of Deuteronomy (but especially Deut 29:1—30:20) could be considered a covenant narrative. The laws of these covenants—including the law codes in Leviticus, Numbers and Deuteronomy—are discussed in the chapter on **legal genres**.

There is also a specific covenant with Phinehas because of his zeal (Num 25:10–18). The most important covenants outside the Torah would be the Davidic covenant and the new covenant. The Davidic covenant as first propounded through Nathan contains unconditional promises to David and his heirs (2 Sam 7:1–29 [=1 Chr 17:1–27]). In 1 Kgs 9:1–9 [=2 Chr 7:11–22], this covenant is extended conditionally to Solomon and his heirs, with Solomon later violating his side of the bargain with ruinous consequences. The end of the Kingdom of Judah, and thus Davidic rule, became the occasion for Psalm 89's bitter contention that YHWH has violated the Davidic covenant. Jeremiah, by contrast, arguably understands the covenant to promise that David never lack a descendant that could rule rather than continuous actual Davidic rulership (Jer 33:14–22). In the same **section of Jeremiah** (Jer 30–33), Jeremiah prophesies that there will be a new covenant (Jer 31:31–34, which in the book of Hebrews is the longest citation of any Hebrew scripture in the New Testament).

The issues here are immense. In addition to the major difference between Jews and Christians concerning the ongoing validity of the Sinai covenant, there are huge interpretative issues concerning the Noahic, Abrahamic, and Davidic covenants that affect Christology and Israelology, not to mention ethics.

Baden, "Morpho-Syntax," 223–37; Drunen, *Biblical Case*; Dumbrell, *Covenant and Creation*; Eichrodt, *Theology of the Old Testament*, 1:36–511; Levenson, "Davidic Covenant," 205–19; Levenson, *Sinai and Zion*;

Mendenhall, "Covenant Forms," 50–76; Nicholson, *God and People*; Niehaus, *God at Sinai*; Novak, *Natural Law*; Williamson, *Abraham, Israel.*

Creation Passage

The Hebrew Bible begins with its major creation narrative (Gen 1:1—2:3 or 2:4a), which after the first two verses is divided into seven sections concerning God's activity on that day (Gen 1:3–5, 6–8, 9–13, 14–19, 20–23, 24–31; 2:1–3). The first six days conclude with the **evening and morning formula** and the lack of this formula in the seventh day indicates a certain timeless quality to the Sabbath.

The first six days also typically have the following features: an **introductory speech formula**, an **exercitive** speech using a jussive construction that calls something into creation, either the **and it was so formula** or another construction demonstrating the efficacy of the divine speech, the **saw it was good formula**, and a naming element. Many of these features are absent in the seventh day. What distinguishes the divine exercitive speeches from that of human characters is that humans can only create social facts (such as marriages, coronations) through speech, but God can create material entities.

The seven part creation structure fits well with the importance in Mesopotamia of the number seven. The Egyptians may have associated the number nine with divine order; and this aspect is present in Gen 1:1—2:3 also because the third and sixth days each have two movements (two sets of divine exercitive speeches, **and it was so formulas** and **saw that it was good formulas**), leading to a total of nine movements in the narrative. Also, the first six-day exhibit something of a two-panel structure: the first and fourth days concern the celestial realm, the second and fifth days concern the sea and the air realms, and the third and sixth days concern the land realm.

Several factors point to the sixth day, and the creation of humans in particular, being a climax: God's deliberation before creating humans in Gen 1:26; the triple use of *bara'* ("to create,") in connection with humans; the poetic triplet in Gen 1:27, repeating that humans are created in the image of God; the blessing on them and an exercitive addressed to humans giving them dominion over living things on earth (Gen 1:28); and the evaluation of the sixth day as not just good but very good (Gen 1:30).

The seventh day also stands out and Gen 1:1—2:3 is partly a pre-Word for the **sabbath law**.

The much debated scholarly issues on this passage include the following: the translation of Gen 1:1 and its relationship to vv. 2–3 (the first *petuchah* or paragraph break in the Hebrew Bible is after v. 5); whether this passage demands a young earth interpretation; the date, authorship, and setting of the passage; whether "let us create" in Gen 1:27 is best understood as a plural of majesty, a pre-indication of the Trinity, God speaking to the angels, or mere self-counseling; and what attributes make humans rather than other animals "in the image of God?"

In addition to the prose account in Gen 1:1—2:3, numerous poetic passages portray creation. Psalm 8 is a **meditation** on the finitude of humans against the vastness of creation; Ps 19 combines the two books of revelation: natural revelation and revelation in Scripture; Ps 29 employs climactic parallelism on "ascribe to the Lord" and "the voice of the Lord" in relation to creation; and Ps 104 discusses the role of the Spirit in creation (Pss 65; 89:5–14; 90; and the **YHWH Kingship Psalms** also help us praise our Creator). In Wisdom Literature, the **creation interrogation subunits** of YHWH's speeches to Job and the great **wisdom appeal** from Lady Wisdom in Prov 8 contribute to creation theology, not to mention the **hymnic fragments** and **divine self-assertion hymns** in Isa 40–55. That the entire cosmos depends on God for its existence and should praise God (Ps 148) is foundational to traditional Jewish and Christian theology.

Beer, "Patristic Understanding," 3–23; Brown, *Structure, Role, Ideology*; Gottlieb, "Creation Theme," 29–36; Hasel, "Polemical Nature," 81–102; Levenson, *Creation*; McCarthy, "Creation Motifs," 393–406; Middleton, *Liberating Image*; Niehoff, "*Creatio ex nihilo*," 37–64; Tsumura, *Earth and Waters in Genesis 1 and 2*; Walton, "Creation," 48–63; Walton, *Lost World*.

Crisis Narrative

These are narratives in which a major character's life is in danger, a frequent genre in world literature. There are two major elements: 1) the crisis and 2) the deliverance, which often testifies to God's providence. Due to space considerations, this entry concentrates on crisis narratives which are clustered together. Certain other narratives not mentioned in this entry might also be considered crisis narratives.

Hagar and Ishmael are dying from thirst but God provides water (Gen 21:8–21; see **separation narrative**). Isaac is about to be sacrificed by Abraham at God's command (see **human sacrifice narrative** for longer discussion and bibliography), but God relents and provides a ram for the sacrifice (Gen 22:1–19; this passage is significant for Christology).

Joseph's brothers throw him in a pit and conspire to kill him, but Judah persuades them to sell Joseph instead (Gen 37:12–36). The good-looking Joseph flees the seduction of Potiphar's wife, is framed and thrown in prison (Gen 39:1–23), and eventually released and appointed as Pharaoh's vizier. YHWH is watching over Joseph (Gen 39:2, 21, 23). In both stories, foes use a garment of Joseph to lie about him. In between, Tamar uses a garment of Judah's to escape execution (Gen 38:12–26; see **sentencing narrative**). Despite obvious differences, Gen 38 is connected thematically to the rest of the Joseph story. Joseph's brothers later proceed from danger to danger: famine, accused of being spies, Simeon thrown in prison, accused of stealing Pharaoh's cup, Benjamin thrown in prison (Gen 42:1—44:17). The climax is Judah's heart-breaking intercession for Benjamin out of concern for a father, Jacob, who only loves the sons born by Rachel (Gen 44:18–34). Then Joseph weeps, reveals his identity, assures his brothers that it was not them who sent him to Egypt but God, and commissions them to deliver a message of salvation to Jacob (Gen 45:1–15).

The early chapters of Exodus involve crises concerning Israelite baby boys and Moses. The midwives Puah and Shiphrah fear God, thwart Pharaoh's first plan to kill Israelite boys at birth, and are rewarded by God (Exod 1:15–21). Moses' **birth narrative** in Exodus 2:1–10 shows Moses being rescued by his mother, sister, and by Pharaoh's own daughter! In an enigmatic incident, YHWH attempts to kill Moses at night. Moses' wife Zipporah intervenes by circumcising their son (Exod 4:24–26), then calling Moses "a bridegroom of blood."

Samson uses his God-given strength to get himself out of certain self-inflicted crises (Judg 15:8–17; 16:1–3, 4–15; **heroic exploits narrative**), but when he is dying of thirst, God rescues him by providing water (Judg 15:18–20). Jonathan is nearly executed for unwittingly breaking his father Saul's foolish oath (**vow narrative**), but Israelite soldiers intervene (1 Sam 14:24–45).

Saul tries to kill David on numerous occasions but David always manages to escape, usually with the help of others. David evades Saul's spear twice (1 Sam 18:1–11). Saul tries over-promoting David but David bonds with his troops, exacerbating Saul's envy against him (1 Sam 18:11–16); then Saul lays a trap for David, offering his daughter in return for military exploits against the Philistines, but with YHWH's aid, David accomplishes twice these exploits (1 Sam 18:17–30). Saul's son, Jonathan, persuades Saul not to kill David (1 Sam 19:1–7), then David eludes another spear attack from Saul (1 Sam 19:8–10), then Saul's daughter, Michal, enables David to escape (1 Sam 19:11–17; **flight narrative**). Saul sends three groups of people to capture David in Ramah but the Spirit of God falls upon each group and they fall into a frenzy; then Saul comes himself to capture David but is foiled when the Spirit of God falls upon him in a frenzy also (1 Sam 18:18–24). Finally, David and Jonathan adopt a complex plan of communication to prevent Saul in another attempt on David's life (1 Sam 20:1–21:1 [NRSV 20:1–42]).

Crisis narratives embedded are layered in 2 Sam 17:15–22. David is in danger so Jonathan and Ahimaaz try to warn him but they in turn are rescued by an unnamed woman who, like Michal in 1 Sam 18, tells a falsehood in doing so. Other examples of crisis are where Elisha is surrounded by a great army but YHWH strikes them with blindness and Elisha evades capture (2 Kgs 6:8–23).

Bekins, "Tamar and Joseph," 375–97; Campbell, *1 Samuel*, 141–51, 167–219; Clines and Eshkanazi, *Queen Michal's Story*; Coats, *Genesis*, 263–94; Coats, *Exodus 1–18*, 25–29, 42–44; Exum, "Every Daughter," 63–82; Frolov, *Judges*, 239–76; Longacre, *Joseph*; Mann, *Run, David*; Mann, "Performative Prayers," 20–40; Propp, "Bloody Bridegroom," 495–518; Winslow, *Early Jewish*.

Curse Narrative

The standard structure has three elements: an offence; an **exercitives subunit** pronouncing a curse; and a **reactions subunit** of the cursed character. Genesis 1–11 has three such narratives. In the **etiological narrative** of Gen 3, the offense is human disobedience at the serpent's prompting (Gen 3:1–7), the reactions come in response to God's accusatory questions (Gen 3:8–13), and God curses the serpent and the ground but not the humans themselves (Gen 3:14–19), although they are banished (**sentencing narrative**). Cain murdered his brother, Abel, and disowns him (Gen 4:8–9), YHWH pronounces a curse upon Cain (Gen 4:10–12), Cain complains that someone will kill him but YHWH ensures that this does not happen (Gen 4:13–16). Genesis 9 is a text tragically abused to justify enslaving people of African descent. The eventual curser, Noah, became drunk lay naked (Gen 9:20–21); Ham, the father of Canaan, sees Noah's nakedness and tells his brothers (Gen 9:22) and Shem and Japheth act nobly by covering Noah's nakedness (Gen 9:23); and Noah blesses Shem and Japheth but mysteriously curses Canaan (Gen 9:24–27), suggesting a gap in the text perhaps where Canaan sins against Noah (castration and sexual violation are common speculations) or that Ham's sin goes beyond publicizing Noah's nakedness. The Bible does not refer back and explain this passage but some points can be made: God blesses Noah's sons, which would include Ham (Gen 9:1); there is no curse on Ham, some of whose descendants lived in Africa; the descendants of the one who is cursed, Canaan, did not live in Africa; the curser is no hero in this narrative; and the narrative likely functioned along with Gen 15:16 as one rationale for the Israelites conquering Canaan.

The Balaam **anti-hero cycle** revolves around the Moabite leader Balak's attempts to get Balaam to curse Israel which rebound to the detriment of Moab (Num 22:1–12; 23:1–12; see **Balaamite Psalm**). For Saul's open-ended curse in 1 Sam 14:24, see **vow narrative**.

Shimei curses a fleeing David for being a man of blood, specifically the blood of the house of Saul (2 Sam 16:5–8), but David reacts with restraint (2 Sam 16:9–14). When David returns triumphantly, Shimei pleads for forgiveness (2 Sam 19:16–20), David swears not to kill Shimei but later instructs Solomon to bring Shimei's grey head down to Sheol (2 Sam 19:21–23; 1 Kgs 2:8–9), Solomon gives Shimei a chance which Shimei blows and Solomon executes him (1 Kgs 2:36–46; see **sentencing narrative**). In 2 Kgs 2:23–25, some boys taunt Elisha, he curses them, and two she-bears tear forty-two of them. Strong **curse subunits** occur in Job's **soliloquy** (Job 3:3–10) and in Jeremiah's **prophetic prayer of complaint** (Jer 20:14–18).

Aaron, "Rabbinic Exegesis," 721–59; Campbell, *2 Samuel*, 138–66; Coats, *Genesis*, 49–66, 86–89; Goldenberg, *Black and Slave*; Knierim and Coats, *Numbers*, 252–63; Robertson, "Current Critical Questions," 177–88.

Death and Burial Narrative

Although there are event of death clauses in the early chapters of Genesis, the first burial narrative in the Bible, and one of the most important, is that of Sarah (Gen 23:1–20). The introduction contains **a length of life formula**, an event of death clause and an action of Abraham mourning (Gen 23:1–2). Then there is a lengthy **dialogue** between Abraham and the Hittites (Gen 23:3–15) with the result that Abraham purchases the land around the cave of Machpelah as a burial plot for Sarah (vv. 16–18) and buries her there (v. 19). The narrator makes a **summarizing comment** that the field and cave were now Abraham's (v. 20) that points to its ongoing significance. Abraham is buried at the same cave by his sons Isaac and Ishmael (Gen 25:7–11), as is Isaac by his sons, Esau and Jacob (Gen 35:27–29). There is a very lengthy death and burial narrative for Jacob (Gen 47:27–50:14) which includes a **blessing narrative** on his grandsons Ephraim and Manasseh (Gen 48) and a **testament narrative** to his twelve sons (Gen 49:1–28), followed by Jacob commanding his sons to bury him at the cave of Machpelah where Abraham, Sarah, Isaac, Rebekah, and Leah were buried (Gen 49:29–33). Jacob then dies, is mourned over, and taken back from Egypt to the cave of Machpelah where his sons bury him (Gen 49:34—50:14). These burial narratives unify the patriarchs and their (most important) wives, and set up an anticipation of when the children of Israel will possess the entire land of Canaan.

There are also narratives of the death and burial of Rebekah's nurse, Deborah (Gen 35:8) and of Rachel who dies giving birth to Benjamin (Gen 35:16–20). Just before his death, Joseph commands that the Israelites carry his bones back to Canaan when God eventually brings the Israelites out of Egypt (Gen 50:22–26), so that the Exodus is again anticipated before the book of the same name begins.

In the other books of the Torah, the main death and burial narratives are those of Miriam (Num 20:1), Aaron (Num 20:22–29, reiterated in 33:38–39) and Moses, whose burial place remains unknown and whose death brings the Torah to a close (Deut 34:1–12).

Other significant death and burial narratives are those of Joshua (Josh 24:29–33 reiterated in Judg 2:6–9), Gideon (Judg 8:32), Jephthah (Judg 12:7), Samson (Judg 16:25–31), who dies bringing the house down on the Philistines, Samuel (1 Sam 25:1) and Saul (1 Sam 31:4–13 [= 1 Chr 10:1–14]). The death of David's son by Bathsheba is poignant for how it characterizes David (2 Sam 12:15b–23) as is the death of Absalom (2 Sam 17:23; see **mourning narrative**).

The death of the unnamed prophet who prophesied the destruction of the Bethel altar is told at length because of its connections to King Josiah (1 Kgs 13:13–22; see 2 Kgs 23:15–18). Kings whose burial included more than just the **death and burial formula** include Ahab (1 Kgs 22:39–40), 22:50 [=2 Chr 21:1]; 2 Kgs 1:17–18; 8:23–24 [=2 Chr 21:12–20]; 9:27–28 [=2 Chr 22:8–9]; 12:20–21 [= 2 Chr 24:25–27]; 13:8–9, 13, 20; 14:15–16, 18–20 [=2 Chr 25:26–28]; 14:29; 15:6–7 [=2 Chr 26:21–23]; 15:21, 38 [=2 Chr 27:7–9]; 16:19–20 [=2 Chr 28:26–27]; 20:21 [=2 Chr 32:32–33]; 21:17–18 [=2 Chr 33:18–20]; 21:23–26 [=2 Chr 33:24–25]; 23:28–30 [=2 Chr 35:20–27]; 1 Chr 10:1–14.

Bailey, *Biblical Perspectives*; Bloch-Smith, *Judahite Burial Practices*; Chapman, *Law and Prophets*, 111–31, 150–66; Coats, *Genesis*, 163–66; Pham, *Mourning*.

Dedication Narrative

After the building (see **construction narrative**) or the restoration (see **building restoration narrative**) of the tabernacle, temple, or second temple, there are dedication ceremonies (Exod 40:16–38; 1 Kgs 8:11–66 [=2 Chr 6:1–7:10]; Ezra 3:1–13; 6:13–18), with dedications of both the first and second temples occurring at Tabernacles (see **festival observance narratives**). Nehemiah organizes a dedication at the rebuilding of the wall of Jerusalem (Neh 12:27–43; see **participant lists**). These narratives typically include a **main actions subunit** and an **exercitives subunit** including a speech of dedication; there is frequently an expressions subunit, where the people sound trumpets and show their joy. In Dan 3:1–7, a Gentile society dedicates its sacred items with similar pageantry.

Knoppers, "Prayer and Propaganda," 57–76; De Troyer, "Sounding Trumpets," 41–58; Weyde, *Appointed Festivals*, 147–62; Yap, "Purpose," 253–64.

Deuteronomistic History Summary

In Judg 2:10–23, the narrator summarizes what is going to happen in the various judge cycles later in the book and its theological significance; in 2 Kgs 17:1–41, the narrator explains the theological reasons why the northern kingdom was exiled (see **exile narrative**); in 2 Kgs 23:25–27, the narrator explains that although Josiah's reign was more righteous than of any king preceding him, YHWH had already determined to exile Judah because of Manasseh's sins. Many scholars regard these passages as evidence of an editor producing a history of the judges and kings evaluated by how well these leaders kept the laws in Deuteronomy (see discussion in overview of Tanak chapter).

Gillmayr-Bucher, "Framework and Discourse," 687–702; Noth, *Deuteronomistic History*.

Dispute Narrative

There are three main elements: 1) the issue causing the dispute, 2) a **dialogue subunit** where the participants state their positions, and 3) outcome of the dispute, either positive or negative. Dispute narratives are extremely common in literature, they usually advance the plot, they have inbuilt tension making them ideal for **stories** rather than **reports** and they have considerable potential for characterization in the dialogue subunits.

They are a major theme in the patriarchal narratives. Abram and Lot dispute grazing areas (see **agricultural/pastoral narrative**) but separate amicably so now Abram has completely separated from his father's house as God had commanded (Gen 13:1–18; see **separation narrative**); Isaac and Abimelech resolve conflict over wells with a treaty (Gen 26:14–33; see **treaty narrative**); Jacob out tricks Laban concerning payment (Gen 30:25–43); a further dispute between them in which Rachel steals missing idols ends with a treaty (Gen 31:25–42; **treaty narrative**); for a resolution of Jacob and Esau's enmity, **see meeting/visit/reunion narrative** (Gen 32:1—33:17); Jacob and his sons dispute taking Benjamin to Egypt and Judah offering himself as surety for Benjamin's safety (Gen 42:29— 43:14).

The dispute between Cis-Jordanian and Trans-Jordanian tribes is resolved when a suspected illegitimate sanctuary is shown not to be an altar (Josh 22:10–34); Gideon placates the Ephraimites by praising their military achievements (Judg 8:1–3); Eli's sons ignore their father's rebuke (1 Sam 2:22–25), "for it was the will of the Lord to put them to death" (1 Sam 2:25), a pre-word that is fulfilled in 1 Sam 4:1–11 (**battle narrative, procession narrative**); a dispute between Samuel and the people concerning a king concludes with YHWH commanding Samuel to give them a king (1 Sam 8:4–22); and a dispute between the people and the nobles concerning various types of property is effectively arbitrated by Nehemiah and ends with the nobles restoring property to the people (Neh 5:1–13). See entry in prophetic narratives chapter.

Coats, Genesis, 116–18, 192–95, 209–33; Mabee, "Jacob and Laban," 192–207; Rickett, "Rethinking," 31–53.

Disqualification Narrative

These narratives explain why a particular character was unsuited for godly leadership. The older brother Cain kills Abel (Gen 4:1–16; see **banishment narrative**). The older brother Esau despises his birthright (Gen 25:29–34). Jacob's eldest son, Reuben, seduces his father's concubine (Gen 35:21–22a); and the next two sons, Simeon and Levi, show themselves vengeance killers (Gen 31:25–31); see the subunits of the **testament narrative** in Gen 49 devoted to Reuben, Simeon and Levi). Eli's sons dishonor the priesthood (1 Sam 2:12–17) as do Samuel's sons (1 Sam 8:1–3). Jeroboam engages in various forms of illegitimate worship (1 Kgs 12:25–33; [=2 Chr 11:13–17]; 13:33–34), setting a pattern for the entire northern kingdom.

Dicou, *Edom*; Krasovec, "Punishment," 5–33.

Divine Command Narrative

The form of this genre is typically a **speech introduction formula** followed by a divine speech issuing directive illocutions to one of YHWH's servants. Addressees include Noah (Gen 6:13–21; 7:1–4); Abraham (Gen 12:1–3; 21:12–13; 22:1–2); Jacob (Gen 35:1–7); Moses and/or Aaron (Exod 33:1–6; Num 1:1–16, 48–53; 2:1–31; 3:5–10, 11–13, 14–15, 40–41, 44–48; 4:1–16, 17–20, 21–33; 17:1–5; 25:19—26:2 [NRSV 26:1–2]; 26:52–56; 33:50–56; 34:1–12); and Joshua (Josh 1:1–9; 6:1–5 [see also **siege narrative**]; 7:10–15 [see also **execution narrative**]; 8:1–2, 18a; 13:1–7; 20:1–6). It is frequently followed by a **compliance narrative**, and the combination of the two highlight the obedience of the servant. In Leviticus especially, God commands Moses to instruct the Israelites via a command to speak formula.

Divine Judgment Narrative

This is a narrative in which YHWH personally brings down judgment upon an individual or group for a specifically mentioned sin. The specific judgment varies significantly: a flood upon everyone except for Noah and his family for the fact that there was evil all the time and that violence filled the earth (Gen 6:1—8:22), division of languages at Babel/Babylon for striving to build a city with its top in the heavens to make a name for themselves (Gen 11:1–9); burning brimstone on Sodom and Gomorrah (and probably Admah and Zeboiim) for wickedness that caused a "great outcry" (Gen 18:16—19:29); consecutive deaths to two sons of Judah, Er and Onan (Gen 38:6–10); smiting the firstborn of all Egyptian households (Exod 12:29–36); causing the Reed Sea to drown the Egyptian armies (Exod 14:1–31); a plague on the Israelites for making the golden calf (Exod 32:15–35); death by fire for the priests Nadab and Abihu who had offered unholy fire (Lev 10:1–3); various deadly punishments in the **revolt narrative** recording the rebellion of Korah, Dathan, and Abiram (Num 16:1—17:15 [NRSV 16:1–50]); a plague on the Israelites who had sexual relations with Moabite women and worshiped their gods (Num 25:1–18); and plagues upon those who disrespected the ark of the covenant, Philistines and Israelites alike (1 Sam 5:1–12; 6:19—7:2). In 2 Sam 24 [=1 Chr 21:1–17], the Israelites suffer a devastating plague because of the sin of their leader, King David.

One purpose of these narratives is to demonstrate YHWH's holiness and consequent intolerance of wickedness. Another is to show that YHWH punishes Israelites and non-Israelites alike for sin. They also provide a partial answer to the question, "Why do the wicked prosper?" showing that the wicked are often punished in the long run.

Harland, "Sin of Babel," 515–33; Walton, "Mesopotamian Background," 155–75.

Dream Epiphany/Theophany

This is a subcategory of **dream narrative** in which there is self-revelation by God or an angel. Two dream theophanies involve Jacob (Gen 28:10–22; see **hieros logos narrative**; 46:1–4) and are both positive. The first establishes Bethel as a sanctuary and fits with the "pillar" motif of Jacob. The second shows a rare explicit participation of YHWH into the Joseph story.

Solomon receives a dream theophany at Gibeon (1 Kgs 3:5–15) which results in him gaining wisdom and hence is also a **wisdom narrative**. First Kings 9:1–9 might be a dream theophany because it states that YHWH "appeared to Solomon a second time, as he had appeared to him at Gibeon." The narrative in which YHWH calls repeatedly to the boy Samuel (1 Sam 3:1–21) is often labeled a dream narrative, but could be simply an **audition**. Its focal point is a **prophecy of punishment** against the house of Eli.

Gnuse, *Dream Theophany*; Long, *2 Kings*, 298–99.

Dream Interpretation Narrative

Dreaming is a common human phenomenon but the Bible primary includes them in two circumstances: the dream emanates from a heavenly figure (**dream epiphany/theophany**) or the dream is interpreted and later comes to pass. The latter occur with regards to Joseph and Daniel, both of whom credit God as the true interpreter. Standard elements are an introduction concerning the dreamer and circumstances, the event which employs "dream" and "behold" words, reactions of audience and interpretation of dream, and fulfillment of interpretation.

The Joseph story contains three paired dreams (Gen 37:2b–11; 40:1–23; 41:1–46). Joseph's own dreams in Gen 37 are skeptically interpreted by Jacob but are somewhat fulfilled when Joseph's brothers perform obeisance to him (**fulfillment narrative**). In Gen 40, Joseph interprets the dreams of Pharaoh's butler and baker, the events come to pass (**fulfillment narrative; banquet narrative**), and this eventually leads to Joseph chance to interpret Pharaoh's dreams in Gen 41. For details of Gen 41 and Daniel's dream interpretations, see **court narrative**. The dreams in Gen 40 and 41 are opaque and need interpreting but the symbolism of the Gen 37 dreams is obvious. Deuteronomy 18:9–14 prohibits various forms of divination and mantic activity but does not specify dream interpretation (divination/sorcery/witchcraft law); and Deut 13 warns against dream interpreters who advocate following false gods (apostasy law).

Bar, *Letter Not Read*; Collins, *Daniel*, 108–9; Ehrlich, *Traum*; Fidler, *Dream Theophanies*; Grossman, "Different Dreams," 717–32; Hasel, "World Empires," 17–30; Husser, *Dream Narratives*; Pirson, *Lord of the Dreams*; Sternberg, *Poetics*, 394–400.

Egyptian Oppression Narrative

This narrates the general suffering (as opposed to the death threats involved in a **crisis narrative**) of the Israelites in bondage and their crying out to God (Exod 1:8–14 2:23–25; 5:6–23) and is similar to the elements in a judges cycle where YHWH hands over Israel to be oppressed by foreigners and then the Israelites cry out to YHWH. Among other purposes, these narratives provide the literary context of the Moses birth narrative and serve as a justification for the plagues upon Egypt that follow.

Exodus 1:6–14 summarizes the transition between Joseph's generation and the generation before Moses. It comprises an event subunit of Joseph's generation dying (Exod 1:6), a summary subunit of the Israelites multiplying (Exod 1:7; see the proleptic summary in Gen 47:27) which functions as a fulfillment narrative to the numerous pre-words of divine promises to multiply the descendants of the patriarchs, an event subunit (Exod 1:8) of a new Pharaoh arising who does not know/care about the negotiations between Joseph and a previous Pharaoh (Gen 47:1–12; negotiations narrative), a commissives subunit (Exod 1:9–10), and a compliance subunit (Exod 1:11–14) narrating the Egyptians oppressing and enslaving the Israelites.

Exodus 2:23–25 summarizes the suffering of the Israelites in Egypt while Moses is in Midian, and the divine experiences subunit (Exod 3:24–25) will motivate God's decision to deliver Israel (Exod 3:7–10) in the immediately following call of Moses (see vocation narrative).

Exodus 5:1–23, which could also be described as a failed negotiations narrative, begins with Moses and Aaron telling Pharaoh, "Thus says the Lord, the God of Israel, 'Let my people go, so that they may celebrate a festival to me in the wilderness'" (Exod 5:1). This second occurrence of the messenger of YHWH formula reinforces the message introduced by the first occurrence in Exodus 4:21–23, namely that the purpose of the Exodus is that the chosen/elect may worship YHWH. The added note in Exodus 5 is that Israel will celebrate a festival, and that will become the festival of weeks, which celebrates the giving of the ten commandments on Mount Sinai in the third month (Exod 19:1—20:21). Salvation history, commandments, and worship are inextricably linked in the Bible.

As foretold in the previous chapter, Pharaoh rejects YHWH's demands, and increases the hardship of Israelite toil—demanding bricks without straw and beating the Israelite supervisors who failed to meet their demand (Exod 5:6–14). Today, the haroset on the Passover Seder plate represents the mortar used by the Israelites in Egypt, and the salt water represents the bitter tears shed there. Deuteronomy is full of post-words concerning YHWH delivering Israel from Egypt (Deut 1:30; 4:20, 34, 37; 5:6, 15; 6:12; 7:8, 18; 13:10; 15:15; 16:1, 3, 12; 20:1; 29:2). YHWH commands the Israelites to recite to their children "We were Pharaoh's slaves in Egypt, but the Lord brought us out of Egypt with a mighty hand" (Deut 6:21; see also Deut 26:5–10).

Baden, "Joseph to Moses," 133–58; Coats, *Exodus 1–18*, 21–25, 33–34; von Rad, *Problem of the Hexateuch*.

Encounter on Journey/Flight Narrative

There are occasions in a **journey narrative**, when there is an unexpected encounter. Some, like Joseph's encounter with the man from Dothan or Saul's encounter with the women at the well are mysteriously unexplained (Gen 37:15–17; 1 Sam 9:11–13; 1 Kgs 13:7–22); others concerning Shimei, Ziba and Mephibosheth form a subplot within the **revolt narrative** of Absalom (2 Sam 16:1–4, 5–14 [see also **curse narrative**]; 19:19b–24 [NRSV 18b–23], 25–31 [NRSV 24–30], 32–40 [NRSV 31–39]); while Elijah's encounter with Obadiah (1 Kgs 18:7–16) serves as background to the encounter between YHWH and Baal (see **confrontation narrative**).

Enlistment Narrative

This is a subsection of a **battle narrative** that focuses on the soldiers enlisting (Judg 3:27–28; 4:6–10; 6:34—7:8; 1 Chr 12:15–22). It focuses on troops' willingness to serve.

Epiphany/Theophany Narrative

A theophany is a manifestation of God; an epiphany is a manifestation of a heavenly being, and thus in its widest sense, epiphany includes the subclass of theophany. An epiphany in a stricter sense refers to an appearance of an angel, but there are numerous narratives involving the angel of YHWH where the YHWH/angel distinction is confused, such as Josh 5:13–15, where Joshua is told to remove his sandals in the presence of the commander of the army of YHWH. We see theophanies in God's call of Moses, Gideon, Isaiah, Jeremiah, and Ezekiel (Exod 3:1—4:19;

Judg 6:7–10, 11–24; Isa 6; Jer 1:4–19; Ezek 1; see glossary on **vocation narratives** for details), before and after the giving and re-giving of the **Decalogue** and Covenant Code on Mount Sinai (Exod 19–20, 24, 34) and to Elijah after his confrontation with the Baal supporters (1 Kgs 19).

Epiphanies/theophanies are standard elements in both **annunciation narratives** (Gen 16:7–14; 17:1–21; 18:1–15; Judg 13:3–23) and in historic apocalypses (Dan 9:20–27; 10:1—12:13). They also occur in episodes where an angel wrestles with Jacob (Gen 32:22–32), Moses is permitted to experience the afterglow of YHWH's glory (Exod 33:12–23), and where YHWH's glory means that Moses cannot enter the tent (Exod 40:34–38). The Angel of YHWH delivers a prophecy of punishment (Judg 2:1–5).

Beckwith, "Daniel 9," 521–42; Collins, *Daniel*, 89–104, 109, 119; Hasel, "Resurrection," 267–84; Jeremias, *Theophanie*; Savran, *Encountering the Divine*.

Etiological Narrative

An etiology is an explanation of the origins of a phenomenon: a custom, a name, a state of affairs. There are etiological elements in numerous narratives—the flood narrative concludes with an etiology for the rainbow, for example—but few are predominately etiological.

The most obvious example is the **paradise narrative** in Gen 2:4—3:24, which tells of the origins of marriage, of clothing, of enmity between the serpent and the woman's seed, of relations between the sexes, of thorns and the difficulty of producing food from the ground, of pain in childbirth, of human death, and of exile from paradise. This nexus of etiologies underlies Christian understanding of Gen 3 as "The Fall," but how great a fall differs between Wesleyan and Eastern Orthodox views, say, and more pessimistic Calvinistic and Augustinian views. Another candidate for an etiological narrative is Gen 32:22–32, which tells of how Israel and Peniel got their names and why Israelites avoid eating the sinews of animals. The purpose of etiological narratives is to explain phenomena experienced in the present.

At the level of liturgical worship, Esther is an etiological narrative for Purim, and the books of Torah are partly etiologies for the Sabbath and the Festivals of Passover/Unleavened Bread, Weeks, and Booths.

Barr, *Garden of Eden*; Golka, "Aetiologies Part 1," 410–28; Golka, "Aetiologies Part 2," 36–47; Long, *Etiological Narrative*; Reno, *Genesis*, 60–97; Sarna, *Genesis*, 16–31.

Exile Narrative

These primarily narrate the exile of Israel by the Assyrians in 722 BCE (2 Kgs 17:7–41) and of Judah by the Babylonians in 587 BCE (2 Kgs 25:8–30 [=Jer 39:1–10; 52:12–27; 2 Chr 36:20–21]), although there is a preliminary Babylonian exile in 597 BCE (in which King Jehoiachin and the prophet Ezekiel are among the exiles). The importance of these events as landmarks in Israelite history can hardly be overstated. The latter prophets, including the individual books of the twelve, must be interpreted in relation to these events. Most prophetic books prophesy one or more of these exiles (pre-word) or reflect back upon them (post-word), with Jeremiah giving a pre-word and describing the event of the Babylonian exile. The exile narrative in 2 Kgs 17 is also the longest **deuteronomistic history summary** and explains why YHWH exiled the northern kingdom. The exile narrative concerning Judah concludes 2 Kings, Chronicles, and Jeremiah. Deuteronomy 30:1–3 is another pre-word to the exile and the book of Lamentations is a post-word. Jeremiah 42:7–43:7 narrates the forced exile of Jeremiah and company into Egypt, despite Jeremiah's warnings.

Becking, *Fall of Samaria*; Brettler, "Ideology," 268–82; Naʿaman, "Historical Background," 206–25; Younger, "Deportations," 201–27; Younger, "Fall of Samaria," 461–82.

Extended Exposition

Narratives in the Hebrew Bible tend to be dominated by actions, events and experiences rather than by expositions. However, there are relatively extended expositions of Moses just before he is granted a glimpse of YHWH's glory (Exod 33:7–11, via a series of **hymnic activities**) and in a **theological evaluation narrative** that concludes the Torah (Deut 34:10–12). We also have an exposition of Israel in the wilderness in Num 9:15–23.

The book of Samuel contains several character portraits, often via their activities: Elkanah and family (1 Sam 1:1–7a), Eli's sons (1 Sam

2:12–17), Hannah and Eli (1 Sam 2:18–20) and Samuel (1 Sam 3:19—4:1a; 7:13–17), the Israelite soldiers (1 Sam 13:19–22), Goliath (1 Sam 17:1–7), Amnon (2 Sam 13:1–3), and Absalom (2 Sam 15:1–6).

Other examples are daily life for Solomon, including banquets (1 Kgs 4:20–5:8 [NRSV 4:20–28]), the wealth of Solomon (1 Kgs 10:14–29 [= 2 Chr 9:13–28]), and Solomon's temple practices (2 Chr 8:12–16). In the autobiographical memoir of Nehemiah, we get a first-person exposition of his activities (Neh 5:14–18); and later in the book we get a third-person account of Levitical activities "in the days of Nehemiah" (Neh 12:44–47).

Fokkelman, *Reading Biblical Narrative*, 55–72; Gunn and Fewell, *Narrative*, 46–89; Sternberg, *Poetics*, 321–64.

Failure to Conquer Narrative

Despite the occasional hyperbole that Joshua and/or the Israelites conquered all the land or wiped out all the Canaanites, numerous statements show that they failed to conquer some part of the land: the Geshurites and Maacathites (Josh 13:13); the Jebusites in Jerusalem (Josh 15:63); the Canaanites in Gezer (Josh 16:10); certain towns in Manasseh's allocated territory (Josh 17:12–13) etc. A summary narrative discusses the various tribes that failed to remove utterly the Canaanites (Judg 1:27–36).

Although Joshua is regarded as a model leader, and there are numerous points of contact between Joshua and the model reforming king Josiah, the various failure to conquer passages within the **campaign to conquer Canaan narrative** provide further evidence even in Joshua's time of Israel's failure to trust YHWH and thus justification of YHWH's eventual decision to exile them. In some ways, they are analogous to Huldah's prophecy that Josiah's reforms cannot reverse YHWH's decision to exile Judah (2 Kgs 22:13–20).

Mullen, "Judges 1:1–36," 33–54; Younger, *Ancient Conquest Accounts*.

Famine/Drought Narrative

Famines and droughts are events and are thus typically mentioned in an **event subunit** which is often also an **introductory subunit**. This is then usually followed by a main actions subunit which describes how the characters deal with the famine/drought and/or a dialogue subunit where they plan to deal with it. In the ancient world, migration was a frequent response to famine and this is reflected in the Hebrew Bible (Gen 12:10–20; 26:1–16; see **sister-wife narratives**; Ruth 1:1–6). Famine narratives are integral to the Joseph story (Gen 41:47—42:5; 47:13–26), forming the rationale for the **journey narratives** of Jacob and his sons to Egypt. In 2 Sam 21:1–14, famine results from Saul having broken a treaty with the Gibeonites (see **treaty narrative**). Famines/droughts underlie several **prophetic miracle narratives** concerning Elijah (1 Kgs 17:1—18:46) and Elisha (2 Kgs 4:38–44; 6:25—8:6).

The **blessing and curse passages** (legal genres) of Lev 26 and Deut 28 regard abundant rain and crops as God's blessing while droughts may signal a curse resulting from disobedience; similarly, famines and droughts may be part of a **prophecy of punishment** (prophetic speech genres). Famine is symbolized in one of the horsemen of the apocalypse (Rev 6:5–6; see also Matt 24:7) and drought is discussed in tractate Ta'anit of the Talmud.

Patai, "Control of Rain," 251–86; Strine, "Famine in Land," 55–69.

Fast Narrative

This is the opposite of a slow narrative and if you read this chapter too fast, you might miss the joke. Fasting occurred as part of mourning (1 Sam 31:13 [=1 Chr 10:12]; 2 Sam 1:12; see **mourning narrative**), or an act of penitence. We see it accompanied by sacrifices (Judg 20:26); or prayer (1 Sam 7:3–6; Dan 9:1–3; Ezra 8:21–23; Neh 1:4–11; 2 Chr 20:1–12; see **prayer narrative**); or by putting on sackcloth and ashes (1 Kgs 21:27–29; Jonah 3:5–10; Est 4:1–17; Dan 9:1–3; Neh 9:1–3). Like the **prayer narratives,** fast narratives would function in part as examples for readers to follow in dire situations. Expectations are inverted in 2 Sam 12:16–23, where David fasts for seven days while his baby son is deathly sick, but when the child dies, David washes his face and eats food. On Yom Kippur, the most solemn fast in Judaism, the afternoon reading from the prophets is the book of Jonah, in which the Ninevites fast and repent and YHWH relents from his threatened punishment. It appears that both Moses (Exod 24:18) and Elijah (1 Kgs 19:8) fast for forty days, as does Jesus in the Temptations narrative (Matt 4:2; Luke 4:2), and fasting is valued in the worship practices of Judaism and Christianity but in different ways.

Lambert, "Fasting as Penitential?" 477–512; Seidler, "Fasting, Sackloth," 117–34.

Festival Observance Narrative

The Israelites observe the Passover under Moses (Exod 12:21–28), Joshua (Josh 5:10–12); and Josiah (2 Kgs 23:21–23 [=2 Chr 35:1–19]); the Second Passover under Hezekiah (2 Chr 30:1–27); the Feast of Tabernacles under Solomon (1 Kgs 8:11–66 [=2 Chr 6:1–7:10]), and Ezra and Nehemiah (Ezra 3:1–7; 6:19–22; Neh 8:1–18). Second Chronicles 15:8–15 may be a festival observance narrative concerning the Feast of Weeks under Asa. The minor festival of Purim is inaugurated under Mordecai and Esther (Est 9:20–32), and in the deuterocanonical books, the minor festival of Hanukkah is inaugurated in 2 Macc 1–2. Several of these narratives occur in the context of **restoration narratives**, thus highlighting the importance of keeping the festivals for restoration of true YHWH worship. For the legal background, see **cultic calendar instruction** in chapter on legal genres. Much of the Gospel of John revolves around Jewish festivals, including Hunukkah/Dedication.

Chavel, "Second Passover," 1–24; Otto, *Das Mazzotfest*; Sweeney, *King Josiah*; de Vries, "Festival Observance," 104–24; Weyde, *Appointed Festivals*, 147–62; Yap, "Purpose and Function," 253–64.

Flight Narrative

This is a subcategory of **journey narrative** in which the protagonist flees from danger or hardship. Frequently a later narrative vindicates the protagonist in some way. In the Torah, Hagar flees from Sarai's persecution (Gen 16:6) and the angel of YHWH announces her son's destiny in the first **annunciation narrative**; Jacob flees in the middle of the night from Laban because of the latter's financial abuse of him (Gen 31:20–30) and Laban has to make a peace treaty with Jacob (**treaty narrative**); Moses flees from Pharaoh after he killed an Egyptian taskmaster (Exod 2:15), and Moses later returns to rescue the Israelites from Egypt. In Judg 9:7–21, Jotham flees from Abimelech who had killed the rest of his brothers (Judg 9:1–6), and Jotham's warning (Judg 9:7b–20; see **fable** in prophetic speech genres) comes down upon Shechem and upon Abimelech (Judg 9:56–57; **fulfillment formula**); Jephthah flees from his clan (Judg 11:3), and they later coming begging him to take leadership. These narratives would be a source of encouragement for believers who had been forced to flee themselves.

David flees from Saul on several occasions (1 Sam 19:8–10, 11–17; 20:1; 21:2–10 [NRSV 1–9], 11–16 [NRSV 10–15]; 22:1–5; 23:14–24a, 24b–28; 27:1–4), many of which are also **crisis narratives** in which Michal or Jonathan save David. David eventually becomes king over all Israel. Absalom flees after killing Amnon (2 Sam 13:34–38) and eventually takes over his father David's throne and harem, fulfilling Nathan's prophecy in 2 Sam 12:11. David's flight from Absalom is paralleled by his return as king (2 Sam 15–19).

Jeroboam flees from Solomon (1 Kgs 11:40) and becomes king over ten tribes of Israel. Elijah flees from Ahab and Jezebel (1 Kgs 19:1–8) and Ahab and Jezebel come to a violent end at the hands of Jehu, who was designated king by Elijah's successor, Elisha. Given this background, it seems that Jonah's flight from YHWH when YHWH commands him to prophesy punishment upon Nineveh (Jonah 1:1–3) marks Jonah as the good guy and YHWH the adversary. The expectation is reversed when the reader finds that YHWH intended Nineveh's repentance and consequent pardon and mercy all along, and that Jonah knew of YHWH's mercy and resented that fact.

Campbell, *1 Samuel*, 203–49; Campbell, *2 Samuel*, 138–66; Frolov, *Judges*, 173–75, 203–29; Kim, "Absalom's Rebellion," 43–63; Mann, *Run, David, Run!*; Teubal, *Hagar the Egyptian*.

Future Temple Vision Narrative

See entry in prophetic narratives chapter.

Genealogical Narrative

Most genealogies are discussed in the chapter on lists but Gen 29:31—30:24 is an extended **birth narrative** with considerable genealogical information that also has many elements of the **annunciation narrative**. The narrative opens with YHWH opening Leah's womb while Rachel remains barren followed by a series of birth reports concerning Leah's first four children: Reuben, Simeon, Levi, and Judah. In response to Rachel's plea to Jacob, "Give me sons," Jacob does not pray to God but retorts, "Am I instead of God?" So Rachel gives Jacob her maidservant, Bilhah, and she adopts the sons that Bilhah bears Jacob, namely Dan and Naphtali. Leah responds in kind and thus adopts Jacob's sons by Leah's handmaiden Zilpah, Gad and Asher. Reuben finds mandrakes which leads to a **negotiation narrative**, the end result of which is that Leah bears two more sons, Issachar and Zebulun, and a daughter, Dinah, and Rachel finally bears Joseph. Rachel bears Jacob a second son, Benjamin, in Gen 35:16–18.

Dinah is the only child whose birth report lacks an etymological speech, suggesting that she was less important in the son-bearing competition between Leah and Rachel. Only Leah and Rachel receive divine aid in enabling them to conceive, and this fits the larger narrative—the sons of the handmaids are less prominent in the Genesis narratives, and the tribal inheritances are at the margins of Israel also. The sons of Jacob are mentioned together in a variety of other genres later with occasional differences in order due to grouping the sons of each mother together and different orders in which the mothers are presented (Gen 35:22–26; 46:8–25; 49:1–28; Exod 1:1–5; Num 1:5–15, 20–47; 2:1–33; 7:12–83; 10:11–28; 13:4–16; 26:5–51; 34:16–29; Deut 27:11–14; 33:1–25; Josh 13–21; Judg 1:1–36; Ezek 48:30–35).

Finlay, *Birth Report Genre*, 115–31; Noth, *System*; Kallai, "Twelve-Tribe Systems," 53–90; Namiki, "Reconsideration," 29–60; Smith, *Role of Mothers*; Weippert, "Geographische," 76–89; Wilson, *Genealogy and History*.

Heroic/Martial Exploit Narrative

These narratives concern military exploits or feats of strength by an individual rather than by an army. Most of the martial exploits in the Hebrew Bible come at the expense of the Philistines, beginning with Shamgar killing 600 Philistines with an ox-goad (Judg 3:31).

The **judge cycle** concerning Samson (Judg 13–16) contains several heroic exploits containing two elements: the predicament that Samson is in (Judg 14:5; 15:9–13) usually because of an attachment to Philistine women (Judg 14:11–18; 15:1–3, 6; 16:1–2, 4–20); and the heroic exploit itself (Judg 14:6, 19; 15:4–5; 16:3–4, 9, 12, 14, 28–30), sometimes discussing the spirit of the Lord coming upon Samson (Judg 13:25; 14:6, 19;

15:14). Exploits include killing a lion, killing thirty men of Ashkelon and using their garments to pay off a wager, killing a thousand more Philistines with the jawbone of a donkey, carrying the Gaza city gate for several miles, and culminate in pushing apart the pillars of the temple dedicated to Dagon, ending his own life but killing more Philistines at his death than he had done during his life.

The pattern continues in the book of Samuel with actions against the Philistines by Jonathan and his armor bearer (1 Sam 14:1–14), and most famously by David against the Philistine champion (1 Sam 17:1–51). See the lists chapter for **hero and exploit record** in the **rosters** of David's warriors (2 Sam 21:15–22 [=1 Chr 20:4–8]; 23:8–23 [=1 Chr 11:10–25]).

Frolov, *Judges*, 287–300; Garsiel, "David's Elite Warriors," 1–28; Johnson, "Spirit of Yhwh," 214–36; Mobley, *Empty Men*.

Hieros Logos Narrative

These are narratives which, in addition to whatever role they play with respect to plot and character development, explain the origin of a particular holy site, such as Bethel (Gen 28:18–22; 35:1–15), Mahanaim (Gen 32:1–2), Peniel (Gen 32:22–30), Succoth (Gen 33:17) and the altar at Orpah (Judg 6:19–24). Many of these concern Jacob and involve etiologies concerning the name of the place (see **etiological narrative**). Jacob may have been a particular hero to the tribe of Ephraim (Gen 48) and these narratives surely informed local practices of Israelite religion prior to the Assyrian exile of the northern kingdom.

Albertz, *Israelite Religion*, 1:139–46; Coats, *Genesis*, 206–9, 223–32, 236–40, 318; Hutton, "Mahanaim, Penuel," 161–78; Long, *Etiological Narrative*; Pury, *Promesse Divine*; Sweeney, "Jacob Narratives," 236–55.

Human Sacrifice Narrative

God tests Abraham by commanding him to sacrifice his son Isaac on Mount Moriah but God relents [see **crisis narrative**] at the last moment as Abraham has demonstrated his obedience, and a ram is sacrificed instead of Isaac (Gen 22:1–19). This famous passage is known as the *Akedah* or "The Binding of Isaac" in Judaism and according to 2 Chr 3:1, Mount Moriah is where the temple later stood. The interpretation of the passage has been hotly disputed. Abraham is often seen as believing from the beginning that he would not have to sacrifice Isaac (in v. 5, he says "we will return to you") but in turn as testing the character of God who cannot permit actual human sacrifice. Christians see Gen 22 a foreshadowing of the sacrifice of Christ (Heb 11:17–19). They see parallels in Isaac being effectively dead to Abraham for three days and carrying the wood himself. Muslims usually regard Ishmael as the son nearly sacrificed.

Some ethicists argue that Abraham should have disobeyed God, others that this is a teleological suspension of the ethical, and others that by the command of God humans may inflict death upon those whom otherwise it would be prohibited. The relationship between this passage and practice of human sacrifice in ancient Canaan is also disputed.

Jephthah vows (see **vow narrative**), conditional upon victory over the Ammonites, to sacrifice whoever comes out of his house to meet him. To his great grief, his daughter comes out but Jephthah fulfills his vow (Judg 11:34–40). The many complex issues raised by this passage include whether human sacrifice was considered acceptable in certain Israelite circles, whether the vow was considered invalid once Jephthah's daughter came to meet him (if human sacrifice was unacceptable), whether Jepthah's daughter was sacrificed or just remained a life-long virgin, and whether the narrator defended or disapproved of Jephthah's action.

King Mesha of Moab sacrificed his oldest son when a battle was going against him (2 Kgs 3:26–27), a stratagem used by several societies in similar circumstances, and the Israelites forces withdrew. See **human sacrifice prohibition** in legal genres chapter.

Banks, *Jephtas Tochter*; Coats, "Abraham's Sacrifice," 389–400; Dewrell, *Child Sacrifice*; Levenson, *Death and Resurrection*; Long, *2 Kings*, 38–48; Trible, *Texts of Terror*, 93–116.

Intercession Narrative

This is a subcategory of **prayer narrative** in which the character intercedes for another party (see also **royal intercession psalm**). On several occasions, YHWH threatens to destroy a people but is persuaded otherwise by the protagonist. Abraham intercedes for Sodom (Gen 18:16–33), YHWH agrees to Abraham's terms but even under them Sodom is destroyed (Gen 19). Several prophets successfully intercede with YHWH on behalf of Israel: Moses (Exod 32:1–14, 30–34; Num 14:13–25), Samuel

(1 Sam 7:3–12) and Amos (Amos 7:1–6). Classical theists analyze all these passages differently than do open and process theists.

Ballentine, "Prophet as Intercessor," 61–73; Filson, "Petition and Intercession," 21–34; Sweeney, "Intercessory Prayer," 213–30.

Interrogation Narrative

An interrogation is a series of non-rhetorical questions by an authority eliciting responses by a character in potential jeopardy. Although series of two or three **inquiries** are common in biblical **dialogues** (see also **question and answer subunit** in the chapter on prophetic genres), full-fledge interrogations are fairly rare. Joseph twice interrogates his brothers (Gen 42:6–25; 44:1–34) to test them and perhaps also to fulfill his dreams (see **dream narrative**). For further examples, see prophetic narratives chapter.

Introductory Regnal Resumé

This is the part of the regnal resumé that occurs at the beginning of a **regnal narrative**. If it is part of a **reign of Israelite King narrative**, it normally contains the **accession formula**, the **length of reign formula**, and perhaps a mention of the capital city. If it is part of a reign of Judahite King narrative, it normally contains an **accession formula**, an **age at accession formula**, a **length of reign formula**, and the name of the queen mother. Usually, the introductory resumé is followed by the **theological evaluation of the reign**. See also **concluding regnal resumé**.

Halpern and Vanderhooft, "Editions of Kings," 179–244.

Journey Narrative

Many narratives begin with an arrival or end with a departure but fewer focus on the journey as a whole. Journey narratives may follow a **commission to get wife narrative** and precede a **marriage narrative** (Gen 24:10–11; 28:10—29:1). The suitor may return to his kin after the marriage narrative (Gen 24:61–65; 33:1–20; Exod 4:18–31). It may be unmotivated (Gen 11:31) or in response to God's command (Gen 12:4–9). Joseph's brothers make journeys because of famine (Gen 42:25–38; 43:1–15; 45:21–25; 46:5–7; 46:28—47:12), as do Naomi and Ruth (Ruth

1:6–19a). Journey narratives mark key narrative transitions during the Exodus and Wilderness Wanderings (Exod 12:37–42; 13:17–22; Num 10:11–36; 21:10–20; 22:1; 33:1–49). Ezra comes from Babylonia to Jerusalem (Ezra 7:1–10). The narratives vary considerably (see also **flight narrative**), but possible elements include preparations for the journey, who accompanied the protagonist, and any encounters (see **encounter narratives**) on the way.

Martin, "Betrothal Journey Narratives," 505–23; Scholz, "Women on Road," 243–46.

Judges Cycle

The cycle of episodes centered around the activities of a judge typically include the following themes: Israel has sinned; YHWH hands Israel over to a foreign nation who oppress the Israelites; the Israelites cry out to YHWH; YHWH raises up a judge/deliverer; the deliverer battles against the enemy, killing the leader; the land has rest; and the judge dies. In Othniel's case, the cycle consists of just one episode (Judg 3:7–11), basically consisting of one formula after another but hitting all the elements.

The Othniel Cycle has a single episode (Judg 3:7–11); the Ehud Cycle has three episodes (Judg 3:12–17, 18–25, 26–30); the Deborah/Barak Cycle has six episodes (Judg 4:1–3, 4–11, 12–15, 16–21, 22–24; 5:1–31); the Gideon Cycle has fourteen episodes (Judg 6:1–6, 7–10, 11–24, 25–32, 33–35, 36–40; 7:1–8, 9–12, 13–23, 24–25; 8:1–3, 4–21, 22–28, 29–35); the Abimelech Anti-Hero Cycle has four episodes (Judg 9:1–6, 7–21, 22–49, 50–57); the Jephthah cycle has six episodes (Judg 10:6–18; 11:1–11, 12–28, 29–33, 34–40; 12:1–7); and the Samson cycle has eight episodes (Judg 13:1–24; 13:25—14:4; 14:5–20; 15:1–8, 9–20; 16:1–3, 4–22, 23–31). Although Samuel is a judge, the narrative of his judgeship (1 Sam 1–7) does not follow this pattern.

Assis, *Self-Interest*; Frolov, *Turn of Cycle*; Frolov, *Judges*, 87–100; Gillmayer-Bucher, "Framework and Discourse," 687–702; Hull, "Finding the Center," 145–58; Kim, *Samson Cycle*; Sterman, "Deborah Narrative," 15–24; Sternberg, *Poetics*, 264–83, 331–37; Toblowsky, "Samuel the Judge," 376–98.

Legislative Speech Narrative

There is no book in the Hebrew Bible containing simply laws. Rather, any laws or law codes are presented within a narrative setting. Occasionally, the legislative speech narrative consists of a **legislative speech subunit** (Exod 12:1–27a, 43–49; 20:1–17; 34:10–26; Num 8:1–2, 5–19; 9:1–3; 28:1—29:39), followed by a **compliance subunit** (Exod 12:27b–28, 50; Num 8:3–4, 20–22; 9:4–5; 30:1 [NRSV 29:40]), **reactions subunit** (Exod 20:18–21), or **divine command subunit** and **compliance subunit** (Exod 34:27–28). More commonly, the genre consists of a **legislative speech subunit** alone (Gen 9:1–7; Exod 13:1, 2–16; 20:1–17; 20:22—23:33; 34:10–28; Lev 1:1—3:17; 4:1—5:13; 5:14–19; 6:1–7, 8–18, 19–23; 6:24—7:21; 7:22–27, 28–38; 11:1–47; 12:1–8; 13:1–59; 14:1–32, 33–57; 15:1–33; 16:1–34; 17:1–16; 18:1–30; 19:1–37; 20:1–27; 21:1–15, 16–24; 22:1–16, 17–33; 23:1–8, 9–22, 23–25, 26–32, 33–44; 24:1–23; 25:1—26:45; 27:1–33; Num 5:1–4, 5–10, 11–31; 6:1–21, 22–27; 8:23–26, 10:1–10; 15:1–16, 17–31, 37–41; 18:1–7, 8–24, 25–32; 19:1–22; 28:1—30:17 [NRSV 28:1—30:16]; 35:1–8, 9–34; Deut 1:6—4:40; 4:44—26:19; 27:1–8; 27:11—28:69 [NRSV 27:11—29:1]; 29:1—30:20 [NRSV 29:2—30:20]; 31:10–13). See legal genres chapter for a discussion of the various laws contained in these narratives.

Legal Case Narrative

Leviticus 24:10–23 presents the story of a soujourner who blasphemed, was held in custody until YHWH's decision was made clear, YHWH tells Moses (see **divine command narrative**) that the blasphemer is to be stoned and specifies other laws for which sojourners must suffer the same penalty as Israelites, and then in a **compliance narrative**, the people obey and stone the man. The passage demonstrates an overriding theme in Leviticus, that of YHWH's holiness, and warns the Israelites to obey the laws and avoid the man's fate. A similar pattern of divine command narrative and compliance narrative occurs in Num 15:32–36 where an Israelite who gathered sticks on the Sabbath is stoned to death by the congregation. Together, these narratives may form part of a pattern in Genesis through Kings where there is a narrative counterpart to each of the ten commandments.

The law concerning the second Passover in Num 9 (see Passover/Unleavened Bread Passage in legal genres) is given in a narrative context, where those who were unable to celebrate the Passover because of ritual uncleanness are permitted to keep it a month later. See also **festival observance narrative** because Hezekiah keeps the Second Passover (2 Chr 30:1–27).

Numbers 27:1–11 discusses the circumstances in which the daughters of Zelophehad succeed in improving an inheritance law which had previously allowed only sons to inherit. In Num 36:1–9, the Manassites remind Moses that Zelophehad's inheritance was to pass on to his daughters and point out that if the daughters marry outside the tribe of Manasseh, this will result in that tribe losing land (Num 36:1–4), and Moses concedes the point, prescribes (from YHWH) that the daughters of Zelophehad may marry any man within the tribe of Manasseh but only within that tribe, and makes it a general legal principle (Num 36:5–9). The narrative concludes with a **compliance subunit** in which Zelophehad's daughters did as YHWH had commanded and their inheritance remained in the tribe of Manasseh (Num 36:10–12).

Burnside, "Sabbath Gatherer," 45–62; Chavel, *Oracular Law*; Fuad, "Curious Case," 51–70; Knierim and Coats, *Numbers*, 117–25, 200–202, 273–75, 329–30; Trevaskis, "Purpose," 295–312.

Marriage Narrative

Most narratives involving a married couple do not narrate how the couple met and got married, but some do. The scenes in Gen 24:10–67 (Rebekah wooed by Abraham's servant for Isaac) and Gen 29:1–30 (Jacob and Rachel, with Leah thrown in during the wedding night) share the following structure: 1) The man goes to a foreign country, having previously been told to take a wife from there; 2) the man arrives at a well and a time reference is given; 3) a difficulty or test with regard to the watering of livestock is mentioned; 4) a woman comes to the well and her name and heritage are mentioned; 5) the test is passed or the obstacle overcome and the livestock are watered; 6) the man the woman interact and family identity is revealed; 7) the woman runs to tell her family the news; 8) the woman's guardian quickly welcomes the man; 9) the man dialogues with the guardian and obtains her as a bride; 10) a bride-price is given; 11) there is a meal or feast; 12) a complication arises which threatens the marriage; 13; the complication is resolved; and 14) the bridegroom takes his wife.

The scenes in Exod 2 (Moses and Zipporah) and in Ruth (Boaz and Ruth) also have many of these elements, as does the narrative in John 4 concerning Jesus and the Samaritan woman (which does not end in a marriage but arguably with a Johannine counterpart, the Samaritan community acknowledging Jesus as the savior of the world). The narratives involving David have different structures but all involving deaths—in 1 Sam 18, David kills 200 Philistines and wins Michal; 1 Sam 25 recounts Nabal's death followed by David marrying Nabal's widow, Abigail (and Abinoam for good measure); and in 2 Sam 11, David commits adultery with Bathsheba, covers it up by having her husband Uriah killed in battle, and then marries her. Othniel's winning of Achsah (told in both Joshua and Judges) is a reward by Achsah's father, Caleb, for military victory; and the Othniel-Achsah-Caleb trio are more harmonious than the David–Michal–Saul trio.

Alter, *Art of Biblical Narrative*, 47–62; Berger, "Ruth," 253–72; Finlay, "Genres, Intertextuality," 165–71; Fuchs, "Structure," 273–81; Schneider, *Judges*, 10–17; Sternberg, *Poetics*, 131–52; Teugels, "Strong Woman," 89–104; Wolde, "Leader Led," 355–75.

Maśśa'

See entry in prophetic narratives chapter.

Meeting/Visit/Reunion Narrative

This is related to **journey narrative**, but the goal is not toward (or from) a place but to a person or party. The climax of the narrative is usually in a **reactions subunit**, when the parties meet or reunite. Genesis 32:4—33:17 [NRSV 32:3—33:17] is an intercalated narrative, overlapping an **epiphany/theophany narrative** which is also an etiological narrative (Gen 32:23–33 [NRSV 22–32]). It begins with Jacob sending news of a gift to Esau who has long sought to kill him, the messengers return with a report that Esau is coming to meet him with 400 men and Jacob reacts in fear (Gen 32:4–9 [NRSV 3–8]). Then comes a **prayer subunit** in which Jacob pleads for deliverance (Gen 32:10–13 [NRSV 9–12], and a lengthy **preparations subunit** (Gen 32:14–22 [NRSV 13–21]). Jacob does obeisance to Esau when they meet (Gen 33:1–3) but Esau "ran to meet him, and embraced him, and fell on his neck and kissed him, and they wept"

(Gen 33:4). There follows a lengthy **dialogue subunit** in which Jacob acts with typical deception, having no intention of remaining with Esau (Gen 33:5–15), and they part ways (Gen 33:12–17).

The reunion of Joseph with his brothers and father (Gen 45:1—46:30) has several stages: Joseph's revelation of his identity and his brothers' reaction (Gen 45:1–15), Pharaoh's reaction (Gen 45:16–19), a **journey narrative** in which the brothers return to Jacob (Gen 45:21–25), Jacob's reaction on hearing news of Joseph (Gen 45:26–28), a **dream narrative** reconfirming God's covenant with Jacob (Gen 46:1–4), and another journey narrative culminating with Jacob's reaction on seeing Joseph (Gen 46:5–30). The unusually strong emphasis on reactions in this narrative brings the characters to life. That Genesis contains three sets of formerly hostile brothers reunite—Isaac and Ishmael in the **death and burial narrative** of their father Abraham in Gen 25, Esau and Jacob in Gen 32–33, and Joseph and his brothers in Gen 45–46 provides a powerful sermon (see Ps 133:1).

The purpose of short meeting/reunion narratives can involve characterization of the participants as friendly or hostile to each other and/or basic transition elements in plot development. The meeting of Moses and Aaron (Exod 4:27–31) largely serves as a joyful transition between events in Sinai and events in Egypt and joins Moses, Aaron and the elders. Likewise, the bittersweet reunion of Naomi with her kinswomen (Ruth 1:19b–22) serves as a transition between the **journey narrative** to Bethlehem (Ruth 1:6–19a) and the **agricultural narratives** in Bethlehem beginning in Ruth 2 which will eventually turn Naomi's bitterness to joy. Less joyful is the reunion of Michal with David, which separates Michal from her doting husband, Palti who weeps profusely but hopelessly (2 Sam 3:14–16). This brief passage gives poignancy to Michal's later complaint against David (2 Sam 6: 16–23). And in the meeting between Solomon and Hiram in 1 Kgs 9:10–14, which differs in style and content from the surrounding material and looks back at the **treaty narrative** in 1 Kgs 5:10–12, Hiram directly voices his complaint to Solomon.

The reunion of Moses with his wife, Zipporah, his sons, Gershom and Eliezer, and his father, Jethro is far more significant in its own right (Exod 18:1–27). Here, the focus lies on Jethro rather than on Zipporah. Zipporah is likewise passive in the **marriage narrative** (Exod 2:15b–21) so this characterization largely fits her but she is the agent of rescue in the **crisis narrative** (Exod 4:24–26). The passage has been interpreted as anti-Moses (Moses can't take care of his family in vv. 1–2, and Jethro initiates the sacrifice in v. 12) or as anti-Jethro (Jethro's criticism of Moses in vv. 17–23). However, the passage shows them in harmony rather than in conflict, Jethro praises what YHWH has done through Moses, and Moses benefits from Jethro's advice, putting it into action.

The reunion of David with Absolom (2 Sam 14:1–33) is a literary masterpiece of characterization through **dialogue**. Joab dialogues with the wise woman of Tekoa (vv. 1–3), the wise woman of Tekoa dialogues with David (vv. 4–20), David dialogues with Joab (vv. 21–24), and Absalom dialogues with Joab (vv. 31–32). Despite the narrator not assigning YHWH one action in this **wisdom narrative**, all this human scheming results with Absalom in David's presence where he can fulfill YHWH's prophecy through Nathan the prophet (2 Sam 12:11–12).

Jeon, "Visit of Jethro," 289–306; Knierim, "Exodus 18," 146–71; Lyke, *King David*; Winslow, *Early Jewish*.

Messenger Narrative

This is a narrative dominated by a **messenger subunit**, i.e. a narrative which focuses on the role of the messenger(s) in conveying the event. In 1 Sam 4:12–18, the narrator describes the tattered state of the messenger and a worried Eli waiting for the news, notes that the city was in uproar at the messenger's news, further describes Eli inquiring about the news, the messenger finally delivering the terrible news, and Eli falling backwards and dying.

In the **monarch behaving badly narrative** of David's affair with Bathsheba, four messages take place in 2 Sam 11:3–6. Then in 2 Sam 11:18–25, Joab gives a messenger precise instructions on what to tell David, including much that the messenger fails to deliver but which reveals a great deal about the characters of Joab and David (and how Israelites viewed Abimelech). Second Samuel 18:19–32 concerns two messengers who want to deliver news to David, one using geographical knowledge to overtake the other, and David's reaction to the two messages. These narratives give readers insight into main characters and unnamed messengers and make the events more vivid.

Finlay, *Birth Report Genre*, 155–59, 220–30; Polzin, *David and Deuteronomist*, 112–17; Sternberg and Perry, "Ironic Eyes," 262–91.

Minor Judge(s) Narrative

Interspersed between the larger narratives concerning judge/deliverers (see **judges cycle**) are three brief narratives summarizing the careers of one, two, and three judges, respectively (Judg 3:31; 10:1–5; 12:8–15). They reflect a pattern in which the legend cycles of Judges tend to get longer. It is debated whether the main purpose of their inclusion is historiographic or literary.

Mullen, "Minor Judges," 185–201; Nelson, "Ideology, Geography," 347–64.

Monarch Acting Badly Narrative

This category does not include **apostasy narratives**, but is limited to where the monarch abuses power for personal gain. The full structure has six elements: the offense by the king; divine punishment; inquiry of prophet or intermediary (the Hebrew Bible sometimes has an **apostolic prophecy narrative** in which YHWH announces punishment instead of the second and third elements); restitution if possible; sacrifices; and appeasement of deity. In Greek literature, Oedipus the King follows this pattern, as does Agamemnon refusing to ransom the priest's daughter in book 1 of the *Illiad*; and the Hittite treaty between Mursilis and Suppiluliumas also shows these motifs. Biblical examples include the Philistine lords' initial treatment of the ark which after consulting they offer gold figures of mice for (1 Sam 5:1–7:1), David committing adultery with Bathsheba and ordering the death of Uriah (2 Sam 11:1–27; in 2 Sam 12, David says the guilty man should restore fourfold, Nathan prophesies punishment, David confesses and in Ps 51 says God does not want sacrifices, and David is restored to a right relationship with God), Saul's broken treaty with the Gibeonites which David makes restitution for (2 Sam 21), David ordering a census against all advice, being rebuked by Gad and offering a sacrifice for (2 Sam 24:1–25 [=1 Chr 21:1–30]), Ahab's introduction of Baal worship and having Naboth executed so that he could take his vineyard, Elijah's rebuke, and Ahab's partial repentance (1 Kgs 16–18, 21); and Hezekiah showing off his wealth to the king of Babylon, with Isaiah's rebuke and prophecy of exile for Judah into Babylon (2 Kgs 20:12–19 [=2 Chr 32:27–31; Isa 39:1–8]). Saul's slaughter of the priests at Nob (1 Sam 22:6–23) does not fit the pattern but Saul had already been rejected (**prophetic dismissal from kingship narratives** in 1 Sam 13 and

15) and this is perhaps an escalation of his depravity. This is another example of a genre showing the prophetic nature of the Former Prophets.

Hanson, "King Crosses Line," 11–25; Homer, *Iliad* 1.1–475; Sophocles, *Oedipus Tyrranos.*

Mourning Narrative

Although many **death and burial narratives** contain an action of mourning, extended mourning narratives are fairly rare. Jacob's mourning over Joseph (Gen 37:33–35) is poignant in its poetic expression but ironic because Joseph is alive. David surprises the audience by refusing to mourn his baby boy after having fasted for him when alive (2 Sam 12:15–23) and by mourning excessively a son that deposed him (2 Sam 19:1–9a [NRSV 18:33–19:8a]).

Olyan, *Biblical Mourning*; Pham, *Mourning.*

Murmuring Narrative

The Israelites murmur or complain against YHWH during the period between the crossing of the Reed Sea and the entry into the promised land (Exod 15:22–27; 16:1–36; 17:1–7; Num 11:1–35; 14:1–45; 20:2–13; 21:4–9). Standard elements include narration of the difficulty, the murmuring of the people, Moses asking YHWH for help, YHWH intervening to resolve the situation, and some rebuke or punishment against offenders. This tradition of Israelite sin and divine patience can be seen in many psalms, including **prayers of complaint**, and as part of the **basis for punishment subunit** in **prophecies of punishment against Israel/Judah**. See also **revolt/rebellion narrative**.

Coats, *Exodus 1–18*, 123–40; Coats, *Rebellion*; Frankel, *Murmuring Stories*; Knierim and Coats, *Numbers*, 174–78, 183–94, 226–29, 237–39, 356.

Negotiations Narrative

The standard pattern is threefold: exposition of issue; a dialogue subunit where the parties negotiate; and resolution of issue. Many of the negotiations occur in Genesis. Abram and Lot negotiate over where to graze flocks (Gen 13:1–12); Abraham and YHWH negotiate over how many righteous men there need be in Sodom for YHWH to spare the city (Gen 18:23–33); Abraham and the Hittites negotiate over the purchase of a burial plot for Sarah (Gen 23:3–18; see also **death and burial narrative**); Abraham's servant and Laban negotiate over Rebekah becoming a bride for Isaac (Gen 24:33–60; see also **marriage narrative**); Esau and Jacob negotiate over Esau's birthright (Gen 25:29–34; see also **disqualification narrative**); Jacob and Laban negotiate over Jacob marrying Rachel (Gen 29:15–19, 25–28; see also **marriage narrative**); Leah and Rachel negotiate over mandrakes (Gen 30:25–34); Shechem and Hamor negotiate with Jacob and his sons regarding Shechem marrying Dinah (Gen 34:4–24; see **rape narrative**); and Judah negotiates with Tamar over sexual relations (Gen 38:12–18). The negotiations narratives serve both to characterize superbly the patriarchs and matriarchs and to illustrate the importance of making wise decisions in negotiations.

In Num 32:1–33, the tribes of Reuben and Gad negotiate for territory east of the Jordan. In Judg 4:4–11, Barak negotiates with Deborah for a condition under which he will lead Naphtali and Zebulun in battle, Deborah concedes but it costs Barak the glory of personally killing the enemy ruler. Jephthah negotiates with the Gileadites the conditions under he will accept leadership (Judg 11:1–11), and then with the Ammonites concerning land from the Arnon to the Jabbok and Jordan (Judg 11:12–28). Boaz negotiates with a close relative of Naomi for the right to marry Ruth (Ruth 4:1–12; see also marriage narrative).

Leuchter, "Genesis 38," 209–27; Rickett, "Rethinking," 31–53.

Offering/Sacrifice Narrative

Moses encourages the Israelites to be generous with their gifts for the construction of the tabernacle (Exod 35:1–29); and after the tabernacle had been constructed, further offerings brought by each tribe are discussed (Num 7:1–89; see lists chapter for further details; this chapter is also a **compliance narrative**). These narratives have been used by Jews and Christians to encourage generosity from their congregations. After the Israelites defeat the Moabites, they give an offering from the plunder (Num 31:25–54).

The Philistines, having learned the cost of disrespecting the ark, send the ark back to Israel with various offerings (1 Sam 6). After YHWH punishes Israel with a plague because of David's census (see **divine judgment**

narrative), David—acting on God's orders this time—builds an altar on Araunah's threshing floor and makes an offering (2 Sam 24:18–25 [=1 Chr 21:18–30]). Ahaz, on the other hand, completely violates divine law by replacing Solomon's altar with a replica of Tiglath-Pileser's one in Damascus on which he makes sacrifices to pagan gods (2 Kgs 16:10–18; 2 Chr 28:22–27).

Of dubious moral worth is Solomon's sacrifice at the high place in Gibeon (2 Chr 1:1–6), just before God grants him wisdom (see **wisdom narrative**). However, his offering (2 Chr 7:1–10) at the **dedication** of the Temple on the Feast of Tabernacles (see **festival offering narrative**) is a model for the reforming kings such as Hezekiah (2 Chr 29:20–36) and Josiah (2 Chr 35:1–19). In post-exilic times, Ezra makes an important offering also (Ezra 8:31–36).

Anderson, *Sacrifices and Offerings*; Beckwith and Selman, *Sacrifice in Bible*; Cohen, "II Samuel 24," 17–40; Milgrom, "The Chieftains Gifts," 221–25.

Opportunity for Regicide Narrative

In narratives whose patterns mirror each other closely, David twice refuses an opportunity to kill Saul (1 Sam 23:19–24:23 [NRSV 23:19—24:22]; 26:1–25). Ziphites tell Saul that David is hiding at the hill of Hachilah (23:19; 26:1), Saul takes three thousand chosen men to seek David (24:3 [NRSV 2]; 26:2), Saul's party stop by road (1 Sam 24:4 [NRSV 3]; 26:3), David's men urge him to kill Saul (24:5 [NRSV 4]; 26:8), David tells them he cannot raise his hand against YHWH's anointed (24:7 [NRSV 6]; 26:9, 11); David takes something from Saul (24:5 [NRSV 4]; 26:11–12), David calls to Saul or Abner (1 Sam 24:9 [NRSV 8]; 26:13–14), Saul replies, "Is that your voice, my son David?" (1 Sam 24:17 [NRSV 16]; 26:17), David declares his innocence (1 Sam 24:12 [NRSV 11]; 26:18), David chides Saul's men (1 Sam 24:10 [NRSV 9]; 26:19), Saul acknowledges guilt (1 Sam 24:18 [NRSV 17]; 26:21), Saul and David part (1 Sam 24:23 [NRSV 22]; 26:25). When these structural similarities are combined with close verbal parallels between the narratives, the likelihood increases that one version is derived from the other, though scholars debate the direction and purpose of borrowing. Setting wise, the two narratives show David's political savvy—he knows that a dynasty built on regicide is extremely shaky—but contrast with the episode between them, where

David is prevented from the political mistake of killing Nabal by Abigail's wise advice (1 Sam 25:18–35).

Edenburg, "Not Murder," 64–85; Koch, *Growth*, 137–48; Polzin, *Samuel and Deuteronomist*, 205–15; Seters, "Two Stories," 93–104; Wearne, "Reading Samuel," 337–54; Wolde, "Leader Led," 355–75.

Oracular Inquiry Narrative

This involves a protagonist going to a prophet to inquire about the future, and the prophet responding with an **oracular prophecy**. The most famous example in the ancient world was that of people inquiring of the oracle at Delphi. In the Hebrew Bible, many inquiries were of YHWH and the answer was presumably received through the Urim and Thummim on the ephod. Frequently, the inquirer asks two questions rather than one. The full pattern of this narrative involved the following elements: the issue needing addressing; the oracular inquiry subunit; the oracular answer subunit; and the fulfillment or results of the oracle.

Oracular inquiry narratives mainly occur outside the latter prophets. Rebekah asks YHWH about her pregnancy (Gen 25:22–23; **annunciation narrative**) and the answer is progressively fulfilled in Israel's history with Edom, the Israelites ask YHWH about which tribe should lead the attack (Judg 1:1–2; 20:18, 23, 26–28; **civil war narrative**) and Judah's leadership bookending Judges is a pre-Word to eventual Judean kingship, Saul asks Samuel an innocuous question about the location of his father's donkeys and is anointed king (1 Sam 9:5–10:8; **coronation narrative**), David asks YHWH whether to battle Philistines and whether the men of Keilah would surrender him and he successfully evades Saul (1 Sam 23:1–13), Saul asks the witch of Endor about Samuel and learns of the impending doom awaiting him and his sons (1 Sam 28:4–25; **prophetic dismissal from kingship narrative**), David asks YHWH which city to enter and is crowned at Hebron (2 Sam 2:1; **coronation narrative** at Hebron) and of whether to go up against the Philistines (2 Sam 5:19 [=1 Chr 14:10]; **battle narrative**), Jehoshaphat inquiring of Micaiah whether to battle against Aram (1 Kgs 22:1–28 [= 2 Chr 18:1–27]; **battle narrative**), King Ben-Hadad of Aram inquires of Elisha if he will recover (2 Kgs 8:7–15), and Josiah's officers inquiring of Huldah concerning the book of the law (2 Kgs 22:14–20 [=2 Chr 34:20–28]; **covenant renewal narrative**). See entry in prophetic narratives chapter for other examples.

Huffmon, "Oracular Process," 449–60; Long, *1 Kings*, 153–57, 254–55; Long, *2 Kings*, 38–48, 100–107, 306–7; Na'aman, "David's Sojourn," 87–97; Parker, "Official Attitudes," 50–68; Zucker, "Micaiah," 156–62.

Paradise Narrative

For Gen 2:4—3:24, which is a narrative concerning events in paradise, see **etiological narrative.** In contast to the Tale of Adapa and other ANE parallels, the reason for expulsion from paradise (see **sentencing narrative**) is human disobedience rather than trickery by superhuman beings. Genesis 3:15 arguably has an eschatological dimension in which the woman's seed gains victory over opposition to God as represented by the serpent.

Plague Narrative

For the narratives concerning the plagues on Egypt, see **sign narrative**. For other plague narratives, see **divine judgment narrative**.

Prayer Narrative

This is a narrative dominated by a prayer subunit. In Psalms, we have numerous prayers without the context (see the chapter on Psalms genres for detailed explanations) in which they were prayed (though see **psalm superscription**). In narratives, short prayers occur in all sorts of contexts, and prayer elements are frequent in **annunciation narratives, dedication narratives, fast narratives, prophetic miracle narratives** and **intercession narratives.**

Concerning the knowledge that his son will build the temple, David gives **a prayer of thanksgiving** (2 Sam 7:18–29 [=1 Chr 17:16–27]), and a **prayer of petition** (1 Chr 29:10–20). Daniel thanks God for revealing mysteries to him (Dan 2:17–23) and gives a **penitential prayer** on behalf of the people (Dan 9:13–19); and prayer narratives concerning Ezra occur both in Ezra and in Nehemiah (Ezra 9:1—10:17; Neh 9:6–37). Jehoshaphat also petitions God (2 Chr 20:5–12). In addition to what they inform the readers about the characters that pray, prayer narratives have a formative aspect, encouraging the readers to do likewise.

Ballentine, *Prayer*; Carson, *Teach Us*; Miller, *They Cried*; Throntveit, *When Kings Speak*.

Preparation Narrative

Preparation narratives are usually a subunit of a larger narrative, and the nature of the preparation depends upon what is being prepared for. The Israelites consecrate themselves (Exod 19:9b–15) in preparation for YHWH's appearance (see **theophany narrative**). More painfully, the Israelites circumcise themselves in preparation for Passover (Josh 5;1–9; see **circumcision narrative**). Joshua has certain tribes prepare descriptions of the remaining land (Josh 10:1–18). Solomon prepares building materials before building the temple (1 Kgs 5:15–26 [NRSV 5:1–12]; 2 Chr 2:1–18). Ezra does the same when building the second temple (Ezra 1:5–11), as does Nehemiah when rebuilding Jerusalem (Neh 2:11–18). There are also preparation subunits in many **battle narratives** and **journey narratives**.

Procession Narrative

Several narratives describe the procession of the ark from one place to the next (Josh 3:1—4:24; 6:6–15; 1 Sam 4:4–5; 2 Sam 6:1–19; 19:9b—20:3 [NRSV 19:8b—20:3]; 1 Kgs 8:1–11 [=2 Chr 5:1–14]; 1 Chr 13:1–14; 15:1—16:3). Much scholarly speculation, since M. Noth, involves the "amphictyony question" concerning the extent to which the tribal arrangement of pre-monarchial Israel around the ark was similar to later Greek sacral leagues. These narratives seems both informational (regarding the movements of the ark) and formational (demonstrating YHWH's sovereignty and holiness). YHWH grants Israel victory at Jericho through a procession but later allows the Philistines to capture the ark when the Israelites become presumptive. YHWH's holiness is demonstrated by punishments on the irreverent but also via the cloud of glory that descends upon Solomon's Jerusalem temple when the ark is laid to rest there.

Campbell, *Ark Narrative*; Frolov, *Turn of Cycle*; Noth, *System*.

Prophetic Dismissal from Kingship Narrative

This narrative involves a **prophecy of punishment against an individual** (see prophetic speech chapter) and typically has a threefold structure: the king's sin; the prophet announcing judgment or rebuking the king; and an aftermath.

The dismissal of Saul, like his **coronation narratives**, is complex. An initial account discusses Saul making a burnt offering himself instead of waiting for Samuel (1 Sam 13:8–10), Samuel's rebuke and Saul's defense (1 Sam 13:11–12), and Samuel's prophecy that Saul's kingdom will be transferred to a man after God's own heart (1 Sam 13:13–15a). Saul's reign continues, but with his son Jonathan acting better than does Saul (1 Sam 13:15b—14:46). Then comes a summary of Saul's reign similar to the ends of **regnal narratives** in 1 and 2 Kings (1 Sam 14:47–52). A second narrative recounts Saul's taking of booty and sparing of the Amalekite king, Agag, contrary to God's command (1 Sam 15:1–9), YHWH telling Samuel what Saul had done (1 Sam 15:10–11), a **dialogue subunit** in which Saul keeps changing his story and Samuel makes clear that YHWH has rejected him (1 Sam 15:13–30), and an aftermath including Samuel executing Agag and eventually crowning David as Saul's successor (1 Sam 15:31—16:13; see **execution narrative, coronation narrative**).

A **conditional prophecy of punishment** (1 Kgs 9:1–9) provides a pre-word to Solomon's dismissal. Then comes an **apostacy narrative** (1 Kgs 11:1–8), the prophecy of punishment which excepts the tribe of Judah as continuing to be ruled by Solomon's descendants (1 Kgs 11:9–13), and an aftermath where YHWH raises two adversaries against Solomon (1 Kgs 11:14–22, 23–25; see **adversary narratives**) and Ahijah symbolizing to Jeroboam that he would rule over ten tribes (1 Kgs 11:26–39; **report of a prophetic symbolic action**). Ironically, Ahijah presides over Jeroboam's dismissal which consists of an **apostacy narrative** (1 Kgs 12:25–33; 13:33–34), an **oracular prophecy narrative** in which Abijah tells Jeroboam's wife that her son Abijah will die and Jeroboam's dynasty end (1 Kgs 14:1–16), and an aftermath in which Abijah and Jeroboam die (1 Kgs 14:17–20) and Baasha ends Jeroboam's dynasty (1 Kgs 15:27–30; **fulfillment subunit**). The dismissal of Baasha in turn contains a **theological evaluation subunit** portraying Baasha as continuing Jer-oboam's apostacy (1 Kgs 15:34), the punishment pronounced by Jehu son of Hanani (1 Kgs 16:1–4), and the aftermath of the end of Baasha and his dynasty (1 Kgs 16:7).

Campbell, *Prophets and Kings*; Campbell, *1 Samuel*, 134–66; Long, *1 Kings*, 120–70; Sternberg, *Poetics*, 482–513.

Prophetic Miracle Narrative

These narratives typically concern either Elijah or Elisha as divine agents performing miracles or as the recipients of miracles that have no human agent (1 Kgs 17:1–7, 8–16, 17–24; 18:30–38, 41–46; 2 Kgs 1:5–12; 2:1–12, 13–18, 19–22; 4:1–7, 8–17, 18–37, 38–41, 42–44; 5:1–19a, 19b–27; 6:1–7, 8–23; 7:1–20; 13:21). They are not intended to be fictional accounts, but whether the reader regards them as recording what actually happens depends greatly upon the reader's attitude toward miracles in general. Many of the miracle narratives involve either a pure act of grace on those suffering or a blessing for those who support the prophet despite opposition or difficulties. Others involve judgment upon those opposed to YHWH. In addition to informational aspects, individual miracle narratives may validate the prophet, warn not to oppose YHWH, and encourage YHWH's servants.

At the level of their contribution to the historical phase of monarchic rule unit in 1 Kgs 13—2 Kgs 17, the seven miracles of Elijah and the fourteen miracles of Elisha validate the granting to Elisha a double portion of the Spirit upon Elijah (2 Kgs 1:9–12), again demonstrating YHWH's sovereignty. Coming in the middle of the last book of the former prophets, they prepare for entire books about individual prophets.

Geisler, *Miracles*; Levine, "Twice as Much," 25–46; Lewis, *Miracles*; Moore, *God Saves*; Olley, "Zealous Prophet," 25–51; Petersen, *Roles*; Rofé, *Prophetical Stories*.

Prophetic Symbolic Action Narrative

For a fuller discussion of the genre, including bibliography, see **report of prophetic symbolic action** in the chapter on prophetic narratives. Outside the writing prophets, we see examples of this genre in Ahijah's tearing of the robe into portions and giving ten to Jeroboam, symbolizing Jeroboam ruling over the ten northern tribes (1 Kgs 11:29–39); and Joash's striking arrows on the ground at Elisha's command, with each action of striking symbolizing a victory over Aram (2 Kgs 13:14–25).

Provision Narrative

David, fulfilling a promise made to Jonathan, brings Mephibosheth to eat at the king's table (2 Sam 9:1–13), an event that foreshadows the ending of the Deuteronomistic History, when King Evil-Merodach does the same for Jehoiachin (2 Kgs 25:27–30 [=Jer 52:31–34]). There is fierce debate as to whether the end of 2 Kings is hopeful or not.

The other provision narratives are a subcategory of **prophetic miracle narratives** in the Elijah-Elisha cycles (1 Kgs 17:1–7, 8–16; 2 Kgs 4:1–7, 38–41, 42–44).

Frolov, "Evil-Merodach," 174–90; Joo, "Fine Balance," 226–43.

Raid Narrative

A raid is a temporary incursion into enemy territory. While a mercenary for the Philistines, David conducts raids Israelite enemies from his base in Ziklag (1 Sam 27:5–12) presented in summary form by the narrator. The Amalekites then raid David's camp and take away the women. David eventually defeats the Amalekites, rescues the women, recovers the booty, and distributes it generously (1 Sam 30:1–31). Similar to the **apology for hero narratives** concerning David, these narratives serve to legitimize David's period as a Philistine mercenary.

Shishak's campaign against Jerusalem is narrated almost as if it were a raid (1 Kgs 14:25–28 [=2 Chr 12:2–12]; as are similar campaigns by Pharaoh Neco (2 Kgs 23:33–34 [=2 Chr 36:3–4], and by King Nebuchadnezzar against Jehoiakim (2 Chr 34:6–7) and Jehoiachin (2 Kgs 24:11–16 [=2 Chr 36:10]).

Shemesh, "David in Service," 73–90.

Rape Narrative

This is a narrative which portrays one character forcing sex upon another character without that character's consent. The thematic structure is threefold, background leading to the event, the act of rape itself, and the aftermath/consequences. The paradigm story is the rape of Tamar in 2 Sam 13. The background consists of Amnon's desire for his half-sister Tamar and his compliance with his friend Jonadab's advice for getting Tamar alone in his room (2 Sam 13:1–9). Then Amnon demands Tamar lie with him, Tamar refuses, and he takes her by force (2 Sam 13:10–14). The aftermath unfolds: Amnon loathes Tamar, Tamar tears her exquisite robe (described in identical terms with Joseph's robe in Gen 37), David is angry but does nothing, and Tamar's brother Absalom avenges her by killing Amnon and then fleeing to Geshur (2 Sam 13:15–39; see **assassination narrative**; **flight narrative**).

In Gen 19, when the men of Sodom want to have carnal knowledge with Lot's guests, Lot offers them his daughters instead to abuse, but that offer is declined; at the end of the narrative, the daughters take their revenge by getting Lot so drunk that "he did not know when she lay down or when she arose," having sex with him and thereby having sons by him. Those sons, Moab and Ben-Ammi, became frequent foes of Israel. In Gen 34, Shechem rapes Dinah but then has genuine feelings for her, Jacob seems to do nothing, and Dinah's brothers, prominently Simeon and Levi, take revenge by annihilating the Shechemites.

In Judg 19:22–30, the men of Gibeah in Benjamin do what the Sodomites declined and rape the *pilegeš* ("concubine") of the visiting Ephraimite and leave her for dead. The Ephraimite then dismembers her body (and it is not clear that she had died before he started the operation), and sends it to the tribes of Israel who muster and almost entirely wipe out the tribe of Benjamin (see **civil war narrative**). The "solution" to aid the tribe of Benjamin recover was for the remaining Benjamites to carry off the daughters of Shiloh at a festival dance (Judg 21:19–23), in a story reminiscent of the "Rape of the Sabine Women" in Roman literature. Israel has fallen very far indeed.

Although power politics were clearly involved in David's relations with Bathsheba (2 Sam 11:1–5), there are enough gaps in the narratives involving David and Bathsheba (including 1 Kgs 1) to allow both the reading that she only slept with David under duress or that she was making a power play of her own. In any case, her behavior is different from Tamar in 2 Sam 13:1–22, who vigorously protests but is forcibly raped by Amnon. Like Jacob, David does nothing but Tamar's brother, Absalom, takes his vengeance by killing Amnon.

The fact that the rapists, and the communities who support them, end up dead in several of these narratives argues that the narratives are partly cautionary for how violent a transgression against the community rape constitutes. Sadly, these narratives also demonstrate how powerless ANE women frequently were.

Absali, "Was It Rape?" 1–15; Blyth, *Narrative of Rape*; Feinglass, "Rape of Tamar," 174–81; Grossman, "Lot's Daughters," 40–57; Schneider, "Achsah," 43–57; Scholz, *Sacred Witness*; Shemesh, "Rape Is Rape," 2–21; Sternberg, *Poetics*, 445–75; Yamada, *Configurations of Rape*.

Regnal Narrative

This narrates the reign of a king and is the dominant genre in most of Samuel, Kings, and Chronicles. The narratives of the three kings of the united monarchy—Saul, David, and Solomon—don't have the sort of definitive beginnings and endings that we see for later monarchs. Saul is acclaimed king in three separate **coronation narratives** (1 Sam 9:1—10:16; 10:17–27; 11:12–15), he is disqualified for kingship in two **disqualification narratives** (1 Sam 13:1–9; 15:1–9) but his **death and burial narrative** is in 1 Sam 31:1–6, long after David has been privately anointed king by Samuel (1 Sam 16:1–13). David is crowned publically by first Judah (2 Sam 2:1–4a) and then all Israel (2 Sam 5:1–5) after having won a civil war against Ish-bosheth whose coronation by Israel is recorded in 2 Sam 2:8–11. Solomon's coronation narrative occurs before David's death and burial narrative.

After the death of Solomon, the regnal narratives are subdivided into two categories: **reign of Israelite King narrative** and **reign of Judahite king narrative**.

Brettler, "1 Kings 1–11," 87–97; Williams, "Once Again," 49–66.

Reign of Athaliah narrative

Neither Kings nor Chronicles regard Athaliah as a legitimate ruler of Judah. She was the daughter of Ahab and married into the royalty of Judah. When her son Ahaziah died, she took the throne and tried to kill all rival claimants, including her grandchildren. Jehosheba, Athaliah's daughter or step-daughter, hides Athaliah's grandson Joash who becomes king after Athaliah is killed in a coup (2 Kgs 11:1–20; 2 Chr 22:10–31).

Long, *2 Kings*, 145–56.

Reign of Israelite King Narrative

As with **reign of Judahite King narratives** with which they are interspersed, the standard pattern is **introductory regnal resumé** (including **theological evaluation**), episodes concerning the king, and **concluding regnal resumé**. The number and complexity of the episodes concerning the king determine whether the narrative is a **report**, **account**, or **story**. These narratives concern only the northern kings of Israel in the divided kingdom period and they do not occur in Chronicles. The reigns covered are those of Jeroboam (1 Kgs 12:25—14:20), Nadab (1 Kgs 15:25–33), Baasha (1 Kgs 15:33—16:7), Elah (1 Kgs 16:8–14), Zimri (1 Kgs 16:15–22), Omri (1 Kgs 16:23–28), Ahab (1 Kgs 16:29—22:40), Ahaziah (1 Kgs 22:52—2 Kgs 2:25), Jehoram (2 Kgs 3:1—9:24), Jehu (2 Kgs 9:25—10:36), Jehoahaz (2 Kgs 13:1–9), Jehoash (2 Kgs 13:10–25), Zachariah (2 Kgs 15:8–12), Jeroboam (2 Kgs 14:23–29), Shallum (2 Kgs 15:13–16), Menachem (2 Kgs 15:17–22), Pekahiah (2 Kgs 15:23–26), Pekah (2 Kgs 15:27–31) and Hoshea (2 Kgs 17:1–6, which leads into an **exile narrative**). The narratives concerning Ahab, Ahaziah, and Jehoram contain several **prophetic miracle narratives** concerning Elijah and Elisha. None of the northern kings receive a positive theological evaluation and 2 Kgs 17 explains why the northern kingdom went into exile.

Reign of Judahite King Narrative

As with **reign of Israelite King narratives** with which they are interspersed in Kings, the standard pattern is **introductory regnal resumé** (including **theological evaluation**), episodes concerning the king, and **concluding regnal resumé**. The number and complexity of the episodes concerning the king determine whether the narrative is a **report**, **account**, or **story**. These concern the kings of the southern kingdom of Judah and are recorded in both Kings and Chronicles: Rehoboam (1 Kgs 14:21–31 [=2 Chr 10:1–12:16]), Abijam (1 Kgs 15:1–8 [=2 Chr 13:1–23]), Asa (1 Kgs 15:9–24 [=2 Chr 14:1–16:14]), Jehoshaphat (1 Kgs 22:41–51 [=2 Chr 17:1—20:37]), Jehoram (2 Kgs 8:16–24 [=2 Chr 21:1–20]), Ahaziah (2 Kgs 8:25—11:20 [=2 Chr 22:1–9]), Jehoash (2 Kgs 12:1–22 [=2 Chr 24:1–27]), Amaziah (2 Kgs 14:1–22 [=2 Chr 25:1–28]), Azariah (2 Kgs 15:1–7 [=2 Chr 26:1–23]), Jotham (2 Kgs 15:32–38 [=2 Chr 27:1–9]); Ahaz (2 Kgs 16:1–20 [=28:1–27]), Hezekiah (2 Kgs 18:1—20:21 [=2 Chr 29:1—32:33]), Manasseh (2 Kgs 21:1–18 [=2 Chr 33:1–20]),

Amon (2 Kgs 21:19–26 [= 2Chr 33:21–25]), Josiah (2 Kgs 22:1—23:30 [=2 Chr 34:1—35:27]), Jehoahaz (2 Kgs 23:31–35 [=2 Chr 36:1–4]), Jehoiakim (2 Kgs 23:36—24:7 =2 Chr 36:5–8]), Jehoiachin (2 Kgs 24:8–17 [=2 Chr 36:9–10]), and Zedekiah (2 Kgs 24:18—25:7 [=Jer 52:1–11; 2 Chr 36:11–21]). For further details, see the book of Kings in the overview of Tanak chapter. The reigns of the reforming kings Hezekiah and Josiah (who reinstituted the second Passover and the regular Passover respectively) are important with regards to the composition of the Deuteronomistic History or Primary History. King Manasseh is blamed in Kings as the one whose apostasy meant a point of no return so that even Josiah's reforms could not prevent the coming exile of Judah.

Ben Zvi, "Reign of Manasseh," 351–74; Eynickel, *Reform of Josiah*; Na'aman, "Kingdom of Judah," 3–71; Provan, *Hezekiah and Kings*; Sweeney, *King Josiah*; de Vries, "Festival Observance," 104–24.

Reprieve Narrative

This is a narrative with the following elements: a **prophecy of punishment** or of an event detrimental to the addressee; a **prayer subunit** or penitential act by the threatened party; and a **prophecy of a reprieve** (see prophetic speech chapter). In 2 Sam 12:7–14, Nathan prophesies punishment against David (12:7–12), David confesses his sin (12:13a; see Ps 51, a **penitential psalm**), and Nathan In 1 Kgs 21:17–29, Elijah delivers YHWH's prophecy of **punishment against an individual**, Ahaz (21:17–24); then, after a **narratorial evaluation subunit** showing the depths of Ahab's evil (21:25–26), Ahab surprisingly fasts and puts on sackcloth (21:27); and YHWH gives a partial reprieve: "Because he has humbled himself before me, I will not bring the disaster in his days; but in his son's days I will bring the disaster on his house" (21:29). In 2 Kgs 20:1–11 [=Isa 38:1–8], Isaiah tells a sick Hezekiah that he will die, Hezekiah prays, and God, because of hearing Hezekiah's prayer and seeing his tears, grants him a fifteen year reprieve. In 2 Chr 12:5–8, Shemaiah delivers a prophecy of punishment, King Rehoboam and his officers humble themselves, and a prophecy of reprieve lessens the punishment.

Request Narrative

Requests, a standard type of **directive illocution**, occur in the **dialogues** of **negotiations narratives** and many other narratives. The full scheme of the request narrative contains three elements: 1) description of the situation; 2) request; 3) affirmative or negative response to the request. Moses's request to the Edomites for Israel to pass through their land is denied (Num 20:14–21), as is a similar request to the Amorites (Num 21:21–23a). These denied requests play a background role in the various **prophecies of punishment against Edom** and the battle against the Amorites respectively.

There are several request narratives in the second half of Joshua. Caleb requests to Joshua Hebron for an inheritance and Joshua grants it (Josh 14:6–15); Achsah requests certain water springs from her father, Caleb, and he grants it (Josh 15:13–19; Judg 1:14–15); the tribe of Joseph requests additional territory from Joshua and he tells them to clear out the Perizzites and the Rephaim and claim it for themselves (Josh 17:14–18); and the Levites ask for various towns and Joshua provides them (Josh 21:1–8). These requests play a pivotal part in the apportionment of land section of the book of Joshua.

The book of kings opens with David granting Nathan and Bathsheba's request for Solomon to be crowned instead of Adonijah (1 Kgs 1:11–31) followed by Solomon's denial of Adonijah's request for Abishag as wife (1 Kgs 2:13–25). Requests also play a significant role in the prophetic miracle stories in the Elijah–Elisha narratives. Elijah requests the widow of Zarephath to give up the last meal for her and her son; she grants the request and miraculously food is provided for her continually (1 Kgs 17:8–16). Elijah requests that Obadiah risk his life by delivering a certain message, which Obadiah does and survives, as Elijah promised (1 Kgs 18:1–16). Elisha asks Elijah for a double portion of the Spirit that was upon him and this request was granted (2 Kgs 2:8–12), and Elisha's fame helps make successful the Shunammite woman's request for her land to be restored (2 Kgs 8:1–6).

Requests help drive the plot in Esther. Vashti refuses the king's request that she appear "in her crown" (Est 1:10–12), and ends up banished. Esther, imperiling her own life, enters the king's inner court to request his presence at her banquet (Est 5:1–4). At that banquet, Esther requests the king and Haman attend another banquet (Est 5:5–8). At the second banquet, Esther requests from the king her life and the lives of her people (Est 7:1–4), a request which is implicitly granted by the king's later actions. Esther again imperils her life by entering the king's inner court to request the king to issue an edict enabling the Jews to survive, which the king grants (Est 8:1–17).

Schneider, "Achsah," 43–57.

Rescue/Release Narrative

This is similar to a crisis narrative but focuses on the rescue from danger. Abram rescues Lot from a coalition of armies (Gen 14:13–16). For other examples, see entry in prophetic narratives chapter.

Revelatory Prophecy Narrative

This is a narrative in which YHWH reveals a prophecy to a servant without commissioning that servant to address a person or group with that prophecy (1 Sam 3:1–18; 2 Chr 20:14–17). See **revelatory prophecy** in the prophetic genres chapter.

Revolt/Rebellion Narrative

Similar to a **murmuring narrative**, this recounts people showing displeasure with a leader, but more intense in that it names individuals who directly challenge the authority of the leader. Miriam and Aaron rebel against Moses on account of his Cushite wife, a marriage which apparently did not disturb YHWH, and YHWH **rebukes** Aaron and Miriam, inflicts leprosy upon Miram who is healed after Moses intercedes for her (Num 12:1–15; see also **intercession narrative**). More serious is the revolt/rebellion by Korah, Dathan, and Abiram (Num 16:1—17:15 [NRSV 16:1–50]) which leads to the deaths of the rebels and 250 of their followers.

Various leaders revolt against David: his beloved son, Absalom (2 Sam 15:7–12), Sheba, a Benjaminite (2 Sam 20:1–2), and Adonijah makes a power play that David treats as a revolt (1 Kgs 1:5–10). Jeroboam leads a successful revolt against Rehoboam (1 Kgs 12:1–20 [=2 Chr 10:1–19]); and Jehu leads a successful revolt against the house of Ahab (2 Kgs 9:14—10:17). Both of these had support from prophets—Ahijah and Elisha, respectively—but the reigns of both Jeroboam and Jehu ultimately end with a negative theological evaluation. During the reign of Athaliah, supporters of her grandson, Jehoash organize a successful coup (2 Kgs 11:4–20 [=2 Chr 23:1–21]).

Coats, *Rebellion*; Mann, *Run, David*; Winslow, *Early Jewish*.

Scene in Ruth

The four main **episodes in Ruth** are divided into scenes, which largely consist of dialogue between characters in a specific locale: Naomi, Ruth and Orpah on the road from Moab (Ruth 1:6–17), Naomi, Ruth and the townswomen at the entrance to Bethlehem (1:18–22), Naomi and Ruth at their place (2:1–2), Boaz, Ruth and Boaz's men in Boaz's field (2:3–17), Naomi and Ruth at their place (2:18–22), a **summary** statement (2:23), Naomi and Ruth at their place (3:1–5), Boaz and Ruth at Boaz's threshing floor (3:6–15), Naomi and Ruth at their place (3:16–18), Boaz, the next of kin, and the elders at the town gate (4:1–12), a birth report (4:13), and Naomi and the townswomen in Bethlehem (4:14–17).

Scouting Narrative

The basic structure is selection or appointment of scouts, sending them with a stated mission, narration of the mission, the return of the scouts and their reports, and aftermath. The failure in faith of the scouts, with the exceptions of Joshua and Caleb, and YHWH's consequent punishment (the 40 years wandering in the wilderness) characterize Num 13:1—14:45 as a **murmuring narrative**. By contrast, the scouts sent by Joshua to Jericho succeed in their mission (Josh 2:1–23) at the cost of a treaty with the Canaanite Rahab, reflecting the situation in the book of Joshua where the conquest as a whole will largely be successful but with Canannite enclaves and a treaty with the Gibeonites (see **conquest narrative**). The scouting narrative in Judg 18:1–10 is part of an **anti-hero cycle** in the epilogue of Judg and precedes the migration of Danites, connecting it with the Samson cycle. In the context of Judges, it disqualifies Dan as the suitable tribe to lead Israel.

Sentencing Narrative

The underlying structure is three parts: 1) a character offends an authority, often in a **main actions subunit**; 2) the authority sentences the character, perhaps via an **exercitives subunit**; and 3) and a **reactions subunit** in which the character accepts or protests the sentence. The sentence can be banishment, execution, or some other punishment. Examples of banishment include YHWH banishing Adam and Eve from the garden for disobedience (Gen 3:1–24), YHWH banishing Cain for murdering Abel (Gen 4:9–15), Solomon banishing Abiathar for his role in crowning Adonijah (1 Kgs 2:26–27; see also **prophecy fulfillment narrative**), and Ahasuerus banishing Vashti for refusing to appear "in her crown" (Est 1:10–22), a development that leads to Esther becoming queen.

Examples of execution include the **legal case narratives** of Lev 24:10–23 and Num 15:32–36 (for blasphemy and sabbath-breaking respectively), Joshua hanging various Canaanite kings after battle (Josh 8:29; 10:22–26), executions performed by Gideon (Judg 8:18–21), Samuel (1 Sam 15:32–33), David (2 Sam 1:1–16; 4:9–12; see **apology for hero narrative**), Solomon (1 Kgs 2:28–34, 39–46) and Ahasuerus (Est 7:1–10). Two innocent people executed are Naboth (1 Kgs 21:8–13) and Zechariah (2 Chr 24:20–21; see also Matt 23:35; Luke 11:51). Although Judah had intended to execute Tamar, she exposed him as the more guilty party (Gen 38:12–26) and became an ancestress of David and the first woman mentioned in the New Testament. Also of interest is the case of Achan who violated the holy ban by taking plunder from Jericho and is executed but not before he gives a full confession, which traditionalists would argue helps his eternal fate. There is complexity and variety in the sentencing narratives and there is not one purpose which covers them all.

Bessette and Feser, *By Man*, 15–100; Byron, *Cain and Abel*; Finlay, "Natural Law," 41–50.

Separation Narrative

Separations can occur with mutual agreement, with one party leaving the other party, or with one party driving the other party away. We see examples of all three in the Hebrew Scriptures. Abram and Lot separate so that both have space for their flocks (Gen 13:1–18; see **negotiations narrative**). After Ishmael "Isaacs" Isaac, Sarah wants Hagar and Ishmael expel-led. Abraham is reluctant to do so, but YHWH tells him to do as

Sarah said, Abraham complies, and eventually Hagar and Ishmael are miraculously saved from dying of thirst (Gen 21:8–21; see **crisis narrative**). Before he dies, Abraham send all the sons he had by concubines away from Isaac (Gen 25:5–6). Jacob stayed at Laban far longer than he intended but did eventually separate from him, though not without difficulty (Gen 31:1–55; see also **treaty narrative**). The tribes of Reuben, Gad, and the half-tribe of Manasseh depart peacefully over the Jordan from the other tribes (Josh 22:1–9). David's troops which had been acting as Philistine mercenaries under Achish are told to leave by the rest of the Philistine army—which unlike the gullible Achish, is rightly suspicious of them (1 Sam 29:1–11).

Mabee, "Jacob and Laban," 192–207; Rickett, "Rethinking," 31–53; Sherwood, "Hagar and Ishmael," 286–304.

Servant Narrative

In this glossary, Gen 24 is treated as a **marriage narrative**; 1 Sam 9 as a **coronation narrative**; Judg 19 as a **rape narrative**; and 2 Kgs 5 as a **prophetic miracle narrative**. However, servants are prominent in all of them and they can be profitably analyzed as a genre. No doubt there are numerous other plausible categories not listed in this glossary.

Settlement Narrative

The Reubenites and Gadites receive permission to settle in the Trans-Jordan rather than the promised land of Canaan, as do part of the tribe of Manasseh (Num 32:34–42; Josh 13:8–14); Caleb's clan settle the Hebron region (Josh 14:6–15) and Debir (Josh 15:13–19); the Danites migrate northwards and settle there (Judg 18:11–31).

There are also narratives in which the Israelites subdue and settle Canaanite territory immediately after a major battle (Josh 10:27–43; 11:12–23; 13:8–14). Similarly, David subdues and garrisons Edomite territory (2 Sam 8:1–14 [=1 Chr 18:1–13]) but does not settle it.

Frolov, *Judges*, 364.

Siege Narrative

Conducting a siege in the ancient Near East was hard work and often ended in failure. The Bible records successful and failed sieges. Joshua besieges Jericho but captures it via a miracle. Abimelech successfully captures Shechem (Judg 9:44–49) but dies ingloriously while besieging Thebez when a townswoman drops a millstone on his head (Judg 9:50–57).

David successfully besieges Jerusalem and makes it his new capital (2 Sam 5:6–12 [=1 Chr 11:4–9]). Joab besieges Rabbah of Ammon, while David lounges in Jerusalem enjoying the delights of Bathsheba (2 Sam 11:1–5). When David orders the death of Bathsheba's husband, Uriah, Joab conducts what he knows is a stupid frontal assault on Rabbah but will result in Uriah's death, and Joab anticipates that David will chide him for not learning from Abimelech's mistake (2 Sam 11:14–21; see **messenger narrative**). Joab continues the siege and graciously allows David to apply the coup-de-grace to the city (2 Sam 12:26–31). [You can read also read about the siege but without all that boring adultery and death warrant stuff in 1 Chr 20:1–3.] On another occasion, Joab besieges Abel Beth Maacah, where the rebel Sheba is holed up. The siege ends when a wise woman has him executed and tosses his head down to Joab (2 Sam 20:10a–22; see also **wisdom narrative**).

Benhadad of Aram besieges Ahab of Samaria, but Ahab breaks up the siege in an attack that catches Benhadad and his leaders drunk (1 Kgs 20:1–21). This does not stop Benhadad from making a second siege against Samaria which also fails (2 Kgs 6:24–7:20). When Hazael of Aram besieges Jehoash in Jerusalem, Jehoash pays tribute to him (2 Kgs 12:17–18). Assyrian records portray Sennacherib as having captured 46 cities and caging Hezekiah like a bird in Jerusalem; the Hebrew Bible records Hezekiah praying to YHWH because of Sennacherib's siege and YHWH sending an angel to destroy the Assyrian army (2 Kgs 18:9—19:37 [=2 Chr 32:1–23; Isa 36:1–37:38]) and Herodotus argues that mice were the real reason for Israel's surprise victory. Where the Assyrians failed, Nebuchadnezzar of Babylon succeeded and Jerusalem fell (2 Kgs 25:1–7 [=Jer 52:1–12; 2 Chr 36:15–19]). See also **battle narrative**.

Eph'al, *City Besieged*.

Sign Narrative

The narratives concerning the first nine plagues upon Egypt (Exod 7:14–25; 7:26—8:11 [NRSV 8:1–15]; 8:12–15 [NRSV 8:16–19], 16–28 [NRSV 20–32]; 9:1–7, 8–12, 13–35; 10:1–20, 21–29; 11:1–10) follow the same pattern as established by Moses's sign of turning his rod into a snake (Exod 7:8–13), namely 1) a **divine command narrative** in which Moses and/or Aaron is commanded to perform a sign/plague; 2) a **compliance narrative**; 3) a narrative about the effects of the sign; 4) possible attempts by Egyptian magicians to reduplicate the sign; 5) an intercession narrative in which YHWH stops the plague; 6) Pharaoh hardening his heart. These narratives serve several purposes: a polemic against the Egyptian gods, many of which are associated with the items being plagued; characterization of Pharaoh as stubborn; and demonstration of YHWH's sovereignty. This series of signs is foreshadowed in the **vocation narrative** of Moses, where YHWH shows various signs to Moses (Exod 4:1–5, 6–7, 8–9) in response to Moses's objections. A similar pattern of signs in response to objections occurs in the **vocation narrative** of Gideon (Judg 6:11–24, 36–40). Several **historical psalms** mention various of these signs/plagues.

Coats, *Exodus 1–18*, 60–79; Grossman, "Structural Paradigm," 588–610; Hoffmeier, "Arm of God," 378–87.

Sister-Wife Narrative

Three narratives (Gen 12:10–20; 20:1–18; 26:6–13) involve the following aspects: 1) there is a famine or natural disaster (Gen 12:10a; missing; 26:1); 2) the patriarch and his wife go to a foreign country (Gen 12:10b; 20:1; 26:2–6); 3) the patriarch fears that the ruler will kill him and take his beautiful wife (Gen 12:11–12; missing; 26:7) 4) the patriarch pretends that the wife is his sister and the matriarch does not act to the contrary (Gen 12:13–16; 20:2; 26:7); 5) the ruler finds out that the matriarch is the patriarch's wife (Gen 12:17; 20:3–7; 26:8); 6) the ruler rebukes the patriarch via a rhetorical question (Gen 12:18–19; 20:8–10; 26:9–11); and 7) the patriarch prospers as the episode concludes (Gen 12:20; 20:14–16; 26:12–13).

Scholars have not reached consensus on what the original version might be, or how to label them (the once popular "threat to the ancestress" does not fit well). These narratives vividly demonstrate the failings of the patriarchs, all of whom are rightly rebuked by Gentiles whose moral standards they had feared. These rebukes imply natural law. God is active throughout (Gen 12:17; 20:3, 6–7, 17–18; 26:2–5, 12), rescuing the patriarchs and blessing them. The narratives show God's covenant faithfulness in the face of human failure.

In addition, each episode serves as plot or character development within the larger story. Genesis 12 motivates Hagar's appearance as Sarah's Egyptian maidservant (made explicit in the Genesis Apocryphon and the Quran). It is the first pre-word to the Exodus event (Israel's family goes to Egypt because of famine, God plagues the Egyptians, and the Israelites leave with Egyptian goods). In Gen 20, Abraham prays that the barren women conceive and immediately afterwards (see **annunciation narrative**), Sarah conceives and bears Isaac. In Gen 26, rather than God revealing to the ruler that the matriarch is married, it is Isaac "sporting" (a play in Hebrew on Isaac's name) with his wife that gives the show away. Genesis 24 records that Isaac loved Rebekah ("X loved Y" is rare in the Bible) and this love prevents him from carrying out his own plan.

Aharoni, "Three Similar Stories," 213–23; Exum, "Who's Afraid?" 91–113; Hoffmeier, "Wives' Tales," 81–99; Speiser, "Wife-Sister Motif," 62–82; Sweeney, "Form Criticism," 17–38.

Song/Poem Narrative

This is a narrative which includes a sizable embedded poem. It typically consists of the speech introduction formula and the poem itself. The poems are treated in the Psalms chapter and the introduction there lists them.

Summary Narrative

The length construction narrative concerning the tabernacle (Exod 35:30–39:43) finishes with a summary (Exod 39:32–43) that describes what the Israelites had built but also moves the narrative forward in that they bring it to Moses for inspection. The conclusion of the **prologue** to the **biblical book** of Judges (Judg 1:1—3:6) is a proleptic summary (Judg 3:1–6) of what will happen in the following **judge cycles** (Judg 3:7—16:31).

Symbolic Dream/Vision Narrative

In contrast to **dream interpretation narrative**, in which the protagonist interprets a ruler's dream, this concerns the protagonist having a dream/vision and a heavenly being interpreting it (hence it is a subcategory of **epiphany narrative**). The symbols in Daniel 7 are four great beasts: a lion with eagles' wings, a bear with three ribs in its mouth, a leopard with four wings on its back, and a terrifying beast with ten horns and great iron teeth. There is general agreement that, though the symbols are very different, these refer to the same four kingdoms of the **dream interpretation narrative** in Daniel 2. The traditional interpretation, both Jewish and Christian, is that they refer to Babylon, Persia, Greece, and Rome; the consensus among critical scholars today is that they refer to Babylon, Media, Persia, and Greece.

The symbols in Dan 8 involve a conflict between Greece and Media-Persia. Beyond that, the angelic command to seal up the vision because it refers to distant events and Daniel's dismay and inability to understand the vision (Dan 8:26–27) leaves the content mysterious. If Antiochus Epiphanes is the referent, the duration of 2,300 evenings and mornings until the sanctuary is restored (8:14) does not easily fit the duration of temple abominations under Antiochus. Philosophical and theological presuppositions play a huge role in how one interprets Daniel.

Beasley-Murray, "Interpretation," 44–58; Collins, *Daniel*, 74–89; Hassler, "Identity," 33–44; Niditch, *Symbolic Vision*.

Tabernacle/Temple Instructions Narrative

YHWH gives exceptionally detailed instructions on how to build the tabernacle (Exod 25:1—31:18) that will be carried out in equally detailed fashion in the construction narrative (Exod 35:1—39:43). The instructions narrative consists of one very long speech by YHWH (Exod 25:1—30:10) followed by six smaller ones (Exod 30:11–16, 17–21, 22–33, 34–48; 31:1–11, 12–17), followed by YHWH's action of giving Moses two tablets of the covenant (Exod 31:18). In terms of content, the material divides into the following sections: instruction concerning a freewill offering (Exod 25:1–9), instruction concerning the ark of the testimony (Exod 25:10–22), instruction concerning the table for the showbread (Exod 25:23–30), instruction concerning the gold lampstand (Exod 25:31–40), instruction concerning the tabernacle (Exod 26:1–37), instruction concerning the altar of burnt offering (Exod 27:1–8), instruction concerning the court of the tabernacle (Exod 27:9–19), instruction concerning the care of the lampstand (Exod 27:20–21), instruction concerning the garments for the priesthood (Exod 28:1–4), instruction concerning the ephod (Exod 28:5–14), instruction concerning the breastplate (Exod 28:15–30), instruction concerning other priestly garments (Exod 28:31–43), instruction concerning the consecration of Aaron and his sons (Exod 29:1–37), instruction concerning the daily offerings (Exod 29:38–46), instruction concerning the altar of incense (Exod 30:1–10), instruction concerning ransom money (Exod 30:11–16), instruction concerning the bronze laver (Exod 30:17–21), instruction concerning the anointing oil (Exod 30:22–33), instruction concerning the incense (Exod 30:34–38), instruction concerning the identity of the artisans (Exod 31:1–11), instruction concerning the Sabbath (Exod 31:12–17).

After the **construction narrative** (Exod 35:30–39:43) concerning the tabernacle, which in its detailed performance functions also as a **compliance narrative**, there is a further tabernacle instructions narrative in Exod 40:1–15.

In 1 Chr 22:1–19, which has no parallel in Kings, David gives Solomon instructions regarding the Temple. Chronicles also contains a different **testament narrative** of David than does Kings, which again focuses on instructions to Solomon regarding the building of the Temple (1 Chr 28:1–29:9).

Hurvitz, "Form," 127–51; Hurvitz, "Priestly Account," 21–30; Klingbeil, "Ritual Space," 59–82; Longacre, "Building," 21–49.

Testing Narrative

The testing of the protagonist's character is one of the most common themes in world literature, and the Hebrew Bible contains several or them. The most famous is the Akedah in which God commands Abraham to sacrifice his son, Isaac (Gen 22:1–19; see **human sacrifice narrative**). Abraham and Isaac demonstrate faith and a **covenant affirmation narrative** ensues.

The stakes are lower when Abraham's servant wants to find a suitable wife for Isaac so he devises a test. Rebekah passes with flying colors, demonstrating hospitality and endurance when she waters ten thirsty camels (Gen 24:12–27). This test forms a fitting counterpart to the obstacles element in the **marriage narrative**.

Joseph demonstrates chastity when he refuses the advances of Potiphar's wife (Gen 39:6b–12), and although he is framed for rape and imprisoned (see rape narrative), this is part of YHWH's plan to bring him to Pharaoh's court.

In Judg 7:1–7, YHWH tests Gideon's faith by telling him to reduce his army. The test proceeds in two stages, in which the remaining troops themselves demonstrate courage and alertness. Similarly, 1 Sam 20:1–42 is at one level a test which Saul fails (showing again his envy of David), and at another level it tests Jonathan's loyalty to David, which he passes.

Daniel and his friends (Shadrach, Meshach and Abednego) refuse the king's food and wine and eat just vegetables, yet end up healthier than the other courtiers (Dan 1:8–16); Daniel's friends refuse to bow down to the king's idol, confessing their faith in God, and escape unharmed from the fiery furnace (Dan 3:1–30); and Daniel continues to pray despite the king's edict prohibiting it, and survives being thrown into a pit of lions (Dan 6:1–29 [NRSV 5:31—6:28]). These are all examples of **court narratives**. They show that one can contribute significantly to a pagan culture but warn against accommodating to the dominant culture to the extent of suppressing faith. They are somewhat similar to the martyr stories in 2 Maccabees but with the exception that God intervenes in the book of Daniel on all three occasions.

Henten, "Reception," 149–69; Koch, *Daniel (1,1–21)*; Lombaard, "Testing Tales," 113–23.

Testament/Farewell Narrative

Large-scale narratives frequently conclude with the leader's parting words (testament or farewell speech) for his descendants. Outside biblical narratives, there are testaments of Moses and of the twelve patriarchs in the Pseudepigrapha. In the Hebrew Bible, Jacob and Moses testaments in poetic prophecy concerning the individual tribes (**tribal blessing subunit**) of Israel (Gen 49:1–27; Deut 33:1–29; see **testament poem** in Psalm genre for details and bibliography). These tribal blessings, especially concerning Joseph and Judah, are a pre-word of later events.

In Josh 23:1–16, Joshua reminds the Israelites of their allotments and exhorts them to obey Mosaic law; in Josh 24:1–28 (see **covenant**

renewal narrative), he gathers the Israelites at Shechem, recites in creedal fashion what YHWH has done for Israel and succeeds in getting Israel to renew their covenant with YHWH. Samuel gives an even longer summary of what YHWH has done historically for Israel (1 Sam 12:1–25). David's advice to Solomon includes exhortations to obey YHWH but focuses, in the fashion of "The Godfather," on the practical aspect on who to trust and how to deal with political enemies (1 Kgs 2:1–9); but the corresponding testament of David in Chronicles is more temple focused and characteristically places David and Solomon in a much better light (1 Chr 29:1–25). The farewell addresses in the Hebrew Bible have a New Testament counterpart in the Farewell Discourse of Jesus in John's account of the Last Supper (John 14–17).

Campbell, *2 Samuel*, 118–28; Coats, *Genesis*, 307–11; Long, *1 Kings*, 41–43, 249; Noth, *Deuteronomistic History*, 78–84.

Theological Evaluation Narrative

The Torah concludes with a highly positive theological evaluation of Moses (Deut 34:10–12), and Joshua and the elders of his time are given a positive theological evaluation also (Josh 24:31). The book of Job begins with a positive theological evaluation of Job (Job 1:1–5). But most theological evaluations are done of kings of Israel and Judah, as an integral part of a **regnal narrative** in the books of Kings and Chronicles and typically occur in the final part of the **introductory regnal resumé**. [An exception is the partial theological appraisal in 1 Kgs 3:2–3 at the beginning of Solomon's reign before his apostasy.] The theological evaluation of the kings of Judah could be either positive or negative and frequently include a **theological evaluation formula**, a **walked after predecessor formula**, and a **high places formula**. The theological evaluations of the kings of Israel are universally negative and typically include a **theological evaluation formula** and a **walked after predecessor formula**.

Scholars have devoted considerable attention to whether the theological evaluation sections either of Israel or of Judah vary in formulation after certain king's reigns. If demonstrated, this could provide evidence of various redactions of a Deuteronomistic History. This would especially be the case if the reigns of Hezekiah and/or Josiah were the points where formulations changed, because these were reforming kings who were involved in canonical processes (collecting Solomonic proverbs or re-promulgating the law). One could certainly imagine scribes under Hezekiah/Josiah producing a history ending in their reigns as ideological support for their reforms and a later editor updating the history to include later monarchs but not sticking to the precise formulations of the previous writers.

Ben Zvi, "Reign of Manasseh," 351–74; Na'aman, "Kingdom," 3–71; Eynickel, *Reform of Josiah*; Provan, *Hezekiah and Kings*; Sweeney, *King Josiah*.

Treaty Narrative

The Hebrew word *berit* (treaty or covenant) can refer to agreements between two humans or between God and humans. For the latter see **covenant narratives**. Abraham makes a treaty with Abimelech, accompanied by Phicol, (Gen 21:22–34) and Isaac makes a treaty with Abimelech, accompanied by Ahuzzath (Gen 26:15–33), both concerning wells. As with the sister-wife narratives involving similarities between Abraham and Isaac, scholars have debated if one narrative is dependent upon another. After a dispute narrative (Gen 31:25–42), Laban and Jacob reconcile their differences enough to make a treaty with each other (Gen 31:43–55).

Joshua makes a treaty with the Gibeonites (Josh 9:1–27), which Saul later breaks, resulting in a famine during David's reign (2 Sam 21:1–14). Solomon makes a treaty with Hiram—building materials for the temple in exchange for twenty cities in the north of Israel—which is initially successful (1 Kgs 5:10–12), but with which Hiram is later unhappy (1 Kgs 9:10–14). This treaty likely is one of the grievances that the northern tribes have with Solomon and which leads to the division of the monarchy.

Blenkinsopp, *Gibeon and Israel*; Hoffmeier, "Wives' Tales," 81–99; McCarthy, *Treaty and Covenant*.

Vocation Narrative

This is a narrative that describes the initiatory call of the prophet/judge to a life of activity specially directed by God (Exod 3–4; Judg 6; Isa 6; Jer 1; Ezek 1). Typical elements within the vocation account include a divine or heavenly appearance (**epiphany/theophany narrative**), a dialogue between YHWH and the prophet in which the prophet often objects, and a reassurance or sign to overcome objections. In Isa 6 and Ezek 1, attention is given to the prophet's vision of YHWH's heavenly realm; in Exod 3–4, Judg 6; Jer 1; and Ezek 2–3, the coming of the word of YHWH is the dominant theme. The teleological cause is to authenticate the prophet as YHWH's spokesman and often to summarize the prophet's overall message.

A different pattern involves the young boy Samuel who hears YHWH's voice and thinks Eli has called him. Eli ironically instructing Samuel on how to receive YHWH's message which is a prophecy of punishment against Eli and his house (1 Sam 3:1–18). Curiously, Elijah bursts on to the scene from nowhere (1 Kgs 17:1), and Elisha's vocation narrative is very brief (1 Kgs 19:19–21) and involves Elijah's mantle rather than YHWH's call. See entry in prophetic narratives chapter.

Buss, "Anthropological Perspective," 9–30; Cohen, "Call of Moses," 256-61; Habel, "Form and Significance," 297–323; Knierim, "Vocation," 47–68.

Vow Narrative

This is a narrative which in which a vow subunit plays a major role. In the **judge cycle** concerning Jephthah, Jephthah makes a vow if YHWH grants victory in battle that results in the sacrifice of his daughter (Judg 11:29–40; see **human sacrifice narrative** for more details). This narrative has parallels with Agamemnon's vow concerning his daughter Iphigenia in various Greek tragedies concerning the Trojan War. Saul makes a similar vow regarding victory in 1 Sam 14, and it would have resulted in the death of his son, Jonathan, had not the Israelite troops intervened.

Other vow narratives are connected with the vow law which enables a father or husband to nullify the vow in certain circumstances (Num 30:3–15). The barren Hannah makes and eventually keeps a vow that if YHWH grants her a son, she will dedicate him as a Nazirite (1 Sam 1:7b–28; see **annunciation narrative**). The son born is Samuel, and Hannah eventually bears five other children of her own. The wives who vowed, contrary to YHWHistic monotheism, to make offerings to the queen of heaven were encouraged by their husbands to do so, and this resulted in a prophecy of punishment for the Judean community in Egypt (Jer 44:24–30).

These stories have two inherent points of tension: whether the condition expressed in the vow will take place and whether the character will keep the vow.

Fidler, "Wife's Vow," 374–88; Hyman, "Acts of Vowing," 231–38; Roi, "Conditional Vows," 3–24; Trible, *Texts of Terror*, 93–116.

Wisdom Narrative

Wisdom themes permeate the story of Joseph: his ability to interpret dreams (Gen 40:1–23; 41:1–36), a theme found in the court narratives of Daniel also; his wise handling of the affairs of Potiphar and even of the prison he was cast into (Gen 39:1–20); and his planning for the years of famine (Gen 41:37–55).

There are numerous references to wisdom in the narratives concerning the successive revolts of Absalom and Sheba (2 Sam 13–20). Amnon's advisor, Jonadab, is described as "wise" (2 Sam 13:1–5); the wise woman of Tekoah skillfully plays the role Joab has hired her for (2 Sam 14:1–20); there is a verbal duel between the wisdom of Ahithophel and the wisdom of Hushai (2 Sam 16:15—17:14); and the wise woman of Abel Beth Maacah saves a city (2 Sam 20:16–22).

Not surprisingly, the reign of Solomon contains several wisdom narratives: his request for wisdom rather than for riches or long life (1 Kgs 3:5–15 [=2 Chr 1:7–13]); his ability to discover which of two prostitutes was the true mother (1 Kgs 3:16–28); Solomon's wise treaty with Hiram (1 Kgs 5:9–14 [NRSV 4:29–34]); and the visit of the Queen of Sheba to test Solomon's wisdom (1 Kgs 10:1–13 [=2 Chr 9:1–12]). These narratives connect well with the superscriptions to Proverbs (Prov 1:1) and Ecclesiastes (Eccl 1:1) and to the two collections of proverbs associated with him (Prov 10:1; 25:1).

In the court narratives concerning Daniel, we see both an exposition of Daniel's wisdom (Dan 1:17–21) and Daniel exhibit that wisdom through **judgment interpretation narratives** (Dan 4:1–34 [NRSV 4–37]; 5:5–30).

Coats, "Joseph Story," 285–97; Crenshaw, "Methods," 129–42; Fox, "Joseph Story," 26–41; Lyke, *King David*; Kim, "Two Mothers," 83–99; Olojede, "Sapiential Elements," 351–68; von Rad, "Joseph Narrative," 439–47; Willey, "Importunate Woman," 115–31; Wills, *Jew in Court*.

Written Document Narrative

These narratives have a simple structure: narration of the writing of the document; the contents of the document. In Dan 3:31–33 [NRSV 4:1–3], Nebuchadnezzar grandiloquently addresses all peoples on the earth, but ends the narrative driven from human society.

The book of Ezra begins by narrating Cyrus's edict which permitted the Jews to rebuild the temple and the city of Jerusalem (Ezra 1:1–4; an abbreviated form of the edict is found in 2 Chr 36:22–23, which concludes the entire Tanak!). That portion of Ezra is in Hebrew but four other letters in Ezra are written in Aramaic, which was the main language used in the Persian Empire. The opponents of the Jews write to Ahasuerus warning of dire consequences if Jerusalem is built (Ezra 4:6–16); Ahasuerus replies to them, decreeing that the building stop (Ezra 4: 17–22); Tattenai the governor informs King Darius about the Jews' claim that Cyrus had permitted them to build Jerusalem and suggests that Darius check the story out (Ezra 5:6–17); Darius does so, finds that Cyrus had issued the edict, and permits the Jews to recommence their rebuilding (6:1–12). The last letter in Ezra is also written in Hebrew, from Artaxerxes to Ezra forbidding the opponents of the Jews to hinder the rebuilding effort (Ezra 7:11–28). These letters play a considerable role in developing the plot concerning the opposition to Ezra (see **adversaries narrative**).

Niditch, *Oral World.*

4

Prophetic Narratives

INTRODUCTION

Partly because of space considerations, the material on prophetic genres has been split between genres of prophetic speech covered in volume 1 and prophetic narratives covered here in volume 2. Recent analysis of prophetic genres looks at larger units also such as prophetic books and the major divisions and smaller sections within those books. This is covered briefly in the Overview of Tanak chapter. The narratives within the latter prophets largely contain the standard subunits found in the narratives chapter (also in volume 2) so putting the prophetic narratives here rather than in the first volume should help reduce the amount of switching between volumes.

FORMULAS IN PROPHETIC NARRATIVE

Measurement Formula "And he measured OBJ N cubits"

This formula is a subcategory of **action** which involves the agent measuring, the object measured, and the length of the measurement. It occurs frequently in the portion of the **vision narrative** concerning the future temple in Ezek 40–42 where the visionary guide measures various aspects of the temple complex (Ezek 40:5, 8, 9, 11, 13, 14, 19, 20, 23, 24, 27, 28, 32, 47, 48; 41:1, 2, 3, 4, 5, 13, 14, 15; 42:16, 17, 18, 19, 20). Sometimes the length of an object is noted as the same as the others rather than restating the number of cubits. The measurement formula also occurs when the visionary guide measures the depth of the flowing waters (Ezek 47:3, 4, 5). Unlike an exposition clause such as "The OBJ was N cubits" which is also frequent in **measurement subunits** of the **scene in vision**, it reports actions and contributes to the vivid sense of dynamism in Ezekiel's visons.

Prophetic Fulfillment Formula: "According to the word of YHWH which PN spoke."

See entry in chapter on narrative genres.

Seeing a Vision Formula: "I lifted up my eyes and saw."

The prophet is the efficient cause of this formula—which sometimes occurs in an abbreviated form "I saw"—and it is used to introduce a **vision report**, just as is the **YHWH showed me formula**. However, the prophet is the subject of the seeing a vision formula (Zech 2:1, 5; 5:1; 6:1), whereas YHWH is the subject of the YHWH showed me formula. The seeing a vision formula is an **assertive** speech act, and is in fact a type of **notice**, the two verbs combining to portray one action. The perlocutionary intent is for the addressee to pay attention to the following vision report.

Spirit Lifted Me Formula "The Spirit Lifted Me Up"

This is a subcategory of tactile experience felt by Ezekiel in the **vision narratives** and is used to introduce a new **scene in vision** (Ezek 3:12, 14; 8:3; 11:1, 24; 43:5), with the alternate form "The Spirit entered into me and set me on my feet" occurring also (Ezek 2:2; 3:24). It can be followed by a new location (Ezek 8:3, 11:1, 24; 43:5) or by an auditory experience or by a speech from a visionary guide (Ezek 2:2; 3:12, 24). It only appears once in Ezek 40–48, where the **visionary guidance formula** dominates, but is prominent in the opening visions of the book.

Visionary Guidance Formula: "And he brought me to LOC."

Although it does not appear in the vision described in Ezek 1–3, this formula is the primary method of introducing **scenes in vision** in the two other **vision narratives** of Ezekiel (Ezek 8:7a, 14a, 16a; 40:2–3a, 17a, 24a, 28a, 32a, 35a, 48a; 41:1a; 42:1a, 15a; 43:1a; 44:1a, 4a; 46:19a, 21a; 47:1a, 2a, 6c). It is frequently followed by a **behold experience**. The formula itself suggests a tactile experience but not so vividly as the **hand of YHWH revelatory formula** or the **spirit lifted me formula**, focusing more on the new location where the next scene is to take place.

Gese, *Verfassungsentwurf*; Hals, *Ezekiel*, 298, 363; Zimmerli, *Ezekiel* 2, 343.

YHWH Showed Me Formula: "This is what he/YHWH showed me."

Like the **seeing a vision formula**, this formula is typically used to introduce a **prophetic vision report**. YHWH is the subject in this formula, unlike the seeing a vision formula in which the prophet is the subject. It is a type of **notice** and is therefore an **assertive**. The prophet is the **efficient cause** of both this formula and the **seeing a vision formula**, but the YHWH showed me formula emphasizes more YHWH's activity rather than the prophet's experience (Jer 24:1; 38:21; Amos 7:1, 4, 7; 8:3; Zech 1:20; 3:1). The **perlocutionary intent** in both cases is for the addressee to pay attention to the following vision report.

SUBUNITS OF PROPHETIC NARRATIVE

Audition

An audition is when a prophet or other character hears a heavenly message without seeing a heavenly messenger or seeing a **vision**. It is likely that many of the units introduced by the **prophetic word formula** or the **speech introduction of YHWH formula** discuss auditions but we do not know which ones. From a form-critical viewpoint, audition reports are considered a variant of vision report but introduced by the audition formula and what is experienced by the prophet is discussed exclusively by auditory means.

Examples include 1 Kgs 19:9b, 11a, 13b; Isa 21:2; Ezek 1:28b—2:1; 2:2–8; 43:6–12; Dan 4:28 [NRSV 31]; 8:13, 16; 10:9.

Bennett, "Vision and Audition," 245–68; Sweeney, *Isaiah 1–39*, 515.

Background Exposition

See exposition subunit in the chapter on narrative genres for a discussion of the genre. In the latter prophets, we see examples providing background information in the following types of narrative: **Assassination narrative** (Jer 40:7–12), **confrontation narrative** (Jer 37:4–5), **interrogation narrative** (Jer 38:14a), **prose sermon narrative** (Jer 34:8b–11; 35:1–11), a **report of a prophetic symbolic action** (Jer 32:2–3a), a **vision report** (Jer 24:1b), and a **written document narrative** (Jer 29:2b–3).

Behold Experience

This is a visual experience involving the Hebrew word *hinnēh* ("behold") and occurs with some frequency in narratives. In the prophetic literature, it is a frequent element in a **scene in vision** in all three **vision narratives** in Ezekiel (Ezek 1:4, 15; 2:9; 3:23; 8:2, 4, 5, 7, 8, 10, 14, 16; 9:2, 11; 10:1, 9; 11:1; 40:3, 5, 17, 24; 42:8; 43:2, 5; 44:4; 46:19, 21; 47:1, 2, 7). Its teleological cause there is to convey vividly to the reader what Ezekiel experienced.

Description of Future Item Subunit

This is a subunit in the **vision narrative** of the future temple (Ezek 40–48), in which Ezekiel describes what certain future items in the temple complex and beyond will be like. These include the future altar, with detailed descriptions of dimensions (Ezek 43:13–17) and a river of water flowing from the future temple that evokes idealistic Eden imagery, including trees who bear fruit every month and whose leaves are for healing (Ezek 47:1–12). Later rabbinic tradition connected this passage with the water ceremony on the seventh day of the Feast of Tabernacles; and it is also part of the background of Rev 21–22 which combines Zion and Eden imagery with Feast of Tabernacles themes, and has a river of life flowing through the city and trees by it whose leaves are for the healing of the nations (Rev 22:1–2). See also Tosephta Sukkah 3:3–18.

Bodi, "Double Current," 22–37; Boyle, "Holiness," 1–21; Dijkstra, "Altar," 22–36.

Description of Temple Subunit

This is a subcategory of **description subunit** in which the object described is the future temple (Ezek 40–42). Together with the **measurement subunit**, this is the main subunit in the **scenes in vision** in Ezek 40–41. It largely consists of **exposition of item** clauses and gives descriptions of various parts of the temple complex without discussing their dimensions (Ezek 40:16, 22–23a, 26–27a, 31, 34, 37–41, 42b–44, 49b; 41:6–7, 16–21, 23–26; 42:5–6, 9–12). For a brief discussion on how these should be interpreted, see the entry on **vision narrative**.

Dialogue Subunit

See entry in chapter on narrative genres for general discussion. This entry discusses dialogue as it occurs most frequently in the latter prophets. On a small level, dialogue occurs in question and answer subunits, and command and compliance subunits. At a larger level, dialogue can occur between YHWH (or angelic representative) and prophet in **dispute narratives, prophetic intercession narratives, report of prophetic symbolic actions, scene in vision, vision reports** and **vocation accounts**; or between prophet and opponent in **confrontation narratives** and **interrogation narratives**; or between prophet and third party in **crisis narratives, oracular inquiry narratives.** Dialogue also occurs between two other parties in **assassination narratives** and **rescue/release narratives**. As with other types of narrative, dialogue is critical in characterization and plot development.

Future Law

YHWH instructs Ezekiel concerning future laws for the altar (Ezek 43:18–27), the outer gate of the sanctuary (Ezek 44:1–3), admission to the temple (Ezek 44:4–14), the Levitical priests (Ezek 44:15–31), the holy district (Ezek 45:1–9), weights and measures (Ezek 45:10–12), offerings (Ezek 45:13–17), festivals (Ezek 45:18–25), Sabbath and new moons (Ezek 46:1–7), the prince (Ezek 46:8–18), and places for priests and kitchen servants (Ezek 46:19–20, 21–24). The extent to which these future laws depart from the laws in Torah is highly debated.

Measurement Subunit

Together with the **description of temple subunit**, this is the standard building block of the **scenes in vision** in Ezek 40–42, and its purpose is to inform the audience of the measurements of various aspects of the temple in Ezekiel's vision. The measurement subunits (Ezek 40:5b–15, 19–21, 23b, 24c-25, 27b, 28b–30, 32b–33, 35b–36, 42a, 47, 48b–49a; 41:1b–4a, 5, 8–15, 22a; 42:2–4, 7–8, 16–20) are composed primarily of **measurement formula clauses** and **exposition of measurement clauses**. For a brief discussion on how these should be interpreted, see **vision narrative**.

Opponent Actions Subunit

This is a subunit discussing the actions of a prophet's adversaries, especially in confrontation narratives (Jer 28:1b–4, 10–11c; 36:20–26; 37:1–3, 11–14; 44:15–19; Amos 7:10–11).

Oracular Inquiry Subunit

In this genre, a character makes an inquiry that only a divine representative would be able to answer. The full pattern may include a **prophetic word formula**, a **speech introduction formula** and the **inquiry** itself. It is the standard first element in an oracular inquiry narrative. Examples in the latter prophets include Jeremiah 16:10; 21:1–2; 42:1–3; and Zech 7:2–3.

Response by Prophet Subunit

This is usually a subcategory of **reactions subunit** in which the prophet is reacting to actions narrated in an **opponent actions subunit** within a confrontation narrative (Jer 28:5–9, 11d–16; 36:27–31; 37:6–10; 44:20–30; Amos 7:12–17)

Response to Oracular Inquiry Subunit

This is the subunit in an **oracular inquiry narrative** which contains the divine response, usually mediated through a prophet. The response may take the form of a prophetic explanation of punishment (Jer 16:11–13), a **branched conditional subunit** offering different outcomes depending on what actions the inquirers take (Jer 21:3b–10), directives to the addressees (Jer 42:7–22), or even question the motive of the inquirers (Zech 7:4–7).

Symbolic Command Subunit

This is a subcategory of divine command subunit in which YHWH commands the prophet to perform an unusual action, thus arousing curiosity in the audience. The explanation is given later in the symbol explanation subunit. It is usually the first of the three standard elements in a prophetic symbolic action narrative. Examples are found in all four books of the latter prophets (Isa 20:2a; Jer 13:1b, 4, 6b; 16:2, 5b, 8; 18:2; 19:1b–2, 10; 20:3c; 25:15b, 27c, 28d; 27:2b–4a; 32:7; 43:9; 51:61b–63 [Jeremiah commanding Baruch's brother Seraiah]; Ezek 3:24–26; 4:1–3a, 4, 6a, 7–12; 5:1–4; 12:1–6, 18; 21:24–25 [NRSV 19–20]; 25:15–16; 37:15–19; Hos 1:2b, 4a, 6b, 9a).

Symbol Explanation Subunit

This is a subunit which explains the significance of a strange action, typically performed by a prophet in compliance with a **symbolic command subunit**, in a **prophetic symbolic action narrative**. Examples are found in all books of the latter prophets (Isa 20:3–6; Jer 13:9b–11; 16:3b–4, 5–7, 9b; 18:6–10; 19:3b–9, 11c–13; 20:4b–6; 25:16, 27d; 27:5–11; 32:13–15; 43:10–13; 51:64a; Ezek 3:27; 4:3b, 5, 6b, 13; 5:5b–17; 12:8–16, 19c–20a; 25:19–27; 37:11b, 20–28; Hos 1:2b, 4b–5, 6c–7, 9b). The explanation is usually in the form of a **prophecy of punishment**.

Visionary Guide Subunit

This subunit concerns the actions of a visionary guide who helps the prophet understand. It occurs in the three major **vision narratives** in Ezekiel. Examples include Ezek 1:19–21; 10:4; 40:4, 45–46; 41:4b, 22b, 13–14; 46:24; 47:6; and 47:8–35, concluding the book.

UNITS OF PROPHETIC NARRATIVE

Assassination Narrative

For the genre as a whole, see entry in narrative genres. The main example in the latter prophets is the assassination of Gedaliah, who has been the object of some scholarly intrigue as to possible royal status or a regent for Jehoiachin, or presiding over a Judean rump state in the aftermath of the Babylonian exile. Appointed by the Babylonians, Gedaliah seems to have been a good man who naively trusted a bad man. The assassination narrative in Jeremiah 40:7—41:3 contains a **background exposition subunit** in which various exiles gather under the governorship of Gedaliah (Jer 40:7–12), a **dialogue** (Jer 40:13–16) between Johanan and Gedaliah, and a main actions subunit in which Ishmael arrives with ten men, eats bread together with Gedaliah, and suddenly assassinates Gedaliah and everyone else (Jer 40:1–3).

Ritzema, "After Zedekiah," 73–91.

Birth Narrative

See the entry in the chapter for narrative genres for the main details on this genre. The birth narratives in the latter prophets (Isa 8:1–4; Hos 1:2–2:2 [NRSV 1:2–11]) are also **reports of prophetic symbolic actions**.

Finlay, *Birth Report Genre*, 162–95.

Confrontation Narrative

See entry in narratives chapter. In the latter prophets, the standard elements are **opponent actions subunits** and **response of prophet subunits**. Isaiah's confrontation with Ahaz (Isa 7:1–25) involves a **prophetic symbolic action narrative** regarding Isaiah's son Shear-jashub "a remnant will return" (Isa 7:1–9), and a confrontation **dialogue** (Isa 7:10–25) revolving around Isaiah's **prophecy of a sign** concerning a woman bearing Immanuel, whose identity is the focus of considerable scholarly dispute.

Confrontation narratives play a major role in the book of Jeremiah where they expand upon what YHWH told Jeremiah in the vocation account: "I for my part have made you today a fortified city, an iron pillar, and a bronze wall, against the whole land—against the kings of Judah, its princes, its priests, and the people of the land" (Jer 1:18). Jeremiah 20:1–6 begins with an **opponent actions subunit** in which Pashhur strikes Jeremiah, puts him in the stocks and releases him (Jer 20:1–3a) followed by a response by prophet (Jer 20:3b–6) which combines elements of **prophecy of punishment against an individual** and **prophecy of punishment against Judah**.

Jeremiah 26 is an intercalated confrontation narrative concerning Jeremiah with the inset passage being another confrontation narrative concerning Uriah (Jer 26:20–23). It contains a **dating formula** followed by a variant of the **prophetic word formula** (Jer 26:1), a **prose sermon** that summarizes the Jeremiah 7 temple sermon (Jer 26:2–6), an **opponent actions subunit** in which the officials demand Jeremiah's death for speaking against the temple (Jer 26:7–11), and a **response by prophet subunit** (Jer 26:12–15), and another **opponent actions subunit** (Jer 26:16–19), an inset **confrontation narrative** in which King Jehoikaim strikes down the prophet Uriah (Jer 26:20–23), and a miniature **rescue narrative** (Jer 26:24) in line with YHWH's reassurance to Jeremiah (Jer 1:18).

Jeremiah 28:1–17 contains a **dating formula** (Jer 28:17a), **opponent actions subunits** in which Hananiah falsely claims to bear a message from YHWH and breaks Jeremiah's yoke (Jer 28:17b–4, 10–11a), **response of prophet subunits** in which Jeremiah points out that events will determine who has spoken truly (Jer 28:5–9, 11b–16) including a **prophecy of punishment against an individual**, Hananiah (Jer 28:15–16), and the **event** of Hananiah dying (Jer 28:17) as Jeremiah had prophesied.

Jeremiah 32 is an intercalated confrontation narrative containing a **dating formula** (Jer 32:1), an **opponent actions subunit** concerning Zedekiah (Jer 32:2–5), an inset **symbolic action narrative** which looks forward to Judah's restoration (Jer 32:6–25), and a resumption of the confrontation narrative with the **response of prophet subunit** which is a **prophecy of punishment and restoration** (Jer 32:26–44) concerning punishment by Nebuchadnezzar of Babylon but eventual restoration in accord with Jeremiah's symbolic actions.

Jeremiah 34:8–22 contains a **prophetic word formula** (Jer 34:8a), an **opponent actions subunit** in which Zedekiah reverses a proclamation of liberty (Jer 34:8b–11), a resumptive **prophetic word formula** (Jer 34:12), and a **response of prophet subunit** (Jer 34:13–22) which culminates in an **announcement of punishment subunit** directed against the nation Judah and the individual Zedekiah (see **prose sermon** for details).

Jeremiah 36:1–32 contains a **dating formula** plus **prophetic word formula** (Jer 36:1), **command subunits** for Jeremiah to write on a scroll earlier prophecies and for Baruch to read the scroll (Jer 36:2–3, 5–7), **compliance subunits** (Jer 36:4, 8–10), an **interrogation narrative** in which Baruch and Jeremiah are warned to hide (Jer 36:11–19), an **opponent actions subunit** in which King Jehoiakim burns the scroll and unsuccessfully attempts to arrest Jeremiah and Baruch (Jer 36:20–26), a **divine command** (Jer 36:27–31) for Jeremiah to write a second scroll and to add a **prophecy of punishment against an individual**, Jehoiakim, and a **compliance subunit** (Jer 36:32). The passage is also a **written document narrative.**

Jeremiah 37:1–21 contains **opponent actions subunits** in which Zedekiah and company refuse to listen to Jeremiah and have him arrested and beaten (Jer 31:1–3, 11–16), an **exposition subunit** (Jer 37:4–5), a **response of prophet subunit** which is a **prophecy of punishment against Judah** (Jer 37:6–10), and an **interrogation narrative** which results in Jeremiah remaining in the court of the guard rather than in the house of the secretary Jonathan (Jer 37:17–21).

Jeremiah 44:1–30 contains a **prophetic explanation of punishment** (Jer 44:1–14) which criticizes the people for making offerings to other gods, an **opponent actions subunit** in which the people determine to continue pouring libations to the queen of heaven (Jer 44:15–19), and a **response of prophet subunit** which is a prophecy of punishment against them (Jer 44:20–30).

The confrontation between Amos and Amaziah (Amos 7:10–17) contains a mini **written document narrative** consisting of Amaziah's report to Jeroboam II of Amos's prophecy of punishment, "Jeroboam shall die by the sword and Israel must go into exile away from his land" (Amos 7:10–11), an **opponent actions subunit** in which Amaziah prohibits Amos from prophesying at Bethel (Amos 7:12–13), and a **response of prophet subunit** (Amos 7:14–17) in which Amos briefly recounts his call (**vocation narrative**), and combines a **prophecy of punishment against an individual**, namely Amaziah, and a **prophecy of punishment against Israel**. For Jonah confronting Nineveh in Jonah 3, see **prophecy of punishment against Assyria/Nineveh** and **fast narrative**.

Irvine, *Isaiah, Ahaz*; Wazana, "Amos against Amaziah," 209–28.

Construction Narrative

For details of the genre, see entry in chapter on narrative genres. Haggai 1:1–15a contains a report of a **disputation speech** (see entry for further details) commanding the building of the temple (Hag 1:1–11), a **compliance subunit** (Hag 1:12), a report of YHWH's encouragement, consisting of the **assistance formula** and the **utterance of YHWH formula** (Hag 1:13), and a further **compliance subunit** (Hag 1:14–15).

Assis, "Build," 514–27.

Crisis Narrative

See the entry in narratives chapter; see also **rescue/release narrative**. Examples within the former prophets include some of the **reports of prophetic miracles** (see entry in narratives chapter), such as when Elisha is surrounded by a great army but YHWH strikes them with blindness so that Elisha evades capture (2 Kgs 6:8–23).

King Zedekiah has Jeremiah thrown into the cistern of Malchiah but Ebed-Melech the Ethiopian eunuch pulls him out before he dies (Jer 38:1–13; see **release/rescue narrative** for details), instantiating YHWH's promise that the Judean kings would fight against Jeremiah but not prevail (Jer 1:18–19).

After Jonah disobeys YHWH's command to prophesy against Nineveh (Jonah 1:1–2), comes a crisis narrative in which YHWH causes a storm which results in Jonah being thrown overboard (Jonah 1:4–16), and YHWH then causes a great fish to swallow Jonah (Jonah 1:17). This new crisis is a **prayer narrative** containing a **prayer subunit** (Jonah 2:1–9) and a **results subunit** (Jonah 2:10). The characterization of the sailors as God-fearing sets up the repentance of the Ninevites later in the book in contrast to Jonah's more problematic relationship with YHWH.

Mann, "Performative Prayers," 20–40.

Dispute Narrative

See the entry in narratives chapter. For Jer 42:1—43:4, see **oracular inquiry narrative**. In Jonah 4, the dispute is between YHWH and Jonah regarding whether Jonah is right to be angry that YHWH has spared Nineveh (the cruel enemies of Israel) and, by implication, whether

YHWH's undisputed attributes of graciousness, mercy, abounding in love etc., are good or not. The passage contains **reactions subunits** displaying Jonah's emotions (Jonah 4:1, 6b, 8b, 9b), a **prayer** (Jonah 4:2–3), **divine responses to prophet** rebuking Jonah at his lack of concern for man or beast (Jonah 4:4, 9a, 10–11), and **main actions** subunits (Jonah 4:5–6a, 7–8a). Jonah turns the divine attributes of mercy and steadfast love into an accusation against YHWH (Jonah 4:3); YHWH answers rhetorically "Should I not be concerned about Nineveh, that great city, in which there are more than a hundred and twenty thousand persons who do not know their right hand from their left, and also many animals?" (Jonah 4:11).

Mann, "Performative Prayers," 20–40; Perry, *Honeymoon Is Over*.

Exile Narrative

See entry in narratives chapter. Jeremiah 39:1–10 and Jer 52:1–30 contain accounts of the Babylonian exile recorded in 2 Kgs 25 and 2 Chr 36.

Fast Narrative

See entry in narratives chapter and read it slowly. In the **confrontation narrative** between Jonah and Nineveh, immediately following the **prophecy of punishment against Assyria/Nineveh** (Jonah 3:1–4), the opponent actions subunit is a **fast narrative** (Jonah 3:5–10). The people and then the king proclaim a fast and putting on sackcloth (Jonah 3:5–6), then there is a **royal decree** commanding humans and animals to fast and put on sackcloth (Jonah 3:7–9), followed by a results subunit in which God relents (Jonah 3:10). This likely means re-reading Jonah's prior prophecy as a **conditional prophecy of punishment** with the implied condition "if you do not repent" being understood (Jer 18:7–8 specifies that nations against whom YHWH has prophesied punishment may avert that disaster by turning from evil). Jews read the book of Jonah on their holiest fast, Yom Kippur, and this passage demonstrating the efficacy of fasting and repentance is the main reason.

Goodhart, "Prophecy, Sacrifice," 43–63; Seidler, "Fasting, Sackcloth," 117–34.

Future Temple Vision Narrative

In Ezek 40–48, the prophet is granted an extensive vision of the future temple in Jerusalem and is instructed about future laws concerning it. It is conceptually similar to the **prophecies of Zion's glorious future** but dwarfs them in magnitude. For an analysis of the units within the narrative see **scene in vision**. The various genres of lists contained in these scenes contribute to the sense of precise order, despite the somewhat bizarre architectural details of the temple and the boundaries between the tribes (which lay in parallel lines and do not correspond to the historical boundaries).

The depiction of the temple differs considerably from both the Solomonic and Second Temples, and there are differences between the **future laws** here (see legal genres chapter) and those in the Mosaic covenant. Further, there is much more of an exclusionary emphasis with regard to the nations than is found in many other eschatological passages. Scholars differ on whether to interpret it as hyperbolic, merely nostalgic, symbolic, a program for the prophet's contemporaries to carry out in the near future, or employing imagery of Eden, cosmic mountain etc., but nevertheless promoting a practical program of temple worship in the Messianic age. It is an important source for New Jerusalem texts in the Dead Sea Scrolls and in Rev 21–22.

Cook and Patton, *Ezekiel's Hierarchical World*; Gese, *Verfassungsentwurf*; Greenberg, "Design and Themes," 181–208; Hals, *Ezekiel*, 289–347; Kasher, "Anthropomorphism," 192–208; Kim, "YHWH Shammah," 187–207; Levenson, *Program of Restoration*; Niditch, "Ezekiel 40–48," 208–34; Niditch, *Symbolic Vision*; Simon, "Ezekiel's Geometric Vision," 411–38.

Interrogation Narrative

See entry in narratives chapter. Jeremiah 37:15–21 exemplifies the three standard elements of interrogation narrative in prophetic literature: a **background exposition subunit** which involves how the prophet came before the interrogator (Jer 37:15–17a), a **dialogue subunit** (Jer 37:17b–20), and a **results subunit** (Jer 37:21). This passage is further discussed in **oracular inquiry narrative**.

Jeremiah 38:14–28 contains a **background exposition** where Zede kiah sends for Jeremiah (Jer 38:14a), a lengthy **dialogue subunit** (Jer 38:14b–26), and a **result narrative subunit** in which the officials fail to find out from Jeremiah much that really happened and Jeremiah remains in the court of the guard (Jer 38:27–28). In the dialogue, Zedekiah swears that he will not put Jeremiah to death (Jer 38:16), Jeremiah makes a **conditional prophecy of salvation** to Zedekiah if he surrenders to Babylon (Jer 38:17–18), and a **conditional prophecy of punishment** otherwise (Jer 38:21–23; see **branched conditional** in legal genres).

Maśśa'

Maśśa' is a Hebrew genre term that is difficult to translate (some translations have "burden," others "oracle"). As a written genre, it is a unit in a prophetic book headed by a maśśa' **superscription** (Isa 21:1–10; Zech 9:1–11:17; 12:1–14:21). The entire books of Nahum, Habakkuk and Malachi are examples of a *maśśa'*. It can also refer to a unit of prophetic speech that is typically recorded in a *maśśa'*.

As a written genre, it typically includes the following: a **citation** of, or reference to, a previously communicated revelation; additional **dialogue** between YHWH and the prophet in which YHWH's will is revealed; narratives that show the continuity between the present situation and the situation to which the previous revelation was addressed; and **exhortations** and **admonitions** to the addressees describing appropriate ways of acting in view of how the previous revelation continues to take effect. In the case of Zech 9–11, the previous revelation is Zech 1–8; and in the case of Zech 12–14, the previous revelation is Zech 1–11. In cases where the entire book is a *maśśa'*, the previous revelation is cited within the book. For example, in Habakkuk the citation of previous revelation is in Hab 1:5–11. In Malachi, the discussion is about how the previous revelation that YHWH loves Jacob (Mal 1:2) continues to operate.

Boda, "Freeing the Burden," 338–57; Floyd, *Minor Prophets 2*, 14–18, 444–52, 631–32; Sweeney, *Isaiah 1–39*, 212–52, 277–79; 534–35; Weis, "Definition of Maśśa'."

Narratives in Isaiah 36–39 and Jermiah 52

Isaiah 36:1—37:38 is a **siege narrative**; Isaiah 38:1–22 is a **reprieve narrative** containing a **psalm**; and Isaiah 39:1–8 is a **monarch behaving badly narrative** (see chapter on narrative genres for further discussion of the individual units and **section of Isaiah** for bibliography of this **section**

of prophetic book). These chapters have a parallel in 2 Kgs 18–20 and are discussed in the chapter on narrative genres. Jeremiah 52 is an appendix and an **exile narrative**.

Person, *Kings-Isaiah*.

Oracular Inquiry Narrative

See entry in narratives chapter. Jeremiah's refusal to marry and have children intended to provoke the people to ask Jeremiah why in an **oracular inquiry subunit** (Jer 16:10), and Jeremiah's **response to oracular inquiry subunit** (Jer 16:11–13) is a **prophetic explanation of punishment** concerning the people's apostasy and idolatry.

Jeremiah 21:1–10 contains an **oracular inquiry subunit** introduced by an expanded **prophetic word formula** (Jer 21:1–2), in which Zedekiah inquires if YHWH will force Nebuchadnezzar to withdraw, and a **response to oracular inquiry subunit** (Jer 21:3b–10 [NRSV 4–10]) yelling "No" and giving the people a **branched conditional** directive (see legal genres chapter) of staying in the city and dying or surrendering and living.

Jeremiah 42:1—43:4 contains an **oracular inquiry subunit** by Johannan and company to Jeremiah concerning where they should go (Jer 42:1–3), a dialogue subunit between Jeremiah and Johannan and (Jer 42:5–6), and an **response to oracular inquiry subunit** (Jer 42:7–22) instructing the people to stay in the land and especially not to go to Egypt(Jer 42:9b–22). In the **noncompliance subunit** (Jer 43:1–4), the leaders falsely accuse Jeremiah and Baruch and ignore the advice.

Zechariah 7:1–7 contains a **dating formula** (Zech 7:1a), a **prophetic word formula** (Zech 7:1b), an **oracular inquiry subunit** on whether or not to fast/weep in the fifth month (Zech 7:2–3; the same fast that the book of Lamentations is read; see overview of Tanak), and a **response to oracular inquiry subunit** (Zech 7:4–7) which questions their motives for fasting.

Floyd, *Minor Prophets* 2, 411–40, 633–34; Huffmon, "Oracular Process," 449–60; Parker, "Official Attitudes," 50–68; Scalise, "Zechariah 7:4–14," 56–65.

Prophetic Intercession Narrative

See **intercession narrative** in narratives chapter. The narrative has three main elements: YHWH issues a **prophecy of punishment** against the target, there is an **objection of prophet subunit**, and a **response of YHWH subunit** in which either YHWH relents or overrides the prophet's objection. See also **prophetic prayer of complaint**.

Two narratives in Jeremiah illustrate the futility of his objections. Jeremiah 5:1–9 contains a **divine command** (Jer 5:1–2) for Jeremiah to see "if you can find one person who acts justly and seeks truth so that I may pardon Jerusalem" anticipating the actions of Diogenes the Cynic (Jer 5:3), an **objection of prophet subunit** hoping that the rich will repent (Jer 5:4–5a), an implied **compliance subunit** in which Jeremiah fails to find a righteous person (Jer 5:5b), and a **prophecy of punishment** (Jer 5:6–9). In Jer 14:11—15:9, YHWH prohibits Jeremiah from interceding (Jer 14:11–12) and issues a **prophecy of punishment on male leaders** (14:14–18), Jeremiah gives **objection of prophet subunits** anyway (14:13, 19–22), and YHWH ends discussion by giving a **prophetic explanation of punishment** (Jer 15:1–9) which states that even intercessions by Moses and Samuel could not prevent YHWH's coming punishment.

By contrast, in the **vision reports** of Amos 7:1–3, 4–6, Amos twice objects to implied punishment on Israel by claiming Jacob cannot stand (7:2b, 5b), and YHWH relents (7:3, 6). See also **intercession subunit** in Psalms chapter.

Ballentine, "Prophet as Intercessor," 61–73; Filson, "Petition and Intercession," 21–34; Sweeney, "Intercessory Prayer," 213–30.

Prose Sermon Narrative

This is a narrative dominated by a **prose sermon**. Jeremiah warns the Judeans (Jer 7:1—8:4; 26:2–6) against thinking that YHWH could not abandon the temple by pointing out that YHWH had let the Philistines capture the ark (1 Sam 4). In Jer 9:11–15 [NRSV 12–16], YHWH will scatter the people because of their disobedience. This and several other prose sermons by Jeremiah use language similar to Deuteronomy.

Jeremiah 11:1–17 is a prose message from YHWH to Jeremiah whose first six verses are a cluster of introductory formulas: the **prophetic word formula** (11:1), **call to attention formulas** (11:2a, 6c), **command to speak formulas** (11:2b–3a, 6b), **messenger of YHWH formula**

(11:3b), **curse formula** (11:3c–5a; legal genres), and variant of the **amen formula** (11:5b; legal genres) and **speech introduction formula** (11:6a). Then comes a **historical reminder subunit** (11:7–8), a further **speech introduction formula** (11:9a), **basis for punishment subunits** (11:9b–10a, 13–14), a **transition subunit** consisting of "therefore" plus **messenger of YHWH formula** (11:11a), a **rhetorical questions subunit** (11:15), and **announcement of punishment subunits** (11:11b–12, 16–17). The message to Jeremiah is not to intercede for Judah because it would be futile; Judah's crimes are so great that punishment is inevitable.

Jeremiah 12:14–17, the last part of a **prophecy of punishment and restoration**, switches to prose and contains a **messenger of YHWH formula** (12:14a), an **announcement of punishment subunit** (12:14b), and a **branched conditional subunit** which offers hope to the enemies of Israel and Judah if they change their ways but destruction otherwise. Jeremiah 17:1–4 is a prose **prophecy of punishment against Judah/Zion** containing a **basis for punishment subunit** (17:1–3a) and an announcement of punishment subunit (17:3b–4). Jeremiah 17:19–27 is another prose prophecy of punishment against Judah Zion, this one beginning with a cluster of prophetic formulas found introducing poetic speech: messenger of YHWH formula (17:19a), commissioning formula (17:19b–20a), call to attention formula (17:20b), and messenger of YHWH formula (17:21a). The main message consists of a **"be careful lest" construction** regarding bearing burdens on the sabbath (17:21b), an **order** not to do work on the sabbath but to keep the sabbath (17:22), a **historical reminder** of the people's disobedience (17:23), and a **branched conditional subunit** offering wellbeing for obedience (17:24–26) and punishment for disobedience (17:27). The **"be careful lest" construction**, the **order**, and the **historical reminder subunit** are frequent legal genres in Deuteronomy.

Jeremiah 25:1–14 begins with a **prophetic word formula** (25:1a), a **dating formula** (25:1b), and an **elaboration clause** (25:2); and the main message consists of a **historical reminder subunit** (25:3–7), a **transition subunit** containing "therefore" plus a **messenger of YHWH formula** (25:8a), and reason and consequences subunits (25:8b–12a, 12c-14) punctuated by an **utterance of YHWH formula** (25:12b). The upshot is that Judah's sin will result in Nebuchadrezzar of Babylon destroying the land but that the Babylonians in turn will be punished for their iniquity.

For Jer 29:4–23, see **written document narrative**. Jeremiah 35:8–22 contains a **prophetic word formula** (34:8a, 12), a **background**

expositions subunit (34:8b–11) informing the audience that Zedekiah had initially proclaimed a year of release for slaves in accordance with the law (see **sabbatical year law**) but then the officials reversed course, a **messenger of YHWH formula** (34:13a), a **historical reminder subunit** (34:13b–15), a **basis for punishment** (34:16), a **transition subunit** consisting of "therefore" plus a **messenger of YHWH formula** (34:17a) and a blistering **announcement of punishment subunit** (34:17b–22). Heinous actions such as these cause YHWH to exile Judah to slavery (34:17b–22).

Jeremiah 35:1–11 could be considered a large **background exposition subunit** for the following prose sermon (Jer 35:12–22). The background consists of a **prophetic word formula** (35:1a), a **dating formula** (35:1b), a **command and compliance subunit** in which Jeremiah tests the Rechabites by offering wine to drink (35:2–5), and a **reactions subunit** in which the Rechabites refuse by recounting the charge of their ancestor Jonadab son of Rechab (35:6–11). The prose sermon contains the following: **prophetic word formula** (35:12), **messenger of YHWH formulas** (35:13a, 18b), **command to speak formula** (35:13b), **rhetorical questions subunit** (35:13c), **utterance of YHWH formula** (35:13d), **historical reminder subunit** which acts as **basis for punishment** for Judah but a **basis for salvation** for the Rechabites (35:14–16), **transition subunits** consisting of "therefore" plus **messenger of YHWH formula** (35:17a, 19a), an **announcement of punishment subunit** directed against Judah and Jerusalem for their disobedience (35:17b), a **speech introduction formula** (35:18a), a **basis for salvation subunit** (35:18b), and an **announcement of salvation subunit** directed at the Rechabites. The prose sermons in Jeremiah have several similarities with his poetic prophecies.

Leuchter, "Manumission Laws," 635–53; McKane, "Jeremiah and Rechabites," 106–23; Weippert, *Prosareden*.

Report of a Prophetic Symbolic Action

The full form of this genre narrates 1) YHWH's command to the prophet to perform a symbolic action (the **symbolic command subunit**); 2) a **compliance subunit** which notes the prophet's actions and frequently includes the **obedience formula**; and 3) the **symbol explanation subunit** which is frequently in the form of a **prophecy of punishment**. There are variations: one of the subunits may be missing and the genre sometimes appears in autobiographical form.

At the performance level, the action may symbolize what YHWH will do in the historical realm (in Jer 19:10–11, breaking the jug symbolizes YHWH breaking the city) or it may anticipate the fate of the onlookers (Isaiah walking naked in Isaiah 20) so that the action functions as a **prophecy**. These actions may have typically been accompanied at the performance level by a speech or some other means of explaining the action's significance; at the literary level, this is usually accomplished by means of a key-word linking the explanation of the significance back to an aspect of YHWH's command or the prophet's action.

Isaiah 7:1–9 contains a **dating formula** (Isa 7:1a), an **exposition subunit** concerning Ahaz's fear at the Syro-Ephraimite alliance (Isa 7:1b–2), a **symbolic command subunit** involving the name of Isaiah's son, Shear-yashub (Isa 7:3), and a **symbol explanation subunit** (Isa 7:4–9). The intent of the prophecy depends on whether the meaning of Shear-yashub is understood as a remnant indeed shall repent (turn to YHWH), a remnant indeed shall return (survive), only a remnant shall repent, or only a remnant shall return.

Isaiah 8:1–4 is also a **birth narrative** and contains a **symbolic command subunit** (Isa 8:1–3a) and a **symbol explanation subunit** concerning the meaning of Isaiah's son Maher-shalal-hash-baz. Isaiah 20 contains an **introductory subunit** (Isa 20:1–2a), a **symbolic command subunit** (Isa 20:2b), a **compliance subunit** wherein Isaiah walks naked and barefoot (Isa 20:2c), and a **symbol explanation subunit** which is both a **prophecy of punishment against Egypt** and a **prophecy of punishment against Ethiopia** (Isa 20:3–6). It prophesies that Assyria will lead the Egyptians and Ethiopians naked and barefoot as symbolized by Isaiah's actions.

Jeremiah 13:1–11 reports the prophet obeying a series of YHWH's commands that result in ruining a loincloth. The passage contains an autobiographical version of the **messenger of YHWH formula** (Jer 13:1a), **symbolic command subunits** (Jer 13:1b, 4, 6), **compliance subunits** (Jer 13:2, 5, 7), versions of the **prophetic word formula** (Jer 13:3, 8), a **messenger of YHWH formula** (Jer 13:9a), and a **symbol explanation subunit** (Jer 13:9b–11) which is a **prophecy of punishment against Judah**.

Jeremiah 16:1–4, 5–7, 8–9 are three units concerning symbolic actions but comprise one YHWH speech and hence omit the **compliance subunit** in all cases. The **symbolic command subunit** prohibiting

Jeremiah from marrying or having children (Jer 16:2) has a **symbol explanation subunit** (Jer 16:3b–4) that announces judgment upon "the sons and daughters who are born in this place, and concerning the mothers who bear them and the fathers who beget them in this land" (Jer 16:3). Jeremiah 16:5–7 contains a **symbolic command subunit** forbidding Jeremiah from entering the house of mourning (Jer 16:5), and a **symbolic explanation subunit** announcing that no one shall lament for the great or small who die in the land (Jer 16:5c-7). Jeremiah 16:8–9 contains a **symbolic command subunit** forbidding Jeremiah from going to the house of feasting (Jer 16:8) and a **symbol explanation subunit** that announces YHWH's banishing of mirth and gladness (Jer 16:9b). These commands are designed to cause an **oracular inquiry narrative** (Jer 16:10–13).

Jeremiah 19:1–11 contains a **symbolic command subunit** commanding Jeremiah to break the potter's jug (Jer 19:10), and a **symbol explanation subunit** in the form of a **comparison announcement**: "So will I break this people and this city, as one breaks a potter's vessel, so that it can never be mended" (Jer 19:11b).

Jeremiah 25:15–29 contains a **symbolic command subunit**: "Take from my hand this cup of the wine of wrath, and make all the nations to whom I send you drink it" (Jer 25:15b), an **explanation of symbol subunit**, "They shall drink and stagger and go out of their minds because of the sword that I am sending among them" (Jer 25:16), a **compliance subunit** (Jer 25:17), a **gentilics list** (Jer 25:18–26a; see entry in chapter on genres of lists), a further **symbolic command subunit** for the king of Sheshach/Babylon to drink (Jer 25:26b), a **command to address** plus expanded **messenger of YHWH formula** in Jeremiah's style (Jer 25:27a), and an **explanation of symbol subunit** plus **utterance of YHWH formula** (Jer 25:27b–29).

Jeremiah 27:1–13 contains a **dating formula** and **prophetic word formula** (Jer 27:1), an autobiographical form of the **prophetic word formula** (Jer 27:2a), a **symbolic command subunit** commanding Jeremiah to make a yoke and put it on his neck (Jer 27:2b–4a), an expanded form of the **messenger of YHWH formula** in Jeremiah's style (Jer 27:4b), a **messenger command** (Jer 27:4c), and a **symbol explanation subunit** (Jer 27:5–12). This last subunit consists of a **prophecy concerning Nebuchadnezzar** (Jer 27:5–7), a **conditional prophecy of punishment** upon those that rebel against Nebuchadnezzar (Jer 27:8), and **parenesis** for people to bring themselves under yoke to Nebuchadnezzar (Jer 27:9–13).

Jeremiah's speech continues in the form of a **disputation speech** (see entry). For the false prophet Hannaniah's counter symbolic action breaking Jeremiah's yoke and Jeremiah's symbolic action in response, see **confrontation narrative.**

Jeremiah 32:1–25 describes Jeremiah's purchase of a field against the background of a **siege narrative.** It is also an oracular inquiry narrative with an **oracular inquiry subunit** (Jer 32:3b–5) and a **response to oracular inquiry subunit** (Jer 32:6–25) which contains the three main elements of a prophetic symbolic action narrative: a **symbolic command subunit** in which the command to buy the field is implied (Jer 32:7), a **compliance subunit** in which Jeremiah buys the field (Jer 32:8–12), and a **symbol explanation subunit** (Jer 32:13–15) which encourages the people that property purchases will again be made in Judah.

Jeremiah 43:8–13 contains a **prophetic word formula** (Jer 43:8), a **symbolic command subunit** (Jer 43:9), a **command to address** and expanded **messenger of YHWH formula** in Jeremiah's style (Jer 43:10a), and a **symbol explanation subunit** that is also a **prophecy of punishment against Egypt** (Jer 43:10b–13) that may refer to an invasion by Nebuchadnezzar of the Nile delta around 568 BCE.

Jeremiah 51:59–64a is unusual in that Jeremiah commands Seraiah (Baruch's brother) to perform a symbolic action. This **written document narrative** contains a superscription (Jer 51:59), an **action** of writing the **prophecies of punishment against Babylon** (Jer 51:60), a speech introduction (Jer 51:61a), a **symbolic command subunit** (Jer 51:61b–3), and a **symbol explanation subunit**: "Thus shall Babylon sink, to rise no more, because of the disasters that I am bringing on her" (Jer 51:64a).

The report of a symbolic action in Ezek 3:22–27 contains a **hand of YHWH revelatory formula** (Ezek 3:22a), a **speech introduction formula** (Ezek 3:22b), a **preparatory command** (Ezek 3:22c), a **compliance subunit** (Ezek 3:23), a **symbolic command subunit** (Ezek 3:24–26) consisting of **the spirit entered me formula** (Ezek 3:24a), a **speech introduction formula** (Ezek 3:24b), a **divine command section** (Ezek 3:24b–26), a **reason subunit** for command, "for they are a rebellious house" (Ezek 3:26b), and what is perhaps a **symbol explanation subunit** (Ezek 3:27) with a divine promise to open Ezekiel's mouth (Ezek 3:27a), a **command to address** the people with the messenger of YHWH formula (Ezek 3:27b), a jussive form of a **two-part invitation** to hear followed by the ominous repetition of "for they are a rebellious house" (Ezek 3:27c).

The symbolic action units in Ezek 4:1–3, 4–6 are part of a larger **divine speech** (Ezek 3:24b—4:12) and thus lack a **compliance subunit**. Symbolic command subunits commands Ezekiel to make a model of siegeworks against Israel (Ezek 4:1–3a) and to lie on his left side for many days (Ezek 4:4) and on his right side for many days (Ezek 4:6a), and the **symbol explanation subunits** (Ezek 4:5, 6b) specify the number of days (390 for Israel and 40 for Judah) and explain their significance (that number of years of punishment). Another **symbolic command subunit** (Ezek 4:7–12) gives further details including baking barley-cakes on human dung and **symbol explanation subunits** function as a **prophecy of punishment against Israel**, (Ezek 4:13) and a **prophecy of punishment against Jerusalem** regarding their lack of bread and water (Ezek 4:16–17).

Ezekiel 5 is entirely divine speech consisting of a **symbolic command subunit** commanding Ezekiel to shave his head and beard, burn one third of the hair inside the city, strike one third of the hair with the sword, and scatter most of the remaining third to the wind but preserving some of them (Ezek 5:1–4); a **messenger of YHWH formula** (Ezek 5:5a); and a **symbol explanation subunit** consisting of a **prophecy of punishment against Jerusalem** (Ezek 5:5b–17).

In Ezek 12:1–16, the **symbolic command subunit** (Ezek 12:1–6) directs Ezekiel to prepare publicly baggage for exile, the **compliance subunit** is quite pedantic (Ezek 12:7), and the **symbol explanation subunit** prophesies the scattering of Israel (Ezek 12:8–16).

As an introduction to a **prophecy of punishment against Jerusalem** (Ezek 21:29–32 [NRSV 24–27]), YHWH commands Ezekiel to mark out a fork in a road (Ezek 21:24–25 [NRSV 19–20] the **symbolic command subunit**), and the following **symbolic explanation subunit** (Ezek 21:26–28 [NRSV 21–23]) prophesies that the king of Babylon will choose to besiege Jerusalem rather than Rabbah of the Ammonites.

The first half of Ezekiel culminates in a symbolic action concerning the death of Ezekiel's wife (Ezek 24:15–27). The **symbolic command subunit** forbids Ezekiel from mourning his wife (Ezek 24:15–17), the **compliance subunit** shows Ezekiel's obedience and is conveyed without emotion (Ezek 24:18), which elicits an **inquiry** from the people and eventually a **symbol explanation subunit** (Ezek 24:21b–27) explains that just as YHWH had taken away Ezekiel's delight so would the delight of their eyes, the sanctuary, be taken away.

After the famous "dry bones" prophecy in Ezek 37:1–14, comes a symbolic action unit on the same theme. The **symbolic command subunit** (Ezek 37:15–17) consists of an autobiographical form of the **prophetic word formula** (Ezek 37:15), and a **divine command subunit** (Ezek 37:16–17), commanding Ezekiel to join together sticks representing Judah and Joseph. In the transition unit (Ezek 37:18–19), YHWH imagines the people's **inquiry** (Ezek 37:18) and commands Ezekiel to give a specific **answer** (Ezek 37:19) that essentially repeats the content in the previous **divine command subunit**. The **symbol explanation subunit** (Ezek 37:20–28) contains an **extended speech introduction** (Ezek 37:20–21a), a **messenger of YHWH formula** (Ezek 37:21b), an **announcement of salvation subunit** (Ezek 37:21c-23) culminating in the **covenant formula** (Ezek 37:23b), a **prophecy concerning David subunit** (Ezek 37:24–25), and an **announcement of salvation subunit** (Ezek 37:26–28) culminating in a **covenant formula** (Ezek 37:27b), and an expanded **recognition formula** (Ezek 37:28).

For Hos 1:2–3, 4–5, 6–7, 8–9, see also **birth narrative**. Regarding Hosea's children, the pattern is for Gomer to bear a child, a **symbolic command subunit** in which YHWH commands Hosea to name the child, and a **symbol explanation subunit** explaining the significance of the name. Hosea 1:2–3 contains a **symbolic command subunit** for Hosea to marry a wife of whoredom (Hos 1:2a), a **symbol explanation subunit** that the land commits whoredom by forsaking YHWH (1:2b) and a **compliance subunit** in which Hosea marries Gomer (1:3). Hosea 3:1–5 contains a **speech report formula** (Hos 3:1a), a **symbolic command subunit** which is a shocking **comparison command**: "Go, love a woman who has a lover and is an adulteress, just as the Lord loves the people of Israel, though they turn to other gods and love raisin cakes" (Hos 3:1b), a **compliance subunit** which omits any reaction on Hosea's part (Hos 3:2–3), and a **symbol explanation subunit** which is a **prophecy of punishment and restoration** for Israel (Hos 3:4–5). It is unclear whether the woman in Hos 3 is Hosea's wife Gomer in Hosea 1.

Zechariah 6:9–15 contains an autobiographical form of the **prophetic word formula** (Zech 6:9), a **symbolic command subunit** involving making a crown and setting it on the head of the high priest (Zech 6:10–11), a **command to address** and **messenger of YHWH formula** (Zech 6:12a), and a **symbol explanation subunit** (Zech 6:12b–15) that concludes with a **conditional prophecy of salvation**: "And the crown shall be in the care of Heldai, Tobijah, Jedaiah, and Josiah son of Zephaniah, as a memorial in the temple of the Lord. Those who are far off shall come and help to build the temple of the Lord; and you shall know that the Lord of hosts has sent me to you. This will happen if you diligently obey the voice of the Lord your God" (Zech 6:14–15).

Zechariah 11:4–17 contains a **messenger of YHWH formula** (Zech 11:4a), a **symbolic command subunit** (Zech 11:4b), a **symbol explanation subunit** (Zech 11:5–6), a **compliance subunit** (Zech 11:7–8), a **symbol explanation subunit** (Zech 11:9) in advance of a symbolic action about to be performed, an implied **compliance subunit** in which Zechariah breaks the staff Favor although YHWH's command to break the staff is not recorded (Zech 11:10–11), a **command and compliance subunit** in which the merchants obey Zechariah's command to give him thirty shekels of silver (Zech 11:12), another **command and compliance subunit** in which Zechariah obeys YHWH's command to throw the thirty shekels of silver into the treasury (Zech 11:13), an implied **compliance subunit** in which Zechariah breaks the staff Unity (Zech 11:14a), a **symbol explanation subunit** (Zech 11:14b), a **speech report formula** and **symbolic command subunit** (Zech 11:15), and a **symbol explanation subunit** (Zech 11:16–17). The passage likely functions as a **prophecy of punishment against (male) leaders.**

Amsler, *Actes des prophètes*; Block, "Beyond the Grave," 113–41; Biwul, *Theological Examination*; Finlay, *Birth Report*, 162–95; Floyd, *Minor Prophets 2*, 646–47; Friebel, *Jeremiah's Sign-Acts*; Fohrer, *Symbolischen Handlungen*; Hals, *Ezekiel*, 354–55; Hasel, *Remnant*, 274–75; Irvine, *Isaiah, Ahaz*; Redditt, "Israel's Shepherds," 631–42; Stacey, *Prophetic Drama*; Sweeney, *Isaiah 1–39*, 536–37; Wong, "Faith," 535–47.

Rescue/Release Narrative

For the genre as a whole, see the entry in the chapter on narrative genres. Jeremiah 38:1–13 consists of an **auditory experience** by various officials (Jer 38:1), Jeremiah's **prophecy of punishment against Jerusalem** (Jer 38:2–3), the **demand** to King Zedekiah by the officials that Jeremiah be put to death (Jer 38:4), Zedekiah's **accession** to their demand by handing him over (Jer 38:5), the officials' **actions** of throwing Jeremiah into a cistern (Jer 38:6a), an **exposition of object** concerning the muddy state of the cistern (Jer 38:6b), the **event** of Jeremiah sinking in the mud (Jer 38:6c), Ebed-Melech the Ethiopian's **auditory experience** of news concerning Jeremiah (Jer 38:7a), an **exposition of location** regarding the king (Jer 38:7b), the **departure** of Ebed-Melech (Jer 38:8a), Ebed-Melech's **intercession** with the king on behalf of Jeremiah (Jer 38:8b–9), the king's positive **response** to the intercession (Jer 38:10), Ebed-Melech's **preparatory actions** to rescue Jeremiah (Jer 38:11), Ebed-Melech's **instruction** to Jeremiah (Jer 38:12a) and Jeremiah's **compliance** (Jer 38:12b), the **actions** that specifically rescue Jeremiah (Jer 38:13a), and the **result**, namely Jeremiah remaining in the court (Jer 38:13b).

Nebuchadrezzar gives a **command** for the imprisoned Jeremiah to be taken good care of (Jer 39:11–12) and this is followed by Nebuzaradan's **compliance** (Jer 39:13–14a) with the **result** that Jeremiah then stays with his own people (Jer 39:14b).

Jeremiah 40:1–6 contains an expanded **prophetic word formula** (Jer 40:1), the captain of the guard's **exercitive speech** releasing Jeremiah to wherever he wants to go (Jer 40:2–5a) and corresponding **action** of release concerning Jeremiah (Jer 40:5b), and the **result narrative subunit** in which Jeremiah stays with Gedaliah (Jer 40:6).

Jeremiah 41:4–14 contains an **arrival** of eighty men (Jer 41:4–5), Ishmael's **actions** of slaughtering all but ten of the men and taking the rest captive (Jer 41:6–10), a brief **battle narrative** preparation of Johanan's forces against Ishmael (Jer 41:11–12), the **result** of the people that Ishmael had taken captive gladly joining with Johanan (Jer 41:13–14), and further **actions** such as Ishmael escaping and Johanan's group departing towards Egypt (Jer 41:15–18).

The appendix to the book of Jeremiah ends with King Evil-Merodach of Babylon's **actions** of showing King Jehoiachin of Judah favor, releasing him from prison, and giving him a special seat with the **result** that Jehoiachin daily dined with the king (Jer 52:31–34 [=2 Kgs 25:27–30]).

Martens, "Narrative Parallelism," 33–49; Ritzema, "After Zedekiah," 73–91.

Scene in Vision

Ezekiel contains three lengthy **vision narratives** (Ezek 1:1—3:15; 8:1—11:25; 40:1—48:35), and each of these divide into various scenes introduced by a **behold experience**, a **spirit lifted me formula** or variation thereof, or a **visionary guidance formula**. See overview of Tanak for further details of the vision narratives. Another standard element is

description subunits of the objects that Ezekiel sees. The scenes (1:4–14, 15–28a; 1:28b-2:1; 2:2–8; 2:9–3:11; 3:12–13, 14–15) in the first vision narrative also contain auditory and tactile experiences, and theophanic and commission elements relevant to the **vocation narrative** concerning Ezekiel. The vision of the divine chariot gave rise to a strand of mystical interpretation in Judaism.

The scenes in Ezek 8:1—11:24 contain numerous divine commands and compliance subunits by Ezekiel as he witnesses the wrath God pours on Jerusalem and the narrative concludes with Ezekiel being translated back to Babylonia.

Ezekiel 40–48 contains ten scenes in Ezek 40–42 which concern the future temple and are dominated by **description subunits** and **measurement subunits** and nine scenes in Ezek 43–48 which display more concern for **future laws** (see entry in legal genres chapter) and future **allotments half-lists** (Ezek 48:1–7, 23–29), **boundary lists**, and **exit lists** (see entries in lists chapter) and frequently contain long **divine speeches** or speeches by Ezekiel's visionary guide.

Vision Narrative

More extensive than vision reports, the narratives in Ezekiel 1:1—3:15; 8:1—11:24; 40:1—48:35 each contain numerous **scenes in vision** and their role in Ezekiel is mentioned in the overview of Tanak chapter. The last narrative is more fully discussed in **future temple vision narrative**.

Vision Report

This glossary reserves the term vision report for briefer narratives than the larger narrative complexes in Ezek 1–3, 8–11, 40–48 which are analyzed in **scene in vision.**

Jeremiah 4:19–31 seems to be a series of three vision reports (Jer 4:19–22, 23–28, 29–31) in which the content of the visions and the rest of the material are not as clearly demarcated as usual. The first report contains Jeremiah's **expression of anguish** at the vision (Jer 4:19a), an **auditory experience** of the trumpet alarm (Jer 4:19b), a **description subunit** concerning the vision (Jer 4:20), a **rhetorical question** (Jer 4:21), and a **basis for punishment subunit** from a divine perspective (Jer 4:22). The second report consists of a series of four **behold experiences** (Jer 4:23,

24, 25, 26), a **messenger of YHWH formula** (Jer 4:27a), an **announcement of punishment subunit** (Jer 4:27b), a **restriction** (Jer 4:27c), an **announcement of punishment subunit** reaching cosmic scale: "Because of this the earth shall mourn, and the heavens above grow black" (Jer 4:28a), and a **divine speech self-authentication formula** (Jer 4:28b). The third report contains a **description subunit** of Judah's forsaken towns (Jer 4:29), a **rhetorical question** and a **taunt** concerning Zion's futile beautification because her lovers seek her life (Jer 4:30), and an **auditory experience** of Zion's anguished cry (Jer 4:31). This series of visions amounts to a prophecy of punishment against Judah in hyperbolic and highly memorable form. This likely dates fairly early in Jeremiah's career and its referent is the siege and destruction of Jerusalem in 587 BCE.

Jeremiah 24:1–10 contains a **YHWH showed me formula** (Jer 24:1a), a **background exposition subunit** (Jer 24:1b), an **experience subunit** (Jer 24:2), a **question and answer subunit** (Jer 24:3), an autobiographical version of the **prophetic word formula** (Jer 24:4), an expanded **messenger of YHWH formula** (Jer 24:5a), and an **explanation of vision subunit** (Jer 24:5b–10). The explanation subdivides into an **announcement of salvation subunit** for the exiles in Babylonia (Jer 24:5b–7a), a **covenant formula** (Jer 24:7b), and an **announcement of punishment subunit** concerning those remaining in Judah (Jer 24:8–10), with the **messenger of YHWH formula** (Jer 24:8b) unusually placed between the protasis and the apodosis.

Ezekiel 37:1–14 contains a **hand of YHWH revelatory formula** (Ezek 37:1a), an **experience subunit** involving a valley of dry bones (Ezek 37:1b–2a), a **behold experience** (Ezek 37:2b), a **question and answer subunit** concerning whether the bones can live (Ezek 37:3), a **command and compliance subunit** (Ezek 37:4–8), in which YHWH commands Ezekiel to prophesy to the bones (Ezek 37:4–6), and Ezekiel complies with the result that the bones come together with skin covering them but no breath yet in them (Ezek 37:7–8). Then comes another **command and compliance subunit** (Ezek 37:9–10) in which YHWH commands Ezekiel to prophesy again (Ezek 37:9) and Ezekiel's compliance results in the bodies living and standing on their feet (Ezek 37:10). Then comes an **explanation of vision subunit** (Ezek 37:11–14) in which the dry bones represent the house of Israel who say "Our bones are dried up, and our hope is lost" (Ezek 37:11) and to whom YHWH replies, "I am going to open your graves, and bring you from your graves, O my people" (Ezek 37:12). Other formulas in this vision report include the **call to attention**

formula (Ezek 37:4c), the **messenger of YHWH formula** (Ezek 37:5a, 9b, 12b), the **recognition formula** (Ezek 37:13a), and the **utterance of YHWH formula** (Ezek 37:14b).

The book of Amos contains five vision reports (Amos 7:1–3, 4–6, 7–9; 8:1–3; 9:1–6). The first two of these are discussed under **report of prophetic intercession**. Amos 7:7–9 contains a **YHWH showed me formula** (Amos 7:7), an **inquiry** by YHWH (Amos 7:8a), an **answer** by Amos (Amos 7:8b), and a **divine speech** that is an **announcement of punishment subunit** (Amos 7:8c–9). Amos 8:1–3 similarly contains a **YHWH showed me formula** (Amos 8:1), an **inquiry** by YHWH (Amos 8:2a), an **answer** by Amos (Amos 8:2b), a **divine speech** that is an **announcement of punishment subunit** containing an **utterance of YHWH formula** (Amos 8:2c–3). Both of these visions contain the **verdict** "The end has come upon my people Israel; I will never again pass them by" (Amos 7:8; 8:2) signaling that intercession will no longer be effective (see **report of prophetic intercession**). Amos 9:1–6 contains a **vision introduction** (Amos 9:1a), a **divine command section** (Amos 9:1b), an **announcement of punishment subunit** (Amos 9:1c–4), and a **hymnic fragment** concluding with the **YHWH of hosts name formula** (Amos 9:5–6).

Seven of the eight visions in the first half of Zechariah have the following basic pattern: an introduction; a description of what Zechariah experienced; Zechariah's inquiry as to the significance; and an interpretation by an angel. Zechariah 1:7–17 contains a **dating formula** (Zech 1:7a), a **prophetic word formula** (Zech 1:7b), **vision introduction** (Zech 1:8a), a **description subunit** concerning a man, later revealed as the angel of YHWH, on a red horse standing among the myrtle trees and behind him were other horses of various colors (Zech 1:8b), and a lengthy **dialogue** (Zech 1:9–17) with its climax the proclamation "I have returned to Jerusalem with compassion; my house shall be built in it, says the Lord of hosts" (Zech 1:16).

Zechariah 2:1–4 [NRSV 1:18–21] contains a **behold experience** of four horns (Zech 2:1 [NRSV 1:18]), an **inquiry** as to what these are (Zech 2:2a [NRSV 1:19a]), and an **answer** by the angel that they are the horns that have scattered Judah, Israel, and Jerusalem (Zech 2:2b [NRSV 1:19b]), a **YHWH showed me formula** concerning four blacksmiths (Zech 2:3 [NRSV 1:20]), an **inquiry**, "What are they coming to do?" (Zech 2:4a [NRSV 1:21a]) and an **answer** that they have come "to strike down the horns of the nations that lifted up their horns against the land of Judah to scatter its people" (Zech 2:4b [NRSV 1:21b]). Zechariah 2:5–9 [NRSV 1–5] contains a **behold experience** of a man with a measuring line (Zech 2:5 [NRSV 1]), a **question and answer subunit** (Zech 2:6 [NRSV 2]), a **behold experience** of another angel (Zech 2:7 [NRSV 3]), and a speech by the angel contains a **commissioning formula** (Zech 2:8a [NRSV 4a]), and an **announcement of salvation subunit** (Zech 2:8b–9 [NRSV 4b–5]) containing the **utterance of YHWH formula** (Zech 2:9b [NRSV 5b]).

Zechariah 3:1–10 contains a **YHWH showed me formula** concerning Joshua and the accuser (Zech 3:1), YHWH's **rebuke** to the accuser (Zech 3:2), a **description subunit** of Joshua's filthy clothes (Zech 3:3), an **angelic command** for the clothes to be removed (Zech 3:4a), an **explanation subunit** that this signifies the removal of Joshua's guilt (Zech 3:4b), a **request** by Zechariah that a clean turban be put on his head (Zech 3:5a), a **compliance subunit** (Zech 3:5b), a **speech introduction** (Zech 3:6), a **messenger of YHWH formula** (Zech 3:7a), a **conditional promise** to Joshua (Zech 3:7b), a **call to attention formula** (Zech 3:8a), and an **announcement of salvation subunit** involving the branch and thus perhaps (although the Hebrew word for "branch" here is different than in Isa 11:1) a **prophecy concerning the Davidic line** (Zech 3:8b–9), a **future event formula** plus **utterance of YHWH formula** (Zech 3:10a), and an **announcement of salvation subunit** (Zech 3:10b).

Zechariah 4:1–14 contains the **action** of the angel waking Zechariah (Zech 4:1), a **question and answer subunit** concerning Zechariah seeing a golden lampstand with seven lamps and two olive trees by it (Zech 4:2–3), a **dialogue** concerning its significance (Zech 4:4–7), climaxing with the word to Zerubbabel, "Not by might, nor by power, but by my spirit, says the Lord of hosts" (Zech 4:6), an autobiographical form of the **prophetic word formula** (Zech 4:8), a **prophecy** that Zerubbabel would complete building the temple (Zech 4:9a), an adapted **recognition formula** (Zech 4:9b), an **explanation subunit** concerning the seven lamps (Zech 4:10), two **inquiries** by Zechariah concerning the significance of the two olive trees (Zech 4:11, 12), a **question and answer subunit** establishing that Zechariah does not know the significance (Zech 4:13), and an **explanation subunit** that these represent the two anointed ones standing by YHWH (Zech 4:14).

Zechariah 5:1–4 contains a **behold experience** of a flying scroll (Zech 5:1), a **question and answer subunit** in which Zechariah states the dimensions of the scroll (Zech 5:2), and an **explanation subunit** (Zech

5:3–4) that it is a curse on those who steal or swear falsely. Zechariah 5:5–11 contains an angelic **command** to see an object (Zech 5:5), a **question and answer subunit** concerning the object (a basket; Zech 5:6a), an **explanation subunit** that it is iniquity in all the land (Zech 5:6b), a **behold experience** of a woman sitting in the basket (Zech 5:7), an **explanation subunit** that "This is wickedness" (Zech 5:8a), an **action** by the angel of putting the woman back into the basket (Zech 5:8b), a **behold experience** of two women with wings lifting up the basket (Zech 5:9), and a **question and answer subunit** informing Zechariah that the basket is headed for the land of Shinar (Zech 5:10–11).

Zechariah 6:1–8 contains a **behold experience** of four chariots emerging between two mountains of bronze (Zech 6:1), a **description subunit** of the four chariots and their variously colored horses (Zech 6:2–3), an **inquiry** as to what these mean (Zech 6:4), an **explanation subunit** that they are the four winds of heaven going out (Zech 6:5–6), a **command and compliance subunit** concerning the horses patrolling the earth (Zech 6:7), and another **explanation subunit** enigmatically proclaiming "Lo, those who go toward the north country have set my spirit at rest in the north country" (Zech 6:8).

Campos, "Structure and Meaning," 2–28; Floyd, *Minor Prophets 2*, 326–410, 644–45; Hals, *Ezekiel*, 266–72, 358; Hayes and Tiemeyer, *Lifted My Eyes*; Horst, "Visionsschilderungen," 193–205; Jeremias, *Nachtgesichte*; Long, "Reports of Visions," 353–65; Niditch, *Symbolic Vision*.

Vocation Account

This is a narrative that describes the initiatory call of the prophet/judge to a life of activity specially directed by God. Examples outside the latter prophets include the calls of Moses (Exod 3–4) and Gideon (Judg 6). Typical elements within the vocation account include a divine or heavenly appearance often involving a **vision report** (including **experiences** by the prophet) and **dialogue** between YHWH and the prophet which may include a **commissioning speech subunit**, a **response of prophet subunit**, and a **reassurance speech** or sign to overcome objections by the prophet. In Isaiah 6 and Ezek 1, attention is given to the prophet's vision of YHWH's heavenly realm; in Exod 3–4; Judg 6; Jer 1; and Ezek 2–3, the coming of the word of YHWH is the dominant theme. The teleological cause is to authenticate the prophet as YHWH's spokesman and often to summarize the prophet's overall message.

Isaiah 6:1–13 begins with a **vision report** (Isa 6:1–4) containing a vague **dating formula** (Isa 6:1a), an **experience of the prophet** (Isa 6:1b), a **description subunit** of the seraphim and the hem of the divine robe (Isa 6:1c–2), a **speech introduction** (Isa 6:3a), the doxological **angelic speech** known as the trisagion: "Holy, holy, holy is the Lord God of Hosts; the whole earth is full of his glory" (Isa 6:3b), and a **description subunit** full of sound and smoke (Isa 6:4). Then comes the **response of the prophet subunit** which is a **woe speech** directed at himself (Isa 6:5), a **reaction of third party subunit** (Isa 6:6–7) which involves a seraph touching a live coal to Isaiah's mouth and performing an **exercitive speech**: "Your guilt has departed and your sin is blotted out" (Isa 6:7b), a question and answer subunit in which YHWH asks "Whom shall I send" and Isaiah volunteers "Here am I; send me!" (Isa 6:8), an enigmatic **divine command subunit** that is the only Scripture quoted in all four Gospels and Acts: "Go and say to this people: 'Keep listening, but do not comprehend; keep looking, but do not understand.' Make the mind of this people dull, and stop their ears, and shut their eyes, so that they may not look with their eyes, and listen with their ears, and comprehend with their minds, and turn and be healed" (Isa 6:9–10), and another **question and answer subunit** consisting of an **inquiry** by the prophet (Isa 6:11a), and an **answer** by YHWH that is an **announcement of punishment subunit** (Isa 6:11b–13).

Jeremiah 1:4–19 contains an autobiographic form of the **prophetic word formula** (Jer 1:4), an **exercitive speech** appointing Jeremiah as a prophet (Jer 1:5), an **objection of prophet subunit** (Jer 1:6), a **response of YHWH subunit** (Jer 1:7–10), a **question and answer subunit** involving the symbol of an almond tree (Jer 1:11), a **symbol explanation subunit** involving a wordplay on the Hebrew words for "almond" and "watch" (Jer 1:12), a **question and answer subunit** regarding the north (Jer 1:13), a **speech report formula** (Jer 1:14a), a **prophecy of punishment against Judah** from the north (Jer 1:14b–16), and a **prophecy of salvation for individual**, concerning Jeremiah (Jer 1:17–19). The **response of YHWH subunit** contains a **speech report formula** (Jer 1:7a), a **reassurance speech** (Jer 1:7b–8) including a **reassurance formula** (Jer 1:8a), **assistance formula** plus **utterance of YHWH formula** (Jer 1:8b), a **narrative introduction** (Jer 1:9a), and an **exercitive speech** appointing Jeremiah "over nations and over kingdoms, to pluck up and to pull down, to destroy and to overthrow, to build and to plant" (Jer 1:9b–10). See also **vision report**.

For Ezek 1:1—3:15, see **scene in vision**.

Bailey, "Jeremiah: Fortified City," 117–38; Buss, "Anthropological Perspective," 9–30; Habel, "Form and Significance," 297–323; Pikor, "Prophet as Witness," 73–95; Sweeney, *Isaiah 1–39*, 542–43.

Written Document Narrative

For comments on the genre as a whole, see the chapter on narrative genres. The **birth narrative** in Isaiah 8:1–4 includes Isaiah having his son's name not only written down on a tablet but attested.

Jeremiah 29:1–23 contains a **superscription** (Jer 29:1), a **background exposition** (Jer 29:2–3), an expanded **messenger of YHWH formula** (Jer 29:4), an **exhortation subunit** to live normal lives but also to seek the welfare of the place in which they have been exiled (Jer 29:5–7), an expanded **messenger of YHWH formula** in Jeremiah's style (Jer 29:8a), an **admonition subunit** not to heed the false prophets (Jer 29:8b–9), a **messenger of YHWH formula** (Jer 29:10a), an **announcement of restoration subunit** after seventy years (Jer 29:10b–14), a **basis for punishment subunit** (Jer 29:15), an expanded and reiterated **messenger of YHWH formula** (Jer 29:16–17a), an **announcement of punishment subunit** on those remaining in Judah plus utterance of YHWH formula (Jer 29:17b–19), a **call to attention formula** addressed to the exiles (Jer 29:20), an expanded **messenger of YHWH formula** (Jer 29:21a), an **announcement of punishment subunit** upon Zedekiah plus **utterance of YHWH formula** (Jer 29:21b–23).

Jeremiah 29:24–32 contains a **command to speak formula** (Jer 29:24), an expanded **messenger of YHWH formula** in Jeremiah's style (Jer 29:25a), an **accusatory action** of Shemiah sending a letter (Jer 29:25b), a **quotation subunit** of the letter's contents which denounced Jeremiah (Jer 29:26–28), an **action** of Zephaniah reading this letter in Jeremiah's hearing (Jer 29:29), a **prophetic word formula** (Jer 29:30), a **command to address** via a letter plus an expanded **messenger of YHWH formula** (Jer 29:31a), and a **reason and consequences subunit** announcing punishment on Shemiah including a **messenger of YHWH formula** and an **utterance of YHWH formula** (Jer 29:31b–32).

Jeremiah 30:1–4 contains a **prophetic word formula** (Jer 30:1), an expanded **messenger of YHWH formula** (Jer 30:2a), a **command** to write in a book "all the words that I have spoken to you" (Jer 30:2b), a **future event formula** plus **utterance of YHWH formula** (Jer 30:3a), an **announcement of restoration subunit** (Jer 30:3b), and a **superscription** to the words that YHWH spoke and which presumably Baruch wrote down (Jer 30:4).

Dearman, "Servants Scribes," 403–21; Dijkstra, "Prophecy by Letter," 319–22; Haran, "Book-Scrolls," 161–73; Lundbom, "Baruch, Seraiah," 89–114; Mastnjak, "Jeremiah as Collection," 25–44; Millard, "Ancient Scribes," 143–53; Holladay, "Identification Two Scrolls," 452–67; Smelik, "Letters to Exiles," 282–95.

Bibliography

Aaron, David H. "Early Rabbinic Exegesis on Noah's Son Ham and the So–Called 'Hamatic Myth.'" *JAAR* 63 (1995) 721–59

———. "The Ruse of Zelophehad's Daughters." *HUCA* 80 (2009) 1–38.

Aasland, Erik. "Two Heads are Better Than One: Using Conceptual Mappings to Analyze Proverb Meaning." *Proverbium* 26 (2009) 1–18.

Aberneth, Andrew T. and Gregory Goswell. *God's Messiah in the Old Testament: Expectations of a Coming King*. Grand Rapids: Baker Academic, 2020.

Abril, Michael Anthony. "Lamentations 5:21 within the Development of Thomas Aquinas' Theology of the Grace of Conversion." *International Journal of Systematic Theology* 16 (2014) 251–72.

Absali, Alexander Izuchukwu. "Was It Rape? The David and Bathsheba Pericope Re-Examined." *VT* 61 (2011) 1–15.

Achenbach, Reinhard. "Das Kyros-Orakel in Jesaja 44,24–45,7 im Lichte altorientalischer Parallelen." *Zeitschrift für altorientalische und biblische Rechtsgeschichte* 11 (2005) 155–94.

Ackerman, Susan. "The Queen Mother and the Cult in Ancient Israel." *JBL* 112 (1993) 385–401.

Adamo, David T. "Ancient Israelite and African Proverbs as Advice, Reproach, Warning, Encouragement and Explanation." *HTS Theological Studies* 71 (2015) 1–11.

Adams, Douglas A. *The Hitchhiker's Guide to the Galaxy*. London: Pan, 1979.

Adams, James W. *The Performative Nature and Function of Isaiah 40–55*. LHBOTS 448. London: T. & T. Clark, 2006.

Adams, Samuel L. *Wisdom in Transition: Act and Consequence in Second Temple Instructions*. JSJSup 125. Leiden: Brill, 2008.

Adeyemi, Femi. "What Is the New Covenant 'Law' in Jeremiah 31:33?" *BSac* 163 (2006) 312–21.

Aejmelaeus, Anneli. "Der Prophet als Klageliedsänger—Zur Funktion des Psalms Jes 63,7—64,11 in Tritojesaja." *ZAW* 107 (1995) 31–50.

———. *The Traditional Prayer in the Psalms*. BZAW 167. Berlin: de Gruyter, 1986.

Aharoni, Reuben. "Concerning Three Similar Stories in the Book of Genesis" (Heb.). *BMik* 24 (1979) 213–23.

———. "The Gog Prophecy and the Book of Ezekiel." *HAR* 1 (1977) 1–27.

Aharoni, Yohanan. *The Land of the Bible: A Historical Geography*. Translated by A. F. Rainey. Philadelphia: Westminster, 1967.

———. "The Province List of Judah." *VT* 9 (1959) 225–46.

Ahn, John. "Psalm 137: Complex Communal Laments." *JBL* 127 (2008) 267–89.

Ahuis, Ferdinand. "Behemot, Leviaton und der Mensch in Hiob 38–42." *ZAW* 123 (2011) 72–91.

———. *Der klagende Gerichtsprophet: Studien zur Klage in der Überlieferung von den alttestamentlichen Gerichtspropheten*. CThM 12. Stuttgart: Calwer Verlag, 1982.

Aitken, Kenneth T. "The Oracles against Babylon in Jeremiah 50–51: Structures and Perspectives." *TynBul* 35 (1984) 25–63.

Albertz, Rainer. *A History of Israelite Religion in the Old Testament Period*. 2 vols. Translated by John Bowden. OTL. Louisville: Westminster John Knox, 1994.

Albright, William F. "The Oracles of Balaam." *JBL* 63 (1944) 207–33.

Aletti, J. N. "Seduction et parole en Proverbs I–IX." *VT* 27 (1977) 129–44.

Alexander, T. D. "The Composition of the Sinai Narrative in Exodus xix 1—xxiv 11." *VT* 49 (1999) 2–20.

Allen, Leslie C. "Disputations in the Book of Jeremiah." *Perspectives in Religious Studies* 35 (2008) 135–46.

Allrik, H. L. "The Lists of Zerubbabel (Nehemiah 7 and Ezra 2) and the Hebrew Numeral Notation." *BASOR* 136 (1954) 21–27.

Alston, William P. *Illocutionary Acts and Sentence Meaning*. Ithaca: Cornell University Press, 2000.

Alt, Albrecht. "The God of the Fathers." In *Essays on Old Testament History and Religion*, 1–100. Translated by Robert A. Wilson. Oxford: Blackwell, 1966.

———. "The Origins of Israelite Law." In *Essays in Old Testament History and Religion*, 79–132. Translated by Robert A. Wilson. Oxford: Blackwell, 1966.

Alter, Robert. *The Art of Biblical Narrative*. New York: Basic Books, 1981.

———. *The Art of Biblical Poetry*. New York: Basic Books, 2011.

———. "How Convention Helps Us Read: The Case of the Bible's Annunciation Type-Scene." *Prooftexts* 3 (1983) 115–30.

Alter, Robert, and Frank Kermode, eds. *The Literary Guide to the Bible*. Cambridge: Harvard University Press, 1987.

Altman, Amnon. "On Some Basic Concepts in the Law of People Seeking Refuge and Sustenance in the Ancient Near East." *ZABR* 8 (2002) 323–42.

Altmann, Peter. *Festive Meals in Ancient Israel: Deuteronomy's Identity Politics in Their Ancient Near Eastern Context*. BZAW 424. Berlin: de Gruyter, 2011.

Amsler, Samuel. *Les actes des prophètes*. Essaies Bibliques 9. Geneva: Labor et Fides, 1985.

Amzallag, Nissim. "The Paradoxical Source of Hope in Isaiah 12." *RB* 123 (2016) 357–77.

———. "Why Is the Cain Genealogy (Gen 4:17–24) Integrated into the Book of Genesis?" *ANES* 55 (2018) 23–50.

Amzallag, Nissim, and Mikhal Avriel. "Complex Antiphony in David's Lament and Its Literary Significance." *VT* 60 (2010) 1–14.

Andersen, Ragnar. "The Elihu Speeches: Their Place and Sense in the Book of Job." *TynBul* 66 (2015) 75–94.

Anderson, Gary A. "King David and the Psalms of Imprecation." *ProEccl* 15 (2006) 267–80.

———. *Sacrifices and Offerings in Ancient Israel: Studies in Their Social and Political Importance*. HSM 41. Atlanta: Scholars, 1987.

Anderson, Gary A., and Joel S. Kaminsky eds., *The Call of Abraham: Essays on the Election of Israel in Honor of Jon D. Levenson*. Notre Dame: University of Notre Dame Press, 2013.

Andersson, Daniel. "Understanding Figurative Proverbs: A Model Based on Conceptual Blending." *Folklore* 124 (2013) 28–44.

Anderson, William H. U. *Qoheleth and Its Pessimistic Theology: Hermeneutic Struggles in Wisdom Literature*. MBPS 54. Lewiston, NY: Mellen Biblical Press, 1997.

Andreasen, Niels-Erik. *The Old Testament Sabbath*. SBLDS 7. Missoula, MT: SBL, 1972.

Angel, Hayyim. "The Literary Significance of the Name Lists in Ezra–Nehemiah." *JBQ* 35 (2007) 143–52.

Ansberry, Christopher B. *Be Wise, My Son, and Make My Heart Glad: An Exploration of the Courtly Nature of the Book of Proverbs*. BZAW 422. Berlin: de Gruyter, 2011.

———. "What Does Jerusalem Have to Do with Athens? The Moral Vision of the Book of Proverbs and Aristotle's Nicomachean Ethics." *HS* 51 (2010) 157–73.

Apple, Raymond. "Addenda to Psalm 145." *JBQ* 44 (2016) 275–93.

———. "The Two Wise Women of Proverbs Chapter 31." *JBQ* 39 (2011) 175–80.

Aquinas, Thomas. *Summa Theologica*. Translated by Fathers of the English Dominican Province. London: Burns, Oates & Washbourne, n.d.

Arnold, Bill T. "Deuteronomy 12 and the Law of the Central Sanctuary *noch einmal*." *VT* 64 (2014) 236–48.

Ashmon, Scott A. *Birth Annunciations in the Hebrew Bible and Ancient Near East: A Literary Analysis of the Forms and Functions of the Heavenly Foretelling of the Destiny of a Special Child*. Lewiston, NY: Edwin Mellen, 2012.

———. "The Covenantal Function of Biblical Birth Annunciations." *CTR* 10 (2012) 41–52.

Assis, Elie. "The Alphabetic Acrostic in the Book of Lamentations." *CBQ* 69 (2007) 710–24.

———. "Chiasmus in Biblical Narrative: Rhetoric of Characterization." *Prooftexts* 22 (2002) 273–304.

———. "From Adam to Esau and Israel: An Anti-Edomite Ideology in 1 Chronicles 1." *VT* 56 (2006) 287–302.

———. *Self-Interest or Communal Interest: An Ideology of Leadership in the Gideon, Abimelech, and Jephthah Narratives (Judges 6–12)*. VTSup 106. Leiden: Brill, 2005.

———. "To Build or Not to Build: A Dispute Between Haggai and His People (Hag 1)." *ZAW* 119 (2007) 514–27.

———. "Why Edom? On the Hostility Towards Jacob's Brother in Prophetic Sources." *VT* 56 (2006) 1–20.

———. "Zechariah 8 and Its Allusions to Jeremiah 30–33 and Deutero-Isaiah." *JHS* 11 (2011) 2–21.

Aster, Shawn Z. "Isaiah 19: The 'Burden of Egypt' and Neo-Assyrian Imperial Policy." *JAOS* 135 (2015) 435–70.

Auerbach, Eric. *Mimesis: The Representation of Reality in Western Literature*. Translated by Willard R. Trask. Princeton: Princeton University Press, 1953.

Austin, J. L. *How to Do Things with Words*. Cambridge: Harvard University Press, 1962.

Ayali-Darshan, Noga. "The Seventy Bulls Sacrificed at Sukkot (Num 29:12–34) in Light of a Ritual Text from Emar (Emar 6, 373)." *VT* 65 (2015) 9–19.

Bach, Robert. *Die Aufforderungen zur Flucht und zum Kampf im alttestamentlichen Prophetenspruch*. WMANT 9. Neukirchen: Neukirchener, 1962.

Baden, Joel S. "The Morpho-Syntax of Genesis 12:1–3: Translation and Interpretation." *CBQ* 72 (2010) 223–37.

———. "From Joseph to Moses: The Narratives of Exodus 1–2." *VT* 62 (2012) 133–58.

Baden, Joel S., and Candida R. Moss. "The Origin and Interpretation of *sara'at* in Leviticus 13–14." *JBL* 130 (2011) 643–62.

Baker, David W. *Tight Fists or Open Hands? Wealth and Poverty in Hebrew Bible Law.* Grand Rapids: Eerdmans, 2009.

Baker, Robin. "Jeremiah and the *Balag*-Lament? Jeremiah 8:18–23 Reconsidered." *JBL* 138 (2019) 587–604.

Bailey, Lloyd R. *Biblical Perspectives on Death.* OBT. Philadelphia: Fortress, 1979.

Bailey, Randall C. "Jeremiah: Fortified City, Bronze Walls, and Iron Pillar against the Whole Land." *HS* 57 (2016) 117–38.

———. "The Redemption of Yhwh: A Literary Critical Function of the Songs of Hannah and David." *BibInt* 3 (1995) 213–31.

Bal, Mieke. *Lethal Love: Feminist Literary Readings of Biblical Love Stories.* Indiana Studies in Biblical Literature. Bloomington: Indiana University Press, 1987.

———. *Murder and Difference: Gender, Genre, and Scholarship on Sisera's Death.* Indiana Studies in Biblical Literature. Bloomington: Indiana University Press, 1988.

———. *Narratology: Introduction to the Theory of Narrative.* Translated by Christine van Boheemen. Toronto: University of Toronto Press, 1985.

Baloian, Bruce Edward. *Anger in the Old Testament.* American University Studies 99. Lausanne: Peter Lang, 1992.

Balfour, Rory J. "'Heavy is the Head': Election, Grace, and Humility in the Climax of the Jacob-Esau Cycle (Genesis 32–33)." *Journal of Theological Interpretation* 16 (2022) 23–39.

Ballentine, Debra Scoggins. *The Conflict Myth and the Biblical Tradition.* Oxford: Oxford University Press, 2015.

Ballentine, Samuel E. "Isaiah 45: God's 'I am,' Israel's 'You Are.'" *HBT* 16 (1994) 103–20.

———. *Prayer in the Hebrew Bible: The Drama of Divine-Human Dialogue.* OBT. Minneapolis: Fortress, 1993.

———. "The Prophet as Intercessor: A Reassessment." *JBL* 103 (1984) 61–73.

Balogh, Csaba. "The Problem with Isaiah's So-Called 'Refrain Poem': A New Look at the Compositional History of Isaiah 9.7–10." *JSOT* 42 (2018) 363–90.

Banks, Michael. *Jephtas Tochter: Traditions-, religions- und rezeptionsgeschichtliche Studien zu Richter 11.29–40.* FAT 71. Tübingen: Mohr Siebeck, 2010.

Bar, Shaul. *A Letter That Has Not Been Read: Dreams in the Hebrew Bible.* Cincinnati: Hebrew Union College Press, 2001.

Bar-Efrat, Shimon. *Narrative Art in the Bible.* BLS 17. Sheffield: Almond, 1989.

Barbiero, Gianni. "The Structure of Job 3." *ZAW* 127 (2015) 43–62.

Barbiero, Gianni, Marco Pavan, and Johannes Schnocks, eds. *The Formation of the Hebrew Psalter: The Book of Psalms Between Ancient Versions, Material Transmission and Canonical Exegesis.* FAT 151. Tübingen: Mohr Siebeck, 2021.

Barcellos, Richard C. *In Defense of the Decalogue: A Critique of New Covenant Theology.* Enumclaw, WA: WinePress, 2001.

Barco, Fancisco Javier del. *Catàlogo de manuscritos hebreos de la Comunidad de Madrid*, vol. 1. Madrid: Centro de Ciencias Humanas y Sociales, 2003.

Barr, James. *The Garden of Eden and the Hope of Immortality.* London: SCM, 1992.

Barré, Lloyd M. "Fasting in Isaiah 58:1–12: A Reexamination." *BTB* 15 (1989) 94–97.

———. "Halelu yah: A Broken Inclusion." *CBQ* 45 (1983) 195–200.

———. "Newly Discovered Literary Devices in the Prayer of Habakkuk." *CBQ* 75 (2013) 446–62.

Bartholomew, Craig G., and Ryan P. O'Dowd. *Old Testament Wisdom Literature: A Theological Introduction*. Downers Grove, IL: IVP Academic, 2011.

Bartlett, John R. *Edom and the Edomites*. JSOTSup 77. Sheffield: JSOT Press, 1989.

———. "Edomite King-List of Genesis 36:31–39 and 1 Chron 1:43–50." *JTS* 16 (1965) 301–14.

Barton, John. "The Day of YHWH in the Minor Prophets." In *Biblical and Near Eastern Essays: Studies in Honour of Kevin J. Cathcart*, edited by Carmel McCarthy and John F. Healy, 68–79. JSOTSup 375. London: T. & T. Clark, 2004.

———. *Ethics in Ancient Israel*. Oxford: Oxford University Press, 2014.

———. *Understanding Old Testament Ethics*. Louisville: Westminster John Knox, 2003.

Baumann, Gerlinde. *Love and Violence: Marriage as Metaphor for the Relationship between YHWH and Israel in the Prophetic Books*. Translated by Linda M. Maloney. Collegeville, MN: Liturgical, 2003.

———. *Die Weisheitsgestalt in Proverbien 1–9: Traditionsgeschichtliche und theologische Studien*. FAT 16. Tübingen: Mohr Siebeck, 1996.

Baumgärtel, Friedrich. "Die Formel *ne'um JHWH*." *ZAW* 73 (1961) 277–90.

Baumgarten, Alfred I. "The Paradox of the Red Heifer." *VT* 43 (1993) 442–51.

Bautch, Richard J. *Developments in Genre between Post-Exilic Penitential Prayers and the Psalms of Communal Lament*. Academia Biblica 7. Atlanta: SBL, 2003.

———. "In Vino Veritas? Critiquing Drunkenness and Deceit in Micah and Isaiah." *ZAW* 129 (2017) 555–67.

Bayer, Bathja. "The Titles of the Psalms: A Renewed Investigation of an Old Testament Problem." In *Yuval Studies of the Jewish Music Research Center*, edited by Israel Adler, 29–123. Yuval Studies 4. Jerusalem: Magnes, 1982.

Beasley-Murray, George R. "The Interpretation of Daniel 7." *CBQ* 45 (1983) 44–58.

Beauchamp, Evode. "Structure strophique des Psaumes." *Recherches de Science Religieuse* 56 (1968) 199–224.

Beaulieu, Stephane A. "Egypt as God's People: Isaiah 19:19–25 and Its Allusions to the Exodus." *PRSt* 40 (2013) 207–18.

Beck, J. A. "Geography and the Narrative Shape of Numbers 13." *BSac* 157 (2000) 271–80.

Becking, Bob. *Between Fear and Freedom: Essays on the Interpretation of Jeremiah 30–31*. OtSt 51. Leiden: Brill, 2004.

———. *The Fall of Samaria: An Historical and Archaeological Study*. SHANE 2. Leiden: Brill, 1992.

Beckwith, Roger T. *Calendar and Chronology, Jewish and Christian: Biblical, Intertestamental and Patristic Studies*. AGAJU 33. Boston: Brill Academic, 2001.

———. *Calendar, Chronology and Worship: Studies in Ancient Judaism and Early Christianity*. AGAJU 61. Leiden: Brill, 2005.

———. "Daniel 9 and the Date of the Messiah's Coming in Essene, Hellenistic, Pharasaic, Zealot and Early Christian Computation." *RevQ* 10 (1981) 521–42.

Beckwith, Roger T., and Martin J. Selman, eds. *Sacrifice in the Bible*. Grand Rapids: Baker, 1995.

Beebee, Thomas O. *The Ideology of Genre: A Comparative Study of Generic Instability*. University Park: Pennsylvania State University Press, 1994.

Beek, Gus W. van. "Frankincense and Myrr." *BA* 23 (1960) 70–95.

Beer, Wynand Vladimir, de. "The Patristic Understanding of the Six Days (Hexaemeron)." *Journal of Early Christian History* 5 (2015) 3–23.

Beetjes, Pancratius C. "Oracles against the Nations: A Central Issue in the Latter Prophets." *BTFT* 50 (1989) 203–9.

Begg, Christopher T. "The Exploits of David's Heroes According to Josephus." *Liber Annus* 47 (1997) 139–69.

Begrich, Joachim. "Das priesterliche Heilsorakel." *ZAW* 52 (1934) 81–92.

———. *Studien zu Deuterojesaja*. Vol 20. Theologische Bücherei. Munich: Kaiser Verlag, 1963.

———. "Die Vertrauensäusserungen im israelitischen Klagenlied des Einzelnen und in seinem babylonischen Gegenstück." *ZAW* 42 (1928) 221–60.

Bekins, Peter. "Tamar and Joseph in Genesis 38 and 39." *JSOT* 40 (2016) 375–97.

Belkin, Samuel. "Levirate and Agnate Marriage in Rabbinic and Cognate Literature." *JQR* 60 (1970) 275–329.

Bellinger, W. H., Jr. "Psalm 137: Memory and Poetry." *HBT* 27 (2005) 5–20.

Belnap, D. "A Comparison of the Communal Lament Psalms and the Treaty-Covenant Formula." *Studies in the Bible and Antiquity* 1 (2009) 1–34.

Bennett, Boyce M. "Vision and Audition in Biblical Prophecy." *Journal of the Academy of Religion and Psychical Research* 3 (1980) 245–68.

Bergant, Diane. "The Challenge of Hermeneutics: Lamentations 1:1–11: A Test Case." *CBQ* 64 (2002) 1–16.

———. "'My Beloved Is Mine and I Am His' (Song 2:16) The Song of Songs and Honor and Shame." *Semeia* 68 (1994) 23–40.

———. *Song of Songs: The Love Poetry of Scripture*. New York: New City Press, 1998.

Berger, Yitzhak. "Ruth and Inner-Biblical Allusion: The Case of 1 Samuel 25." *JBL* 128 (2009) 253–72.

Berlin, Adele. *The Dynamics of Biblical Parallelism*. Bloomington: Indiana University Press, 1985.

———. *Lamentations*. OTL. Louisville: Westminster John Knox, 2002.

———. *Poetics and Interpretation of Biblical Narrative*. BLS 9. Sheffield: Almond, 1983.

Berlinerblau, Jacques. *The Vow and the "Popular Religious Groups" of Ancient Israel: A Philological and Sociological Inquiry*. JSOTSup 210. Sheffield: Sheffield Academic, 1996.

Berman, Joshua. "Criteria for Establishing Chiastic Structure: Lamentations 1 and 2 as Test Cases." *Maarav* 21 (2014) 57–69.

Bernat, David. "Biblical Wasfs beyond Song of Songs." *JSOT* 28 (2004) 327–49.

Beuken, Willem A. M. "YHWH's Sovereign Rule and His Adoration on Mt. Zion: A Comparison of Poetic Visions in Isaiah 24–27, 52 and 66." In *The Desert Will Bloom: Poetic Visions in Isaiah*, edited by A. Joseph Everson and Hyun Chul Paul Kim, 91–107. AIL 4. Atlanta: SBL, 2009.

Beyerlein, Walter. *Der 52. Psalm: Studien zu seiner Einordnung*. BWANT 111. Stuttgart: Kohlhammer, 1980.

Biddle, Mark E. "Lady Zion's Alter Egos: Isaiah 47:1–15 and 57:6–13 as Structural Counterparts." In *New Visons of Isaiah*, edited by Roy F. Melugin and Marvin A. Sweeney, 124–39. JSOTSup 214. Sheffield: Sheffield Academic, 1996.

Bienkowski, Piotr, ed. *Early Edom and Moab: The Beginning of the Iron Age in Southern Jordan*. Sheffield Archeological Monographs 7. Sheffield: Collins, 1992.

Bier, Miriam, and Tim Bulkeley, eds. *Spiritual Complaint: The Theology and Practice of Lament*. Cambridge: James Clarke, 2014.

Bigger, Stephen F. "The Family Laws of Leviticus 18 in Their Setting." *JBL* 98 (1979) 187–203.

Bin-Nun, Shoshana R. "Formulas from Royal Records of Israel and Judah." *VT* 18 (1968) 414–32.

Birnbaum, Aiton. "Political Assassination in Biblical Israel." *JBQ* 43 (2015) 191–99.

Biwul, J. K. T. *A Theological Examination of Symbolism in Ezekiel with Emphasis on the Shepherd Metaphor*. London: Langham Monographs, 2013.

Bland, Dave L. *Proverbs and the Formation of Character*. Eugene, OR: Cascade Books, 2015.

Blenkinsopp, Joseph. "Ecclesiastes 3:1–15: Another Interpretation." *JSOT* 20 (1995) 55–64.

———. *Gibeon and Israel: The Role of Gibeon and the Gibeonites in the Political and Religious History of Early Israel*. Cambridge: Cambridge University Press, 1972.

———. *A History of Prophecy in Israel*. Philadelphia: Westminster John Knox, 1996.

———. "The Social Context of the 'Outsider Woman' in Proverbs 1–9." *Bib* 72 (1991) 457–73.

Bloch, Abraham P. *The Biblical and Historical Background of the Jewish Holy Days*. New York: Ktav, 1978.

Bloch, Ariel, and Chana Bloch. "From in the Garden of Delights." *Judaism* 44 (1995) 36–63.

Bloch-Smith, Elizabeth. *Judahite Burial Practices and Beliefs about the Dead*. JSOTSup 123. Sheffield: JSOT Press, 1992.

Block, Daniel I. "Beyond the Grave: Ezekiel's Vision of Death and the Afterlife." *BBR* 2 (1992) 113–41.

———. "*Bny ʿamwn*: The Sons of Ammon." *AUSS* 22 (1984) 197–212.

———. "The Burden of Leadership: The Mosaic Paradigm of Kingship (Deut 17:14–20)." *BSac* 162 (2005) 259–78.

———. "Israel's House: Reflections on the Use of *byt ysr'l* in the Old Testament in Light of Its Ancient Near Eastern Environment." *JETS* 28 (1985) 257–75.

Blyth, Caroline. *The Narrative of Rape in Genesis 34: Interpreting Dinah's Silence*. Oxford: Oxford University Press, 2010.

Boadt, Lawrence. *Ezekiel's Oracles Against Egypt*. BibOr 37. Rome: Pontifical Biblical Institute, 1980.

Boda, Mark J. "Babylon in the Book of the Twelve." *Hebrew Bible and Ancient Israel* 3 (2014) 225–48.

———. "Chiasmus in Ubiquity: Symmetrical Mirages in Nehemiah 9." *JSOT* 21 (1996) 55–70.

———. "Freeing the Burden of Prophecy: Maśśā' and the Legitimacy of Prophecy in Zech 9–14." *Bib* 87 (2006) 338–57.

———. "From Fasts to Feasts: The Literary Function of Zechariah 7–8." *CBQ* 65 (2003) 390–407.

———. "The Priceless Gain of Penitence: From Communal Lament to Penitential Prayer in the 'Exilic' Liturgy of Israel." *HBT* 25 (2003) 51–75.

———. *"Return to Me": A Biblical Theology of Repentance.* New Studies in Biblical Theology 35. Downers Grove, IL: InterVarsity, 2015.

Bodi, Daniel. "The Double Current and the Tree of Healing in Ezekiel 47:1–12 in Light of Babylonian Iconography and Texts." *Die Welt des Orients* 45 (2015) 22–37.

Bøe, Sverre. *Gog and Magog: Ezekiel 38–39 as Pre-Text for Revelation 19,17–21 and 20,7–10.* WUNT 2/135. Tübingen: Mohr Siebeck, 2001.

Boecker, Hans Jochen. *Law and the Administration of Justice in the Old Testament and Ancient East.* Translated by Jeremy Moiser. Minneapolis: Augsburg, 1980.

———. *Redeformen des Rechtsleben im Alten Testament.* 2nd ed. WMANT 14. Neukirchen-Vluyn: Neukirchener, 1970.

Boling, Robert G. "In Those Days, There Was No King in Israel." In *A Light Unto My Path: Old Testament Studies in Honor of Jacob M. Myers,* edited by Howard N. Bream et al., 33–48. Gettysburg Theological Studies 4. Philadelphia: Temple University Press, 1974.

Boloje, Blessing Onoriode, and Alphonso Greenwald. "Malachi's Eschatological Day of YHWH: Its Dual Roles of Cultic Restoration and Enactment of Social Justice (Mal 3:1–5; 3:16–4:6." *OTE* 27 (2014) 53–81.

Borowski, Oded. *Agriculture in Iron Age Israel.* Winona Lake, IN: Eisenbrauns, 1987.

Bosman, Hendrik Jan. "Being Wise Betwixt Order and Mystery: Keeping the Commandments and Fearing the Lord." *Scriptura* 111 (2012) 433–39.

Bosman, Hendrik Jan, and Harm van Grol, eds. *Studies in Isaiah 24–27.* OtSt 43. Leiden: Brill, 2000.

Bosworth, David. "Daughter of Zion and Weeping in Lamentations 1–2." *JSOT* 38 (2013) 217–37.

Bowen, Nancy R. "The Daughters of Your People: Female Prophets in Ezekiel 13:17–23." *JBL* 118 (1999) 417–33.

Bourke, J. "Le jour de Yahvé dans Joël." *RB* 66 (1959) 5–31.

Bouzard, Walter C. *We Have Heard with Our Ears, O God: Sources of the Communal Laments in the Psalms.* SBLDS 159. Atlanta: Scholars, 1997.

Bovell, Carlos. "Symmetry, Ruth and Canon." *JSOT* 28 (2003) 175–91.

Boyd, Samuel L. "The Rhetoric of Memory and the Formation of Identity in Psalm 78 and Deuteronomy 32." *BR* 66 (2021) 7–30.

Boyle, Brian. "'Holiness Has a Shape': The Place of the Altar in Ezekiel's Visionary Plan of Sacral Space (Ezekiel 43:1–12, 13–17, 18–27)." *ABR* 57 (2009) 1–21.

Braun, Joachim. *Music in Ancient Israel/Palestine: Archeological, Written, and Comparative Sources.* Translated by Douglas W. Stott. Grand Rapids: Eerdmans, 2002.

Braun, Roddy L. "1 Chronicles 1–9 and the Reconstruction of the History of Israel: Thoughts on the Use of Genealogical Data in Chronicles and the Reconstruction of the History of Israel." In *The Chronicler as Historian,* edited by M. Patrick Graham et al, 93–105. JSOTSup 238. Sheffield: Sheffield Academic, 1997.

Brenner, Athalya. "Aromatics and Perfumes in the Song of Songs." *JSOT* 25 (1983) 75–81.

———. "'Come Back, Come Back the Shulammite' (Song of Songs 7,1–10): A Parody of the Wasf Genre." In *On Humour and the Comic in the Hebrew Bible,* edited by Yehoshua Radday and Athalya Brenner, 251–75. JSOTSup 92. Sheffield: Almond, 1990.

———. "Female Social Behavior: Two Descriptive Patterns within the 'Birth of the Hero' Paradigm." *VT* 36 (1986) 257–73.

———, ed. *A Feminist Companion to the Song of Songs*. FCB 1. Sheffield: JSOT Press, 1993.

———. "Gazing Back at the Shulammite, Yet Again." *BibInt* 11 (2003) 295–300.

———. "God's Answer to Job." *VT* 31 (1981) 129–37.

———. "Job the Pious? The Characterization of Job in the Narrative Framework of the Book." *JSOT* 43 (1989) 37–52.

Brettler, Mark Z. "Ideology, History and Theology in 2 Kings XVII 7–23." *VT* 39 (1989) 268–82.

———. "Never the Twain Shall Meet? The Ehud Story as History and Literature." *HUCA* 62 (1991) 285–304.

———. "The Structure of 1 Kings 1–11." *JSOT* 49 (1991) 87–97.

Brettler, Mark Z. and Amy-Jill Levine. "Isaiah's Suffering Servant: Before and After Christianity." *Int* 73 (2019) 158–73.

Breuer, Yochanan. "The System of Dividing Lists into Verses." *VT* 61 (2011) 184–226.

Bricker, Daniel P. "The Doctrine of the 'Two Ways' in Proverbs." *JETS* 38 (1995) 501–17.

———. "Proverbs 28.1–11: A Small Poem?" *JSOT* 34 (2010) 313–30.

Briggs, Richard S. "Reading the Historical Books as Part of the Primary History." In *The Oxford Handbook of the Historical Books of the Hebrew Bible*, edited by Brad E. Kelle and Brent A. Strawn, 323–38. Oxford: Oxford University Press, 2020.

Bright, John. "The Apodictic Prohibition: Some Observations." *JBL* 92 (1973) 185–204.

———. "The Date of the Prose Sermons of Jeremiah." *JBL* 70 (1951) 15–35.

———. *A History of Israel*. 2nd ed. Philadelphia: Westminster, 1972. 3rd ed., 1981.

Brin, Gershon. *Studies in Biblical Law: From the Hebrew Bible to the Dead Sea Scrolls*. JSOTSup 176. Sheffield: JSOT Press, 1994.

Broderson, Alma. *The End of the Psalter: Psalms 146–50 in the Masoretic Text, the Dead Sea Scrolls, and the Septuagint*. BZAW 505. Berlin: de Gruyter, 2017.

Brodsky, Harold. "The Utopian Map in Ezekiel 48:1–35." *JBQ* 34 (2006) 20–26.

Bronner, Leila Leah. *The Stories of Elijah and Elisha as Polemics against Baal Worship*. Pretoria Oriental Studies 6. Leiden: Brill, 1968.

Brouwer, Wayne. "Understanding Chiasm and Assessing Macro-Chiasm as a Tool of Biblical Interpretation." *Calvin Theological Journal* 53 (2018) 99–127.

Brower, Wayne. "Understanding Chiasm and Assessing Macro–Chiasm as a Tool of Biblical Interpretation." *Calvin Theological Journal* 53 (2018) 99–127.

Brown, John P. "The Mediterranean Vocabulary of the Vine." *VT* 19 (1969) 146–70.

Brown, Ken. *The Vision in Job 4 and Its Role in the Book*. FAT 2/75. Tübingen: Mohr Siebeck, 2015.

Brown, Raymond E. *The Birth of the Messiah*. New Haven: Yale University Press, 1999.

Brown, William P. *Character in Crisis: A Fresh Approach to the Wisdom Literature of the Old Testament*. Grand Rapids: Eerdmans, 1996.

———. "The Didactic Power of the Metaphor in the Aphoristic Sayings of Proverbs." *JSOT* 29 (2004) 133–54.

———. "The So-Called Refrain in Isaiah 5:25–30 and 9:7–10:4." *CBQ* 40 (1990) 432–43.

———. *Structure, Role, and Ideology in the Hebrew and Greek Texts of Genesis 1:1—2:3*. SBLDS 132. Atlanta: SBL Press, 1993.

———. "'Whatever Your Hand Finds to Do': Qoheleth's Work Ethic." *Int* 55 (2001) 271–84.

———. *Wisdom's Wonder: Character, Creation, and Crisis in the Bible's Wisdom Literature*. Grand Rapids: Eerdmans, 2014.

Brownlee, William H. "Ezekiel's Parable of the Watchman and the Editing of Ezekiel." *VT* 28 (1978) 392–408.

———. "Ezekiel's Poetic Indictment of the Shepherds." *HTR* 51 (1958) 191–203.

———. "Psalms 1–2 as a Coronation Liturgy." *Bib* 52 (1971) 321–36.

———. "'Son of Man Set Your Face,' Ezekiel the Refugee Prophet." *HUCA* 54 (1983) 83–110.

Broyles, Craig C. *The Conflict of Faith and Experience: A Form-Critical and Theological Study of Selected Lament Psalms*. JSOTSup 52. Sheffield: JSOT Press, 1989.

Brueggemann, Walter. "The Costly Loss of Lament." *JSOT* 36 (1986) 57–71.

———. "Jeremiah's Use of Rhetorical Questions." *JBL* 92 (1973) 358–74.

Brueggemann, Walter, and Patrick D. Miller, Jr. "Psalm 73 as a Canonical Marker." *JSOT* 72 (1996) 45–56.

Brug, John F. "Biblical Acrostics and Their Relationship to Other Ancient Near Eastern Acrostics." In *The Bible in the Light of Cuneiform Literature: Scripture in Context III*, edited by William W. Hallo et al., 283–304. Ancient Near Eastern Texts and Studies 8. Lewiston, NY: Mellen, 1990.

———. *A Literary and Archeological Study of the Philistines*. BARIS 265. Oxford: Shangri-La, 2002.

Bryan, David T. "A Reevaluation of Gen 4 and 5 in Light of Recent Studies in Genealogical Fluidity." *ZAW* 99 (1987) 180–88.

Bryce, Glendon E. *A Legacy of Wisdom: The Egyptian Contribution to the Wisdom of Israel* Lewisburg, NY: Bucknell University Press, 1979.

Budde, Karl. *Das Lied Moses Deut. 32*. Tübingen: Mohr Siebeck, 1920.

Budin, Stephanie Lynn. *The Myth of Sacred Prostitution in Antiquity*. Cambridge: Cambridge University Press, 2008.

Bullinger, E. W. *Figures of Speech Used in the Bible Explained and Illustrated*. London: Eyre & Spottiswoode, 1898.

Budziszewski, Jay. *What We Can't Not Know: A Guide*. San Francisco: Ignatius, 2011.

Burkes, Shannon. *Death in Qoheleth and Egyptian Biographies of the Late Period*. SBLDS 170. Atlanta: SBL, 1999.

Burnbright, John D. "Does Eliphaz Really Begin 'Gently'? An Intertextual Reading of Job 4,2–11." *Bib* 95 (2014) 347–70.

Burnett, Joel S. "Forty-Two Songs for Elohim: An Ancient Near Eastern Organizing Principle in the Shaping of the Elohistic Psalter." *JSOT* 31 (2006) 81–101.

Burnside, Jonathan P. "At Wisdom's Table: How Narrative Shapes the Biblical Food Laws and Their Social Function." *JBL* 135 (2016) 223–45.

———. "Exodus and Asylum: Uncovering the Relationship between Biblical Law and Narrative." *JSOT* 34 (2010) 243–66.

———. "'What Shall we Do with the Sabbath-Gatherer?' A Narrative Approach to a 'Hard Case' in Biblical Law (Numbers 15:32–36)." *VT* 60 (2010) 45–62.

Burrows, Millar. "Nehemiah 3:1–32 as a Source for the Topography of Ancient Jerusalem." *AASOR* 14 (1933–34) 115–40.

Buss, Martin J. "An Anthropological Perspective on Prophetic Call Narratives." *Semeia* 21 (1981) 9–30.

———. "The Distinction between Civil and Criminal Law in Ancient Israel." In *Proceedings of the Sixth World Congress of Jewish Studies I*, 51–62. Jerusalem: Academic Press, 1977.

———. "Potential and Actual Interactions between Speech Act Theory and Biblical Studies." *Semeia* 41 (1987) 125–32.

———. "The Psalms of Asaph and Korah." *JBL* 82 (1963) 382–91.

Butler, Trent C. "A Forgotten Passage from a Forgotten Era (1 Chr XVI 8–36)." *VT* 28 (1978) 142–50.

Byron, John. *Cain and Abel in Text and Tradition: Jewish and Christian Interpretations of the First Sibling Rivalry*. Themes in Biblical Narrative: Jewish and Christian Traditions 14. Leiden: Brill Academic, 2011.

Callow, John. "Units and Flow in the Song of Songs 1:2—2:6." In *Biblical Hebrew and Discourse Linguistics*, edited by Robert L. Bergen, 462–86. Dallas: Summer Institute of Linguistics, 1994.

Camp, Claudia V. "Proverbs and the Problems of the Moral Self." *JSOT* 40 (2015) 25–42.

———. *Wisdom and the Feminine in the Book of Proverbs*. BLS 11. Sheffield: Sheffield Academic, 1985.

Campbell, Antony F. *1 Samuel*. FOTL 7. Grand Rapids: Eerdmans, 2003.

———. *2 Samuel*. FOTL 8. Grand Rapids: Eerdmans, 2005.

———. *The Ark Narrative, 1 Sam 4–6, 2 Sam 6: A Form-Critical and Traditio-Historical Study*. SBLDS 16. Missoula: Scholars, 1975.

———. *Of Prophets and Kings: A Late Ninth-Century Document (1 Samuel 1–2 Kings 10)*. Catholic Biblical Quarterly Monograph Series 17. Washington, DC: Catholic Biblical Association of America, 1986.

Campos, Martha. *Explanations for Exile in Amos*. Hebrew Bible Monographs 16. Sheffield: Sheffield Phoenix, 2021.

———. "Structure and Meaning in the Third Vision of Amos (7:7–17)." *JHebS* 11 (2011) 2–28.

Carasik, Michael. "Who Were the 'Men of Hezekiah' (Proverbs xxv 1)." *VT* 44 (1994) 289–300.

Carmichael, Calum M. *Law and Narrative in the Bible: The Evidence of the Deuteronomic Laws and the Decalogue*. Ithaca: Cornell University Press, 1985.

———. *The Laws of Deuteronomy*. Ithaca: Cornell University Press, 1974.

———. "The Three Laws on the Release of Slaves (Ex 21:2–11; Deut 15:12–18; Lev 25:39–46)." *ZAW* 112 (2000) 509–25.

Carr, Davi M. "Canonization in the Context of Community: An Outline of the Formation of the Tanakh and the Christian Bible." In *A Gift of God in Due Season: Essays on Scripture and Community in Honor of James A. Sanders*, edited by Richard D. Weis and David M. Carr, 22–65. JSOTSup 225. Sheffield: Sheffield Academic, 1996.

Carroll R, M. Daniel, and Jacqueline E. Lapsley, eds. *Character Ethics and the Old Testament: Moral Dimensions of Scripture*. Louisville: Westminster John Knox, 2007.

Carson, Donald A., ed. *Teach Us to Pray: Prayer in the Bible and the World*. Grand Rapids: Baker, 1990.

Cartledge, Tony W. *Vows in the Hebrew Bible and the Ancient Near East*. JSOTSup 147. Sheffield: JSOT Press, 1992.

Case, M. L. "Cunning Linguists: Oral Sex in the Song of Songs." *VT* 67 (2016) 171–86.

Caspari, W. "Kultpsalm 50." *ZAW* 45 (1927) 254–66.

Cassuto, Umberto. "The Function of Chiasmus in Hebrew Poetry." *CBQ* 40 (1978) 1–40.

Caulley, Thomas Scott. "Balaam's 'Star' Oracle in Jewish and Christian Prophetic Tradition." *ResQ* 56 (2014) 28–40.

Ceresko, Anthony R. "Psalm 149: Poetry, Themes (Exodus and Conquest), and Social Function." *Bib* 67 (1986) 177–94.

Chapman, Stephen B. *The Law and the Prophets: A Study in Old Testament Canon Formation*. FAT 27. Tübingen: Mohr Siebeck, 2009.

Charney, Davida. "Maintaining Innocence Before a Divine Hearer: Deliberative Rhetoric in Psalm 22, Psalm 17, and Psalm 7." *BibInt* 21 (2013) 33–63.

Chavel, Simeon. *Oracular Law and Priestly Historiography in the Torah*. FAT 2/71. Tübingen: Mohr Siebeck, 2014.

———. "The Second Passover, Pilgrimage, and the Centralized Cult." *HTR* 102 (2009) 1–24.

Childs, Brevard S. *The Book of Exodus: A Critical, Theological Commentary*. OTL. Philadelphia: Westminster, 1974.

———. *Isaiah and the Assyrian Crisis*. SBT 2/3. London: SCM, 1967.

———. *Memory and Tradition in Israel*. SBT 1/37. Naperville: Allenson, 1962.

———. *Myth and Reality in the Old Testament*. SBT 27. Naperville: Alec R. Allenson, 1960.

———. "Psalm Titles and Midrashic Exegesis." *JSS* 16 (1971) 137–50.

———. "A Study of the Formula 'Until this Day.'" *JBL* 82 (1963) 279–92.

Chisholm, Robert B., Jr. "Ehud: Evaluating an Assassin." *BSac* 168 (2011) 274–82.

Cho, Paul K. "The Integrity of Job 1 and 42:11–17." *CBQ* 76 (2014) 230–51.

———. "Job 2 and 42:7–10 as Narrative Bridge and Theological Pivot." *JBL* 136 (2017) 857–77.

Chrichigno, Gregory. *Debt-Slavery in Israel and the Ancient Near East*. JSOTSup 141. Sheffield: Sheffield Academic, 1993.

Claasens, Juliana. "'Give Us a Portion among Our Father's Brothers': The Daughters of Zelophehad, Land, and the Quest for Human Dignity." *JSOT* 37 (2013) 319–37.

Claissé-Walford, Nancy L. de, ed. *The Shape and Shaping of the Book of Psalms: The Current State of Scholarship*. AIL 20. Atlanta: SBL Press, 2014.

Clements, Roland E. "The Form and Character of Prophetic Woe Oracles." *Semitics* 8 (1982) 17–29.

———. "The Immanuel Prophecy of Isa. 7:10–17 and its Messianic Interpretation." In *Die Hebräische Bibel und ihre zweifache Nachgeschichte: Festschrift für Rolf Rendtorff zum 65. Geburtstag*, edited by Erhard Blum et al., 225–40. Neukirchen-Vluyn: Neukirchener, 1990.

———. "The Messianic Hope in the Old Testament." *JSOT* 43 (1990) 3–19.

———. *Wisdom for a Changing World: Wisdom in Old Testament Theology*. Berkeley Lecture Series 2. Berkeley: Bibal, 1990.

Clifford, Richard J. "The Use of *hoy* in the Prophets." *CBQ* 28 (1986) 458–64.

———. *Wisdom Literature in Mesopotamia and Israel*. SBL Symposium Series 36. Atlanta: SBL Press, 2007.

Clines, David J. A. *The Theme of the Pentateuch*. 2nd ed. JSOTSup 10. Sheffield: Academic, 1997.

Clines, David J. A., and Tamara C. Eshkanazi, eds. *Telling Queen Michal's Story: An Experiment in Comparative Interpretation*. JSOTSup 119. Sheffield: JSOT Press, 1991.

Coats, George W. "Abraham's Sacrifice of Faith: A Form-Critical Study of Gen 22." *Int* 27 (1973) 389–400.

———. *Exodus 1–18*. FOTL 2A. Grand Rapids: Eerdmans, 1999.

———. *Genesis: With an Introduction to Narrative Literature*. FOTL 1. Grand Rapids: Eerdmans, 1983.

———. *Rebellion in the Wilderness: The Murmuring Motif in the Wilderness Traditions of the Old Testament*. Nashville: Abingdon, 1968.

———, ed. *Saga, Legend, Tale, Novella, Fable: Narrative Forms in Old Testament Literature*. JSOTSup 35. Sheffield: JSOT, 1985.

Cocco, Francesco. *The Torah as a Place of Refuge: Biblical Criminal Law and the Book of Numbers*. FAT 2/84. Tübingen: Mohr Siebeck, 2016.

Cogan, Morton. *Imperialism and Religion: Assyria, Judah, and Israel in the Eighth and Seventh Centuries B.C.E.* SBLMS 19. Missoula, MT: Scholars, 1974.

———. "Raising the Walls of Jerusalem (Nehemiah 3:1–32): The View from Dur-Sharrukin." *IEJ* 56 (2006) 84–95.

Cohen, Abraham. *The Five Megilloth*. London: Soncino, 1961.

Cohen, Jeffrey M. "The Call of Moses." *JBQ* 20 (1992) 256–61.

Cohen, Mark E. *The Canonical Lamentations of Ancient Mesopotamia*. Potomac: Capital Decisions, 1988.

———. *The Cultic Calendars of the Ancient Near East*. Bethesda: Capital Decisions, 1993.

Cohen, Matty. "II Samuel 24 ou l'histoire d'un royal avorté." *ZAW* 113 (2001) 17–40.

Cohen, Menahem. לדמותם הקונסונאנטית של דפוסי המקרא הראשונים. המהדורה הראשונה של התנ"ך השלם דפוס סונצ'ינו משנת 1488. *Bar Ilan* 18–19 (1981) 47–67.

Cole, Robert. *Psalms 1–2: Gateway to the Psalter*. Hebrew Bible Monographs 37. Sheffield: Phoenix, 2013.

Collins, Adela Yarbro, and John J. Collins. *King and Messiah as Son of God: Divine, Human and Angelic Messianic Figures in Biblical and Related Literature*. Grand Rapids: Eerdmans, 2008.

Collins, John J. "The Court-Tales in Daniel and the Development of Apocalyptic." *JBL* 94 (1975) 218–34.

———. *Daniel: With an Introduction to Apocalyptic Literature*. FOTL 20. Grand Rapids: Eerdmans, 1984.

Condren, Janson C. "Is the Account of the Organization of the Camp Devoid of Organization? A Proposal for the Literary Structure of Numbers 1.1—10.10." *JSOT* 37 (2013) 423–52.

Conrad, Edgar W. *Fear Not Warrior: A Study of* 'al tira' *Pericopes in the Hebrew Scriptures*. BJS 75. Chico, CA: Scholars, 1985.

Coogan, Michael David. "A Structural and Literary Analysis of the Song of Deborah." *CBQ* 40 (1978) 143–66.

Cook, Gregory D. "Power, Mercy, and Vengeance: The Thirteen Attributes in Nahum." *Journal for the Evangelical Study of the Old Testament* 5 (2016) 27–37.

Cook, Stephen L. "Innerbiblical Interpretation in Ezekiel 44 and the History of Israel's Priesthood." *JBL* 114 (1995) 193–208.

Cook, Stephen L. and Corrine Patton, eds. *Ezekiel's Hierarchical World: Wrestling with a Tiered Reality*. Atlanta: SBL, 2004.

Cooke, Gerald. "The Israelite King as Son of God." *ZAW* 73 (1961) 202–25.

Cooper, Jerrold S. "New Cuneiform Parallels to the Song of Songs." *Journal of Near Eastern Studies* 90 (1971)157–62.

Copan, Paul and Matt Flannagan. *Did God Really Command Genocide?: Coming to Terms with the Justice of God*. Ada: Baker, 2014.

Corral, Martin Alonso. *Ezekiel's Oracles against Tyre: Historical Reality and Motivations*. BibOr 46. Rome: Pontifical Institute, 2002.

Cotter, David W. *A Study of Job 4–5 in the Light of Contemporary Literary Theory*. SBLDS 124. Atlanta: Scholars Press, 1992.

Cotterell, Peter. "The Greatest Song: Some Linguistic Considerations." *The Bible Translator* 47 (1996) 101–8.

Couy, J. Blake. "Amos vii 10–17 and Royal Attitudes toward Prophecy in the Ancient Near East." *VT* 58 (2008) 300–14.

Cox, Dermot. "Fear or Conscience? Yir'at YHWH in Proverbs 1–9." *Studia Hieroslymitana* 3 (1982) 83–90.

Craig, Kenneth M., Jr. *Reading Esther: A Case for the Literary Carnivalesque*. Louisville: Westminster John Knox, 1995.

Craigie, Peter C. *The Problem of War in the Old Testament*. Grand Rapids: Eerdmans, 1978.

Creach, Jerome F. D. *The Destiny of the Righteous in the Psalms*. St. Louis: Chalice, 2008.

Crenshaw, James L. "The Expression *mî yôde*[set macron over e]*a*ʻ in the Hebrew Bible." *VT* 36 (1986) 274–88.

———. *Hymnic Affirmation of Divine Justice: The Doxologies of Amos and Related Texts in the Old Testament*. SBLDS 24. Missoula: Scholars, 1975.

———. "A Mother's Instruction to Her Son (Proverbs 31:1–9)." In *Urgent Advice and Probing Questions: Collected Writings on Old Testament Wisdom*, 382–95. Macon, GA: Mercer University Press, 1995.

———. *Old Testament Wisdom: An Introduction*. Rev. ed. Louisville: Westminster John Knox, 1998.

———. "Wisdom Psalms?" *CurBR* 8 (2000) 9–17.

Crim, Keith R. "Your Neck Is Like the Tower of David (The Meaning of Simile in the Song of Solomon 4:4)." *The Bible Translator* 22 (1971) 70–74.

Cross, Frank Moore. "The Priestly Tabernacle and the Temple of Solomon." In *From Epic to Canon: History and Literature in Ancient Israel*, 84–95. Baltimore: Johns Hopkins University Press, 1998.

Cross, Frank Moore, and David Noel Freedman. *Studies in Ancient Yahwistic Poetry*. SBLDS 21. Missoula, MT: Scholars, 1975.

Cross, Frank Moore, and G. Ernest Wright. "The Boundary and Province Lists of the Kingdom of Judah." *JBL* 75 (1956) 202–26.

Crouch, Carly L. *War and Ethics in the Ancient Near East: Military Violence in Light of Cosmology and History*. BZAW 407. Berlin: de Gruyter, 2009.

Crow, Loren D. *The Songs of Ascents (Psalms 120–134): Their Place in Israelite History and Religion*. SBLDS 148. Atlanta: Scholars, 1996.

Crüsemann, Frank. *Studien zur Formgeschichte von Hymnus und Danklied in Israel*. WMANT 32. Neukirchen-Vluyn: Neukirchener, 1969.

Curkpatrick, Stephen. "Between Mashal and Parable: 'Likeness' as a Metonymic Enigma." *HBT* 24 (2002) 58–71.

Curtis, John Briggs. "On Job's Witness in Heaven." *JBL* 102 (1983) 549–62.

Curtis, Edward M. *Interpreting the Wisdom Books: An Exegetical Handbook*. Grand Rapids: Kregel Academic, 1995.

Daniélou, Jean. "Le symbolism eschatologique de la Fête des Tabernacles." *Irénicon* 31 (1958) 19–40.

Daniels, Dwight R. "Is There a 'Prophetic Lawsuit' Genre?" *ZAW* 37 (1987) 339–60.

Daube, David. "The Civil Law of the Mishnah: The Arrangement of the Three Gates." *Tulane Law Review* (1943–44) 351–407.

Davage, David Willgren. "What Could We Agree On? Outlining Five Fundaments in the Research of the 'Book' of Psalms." In *The Formation of the Hebrew Psalter: The Book of Psalms Between Ancient Versions, Material Transmission and Canonical Exegesis*, edited by Gianni Barbiero et al., 1–36. FAT 151. Tübingen: Mohr Siebeck, 2021.

Davies, Eryl W. "Inheritance Rights and the Hebrew Levirate Marriage." *VT* 31 (1981) 138–44, 257–68.

Davies, G. I. "The Wilderness Itinerary." *TynBul* 25 (1974) 46–81.

Davis, Barry C. "Ecclesiastes 12:1–8—Death, an Impetus for Life." *BSac* 148 (1991) 298–318.

Day, John. *God's Conflict with the Dragon and the Sea: Echoes of a Canaanite Myth in the Old Testament*. University of Cambridge Oriental Publications 35. Cambridge: Cambridge University Press, 1985.

———. *Molech: A God of Human Sacrifice in the Old Testament*. University of Cambridge Oriental Publications 41. Cambridge: Cambridge University Press, 1989.

Day, John, R. P. Gordon, and H. G. M. Williamson, eds. *Wisdom in Ancient Israel: Essays in Honour of J. A. Emerton*. Cambridge: Cambridge University Press, 1995.

Day, John N. "The Imprecatory Psalms and Christian Ethics." *BSac* 159 (2002) 166–86.

Day, John, ed. *King and Messiah in Israel and the Ancient Near East: Proceedings of the Oxford Old Testament Seminar*. JSOTSup 270. Sheffield: JSOT Press, 1998.

Dearman, J. Andrew. "My Servants the Scribes: Composition and Context in Jeremiah 36." *JBL* 109 (1990) 403–21.

Declaissé-Walford, Nancy, ed. *The Shape and Shaping of the Book of Psalms: The Current State of Scholarship*. AIL 20. Atlanta: SBL Press, 2014.

Dell, Katherine J. "A Wise Man Reflecting on Wisdom: Qoheleth/Ecclesiastes." *TynBul* 71 (2020) 137–52.

Dell, Katherine J., and Will Kynes, eds. *Reading Job Intertextually*. LHBOTS 574. New York: Bloomsbury, 2013.

Delekat, Lienhard. "Probleme der Psalmenüberschriften." *ZAW* 76 (1964) 280–97.

Destro, Adriana. *The Law of Jealousy: Anthropology of Sotah*. BJS. Providence: Brown University Press, 2020.

De Vries, Simon J. *1 and 2 Chronicles*. FOTL 11. Grand Rapids: Eerdmans, 1989.

———. "Festival Observance in Chronicles." In *Problems in Biblical Theology: Essays in Honor of Rolf Knierim*, edited by Henry T. C. Sun and Keith L. Eades, 104–24. 1997. Reprint, Eugene, OR: Wipf & Stock, 2011.

———. "Moses and David as Cult Founders in Chronicles." *JBL* 107 (1988) 619–39.

———. *From Old Revelation to New: A Tradition-Historical and Redaction-Critical Study of Temporal Transpositions in Prophetic Prediction*. Grand Rapids: Eerdmans, 1995.

Dewrell, Heath D. *Child Sacrifice in Ancient Israel*. EANEC. Winona Lake, IN: Eisenbrauns, 2017.

———. "'Swearing to YHWH, but Swearing by Mōlek–Sacrifices': Zephaniah 1:5b." *VT* 60 (2019) 737–41.

Dharamraj, Havilah. "Green-Eyed Lovers: A Study of Jealousy in Song of Songs 8:5–7." *Priscilla Papers* 32 (2018) 3–8.

Dhorme, Paul. "Les chapitres XXV–XXVIII du livre de Job." *RB* 33 (1924) 343–56.

Diamond, A. R. Pete. *The Confessions of Jeremiah in Context: Scenes of Prophetic Drama*. JSOTSup 45. Sheffield: Academic, 1987.

Dick, Michael Brennan. "Job 31, the Oath of Innocence, and the Sage." *ZAW* 95 (1983) 31–53.

Dicou, Bert. *Edom, Israel's Brother and Antagonist: The Role of Edom in Biblical Prophecy and Story*. JSOTSup 169. Sheffield: Sheffield Academic, 1994.

Diethelm, Michel. *Untersuchungen zur Eigenart des Buches Qohelet*. BZAW 183. Berlin: de Gruyter, 1989.

Dijk, H. J. van. *Ezekiel's Prophecy on Tyre (Ez 26,1—28,19): A New Approach*. BibOr 20. Rome: Pontifical Biblical Institute, 1968.

Dijkstra, Meindert. "The Altar of Ezekiel: Fact or Fiction?" *VT* 42 (1992) 22–36.

———. "Is Balaam also among the Prophets?" *JBL* 114 (1995) 43–64.

———. "Prophecy by Letter (Jeremiah xxix 24–32)." *VT* 33 (1983) 319–22.

Dim, Emmanuel Uchenna. *The Eschatological Implications of Isa 65 and 66 as the Conclusion of the Book of Isaiah*. Bible in History 3. Bern: Lang, 2005.

Dion, Paul-Eugène. "The 'Fear Not' Formula and Holy War." *CBQ* 32 (1970) 565–70.

Dobbs-Allsopp, F. W. "The Delight of Beauty and Song of Songs 4:1–7." *Int* 59 (2005) 260–77.

———. "The Effects of Enjambment in Lamentations (Part II)." *ZAW* 113 (2001) 370–85.

———. "The Enjambing Line in Lamentations: A Taxonomy (Part I)." *ZAW* 113 (2001) 219–39.

———. *Lamentations*. IBC. Louisville: Westminster John Knox, 2002.

———. "R(az/ais)ing Zion in Lamentations 2." In *David and Zion: Biblical Studies in Honor of J. J. M. Roberts*, edited by Kathryn L. Roberts and Bernard F. Batto, 21–68. Winona Lake, IN: Eisenbrauns, 2004.

———. *Weep, O Daughter of Zion: A Study of the City-Lament Genre in the Hebrew Bible*. BibOr 44. Rome: Editrice Pontificio Istituto Biblico, 1993.

Dohmen, Christof. "Das Immanuelzeichen: ein jesajanisches Drohwort und seine inner alttestamentliche Rezeption." *Bib* 68 (1987) 305–29.

Dorsey, David A. "Literary Structuring in the Song of Songs." *JSOT* 46 (1990) 81–96.

Dothan, Trude. *The Philistines and their Material Culture*. New Haven: Yale University Press, 1982.

Douglas, Mary. *Purity and Danger: An Analysis of the Concepts of Pollution and Taboo*. London: Routledge, 1966.

Dow, L. K. Fuller. *Images of Zion: Biblical Antecedents for New Jerusalem*. NTM 25. Sheffield: Sheffield Phoenix, 2010.

Dozeman, Thomas B. *God on the Mountain: A Study of Redaction, Theology, and Canon in Exodus 19–24*. SBLMS 37. Atlanta: Scholars, 1997.

Draper, J. A. "The Heavenly Feast of Tabernacles: Revelation 7.1–17." *JSNT* 19 (1983) 133–47.

Drunen, David Van. *A Biblical Case for Natural Law*. Grand Rapids: Acton Institute, 2006.

Dubarle, André-Marie. "La manifestation théophanique de Dieu dans la liturgie d'Israël." *Lex Orandi* 40 (1967) 9–23.

Dubovsky, Peter. "Usual and Unusual Concluding Formulas in 2 Kings 13–14: A Reconstruction of the Old Greek and Its Implications for the Literary History." *Bib* 101 (2020) 321–29.

Dubrow, Heather. *Genre*. The Critical Idiom 42. London: Methuen, 1982.

Duggan, Michael W. *The Covenant Renewal in Ezra-Nehemiah (Neh 7:72b—10:40): An Exegetical, Literary, and Theological Study*. SBLDS 164. Atlanta: SBL, 2001.

Duhm, Bernard. *Das Buch Jesaja*. Göttingen: Vandenhoeck & Ruprecht, 1982.

Dumbrell, William J. *Covenant and Creation: A Theology of the Old Testament Covenants*. Grand Rapids: Baker, 1984.

———. "Jer 49.28–33; An Oracle against a Proud Desert Power." *AJBA* 2 (1972) 99–109.

Dupont, Jacques. "Beatitudes egyptiennes." *Bib* 57 (1976) 154–67.

Eaton, John H. *Kingship and the Psalms*. SBT 2/32. London: SCM, 1986.

Eberhart, Christian. *Studien zur Bedeutung der Opfer im Alten Testament: Die Signifikanz von Blut- und Verbrennungsriten im kultischen Rahmen*. WMANT 94. Neukirchen-Vluyn: Neukirchener, 2002.

Edelman, Diana. "The Asherite Genealogy in 1 Chronicles 7:3–40." *BR* 33 (1988) 13–23.

Edenburg, Cynthia. "How (Not) to Murder a King: Variations on a Theme in 1 Sam 24; 26." *SJOT* 12 (1998) 64–85.

———. "Ideology and Social Context of the Deuteronomic Women's Sex Laws (Deuteronomy 22:13–29)." *JBL* 128 (2009) 43–60.

Ehrlich, Ernst Ludwig. *Der Traum im Alten Testament*. BZAW 73. Berlin: de Gruyter, 2020.

Eichler, Raanan. "A Sin is Borne: Clearing up the Law of Women's Vows (Numbers 20)." *VT* 71 (2021) 317–28.

Eichrodt, Walter. *Theology of the Old Testament*. 2 vols. Translated by J. A. Baker. OTL. London: SCM, 1961.

Eissfeldt, Otto. *Der Maschal im Alten Testament: Eine wortgeschichtliche Untersuchung nebst einer literargeschichtlichen Untersuchung der mashal genannten Gattungen "Volkssprichwort" und "Spottlied."* BZAW 24. Giessen: Töpelmann, 1913.

Embry, Brad, ed. *Megilloth Studies: The Shape of Contemporary Scholarship*. Sheffield: Phoenix, 2016.

Emerton, J. A. "The Teaching of Amenemope and Proverbs xxii 17—xxiv 22: Further Reflections on a Long-standing Problem." *VT* 51 (2001) 431–65.

Eph'al, Israel. *The Ancient Arabs: Nomads on the Borders of the Fertile Crescent, 9th–5th Centuries B.C.* Jerusalem: Magnes, 1984.

———. *The City Besieged: Siege and Its Manifestations in the Ancient Near East*. CHANE 36. Leiden: Brill, 2009.

Epstein, Louis M. *Marriage Laws in the Bible and the Talmud*. Cambridge: Harvard University Press, 1942.

Eschelbach, Michael A. "Song of Songs: Increasing Appreciation of and Restraint in Matters of Love." *AUSS* 42 (2004) 305–24.

Eslinger, Lyle M. "Ezekiel 20 and the Metaphor of Historical Teleology: Concepts of Biblical History." *JSOT* 23 (1998) 93–125.

Eversmann, Anke. "Gottesbefragung und Bruderkrieg in Ri 20." *BN* 136 (2008) 17–30.

Everson, A. Joseph, and Hyun Chul Paul Kim., eds. *The Desert Will Bloom: Poetic Visions in Isaiah*. AIL 4. Atlanta: SBL, 2009.

Eynickel, Erik. *The Reform of King Josiah and the Composition of the Deuteronomistic History*. OTS 33. Leiden: Brill, 1996.

Exum, J. Cheryl. "A Literary and Structural Analysis of the Song of Songs." *ZAW* 85 (1973) 47–79.

———. "Asseverative *'l* in Canticles 1:6?" *Bib* 62 (1981) 416–19.

———. "Who's Afraid of 'The Endangered Ancestress.'" In *The New Literary Criticism and the Hebrew Bible*, edited by J. Cheryl Exum and David J. A. Clines, 91–113. Sheffield: JSOT Press, 1993.

———. "'You Shall Let Every Daughter Live': A Study of Exodus 1:8—2:10." *Semeia* 28 (1983) 63–82.

———. *Song of Songs*. OTL. Louisville: Westminster John Knox, 2005.

Falk, Marcia. *Love Lyrics from the Bible: A Translation and Literary Study of the Song of Songs*. BLS 4. Sheffield: Almond, 1982.

Falk, Zeev W. *Hebrew Law in Biblical Times*. Jerusalem: Wahrmann, 1964.

Feinglass, A. "The Rape of Tamar." *JBQ* 20 (1992) 174–81.

Fensham, F. Charles, and P. A. H. de Boer. "Treaty between Solomon and Hiram and the Alalakh Tablets." *JBL* 79 (1960) 59–60.

Ferris, Paul W. *The Genre of Communal Lament in the Bible and the Ancient Near East*. SBLDS 127. Atlanta: Scholars, 1992.

Feser, Edward. *Neo-Scholastic Essays*. South Bend: St. Augustines, 2015.

Feser, Edward C., and Joseph M. Bessette. *By Man Shall His Blood Be Shed: A Catholic Defense of the Death Penalty*. San Francisco: Ignatius, 2017.

Fewell, Danna Nolan. *Circle of Sovereignty: A Story of Stories in Daniel 1–6*. JSOTSup 72. Sheffield: Almond, 1988.

Fewell, Danna Nolan, and David M. Gunn. "'A Son is Born to Naomi! Literary Allusions and Interpretation in the Book of Ruth." *JSOT* 40 (1988) 99–108.

Fidler, Ruth. *"Dreams Speak Falsely"? Dream Theophanies in the Bible: Their Place in Ancient Israelite Faith and Tradition*. Jerusalem: Magnes, 2005.

———. "A Wife's Vow—The Husband's Woe?: The Case of Hannah and Elkanah 1 Samuel 1,21.23." *ZAW* 118 (2006) 374–388.

Filson, Floyd V. "Petition and Intercession: The Biblical Doctrine of Prayer (2)." *Int* 8 (1954) 21–34.

Finkelstein, Israel. "The Historical Reality behind the Genealogical Lists in 1 Chronicles." *JBL* 131 (2012) 65–83.

Finkelstein, Israel, and Neil Asher Silberman. *The Bible Unearthed: Archeology's New Vision of Ancient Israel and the Origin of Its Sacred Texts*. New York: Free Press, 2001.

Finkelstein, Jacob J. *The Ox That Gored*. Transactions of the American Philosophical Society 71.2. Philadelphia: American Philosophical Society, 1981.

Finlay, Timothy D. *The Birth Report Genre in the Hebrew Bible*. FAT 2/11. Tübingen: Mohr Siebeck, 2006.

———. "Genres, Intertextuality, Bible Software, and Speech Acts." In *Second Wave Intertextuality and the Hebrew Bible*, edited by Marianne Grohmann and Hyun Chul Paul Kim, 153–71. Atlanta: SBL, 2019.

———. "Natural Law Recorded in Divine Revelation: A Critical and Theological Reflection on Genesis 9:1–7." In *Partners with God: Theological and Critical Readings of the Bible in Honor of Marvin A. Sweeney*, edited by Shelly L. Birdsong and Serge Frolov, 41–50. Claremont: Claremont Press, 2017.

Finsterbusch, Karin. "The First-born Between Sacrifice and Redemption in the Hebrew Bible." In *Human Sacrifice in Jewish and Christian Tradition*, edited by Karin Finsterbusch, Armin Lange and Diethard Römheld, 87–108. Studies in the History of Religions 112. Leiden: Brill, 2006.

Finsterbusch, Karin, Armin Lange, and Diethard Römheld, eds. *Human Sacrifice in Jewish and Christian Tradition*. Studies in the History of Religions 112. Leiden: Brill, 2006.

Firmage, Edwin. "The Biblical Dietary Laws and the Concept of Holiness." In *Studies in the Pentateuch*, edited by J. Emerton, 177–208. VTSup 41. Leiden: Brill, 1990.

Firmage, Edwin, Bernard G. Weiss, and John W. Welch, eds. *Religion and Law: Biblical-Judaic and Islamic Perspectives*. Winona Lake, IN: Eisenbrauns, 1990.

Firth, David G. *Surrendering Retribution in the Psalms: Responses to Violence in Individual Complaints*. Paternoster Biblical Monographs. Milton Keynes, UK: Paternoster, 2005.

Fishbane, Michael A. "Sin and Judgment in the Prophecies of Ezekiel." *Int* 38 (1984) 131–50.

Fitzpatrick, Paul E. *The Disarmament of God: Ezekiel 38–39 in Its Mythic Context*. Vol. 37. CBQMS 37. Washington: Catholic Biblical Association, 2004.

Fitzpatrick-McKinley, Anne. *The Transformation of Torah from Scribal Advice into Law*. JSOTSup 287. Sheffield: Sheffield Academic, 1999.

Fleming, Daniel E. "The Biblical Tradition of Anointing Priests." *JBL* 117 (1998) 411–14.

Flint, Peter W. *The Dead Sea Psalms Scrolls and the Book of Psalms*. Studies on the Texts of the Desert of Judah 17. Leiden: Brill, 1997.

Flint, Peter W., and Patrick D. Miller, eds. *The Book of Psalms: Composition and Reception*. VTSup 99. Leiden: Brill, 2005.

Floyd, Michael. *Minor Prophets: Part 2*. FOTL 22. Grand Rapids: Eerdmans, 2000.

Floyd, Michael H. "Prophetic Complaints about the Fulfillment of Oracles in Habakkuk 1:2–17 and Jeremiah 15:10–18." *JBL* 110 (1991) 397–418.

Floysvik, Ingvar. *When God Becomes My Enemy: The Theology of the Complaint Psalms*. St Louis: Concordia Academic, 1997.

Flusser, David. "The Four Empires in the Fourth Sibyl and in the Book of Daniel." *Israel Oriental Studies* 2 (1972) 148–75.

Fohrer, Georg. *Die symbolischen Handlungen der Propheten*. 2nd ed. Abhandlungen zur Theologie des Alten Neuen Testaments 54. Zurich: Zwingli, 1968.

Fokkelman, Jan P. *Reading Biblical Narrative: An Introductory Guide*. Philadelphia: Westminster John Knox, 2000.

———. "Stylistic Analysis of Isaiah 40:1–11." *OtSt* 21 (1981) 68–90.

Follis, Elaine R., ed. *Directions in Biblical Hebrew Poetry*. JSOTSup 40. Sheffield: JSOT Press, 1987.

———. "The Holy City as Daughter." In *Directions in Biblical Hebrew Poetry*, 173–84. JSOTSup 40. Sheffield: JSOT Press, 1987.

Fontaine, Carole. *Traditional Sayings in the Old Testament*. BLS. Sheffield: Almond, 1982.

———. *Smooth Words: Women, Proverbs and Performance in Biblical Wisdom*. JSOTSup 356. Sheffield: Sheffield Academic, 2002.

Foster, Robert L. "Shepherds, Sticks, and Social Destabilization: A Fresh Look at Zechariah 11:4–17." *JBL* 126 (2007) 735–53.

Fountain, Thomas E. "A Parabolic View of the Song of Solomon." *JETS* 9 (1966) 97–101.
Fowler, Alastair. *A History of English Literature: Forms and Kinds from the Middle Ages to the Present*. Oxford: Blackwell, 1987.
———. *Kinds of Literature: An Introduction to the Theory of Genres and Models*. Cambridge: Harvard University Press, 1982.
———. "The Life and Death of Literary Forms." *New Literary History* 2 (1971) 199–216.
Fox, Michael V. "Aging and Death in Qoheleth 12." *JSOT* 42 (1988) 55–77.
———. "The Formation of Proverbs 22:17—23:11." *Die Welt des Orients* 38 (2008) 22–37.
———. "Frame-Narrative and Composition in the Book of Qohelet." *HUCA* 48 (1977) 83–106.
———. "God's Answer and Job's Response." *Bib* 94 (2013) 1–23.
———. "Ideas of Wisdom in Proverbs 1–9." *JBL* 116 (1997) 613–33.
———. "The Pedagogy of Proverbs 2." *JBL* 113 (1994) 233–43.
———. *Qohelet and His Contradictions*. Sheffield: Almond, 1989.
———. "Reading the Tale of Job (Job1:1—2:13 + 42:7–17)." In *A Critical Engagement: Essays on the Hebrew Bible in Honour of J. Cheryl Exum*, edited by David J. A. Clines and Ellen J. van Wolde, 162–79. HBM 38. Sheffield: Sheffield Phoenix, 2010.
———. "The Sign of the Covenant: Circumcision in the Light of the Priestly *'ôt* Etiologies." *RB* 81 (1974) 557–96.
———. *The Song of Songs and the Ancient Egyptian Love Songs*. Madison: University of Wisconsin Press, 1985.
———. "Wisdom in the Joseph Story." *VT* 51 (2001) 26–41.
Franke, Chris A. "Reversals of Fortune in the Ancient Near East: A Study of the Babylon Oracles in the Book of Isaiah." In New Visions of Isaiah, edited by Roy F. Melugin and Marvin A. Sweeney, 104–23. JSOTSup 214. Sheffield: Sheffield Academic, 1996.
Frankel, David. *The Murmuring Stories of the Priestly School: A Retrieval of Ancient Sacerdotal Lore*. VTSup 89. Leiden: Brill, 2002.
Fredericks, Daniel C. *Coping with Transience: Ecclesiastes on Brevity in Life*. BibSem 18. Sheffield: JSOT Press, 1993.
Freedman, David Noel. "Acrostic Poems in the Hebrew Bible." *CBQ* 48 (1986) 408–31.
———. "Acrostics and Meter in Hebrew Poetry." *HTR* 65 (1972) 367–92.
———. "Headings in the Books of the Eighth-Century Prophets." *AUSS* 25 (1987) 9–26.
———. *Psalm 119: The Exaltation of Torah*. Winona Lake, IN: Eisenbrauns, 1999.
———. *The Relationship between Herodotus'* History *and Primary History*. Winona Lake, IN: Eisenbrauns, 1981.
———. "The Structure of Job 3." *Bib* 49 (1968) 503–08.
———. "The Structure of Psalm 119." *HAR* 14 (1994) 55–87.
———. *The Unity of the Hebrew Bible*. Ann Arbor: University of Michigan Press, 1991.
Frei, Hans. *The Eclipse of Biblical Narrative: A Study in Eighteenth and Nineteenth Century Hermeneutics*. New Haven: Yale University Press, 1974.
Fretheim, Terence E. "'I Was Only a Little Angry': Divine Violence in the Prophets." *Int* 58 (2004) 365–75.
———. "Nature's Praise of God in the Psalms." *Ex Auditu* 3 (1987) 16–30.
Friebel, Kelvin G. *Jeremiah's and Ezekiel's Sign-Acts: Rhetorical Nonverbal Communication*. LHBOTS 283. Sheffield: Academic, 1993.

Fried, Lisbeth S. "Cyrus the Messiah? The Historical Background to Isaiah 45:1." *HTR* 95 (2002) 373–93.

Fritz, Volkmar. "Abimelech und Sichem in Jdc. IX." *VT* 32 (1982) 129–44.

Frolov, Serge. "Evil-Merodach and the Deuteronomist: The Socio-Historical Setting of Dtr in the Light of 2 Kings 25,27–30." *Bib* 88 (2007) 174–90.

———. "How Old Is the Song of Deborah?" *JSOT* 36 (2011) 163–84.

———. *Judges*. FOTL 6B. Grand Rapids; Eerdmans, 2013.

———. *The Turn of the Cycle: 1 Samuel 1–8 in Synchronic and Diachronic Perspectives*. BZAW 342. Berlin: de Gruyter, 2004.

Frolov, Serge, and Mikhail Stetckevitch. "Repentance in Judges: Assessing the Reassessment." *Hebrew Studies* 60 (2019) 129–39.

Frow, John. *Genre*. New Critical Idiom. New York: Routledge, 2015.

Fuad, Chelcent. "The Curious Case of the Blasphemer: Ambiguity as Literary Device in Leviticus 24:10–23." *HBT* 41 (2019) 51–70.

———. "What Has Leviticus 17 to Do with Deuteronomy 12.20–27? The Literary Relationship Between the Deuteronomic and Holiness Codes on Cult Centralization and Animal Slaughter." *JSOT* 45 (2020) 20–33.

Fuchs, Esther. "Structure, Ideology and Politics in the Betrothal Type-Scene." In *A Feminist Companion to Genesis*, edited by Athalya Brenner, 273–81. FCB 2. Sheffield: Sheffield Academic, 1993.

Fuente, O. Garcia de la. ""Liturgias de entrada, normas de asilo o exhortaciones proféticas: A propósito de los Salmos 15 y 24." *Augustinianum* 9 (1969) 266–98.

Furman, Nelly. "His Story Versus Her Story: Male Genealogy and Female Strategy in the Jacob Cycle." *Semeia* 46 (1989) 141–50.

Gabelein, Paul W., Jr. "Psalm 34 and other Biblical Acrostics: Evidence from the Aleppo Codex." *Maarav* 5–6 (1990) 127–43.

Galil, Gershon. *The Chronology of the Kings of Israel and Judah*. SHANE 9. Leiden: Brill, 1996.

———. "The Sons of Judah and the Sons of Aaron in Biblical Historiography." *VT* 35 (1985) 488–95.

Galling, Kurt. "The 'Gola-list' According to Ezra 2 and Nehemiah 7." *JBL* 70 (1951) 149–58.

Gammie, John G. "Behemoth and Leviathan: On the Didactic and Theological Significance of Job 40:15—41:26." In *Israelite Wisdom: Theological and Literary Essays in Honor of Samuel Terrien*, edited by John G. Gammie et al., 217–31. Homage Series 3. Missoula, MT: Scholars, 1978.

Ganzel, Tova. "Isaiah's Critique of Shebna's Trespass: A Reconsideration of Isaiah 22.15–25." *JSOT* 39 (2015) 469–87.

Garcia, R. M. Alonso. "Ex 34,10–28: Un studio histórico-literario." *EstBib* 56 (1998) 433–64.

Gardner, Anne E. "Isaiah 66:1–4: Condemnation of Temple and Sacrifice or Contrast between the Arrogant and the Humble." *RB* 113 (2006) 506–28.

Garroway, Kristine Henriksen, Christine Elizabeth Palmer, and Angela Roskop Erisman, eds. *Essays on Dress and the Body in the Bible and Ancient Near East in Honor of Nili S. Fox*. Cincinnati: Hebrew Union College Press, 2022.

Garsiel, Moshe. "David's Elite Warriors and Their Exploits in the Books of Samuel and Chronicles." *JHebS* 11 (2011) 1–28.

Gärtner, Judith. "The Historical Psalms: A Study of Psalms 78; 105; 106; 135; and 136 as Key Hermeneutical Texts in the Psalter." *HBAI* 4 (2015) 373–99.

Gärtner, Judith and Anja Klein. "Editorial: The Historical Psalms." *HBAI* 4 (2015) 369–72.

Gass, Erasmus. "Modes of Divine Communication in the Balaam Narrative." *BN* 139 (2008) 19–38.

Gault, Brian P. "An Admonition against 'Rousing Love': The Meaning of the Enigmatic Refrain in Song of Songs." *BBR* 20 (2010) 161–84.

———. "A 'Do Not Disturb' Sign? Re-examining the Adjuration Refrain in Song of Songs." *JSOT* 36 (2011) 93–104.

Geisler, Norman L. *Miracles and the Modern Mind.* Grand Rapids: Baker, 1992.

Genette, Gérard. *Paratexts: Thresholds of Interpretation.* Translated by Jane E. Lewin. Literature, Culture, Theory 20. Cambridge: Cambridge University Press, 1997.

Gerhard, Albert, and Clemens Leonhard, eds. *Jewish and Christian Liturgy and Worship: New Insights into Its History and Interaction.* Jewish and Christian Perspectives 15. Leiden: Brill, 2007.

Gerhard, M. "The Dilemma of the Text: How to 'Belong' to a Genre." *Poetics* 18 (1989) 355–73.

Gerstenberger, Erhard S. *Der bittende Mensch: Bittritual und Klagelied des Einzelnen im Alten Testament.* WMANT 51. 1980. Reprint, Eugene, OR: Wipf & Stock, 2010.

———. *Charting the Course of Psalms Research.* Essays on Psalms, vol. 1. Edited by K. C. Hanson. Eugene, OR: Cascade Books, 2022.

———. *Comparative Perspectives on the Psalms.* Essays on the Psalms, vol. 3. Edited by K. C. Hanson. Eugene, OR: Cascade Books, 2025.

———. "The Enemies in the Psalms: A Challenge to Christian Preaching." *HBT* 4/5 (1982–83) 61–78.

———. *Praise and Petition in the Old Testament.* Essays on the Psalms, vol. 2. Edited by K. C. Hanson. Eugene, OR: Cascade Books, 2024.

———. *Psalms Part 1: With an Introduction to Cultic Poetry.* FOTL 14. Grand Rapids: Eerdmans, 1988.

———. *Psalms Part 2, and Lamentations.* FOTL 15. Grand Rapids: Eerdmans, 2001.

———. "The Woe-Oracles of the Prophets." *JBL* 81 (1962) 249–63.

Gese, Hartmut. *Der Verfassungsentwurf des Ezekiel.* BHT 25. Tübingen: Mohr Siebeck, 1957.

———. *Vom Sinai zum Zion: Alttestamentliche Beiträge zur bilbischen Theologie.* BEvT 64. Munich: Kaiser, 1974.

Geyer, John B. "Mythology and Culture in the Oracles against the Nations." *VT* 36 (1986) 129–45.

———. "The Night of Dumah (Isaiah XXI: 11–12)." *VT* 42 (1992) 317–39.

Giffone, Benjamin D. "A 'Perfect' Poem: The Use of the Qatal Verbal Form in the Biblical Acrostics." *Hebrew Studies* 51 (2010) 49–72.

Gilders, William K. *Blood Ritual in the Hebrew Bible: Meaning and Power.* Baltimore: Johns Hopkins University Press, 2004.

Gileadi, Avraham, ed. *Israel's Apostasy and Restoration: Essays in Honor of Roland K. Harrison* Grand Rapids: Baker, 1988.

Giles, Terry, and Bill Doan. *Twice Used Songs: Performance Criticism of the Songs of Ancient Israel.* Peabody, MA: Hendrickson, 2009.

Gillingham, Susan E. *A Journey of Two Psalms: The Reception of Psalms 1 & 2 in Jewish and Christian Tradition*. Oxford: Oxford University Press, 2013.

———. "The Zion Tradition and the Editing of the Hebrew Psalter." In *Temple and Worship in Biblical Israel*, edited by John Day, 308–41. LHBOTS 422. London: T. & T. Clark, 2005.

Gillmayr-Bucher, Susanne. "Framework and Discourse in the Book of Judges." *JBL* 128 (2009) 687–702.

Gilmer, Harry W. *The If-You Form in Israelite Law*. SBLDS 15. Missoula, MT: Scholars, 1975.

Gitay, Yehoshua. *Prophecy and Prophets: The Diversity of Contemporary Issues in Scholarship*. Atlanta: Scholars, 1997.

Glatt-Gilad, David A. "Genealogy Lists as a Window to Historiographic Periodization in the Book of Chronicles." *Maarav* 21 (2014) 71–79.

———. "Regnal Formulae as a Historiographic Device in the Book of Chronicles." *RB* 108 (2001) 184–209.

Gnuse, Robert Karl. *Dream Theophany of Samuel: Its Structure in Relation to Ancient Near Eastern Dreams and Its Theological Significance*. Lanham, MD: University Press of America, 1984.

Goering, Greg S. "Proleptic Fulfillment of the Prophetic Word: Ezekiel's Dirges over Tyre and its Ruler." *JSOT* 36 (2012) 483–505.

Goff, Matthew. "Qumran Wisdom Literature and the Problem of Genre." *DSD* 17 (2010) 315–35.

Goh, Samuel T. S. "Ruth as a Superior Woman of חיל? A Comparison between Ruth and the 'Capable' Woman in Proverbs 31.10–31." *JSOT* 38 (2014) 487–500.

Goldenberg, David M. *Black and Slave: The Origins and History of the Curse of Ham*. SBR 10. Berlin: de Gruyter, 2017.

Goldenstein, J. *Das Gebet der Gottesknechte: Jes 63,7—64,11 im Jesajabuch*. WMANT 92. Neukirchen-Vluyn: Neukirchener, 2001.

Goldingay, John. "The Arrangement of Isaiah xli–xlv." *VT* 29 (1979) 289–99.

———. "The Significance of Circumcision." *JSOT* 88 (2003) 3–18.

Goldstein, Aaron. "Large Census Numbers in Numbers: An Evaluation of Current Proposals." *Presbyterion* 38 (2012) 99–108.

Goldstein, Bernard R. and Alan Cooper. "The Festivals of Israel and Judah and the Literary History of the Pentateuch." *JAOS* 110 (1990) 19–31.

Golka, Friedemann W. "The Aetiologies in the Old Testament Part 1." *VT* 26 (1976) 410–28.

———. "The Aetiologies in the Old Testament Part 2." *VT* 27 (1977) 36–47.

Good, Edwin M. "Capital Punishment and Its Alternatives in Ancient Near Eastern Law." *Stanford Law Review* 19 (1967) 94–77.

———. "Ezekiel's Ship: Some Extended Metaphors in the Old Testament." *Semitics* 1 (1970) 79–103.

Goodhart, Sandor. "Prophecy, Sacrifice and Repentance in the Story of Jonah." *Semeia* 33 (1985) 43–63.

Goodwin, Robert P. *Selected Writing of St. Thomas Aquinas*. Indianapolis: Bobbs-Merrit, 1965.

Gorman, Frank H., Jr. *Ideology of Ritual: Space, Time and Status in the Priestly Theology*. LHBOTS 91. Sheffield: Sheffield Academic, 1990.

Gordis, Robert. "Conclusion of the Book of Lamentations (5:22)." *JBL* 93 (1974) 289–93.

———. "The Lord out of the Whirlwind: The Climax and Meaning of Job." *Judaism* 13 (1964) 48–63.

———. "Quotations in Wisdom Literature." *JQR* 30 (1939–40) 123–47.

———. "A Rhetorical Use of Interrogative Sentences in Biblical Hebrew." *AJSL* 49 (1933) 212–17.

———. *The Song of Songs and Lamentations: A Study, Modern Translation and Commentary*. Rev. ed. New York: Ktav, 1974.

———. "Studies in the Esther Narrative." *JBL* 95 (1976) 43–58.

Gosse, Bernard. *L'espérance messianique davidique et le structuration du Psautier*. Supplément à Transeuphratène 21. Pendé: Gabalda, 2015.

———. "Le 'moi' prophétique de l'oracle contre Babylone d'Isaïe XXI, 1–10." *RB* 93 (1986) 70–84.

———. "Les introductions des Psaumes 93–94 et Isaïe 59,15b–20." *ZAW* 106 (1994) 303–6.

Gössmann, Felix. "Der siggaion." *Augustinianum* 8 (1968) 367–81.

Gottlieb, Fred. "The Creation Theme in Genesis 1, Psalm 104, and Job 38–42." *JBQ* 44 (2016) 29–36.

Gottwald, Norman. "Immanuel as the Prophet's Son." *VT* 8 (1958) 36–47.

———. *The Tribes of Yahweh: A Sociology of the Religion of Liberated Israel, 1250–1050 B.C.E.* Maryknoll, NY: Orbis, 1979.

Goulder, Michael D. *The Prayers of David*. JSOTSup 102. Sheffield: Sheffield Academic, 1990.

———. *The Psalms of Asaph and the Pentateuch*. JSOTSup 20. Sheffield: JSOT Press, 1982.

———. *The Psalms of the Sons of Korah*. JSOTSup 20. Sheffield: JSOT Press, 1982.

———. *The Song of Fourteen Songs*. JSOTSup 36. Sheffield: JSOT Press, 1986.

Gordon, Cyrus H. "Leviathan: Symbol of Evil." In *Biblical Motifs: Origins and Transformations*, edited by A. Altmann, 1–9. Cambridge: Harvard University Press, 1966.

Gottlieb, Fred. "The Creation Theme in Genesis 1, Psalm 104 and Job 38–42." *JBQ* 44 (2016) 29–36.

Gowan, Donald E. "God's Answer to Job: How Is It an Answer?" *HBT* 8 (1986) 85–102.

Grabbe, Lester L. "The Scapegoat Tradition: A Study in Early Jewish Interpretation." *JSJ* 18 (1987) 152–67.

Grabill, Stephen J. *Rediscovering the Natural Law in Reformed Theological Ethics*. Grand Rapids: Eerdmans, 2006.

Graffy, Adrian. *A Prophet Confronts His People*. AnBib 104. Rome: Biblical Institute Press, 1984.

Green, Alberto R. "Regnal Formulas in the Hebrew and Greek Texts of the Book of Kings." *JNES* 42 (1983) 167–80.

Greenberg, Moshe. "The Design and Themes of Ezekiel's Program of Restoration." In *Interpreting the Prophets*, edited by James Luther Mays and Paul J. Achtemeier, 215–36. Philadelphia: Fortress, 1987.

———. "Ezekiel 17 and the Policy of Psammetichus II." *JBL* 76 (1957) 304–09.

———. "Idealism and Practicality in Numbers 35:4–5 and Ezekiel 48." *JAOS* 88 (1968) 59–66.

Greenspahn, Frederick E. “Deuteronomy and Centralization.” *VT* 64 (2014) 227–35.
———. “Theology of the Framework in the Book of Judges.” *VT* 36 (1986) 385–96.
Greenstein, Edward L. “The Riddle of Samson.” *Prooftexts* 1 (1981) 237–60.
Greenwood, Kyle. “Debating Wisdom: The Role of Voice in Ecclesiastes.” *CBQ* 74 (2012) 476–91.
Grimes, Ronald L. “Infelicitous Performances and Ritual Criticism.” *Semeia* 41 (1987) 103–22.
Grinz, Y. M. “Archaic Terms in the Priestly Code.” *Leshonenu* 39 (1974) 5–30, 163–80.
Grohmann, Marianne. *Fruchtbarkeit und Geburt in Den Psalmen*. FAT 53. Tübingen: Mohr Siebeck, 2007.
———. “Psalm 113 and the Song of Hannah (1 Samuel 2:1–10): A Paradigm for Intertextual Reading?” In *Reading the Bible Intertextually*, edited by Richard B. Hays et al., 119–35. Waco: Baylor University Press, 2009.
Grossberg, Daniel. “Nature, Humanity, and Love in Song of Songs.” *Int* 59 (2005) 229–42.
Grossman, Jonathan. “‘Associative Meanings’ in the Character Evaluation of Lot’s Daughters.” *CBQ* 76 (2014) 40–57.
———. “Different Dreams: Two Models of Interpretation for Three Pairs of Dreams.” *JBL* 135 (2016) 717–32.
———. “The Structural Paradigm of the Ten Plagues Narrative and the Hardening of Pharaoh’s Heart.” *VT* 64 (2014) 588–610.
Grüneberg, Keith N. *Abraham, Blessing and the Nations: A Philological and Exegetical Study of Genesis 12:3 in Its Narrative Context*. BZAW 332. Berlin: de Gruyter, 2014.
Grünwaldt, Klaus. *Das Heiligketisgesetz Leviticus 17–26: Ursprüngliche Gestalt, Tradition und Theologie*. BZAW 271. Berlin: de Gruyter, 1999.
Guillaume, Philippe. “Lamentations 5: The Seventh Acrostic.” *JHebS* 9 (2009) 2–6.
Gunkel, Hermann. “The Close of Micah.” In *What Remains of the Old Testament and Other Essays*, 115–29. New York: Macmillan, 1928.
———. *Creation and Chaos in the Primeval Era and the Eschaton: A Religio-Historical Study of Genesis 1 and Revelation 12*. Translated by K. William Whitney Jr. Foreword by Peter Machinist. Grand Rapids: Eerdmans, 2006.
———. *The Folktale in the Old Testament*. Sheffield: Almond, 1987.
———. *The Legends of Genesis*. Translated by W. H. Carruth. New York: Schocken, 1964.
———. *The Psalms: A Form-Critical Introduction*. Translated by Thomas M. Horner. Philadelphia: Fortress, 1967.
———. *Schöpfung und Chaos in Urzeit und Endzeit: Eine religionsgeschichtliche Untersuchen über Gen 1 und Ap. Jon 12*. Göttingen: Vandenhoeck & Ruprecht, 1895.
Gunkel, Hermann, and Joachim Begrich. *Introduction to Psalms: The Genres of the Religious Lyric of Israel*. Translated by James D. Nogalski. Mercer Library of Biblical Studies. Reprint, Eugene, OR: Wipf & Stock, 2020.
Gunn, David M., and Danna Nolan Fewell. *Narrative in the Hebrew Bible*. Oxford Bible Series. Oxford: Oxford University Press, 1993.
Gunn, George A. “Psalm 2 and the Reign of the Messiah.” *BSac* 169 (2012) 427–42.
Guthrie, Harvey H, Jr. “Ezekiel 21.” *ZAW* 74 (1962) 268–81.
———. *Theology as Thanksgiving*. New York: Seabury, 1981.

Haas, Peter. "'Die He Shall Surely Die': The Structure of Homicide in Biblical Law." *Semeia* 45 (1988) 67–88.

Habel, Norman C. "Appeal to Ancient Tradition as a Literary Form." *ZAW* 88 (1976) 253–72.

———. "The Form and Significance of the Call Narratives." *ZAW* 77 (1965) 297–323.

———. "'Only the Jackal Is My Friend': On Friends and Redeemers in Job." *Int* 31 (1977) 227–36.

Hadad, Eliezer. "'Unintentionally' (Numbers 35:11) and 'Unwittingly' (Deuteronomy 19:4): Two Aspects of the Cities of Refuge." *AJSR* 41 (2017) 155–73.

Koenen, Klaus. *Ethik und Eschatologie im Tritojesajabuch: Eine literarkritische und redaktionsgeschichtliche Studie.* WMANT 62. Neukirchen-Vluyn: Neukirchener, 1990.

Hahn, Scott. "Covenant in the Old and New Testaments." *CurBS* 3 (2005) 263–92.

Hallo, William W. "For Love Is Strong as Death." *Journal of the Ancient Near Eastern Society* 22 (1993) 45–50.

Hallo, William W., ed. *The Context of Scripture.* 3 vols. Leiden: Brill, 1997–2002.

Halpern, Baruch. *The Constitution of the Monarchy in Israel.* HSM 25. Chico: Scholars, 1981.

———. "Why Manasseh Is Blamed for the Babylonian Exile: The Evolution of a Biblical Tradition." *VT* 48 (1998) 473–514.

Halpern, Baruch, and David S. Vanderhooft. "The Editions of Kings in the 7th–6th Centuries." *HUCA* 62 (1991) 179–244.

Halpern, Baruch, and Deborah W. Hobson, eds. *Law and Ideology in Monarchic Israel.* JSOTSup 124. Sheffield: JSOT Press, 1991.

Hals, Ronald M. *Ezekiel.* FOTL 19. Grand Rapids: Eerdmans, 1989.

Ham, T. C. "The Gentle Voice of God in Job 38." *JBL* 132 (2013) 527–41.

———. "Songs of Brokenness to the Healing God." *Journal of Spiritual Formation and Soul Care* 9 (2016) 233–46.

Hamilton, James. "The Seed of the Woman and the Blessing of Abraham." *TynBul* 58 (2014) 253–73.

Hamilton, Jeffries M. *Social Justice and Deuteronomy: The Case of Deuteronomy 15.* SBLDS 136. Atlanta: Scholars, 1992.

Hamilton, Mark W. "Elite Lives: Job 29–31 and Traditional Authority." *JSOT* 32 (2007) 69–89.

Hamme, Joel T. "The Penitential Psalms and Wholeness: Penitential Psalms in the Context of Ancient Near Eastern Penitential Prayers." *Pneuma* 38 (2016) 330–48.

Hancher, Michael. "Performative Utterance, the Word of God, and the Death of the Author." *Semeia* 41 (1987) 26–40.

Hanson, K. C. "Alphabetic Acrostics: A Form-Critical Study." PhD diss., Claremont Graduate School, 1984.

———. "Blood and Purity in Leviticus and Revelation." *Listening: Journal of Religion and Culture* 28 (1993) 215–30.

———. "'How Honorable!' 'How Shameful!': A Cultural Analysis of Matthew's Makarisms and Reproaches." *Semeia* 68 (1996) 83–114.

———. "When the King Crosses the Line: Royal Deviance and Restitution in Levantine Ideologies." *BTB* 26 (1996) 11–25.

Haran, Menahem. "Book-Scrolls in Israel in Pre-Exilic Times." *JJS* 33 (1982) 161–73.

———. "The Complex of Ritual Acts Performed inside the Tabernacle." *ScrHier* 8 (1961) 272–301.

———. "The Graded Numerical Sequence and the Phenomenon of 'Automatism' in Biblical Poetry." In *Congress Volume: Uppsala, 1971*, 238–67. VTSup 22. Leiden: Brill, 1972.

———. "The Law Code of Ezek xl–xlviii and Its Relation to the Priestly School." *HUCA* 50 (1979) 59–71.

———. *Temples and Temple Services in Ancient Israel.* Oxford: Clarendon, 1978.

Hartley, John E. "The Use of Typology Illustrated in a Study of Isaiah 9:1–7." In *Interpreting God's Word for Today: An Inquiry into Hermeneutics from a Biblical Theological Perspective*, 195–229. Wesleyan Theological Perspectives 2. Anderson, IN: Warner, 1982.

———. "Some Aspects of the Exegesis of Jeremiah 31:31–34." In *When Jews and Christians Meet*, edited by Jakob J. Petuchowski, 87–97. Albany: SUNY Press, 1988.

Harland, P. J. "Vertical or Horizontal: The Sin of Babel." *VT* 48 (1998) 515–33.

Harner, Philip B. "The Salvation Oracle in Second Isaiah." *JBL* 88 (1969) 418–34.

Hartley, John E. "From Lament to Oath: A Study of Progression in the Speeches of Job." In *The Book of Job*, edited by W. A. M. Beuken, 79–100. BETL 114. Leuven: Leuven University Press, 1994.

———. *Leviticus.* WBC 3. Dallas: Word, 1992.

Hasel, Gerhard F. "The Four World Empires of Daniel 2 Against Its Near Eastern Environment." *JSOT* 12 (1979) 17–30.

———. "The Polemical Nature of the Genesis Cosmology." *EvQ* 46 (1974) 81–102.

———. *The Remnant: The History and Theology of the Remnant Idea from Genesis to Isaiah.* Berrien Springs, MI: Andrews University Press, 1972.

———. "Resurrection in the Theology of Old Testament Apocalyptic." *ZAW* 92 (1980) 267–84.

Hassan, Musa. "Job's Lament: Towards the Theological-Ethical Significance of Job 29–31." *Journal of Biblical Theology* 3 (2020) 196–217.

Hassler, Mark A. "The Identity of the Little Horn in Daniel 8: Antiochus IV Epiphanes, Rome, or the Antichrist?" *Masters Seminary Journal* 27 (2016) 33–44.

———. "Isaiah 14 and Habakkuk 2: Two Taunt Songs against the same Tyrant?" *Masters Seminary Journal* 26 (2015) 221–29.

Hatton, Peter. "A Cautionary Tale: The Acts-Consequence 'Construct.'" *JSOT* 35 (2011) 375–84.

Hauser, Alan J. "Two Songs of Victory: A Comparison of Exodus 15 and Judges 5." In *Directions in Biblical Hebrew Poetry*, edited by Elaine R. Follis, 265–84. JSOTSup 40. Sheffield: JSOT Press, 1987.

Hauser, Alan J., and Russell Gregory. *From Carmel to Horeb: Elijah in Crisis.* JSOTSup 85. Sheffield: Almond, 1990.

Havea, Jione. *Elusions of Control: Biblical Law on the Words of Women.* SemeiaSt 41. Atlanta: SBL, 2003.

Hayes, Elizabeth R. "The Unity of the Egyptian Hallel: Psalms 113–18." *BBR* 9 (1999) 145–56.

Hayes, Elizabeth R., and Lena-Sofia Tiemeyer, eds. *"I Lifted My Eyes and Saw": Reading Dream and Vision Reports in the Hebrew Bible.* LHBOTS 584. London: T. & T. Clark, 2014.

Hayes, John H. "The Tradition of Zion's Inviolability." *JBL* 82 (1963) 419–26.

———. "The Usage of Oracles against Foreign Nations in Ancient Israel." *JBL* 87 (1968) 81–92.

Hays, Christopher B. "The Covenant with Mut: A New Interpretation of Isaiah 28:1–22." *VT* 60 (2010) 212–40.

———. "Re-Excavating Shebna's Tomb: A New Reading of Isa 22, 15–19 in Its Ancient Near Eastern Context." *ZAW* 122 (2010) 558–75.

Hebrew Bible and Ancient Israel 4 (2015) Thematic issue: The Historical Psalms.

Heger, Paul. *The Three Biblical Altar Laws: Developments in the Sacrificial Cult in Practice and Theology: Political and Economic Background.* BZAW 279. New York: de Gruyter, 1999.

Heim, Knut Martin. *Like Grapes of Gold Set in Silver: An Interpretation of Proverbial Clusters in Proverbs 10:1—22:16.* BZAW 273. Berlin: de Gruyter, 2001.

Helm, Robert. "Azazel in Early Jewish Tradition." *AUSS* 32 (1994) 217–26.

Hempfer, Klaus W. *Gattungstheorie: Information und Synthese.* Uni-Taschenbücher 133. Munich: Fink, 1973.

Hendel, Ronald S. *The Epic of the Patriarch: The Jacob Cycle and the Narrative Traditions of Canaan and Israel.* HSM 42. Atlanta: Scholars, 1987.

Henderson, Ruth. "The Concentric Structure of the Wisdom Poem in Job 28." *Journal of Ancient Judaism* 9 (2018) 26–45.

Hendrix, Ralph E. "A Literary Structural Overview of Exod 25–40." *AUSS* 30 (1992) 123–38.

Hensel, Benedikt, ed. *The History of the Jacob Cycle (Genesis 25–35): Recent Research on the Compilation, the Redactions, and the Reception of the Biblical Narrative and Its Historical and Cultural Contexts.* Archaeology and Bible 4. Tübingen: Mohr Siebeck, 2021.

Henten, J. W. van. "Reception of Daniel 3 and 6 in Early Christian Literature." In *The Book of Daniel: Composition and Reception*, edited by John J. Collins and Peter W. Flint, 149–69. VTSup 83. Leiden: Brill, 2001.

Heschel, Abraham Joshua. *The Prophets.* Philadelphia: JPS, 1962.

———. *The Sabbath: Its Meaning for Modern Man.* New York: Noonday, 1975.

Hess, Richard S. "The Book of Joshua as a Land Grant." *Bib* 83 (2002) 493–506.

———. "The Genealogies of Genesis 1–11 and Comparative Literature." *Bib* 70 (1989) 241–54.

———. "A Typology of West-Semitic Place Name Lists with Special Reference to Joshua 13–21." *BA* 59 (1996) 160–70.

Hess, Richard S., and Gordon J. Wenham, eds. *Zion: City of Our God.* Grand Rapids: Eerdmans, 1999.

Heiser, Michael S. *Supernatural: What the Bible Teaches about the Unseen World—And Why It Matters.* Bellingham, WA: Lexham, 2015.

———. *The Unseen Realm: Recovering the Supernatural Worldview of the Bible.* Bellingham, WA: Lexham, 2015.

Hibbard, J. Todd, and Hyun Chul Paul Kim, eds. *Formation and Intertextuality in Isaiah 24–27: The Reuse and Evocation of Earlier Texts and Traditions.* AIL 17. Atlanta: Society of Biblical Literature, 2013.

Hildebrandt, Ted A. "Motivation and Antithetic Parallelism in Proverbs 10–15." *JETS* 35 (1992) 433–44.

Hillers, Delbert R. *Lamentations.* AB 7A. Garden City, NY: Doubleday, 1992.

———. "A Study of Psalm 148." *CBQ* 40 (1978) 323–34.

Hobbs, T. R. *A Time for War: A Study of Warfare in the Old Testament*. Old Testament Studies 3. Wilmington, DE: Glazier, 1989.

Hodge, Carleton Taylor. "Miktam." *Language* 78 (2002) 156–60.

Hoffmann, Yair. "The Day of the Lord as a Concept and a Term in the Prophetic Literature." *ZAW* 93 (1981) 37–50.

Hoffmeier, James K. "The Arm of God versus the Arm of Pharaoh in the Exodus Narratives." *Bib* 67 (1986) 378–87.

———. "The Wives' Tales of Genesis 12, 20 & 26 and the Covenants at Beersheba." *TynBul* 43 (1992) 81–99.

Hoffner, Harry A., Jr. "Incest, Sodomy and Bestiality in the Ancient Near East." In *Orient and Occident: Essays Presented to Cyrus H. Gordon on the Occasion of His Sixty-fifth Birthday*, edited by Harry A. Hoffner, 81–90. AOAT 22. Neukirchen-Vluyn: Neukirchener, 1973.

Hofstadter, Douglas R. *Gödel, Escher, Bach: An Eternal Golden Braid*. New York: Basic Books, 1999.

Høgenhavn, Jesper. "The Opening of the Psalter: A Study in Jewish Theology." *SJOT* 15 (2001) 169–80.

Holbert, John C. "'The Skies Will Uncover his Iniquity': Satire in the Second Speech of Zophar (Job xx)." *VT* 31 (1981) 171–79.

———. *The Ten Commandments: A Preaching Commentary*. Nashville: Abingdon, 2002.

Holladay, William L. "Form and Word-Play in David's Lament over Saul and Jonathan." *VT* 20 (1970) 153–89.

———. "A Fresh Look at 'Source B' and 'Source C' in Jeremiah." *VT* 25 (1975) 392–96, 402–12.

———. "The Identification of the Two Scrolls of Jeremiah." *VT* 30 (1980) 452–67.

———. *Jeremiah 1: A Commentary on the Book of the Prophet Jeremiah, Chapters 1–25*. Hermeneia. Minneapolis: Fortress, 1986.

———. *Jeremiah 2: A Commentary on the Book of the Prophet Jeremiah, Chapters 26–52*. Hermeneia. Minneapolis: Fortress, 1989.

———. "Prototype and Copies: A New Approach to the Poetry-Prose Problem in the Book of Jeremiah." *JBL* 79 (1960) 351–67.

Hom, Mary Katherine Y. H. "On the Use of *wytba* + *bkvyw* and *rbq* Formulae in the Book of Kings." *BN* 172 (2017) 3–12.

Horst, Friedrich. "Die Formen des althebräischen Liebesliedes." In *Gottes Recht: Gesammelte Studien*, 176–87. Theoligische Bücherei 12. Munich: Kaiser, 1961.

———. "Die Visionsschilderungen des alttestamentliche Propheten." *EvT* 20 (1960) 193–205.

Horne, Milton. "From Ethics to Aesthetics: The Animals in Job 38:39—39:30." *RevExp* 102 (2005) 127–42.

Hossfeld, Frank-Lothar, and Erich Zenger. "The So-Called Elohistic Psalter: A New Solution for an Old Problem." In *A God so Near: Essays on Old Testament Theology in Honor of Patrick D. Miller*, edited by Brent A. Strawn and Nancy R. Bowen, 35–51. Winona Lake, IN: Eisenbrauns, 2003.

Houston, Walter C. *Purity and Monotheism: Clean and Unclean Animals in Biblical Law*. JSOTSup 140. Sheffield: JSOT Press, 1993.

———. "What Did the Prophets Think They Were Doing? Speech Acts and Prophetic Discourse in the Old Testament." *BibInt* 1 (1993) 167–88.

Howard, David M. *The Structure of Psalms 93–100*. BJUCSD 5. Winona Lake, IN: Eisenbrauns, 1997.

Hoyt, JoAnna. "Reassessing Repentance in Judges." *BSac* 169 (2012) 143–57.

Hristova-Gotthard, Hrisztalina, and Melita Aleksa Varga, eds. *Introduction to Paremiology: A Comprehensive Guide to Proverb Studies*. Berlin: de Gruyter, 2014.

Huffmon, Herbert B. "The Covenant Lawsuit in the Prophets." *JBL* 78 (1959) 285–95.

———. "The Oracular Process: Delphi and the Near East." *VT* 57 (2007) 449–60.

Hull, John H., Jr. "Finding the Center: The Abimelech Account and the Gideon/Abimelech Cycle as the Turning Point in Judges." In *The Genre of Biblical Commentary: Essays in Honor of John E. Hartley on the Occasion of His 75th Birthday*, edited by Timothy D. Finlay and William Yarchin, 145–58. Eugene, OR: Pickwick Publications, 2015.

Hullinger, Jerry M. "The Divine Presence, Uncleanness, and Ezekiel's Millennial Sacrifices." *BSac* 163 (2006) 405–22.

Hunt, Patrick N. "Sensory Images in Song of Songs 1:12—2:16." In *Dort ziehen Schiffe dahin: Collected Communications to the XIVth Congress of the International Organization for the Study of the Old Testament*, edited by Matthias Augustin and Klaus-Dietrich Schunck, 69–78. Beiträge zur Erforschung des Alten Testaments und des antiken Judentums 28. New York: Lang, 1996.

Hunter, A. Vanlier. *Seek the Lord! A Study of the Meaning and Function of the Exhortations in Amos, Hosea, Isaiah, Micah, and Zephaniah*. Baltimore: St. Mary's Seminary and University, 1982.

Hunter, Alastair G. "Yahweh Comes Home to Zion." In *Psalms*, 173–258. Old Testament Readings. London: Routledge, 1999.

Hurvitz, Victor (Avigdor). "The Form and Fate of the Tabernacle: Reflections on a Recent Proposal." *JQR* 86 (1995) 127–51.

———. *A Linguistic Study of the Relationship between the Priestly Source and the Book of Ezekiel*. CahRB 20. École Biblique: Rome, 1982.

———. "The Priestly Account of Building the Tabernacle." *JAOS* 105 (1985) 21–30.

———. "Wisdom Vocabulary in the Hebrew Psalter: A Contribution to the Study of 'Wisdom Psalms.'" *VT* 38 (1988) 41–51.

Husser, Jean-Marie. *Dreams and Dream Narratives in the Biblical World*. BibSem 63. Sheffield: Sheffield Academic, 1999.

Hutton, Jeremy M. "Mahanaim, Penuel and Transhumance Routes: Observations on Genesis 32–33 and Judges 8." *JNES* 65 (2006) 161–178.

Hutton, Rodney R. "Declaratory Formulae: Forms of Authoritative Pronouncement in Ancient Israel." Ph.D. diss., Claremont Graduate School, 1983.

Hyman, Ronald T. "Four Acts of Vowing in the Bible." *JBQ* 37 (2009) 231–38.

Irvine, Stuart A. *Isaiah, Ahaz, and the Syro-Ephraimitic Crisis*. SBLDS 123. Atlanta: Scholars, 1990.

Issler, Klaus. "Lending and Interest in the OT: Examining Three Interpretations to Explain the Deuteronomy 23:19–20 Distinction in Light of the Historical Usury Debate." *JETS* 59 (2016) 761–89.

Ittmann, Norbert. *Die Konfessionen Jeremias: Ihre Bedeutung für die Verkündigung des Propheten*. WMANT 54. Neukirchen–Vluyn: Neukirchener Verlag, 1981.

Iwanski, Dariusz. *The Dynamics of Job's Intercession*. AnBib 161. Rome: Pontifical Biblical Institute, 2006.

Jackson, Bernard S. "Law, Wisdom, and Narrative." In *Narrativity in Biblical and Related Texts*, edited by George J. Brooke and Jean-Daniel Kaestli, 31–51. BETL 149. Leuven: Peeters, 2000.

———. "The Problem of Exod. 21:22–5 (Ius Talionis)." *VT* 23 (1973) 273–304.

Jagersma, H. *A History of Israel in the Old Testament Period*. Translated by John Bowden. Philadelphia: Fortress, 1983.

———. "The Tithes in the Old Testament." *OTS* 21 (1981) 116–28.

Janowski, Bernd, and Peter Stuhlmacher, eds. *The Suffering Servant: Isaiah 53 in Jewish and Christian Sources*. Grand Rapids: Eerdmans, 2004.

Janzen, Waldemar. "*'Ashre* in the Old Testament." *HTR* 58 (1965) 215–26.

———. *Mourning Cry and Woe Oracle*. BZAW 125. Berlin: de Gruyter, 1972.

Japhet, Sara. "The Historical Reliability of Chronicles: The History of the Problem and Its Place in Biblical Research." *JSOT* 33 (1985) 83–107.

———. *The Ideology of the Book of Chronicles and Its Place in Biblical Thought*. BEATAJ 9. Frankfurt: Lang, 1989.

Jarick, John, ed. *Perspectives on Israelite Wisdom: Proceedings of the Oxford Old Testament Seminar*. LHBOTS 618. London: Bloomsbury T. & T. Clark, 2016.

Jemielity, Thomas. *Satire and the Hebrew Prophets*. Literary Currents in Biblical Interpretation. Louisville: Westminster John Knox, 1992.

Jenei, Péter. "Strategies of Stranger Inclusion in the Narrative Traditions of Joshua-Judges: The Cases of Rahab's Household, the Kenites and the Gibeonites." *OTE* 32 (2019) 127–54.

Jeon, Jaeyoung. "The Visit of Jethro (Exodus 18): Its Composition and Levitical Reworking." *JBL* 136 (2017) 289–306.

Jeremias, Christian. *Die Nachtgesichte des Sacharja*. FRLANT 117. Göttingen: Vandenhoeck & Ruprecht, 1977.

Jeremias, Joachim. *Das Königtum Gottes in den Psalmen: Israels Begegnung mit dem kanaanäischen Methos in den Jahwe-König-Psalmen*. FRLANT 141. Göttingen: Vandenoeck & Ruprecht, 1987.

———. *Theophanie: Die Geschichte einer alttestamentlichen Gattung*. WMANT 10. Neukirchen-Vluyn: Neukirchener, 1965.

Jerusalmi, Isaac. *The Story of Joseph: A Philological Commentary*. Cincinnati: Hebrew Union College, 1968.

Jindo, Job Y. "On the Biblical Notion of the 'Fear of God' as a Condition for Human Existence." *BibInt* 19 (2011) 433–53.

Johnson, Dylan. "The 'Spirit of Yhwh' and Samson's Martial Rage: A *Leitmotif* of the Biblical Warrior Tradition." *VT* 72 (2022) 214–36.

Johnson, John Edgar. "An Analysis of Proverbs 1:1–7." *BSac* 144 (1987) 419–32.

Johnson, Marshall D. *Making Sense of the Bible: Literary Type as an Approach to Understanding*. Grand Rapids: Eerdmans, 2002.

———. *The Purpose of the Biblical Genealogies with Special Reference to the Setting of the Genealogies of Jesus*. Society for New Testament Studies Monograph Series 8. Cambridge: Cambridge University Press, 1969.

Joffe, Laura. "The Answer to the Meaning of Life, the Universe and the Elohistic Psalter." *JSOT* 27 (2002) 223–35.

———. "The Elohistic Psalter: What, How and Why?" *SJOT* 15 (2001) 142–66.

Johannes, Gottfried. "Unvergleichlichkeitsformulierungen im Alten Testament." PhD diss., Mainz, Gutenburg University, 1968.

Jones, Brian C. *Howling over Moab: Irony and Rhetoric in Isaiah 15–16*. SBLDS 157. Atlanta: Scholars, 1996.

Jones, Scott C. *Rumors of Wisdom: Job 28 as Poetry*. BZAW 398. Berlin: de Gruyter, 2009.

Jong, Matthijs. J. de. "Biblical Prophecy—A Scribal Enterprise: The Old Testament Prophecy of Unconditional Judgment Considered as a Literary Phenomenon." *VT* 61 (2011) 39–70.

Joo, Samantha. "A Fine Balance between Hope and Despair: The Epilogue to 2 Kings (25:27–30)." *BibInt* 20 (2012) 226–43.

Joosten, Jan. *People and Land in the Holiness Code: An Exegetical Study of the Ideational Framework of the Law in Leviticus 17–26*. VTSup 67. Leiden: Brill, 1996.

Joukowsky, Martha S., ed. *The Heritage of Tyre: Essays on the History, Archeology, and Preservation of Tyre*. Dubuque: Kendall/Hunt, 1992.

Kahle, Paul. "The Hebrew Text of the Complutensian Polyglot." In *Homeahe a Millds-Vallicrosa*, vol. 1, 741–51. Barcelona: Consejo Superior de Investigaciones Cientificas, 1954.

Kaiser, Barbara Bakke. "Poet as Female Impersonator: The Image of Daughter Zion as Speaker in Biblical Poems of Suffering." *JR* 67 (1987) 164–82.

Kaiser, Walter C., Jr. *A History of Israel from the Bronze Age Through the Jewish Wars*. Nashville: Broadman & Holman, 1998.

———. *The Messiah in the Old Testament*. Grand Rapids: Zondervan, 1995.

———. "The Unfailing Promises to David." *JSOT* 45 (1989) 91–98.

Kallai, Zecharia. "The Boundaries of Canaan and the Land of Israel in the Bible." *ErIsr* 12 (1975) 27–34.

———. "The Twelve-Tribe Systems of Israel." *VT* 47 (1997) 53–90.

Kalmanofsky, Amy. "The Dangerous Sisters of Jeremiah and Ezekiel." *JBL* 130 (2011) 299–312.

Kaminsky, Joel S. *Yet I Loved Jacob: Reclaiming the Biblical Concept of Election*. Nashville: Abingdon, 2007.

Kaplan, Jonathan. "The Credibility of Liberty: The Plausibility of the Jubilee Legislation of Leviticus 25 in Ancient Israel and Judah." *CBQ* 81 (2019) 183–203.

Kaplan, L. J. "Maimonides, Dale Patrick, and Job XLII 6." *VT* 28 (1978) 356–58.

Kartveit, Magnar. *Motive und Schichten der Landtheologie in 1 Chronik 1–9*. ConBOT 28. Stockholm: Almquist & Wiksell, 1989.

Kasher, Rimon. "Anthropomorphism, Holiness and Cult: A New Look at Ezekiel 40–48." *ZAW* 110 (1998) 192–208.

———. "The Sitz im Buch of the Story of Hezekiah's Illness and Cure (II Reg 20,1–11; Isa 38,1–22)." *ZAW* 113 (2001) 41–55.

Kazen, Thomas. "Explaining Discrepancies in the Purity Laws on Discharges." *RB* 114 (2007) 348–71.

Kearney, Peter J. "Creation and Liturgy: The P Redaction of Ex 25–40." *ZAW* 89 (1977) 375–87.

Keefer, Arthur J. "Phonological Patterns in the Hebrew Bible: A Century of Studies in Sound." *CurBR* 15 (2016) 42–64.

———. "A Shift in Perspective: The Intended Audience and Coherent Reading of Proverbs 1:1–7." *JBL* 136 (2017) 103–16.

Keel, Othmar. *The Song of Songs*. Translated by Frederick J. Gaiser. Continental Commentaries. Minneapolis: Fortress, 1994.

Keel, Othmar, and Christoph Uehlinger. *Gods, Goddesses and Images of God in Ancient Israel*. Translated by Thomas H. Trapp. Minneapolis: Fortress, 1998.

Keiser, Evelien, and Hella Olbertz, eds. *Recent Developments in Functional Discourse Grammar*. Studies in Language Companion Series 205. Amsterdam: Benjamins.

Kelle, Brad E., and Brent A. Strawn, eds. *The Oxford Handbook of the Historical Books of the Hebrew Bible*. Oxford: Oxford University Press, 2020.

Kelle, Brad E., and Frank Richtel Ames, eds. *Writing and Reading War: Rhetoric, Gender and Ethics in Biblical and Modern Contexts*. SBL Symposium Series 42. Atlanta: SBL, 2008.

Kermode, Frank. *The Genesis of Secrecy: On the Interpretation of Narrative*. Cambridge: Harvard University Press, 1983.

Kessler, Martin. "The Judgment–Promise Dialectic in Jeremiah 26–36." *ACEBT* 16 (1977) 60–72.

Kilchör, Benjamin. "The Meaning of Ezekiel 44,6–14 in Light of Ezekiel 1–39." *Bib* 98 (2017) 191–207.

Kilian, Rudolf. *Literarkritische und Formgeschictliche Untersuchung des Heiligketisgestzes*. BBB 19. Bonn: Hanstein, 1963.

Kim, Daewook. "Absalom's Rebellion and David's Flight (2 Sam 15) The Emergence of the Ideal King David." *BZ* 67 (2023) 43–63.

Kim, Jichan. *The Structure of the Samson Cycle*. Kampen: Kok Pharos, 1993.

Kim, Hyun Chul Paul. "City, Earth, and Empire in Isaiah 24–27." In *Formation and Intertextuality in Isaiah 24–27: The Reuse and Evocation of Earlier Texts and Traditions*, edited by J. Todd Hibbard and Hyun Chul Paul Kim, 25–48. AIL 17. Atlanta: SBL, 2013.

———. "Two Mothers and Two Sons: Reading 1 Kings 3:16–28 as a Parody on Solomon's Coup (1 Kings 1–2)." In *Partners with God: Theological and Critical Readings of the Bible in Honor of Marvin A. Sweeney*, edited by Shelley L. Birdsong and Serge Frolov, 83–99. Claremont Studies in Hebrew Bible and Septuagint 2. Claremont: Claremont Press, 2017.

Kim, Soo J. "YHWH Shammah: The City as Gateway to the Presence of YHWH." *JSOT* 39 (2014) 187–207.

Kim, Young Hye. "The Third Messiah in the Book of Malachi: An Analysis on Malachi 4:4–6." *Korean Journal of Christian Studies* 93 (2014) 25–42.

Kimelman, Reuven. "Psalm 145: Theme, Structure, and Impact." *JBL* 113 (1994) 37–58.

King, Andrew M. "A Remnant Will Return: An Analysis of the Literary Function of the Remnant Motif in Isaiah." *JETS* 4 (2015) 145–69.

King, Greg A. "The Remnant in Zephaniah." *BSac* 151 (1994) 414–27.

Kislev, Itamar. "The Number of Numbers: The Census Accounts in the Book of Numbers." *ZAW* 128 (2016) 189–204.

Kiss, Jenö. *Die Klage Gottes und des Propheten; Ihre Rolle in der Komposition und Redaktion von Jer 11–12, 14–15 und 18*. WMANT 99. Neukirchen-Vluyn: Neukirchener Verlag, 2003.

Kissling, Paul J. *Reliable Characters in the Primary History: Profiles of Moses, Joshua, Elijah and Elisha*. JSOTSup 224. Sheffield: Sheffield Academic, 1996.

Kitchen, Kenneth A. *On the Reliability of the Old Testament*. Grand Rapids: Eerdmans, 2003.

———. "The Tabernacle—A Bronze Age Artifact." *ErIsr* 24 (1993) 119–29.

———. *The Third Intermediate Period in Egypt (1100–650 BC)*. Warminster: Aris & Phillips, 1972.

Kiuchi, N. *The Purification Offering in the Priestly Literature: Its Meaning and Function*. JSOTSup 56. Sheffield: JSOT Press, 1987.

Klein, Reuven Chaim. "Reconciling the Sacrifices of Ezekiel with the Torah." *JBQ* 43 (2015) 211–22.

Kleinig, John W. "Bach, Chronicles, and Church Music." *Logia* 9 (2000) 7–10.

———. *The Lord's Song: The Basis, Function, and Significance of Choral Music in Chronicles*. JSOTSup 156. Sheffield: JSOT Press, 1993.

Klingbeil, Gerald A. "Ritual Space in the Ordination Ritual of Aaron and His Sons as Found in Leviticus 8." *JNSL* 21 (1995) 59–82.

Knauf, Ernst Axel. "Alter und Herkunft der edomitischen Königsliste Gen 36:31–39." *ZAW* 97 (1985) 245–53.

Knierim, Roff P. "Exodus 18 and Neuordnung der mosäischen Gerichtsbarkeit." *ZAW* 73 (1961) 146–71.

———. *Die Hauptbegriffe für Sünde im alten Testament*. Gütersloh: Mohn, 1967.

———. "'I Will Not Cause It to Return,' in Amos 1 and 2." In *Canon and Authority: Essays in Old Testament Religion and Theology*, edited by George W. Coats and Burke O. Long, 163–75. Philadelphia: Fortress, 1976.

———. "Old Testament Form Criticism Reconsidered." *Int* 27 (1973) [435–68 in Reprint]

———. "The Problem of Ancient Israel's Prescriptive Legal Traditions." *Semeia* 45 (1988) 5–26.

———. *The Task of Old Testament Theology: Substance, Method, and Cases: Essays*. Grand Rapids: Eerdmans, 1995.

———. *Text and Concept in Leviticus 1:1–9*. FAT 2. Tübingen: Mohr Siebeck, 1992.

———. "The Vocation of Isaiah." *VT* 18 (1968) 47–68.

Knierim, Rolf P., and George W. Coats. *Numbers*. FOTL 4. Grand Rapids: Eerdmans, 2005.

Knierim, Rolf P., and Gene M. Tucker. "Editor's Foreword." In Marvin Sweeney, *Isaiah 1–39 with an Introduction to Prophetic Literature*, xv–xvii. FOTL 16. Grand Rapids: Eerdmans, 1996.

Knohl, Israel. "The Original Version of Deborah's Song, and Its Numerical Structure." *VT* 66 (2016) 45–65.

———. "The Priestly Torah Versus the Holiness School: Sabbath and the Festivals." *HUCA* 58 (1987) 65–117.

———. *The Sanctuary of Silence: The Priestly Torah and the Holiness School*. Minneapolis: Fortress, 1995.

Knoppers, Gary N. "The Deuteronomist and the Deuteronomic Law of the King: A Reexamination of a Relationship." *ZAW* 108 (1996) 329–46.

———. "Prayer and Propaganda: Solomon's Dedication of the Temple and the Deuteronomistic Program." *CBQ* 57 (1995) 57–76.

Knowles, Melody. "Pilgrimage Imagery in the Returns in Ezra." *JBL* 123 (2004) 57–74.

Koch, Klaus. *Daniel (1,1–21)*. BKAT 22/1. Neukirchen-Vluyn: Neukirchener, 1986.

———. *The Growth of the Biblical Tradition*. Translated by S. Cupitt. New York: Scribner, 1969.

———. *Die Priesterschrift von Exodus 25 bis Leviticus 16*. FRLANT 53. Göttingen: Vandenhoeck & Ruprecht, 1959.

———. "Die Rolle der hymnischen Abschnitte in der Komposition des Amos-Buches." *ZAW* 86 (1974) 504–37.

———. "Der Spruch 'Sein Blut bleibe auf seinem Haupt' und die israelitische Auffasung vom vergossenen Blut." *VT* 12 (1962) 396–416.

———. "Tempeleinlassliturgien und Dekaloge." In *Studien zur Theologie der alttestamentlichen Überlieferungen*, edited by Klaus Koch and Rolf Rendtorff, 46–60. Neukirchen-Vluyn: Neukirchener, 1961.

Koenen, Klaus. *Ethik und Eschatologie im Tritojesajabuch*. WMANT 62. Neukirchener-Vluyn: Neukirchener, 1990.

Kooten, George H. van, and Jacques van Ruiten, eds. *The Prestige of the Pagan Prophet Balaam in Judaism, Early Christianity and Islam*. Themes in Biblical Narrative 11. Leiden: Brill, 2008.

Koh, Y. V. *Royal Autobiography in the Book of Qoheleth*. BZAW 369. Berlin: de Gruyter, 2006.

Kraft, Charles Franklin. *The Strophic Structure of Hebrew Poetry: As Illustrated in the First Book of the Psalter*. Chicago: University of Chicago Press, 1938.

Kramer, Samuel Noah. *Lamentation over the Destruction of Ur*. AS 12. Chicago: University Press, 1940).

———. *Mythologies of the Ancient World*. Garden City: Doubleday, 1961.

———. "Sumerian Similes: A Panoramic View of Some of Man's Oldest Literary Images." *JAOS* 89 (1969) 1–10.

Krasovec, José. *Antithetic Structure in Biblical Hebrew Poetry*. VTSup 35. Leiden: Brill, 1984.

———. "Punishment and Mercy in the Primeval History (Gen 1–11)." *ETL* 70 (1994) 5–33.

Kratz, Reinhard G. "Die Tora Davids: Psalm 1 und die doxologische Fünfteilung des Psalters." *ZTK* 93 (1996) 1–34.

Kratz, Reinhard G., and Hermann Spieckermann, eds. *Divine Wrath and Divine Mercy in the World of Antiquity*. FAT 2/33. Tübingen: Mohr Siebeck, 2008.

Krauss, Hans-Joachim. *Die Königsherrschaft Gottes im Alten Testament: Untersuchungen zu den Liedern von Jahwes Thronbesteigung*. BHT 13. Tübingen: Mohr Siebeck, 1951.

Kugel, James L. *The Idea of Biblical Poetry: Parallelism and Its History*. New Haven: Yale University Press, 1981.

———. "Qohelet and Money." *CBQ* 51 (1989) 32–49.

Kuntz, John K. "The Canonical Wisdom Psalms of Ancient Israel—Their Rhetorical, Thematic, and Formal Dimensions." In *Rhetorical Criticism: Essays in Honor of James Muilenburg*, edited by Jared J. Jackson and Martin Kessler, 186–222. Pittsburgh Theological Monograph Series 1. Pittsburgh: Pickwick Publications, 1974.

———. "Reclaiming Biblical Wisdom Psalms: A Response to Crenshaw." *CurBS* 1 (2003) 145–54.

Kynes, Will. *My Psalm Has Turned into Weeping: Job's Dialogue with the Psalms*. BZAW 437. Berlin: de Gruyter, 2012.

———. *An Obituary for "Wisdom Literature": The Birth, Death, and Intertextual Reintegration of a Biblical Corpus*. Oxford: Oxford University Press, 2019.

Laato, Antti. "The Levitical Genealogies in 1 Chronicles 5–6 and the Formation of Levitical Idelology in Post-Exilic Judah." *JSOT* 19 (1994) 77–99.

———. *A Star is Rising: The Historical Development of the Old Testament Royal Ideology and the Rise of the Jewish Messianic Expectation*. International Studies in Formative Christianity and Judaism 5. Atlanta: Scholars, 1997.

———. *Who Is Immanuel? The Rise and Foundering of Isaiah's Messianic Expectations*. A[set ring over a]bo: A[set ring over a]bo Academy, 1988.

Labahn, Antje. "Fire from Above: Metaphors and Images of God's Actions in Lamentations 2:1–9." *JSOT* 31 (2006) 239–56.

Labuschagne, C. J. *The Incomparability of Yahweh in the Old Testament*. Pretoria Oriental Series 5. Leiden: Brill, 1966.

Lambert, David A. "Fasting as a Penitential Rite: A Biblical Phenomenon?" *HTR* 96 (2004) 477–512.

———. *How Repentance Became Biblical: Judaism, Christianity, and the Interpretation of Scripture*. New York: Oxford University Press, 2016.

Lappin, Shalom, and Elabbas Benmamoun. *Fragments: Studies in Ellipsis and Gapping*. New York: Oxford University Press, 1999.

Lauber, Stephan. "Hi 32 als hellenistisches Proömium." *ZAW* 125 (2013) 607–21.

Lee, Eunny P. *The Vitality of Enjoyment in Qohelet's Theological Rhetoric*. BZAW 353. Berlin: de Gruyter, 2005.

Leeuwen, Raymond C. van. *Context and Meaning in Proverbs 25–27*. SBLDS 96. Atlanta: Scholars, 1996.

Legget, Donald A. *The Levirate and Goel Institutions in the Old Testament with Special Attention in the Book of Ruth*. Cherry Hill, NY: Mack, 1974.

Lemardelé, Christophe. *Les cheveux du Nazir. De Samson à Jacques, frère de Jésus*. Paris: Cerf, 2016.

Lenzi, Alan C. "Proverbs 8:22–31: Three Perspectives on its Composition." *JBL* 125 (2006) 687–714.

Leuchter, Mark. "The Ambiguous Details in the Blasphemer Narrative: Sources and Redaction in Leviticus 24:10–23." *JBL* 130 (2011) 431–50.

———. "Genesis 38 in Social and Historical Perspective." *JBL* 132 (2013) 209–27.

———. "The Manumission Laws in Leviticus and Deuteronomy: The Jeremiah Connection." *JBL* 127 (2008) 635–53.

———. "The Royal Background of Deut 18,15–18." *ZAW* 130 (2018) 364–83.

Leuenberger, Martin. *Konzeptionen des Königtums Gottes im Psalter: Untersuchungen zu Komposition und Redaktion der theokratischen Bücher IV–V im Psalter*. Abhandlungen zur Theologiedes Alten und Neuen Testaments 83. Zurich: TVZ, 2004.

Levenson, Jon D. *Creation and the Persistence of Evil: The Jewish Drama of Divine Omnipotence*. Princeton: Princeton University Press, 1988.

———. "The Davidic Covenant and Its Modern Interpreters." *CBQ* 41 (1979) 205–19.

———. *Resurrection and the Restoration of Israel: The Ultimate Victory of the God of Life*. New Haven: Yale University Press, 2008.

———. *Sinai and Zion: An Entry into the Jewish Bible*. Minneapolis: Winston, 1985.

———. "The Sources of Torah: Psalm 119 and the Modes of Revelation in Second Temple Judaism." In *Ancient Israelite Religion: Essays in Honor of Frank Moore Cross*, Jr., edited by Patrick D. Miller Jr. et al., 559–74. Philadelphia: Fortress, 1987.

———. *Theology of the Program of Restoration of Ezekiel 40–48*. HSM 10. Missoula, MT: Scholars, 1976.

Levin, Christoph. "Die Entstehung er Büchereinteilung des Psalters." *VT* 54 (2004) 83–90.

———. "Psalm 136 als Zeitwilige Schlussdoxologie des Psalters." *SJOT* 14 (2000) 17–27.

Levin, Yigal. "From Lists to History: Chronological Aspects of the Chronicler's Genealogies." *JBL* 123 (2004) 601–36.

———. "Numbers 34:2–12, the Boundaries of the Land of Canaan, and the Empire of Necho." *JANES* 30 (2006) 55–76.

———. "Understanding Biblical Genealogies." *CurBS* 9 (2001) 11–46.

Levine, Baruch A. "The Descriptive Tabernacle Texts of the Pentateuch." *JAOS* 85 (1965) 307–18.

———. *Leviticus*. JPS Torah Commentary. Philadelphia: Jewish Publication Society, 1989.

Levine, Nachman. "Twice as Much as Your Spirit: Pattern, Parallel and Paronomasia in the Miracles of Elijah and Elisha." *JSOT* 85 (1999) 25–46.

Levinson, Bernard M. *Deuteronomy and the Hermeneutics of Legal Innovation*. Oxford: Oxford University Press, 1997.

———. "The Birth of the Lemma: The Restrictive Reinterpretation of the Covenant Code's Manumission Law by the Holiness Code." *JBL* 124 (2005) 617–39.

Levinson, Bernard M., ed. *Theory and Method in Biblical and Cuneiform Law: Revision, Interpolation and Development*. JSOTSup 181. Sheffield: Sheffield Academic, 2006.

Levy, Thomas E., Mohammad Najjar, and Erez Ben-Yosef. *New Insights into the Iron Age Archaeology of Edom, Southern Jordan*. Monumenta Archaeologica 35. Los Angeles: Cotsen Institute of Archaeology, 2016.

Lewis, C. S. *Miracles*. London: Fontana, 1966.

Lichtheim, Miriam. *Egyptian Wisdom Literature in the International Context: A Study of Demotic Instructions*. OBO 52. Göttingen: Vandenhoeck & Ruprecht.

Linafelt, Tod. "The Refusal of a Conclusion in the Book of Lamentations." *JBL* 120 (2001) 340–43.

Lindblom, Johannes. *Prophecy in Ancient Israel*. Philadelphia: Fortress, 1963.

Lindstrøm, Fredrik. *Suffering and Sin: Interpretations of Illness in the Individual Complaint Psalms*. ConBOT 37. Stockholm: Almqvist & Wicksell, 1994.

Lipinski, Edward. *The Arameans: Their Ancient History, Culture, and Religion*. OLA 100. Leuven: Peeters, 2000.

———. "Macarismes et psaumes de congratulation." *RB* (1968) 321–67.

Liverani, Mario. "The Trade Network of Tyre according to Ezek 27." In *Ah, Assyria: Studies in Assyrian History and Ancient Near Eastern Historiography Presented to Hayim Tadmor* Scripta Hierosolymitana, edited by Mordechai Cogan and Israel Ephal, 65–79. Jerusalem: Magnes, 1991.

Lohfink, Norbert. "Freu dich, Jüngling—doch nicht, weil du jung bist: Zum Formproblem im Schlussgedicht Kohelets (Koh 11,9—12,8)." *BibInt* 3 (1995) 158–80.

———. *Krieg und Staat im alten Israel*. Beiträge zur Friedensethik 14. Barsbüttel: Institut für Theologie und Friden, 1992.

Lohr, Joel N. *Chosen and Unchosen: Concepts of Election in the Pentateuch and Jewish-Christian Interpretation*. Winona Lake, IN: Eisenbrauns, 2009.

Lombaard, Christo. "Testing Tales: Genesis 22 and Daniel 3 and 6." In *Prayers and the Construction of Israelite Identity*, edited by Susanne Gillmayr-Bucher and Maria Häusl, 113–123. AIL 35. Atlanta: SBL, 2019.

Long, Burke O. *1 Kings: With an Introduction to Historical Literature*. FOTL 9. Grand Rapids: Eerdmans, 1984.

———. *2 Kings*. FOTL 10. Grand Rapids: Eerdmans, 1991.

———. *The Problem of Etiological Narrative in the Old Testament*. BZAW 108. Berlin: de Gruyter, 1968.

———. "Reports of Visions Among the Prophets." *JBL* 95 (1976) 353–65.

Longacre, Robert E. "Building for the Worship of God: Exodus 25:1—30:10." In *Discourse Analysis of Biblical Literature: What It Is and What It Offers*, edited by Walter R. Bodine, 21–49. Semeia Studies. Atlanta: Scholars, 1995.

———. *Joseph: A Story of Divine Providence*. Winona Lake, IN: Eisenbrauns, 2003.

Longman, Tremper, III. *Song of Songs*. NICOT. Grand Rapids: Eerdmans, 2001.

Lopez, René. "The Meaning of 'Behemoth' and 'Leviathan' in Job." *BSac* 173 (2016) 401–24.

Lord, Albert B. *The Singer of Tales*. Cambridge: Harvard University Press, 1960.

Low, Katherine B. "Implications Surrounding Girding the Loins in Light of Gender, Body, and Power." *JSOT* 36 (2011) 3–30.

Lowenthal, Eric I. *The Joseph Narrative in Genesis*. New York: Ktav, 1973.

Lowery, R. H. *The Reforming Kings: Cult and Society in First Temple Judah*. JSOTSup 120. Sheffield: Academic, 1991.

Lowth, Robert. *De sacra poesi hebraeorum*. Oxford, 1753.

Lund, Nils W. "The Presence of Chiasmus in the Old Testament." *American Journal of Semitic Languages and Literature* 46 (1929–30) 104–26.

Lundbom, Jack R. "Baruch, Seraiah, and Expanded Colophons in the Book of Jeremiah." *JSOT* 11 (1986) 89–114.

———. "Mary Magdalene and Song of Songs 3:1–4." *Int* 49 (1995) 172–75.

Lyke, Larry. "The Song of Songs, Proverbs, and the Theology of Love." In *Theological Exegesis: Essays in Honor of Brevard Childs*, edited by Christopher Seitz and Katherine Green-McCreight, 208–23. Grand Rapids: Eerdmans, 1999.

———. *King David with the Wise Woman of Tekoa: The Resonance of Tradition in Parabolic Narrative*. JSOTSup 255. Sheffield: Academic, 1997.

Lyu, Sun Myung. *Righteousness in the Book of Proverbs*. FAT 2/55. Tübingen: Mohr Siebeck, 2012.

Mabee, Charles. "Jacob and Laban: The Structure of Judicial Proceedings (Genesis 31:25–42)." *VT* 30 (1980) 192–207.

MacDonald, Burton, and Randall W. Younker, eds. *Ancient Ammon*. SHANE 17. Leiden: Brill, 1999.

Macintosh, A. A. *Isaiah XXI: A Palimpsest*. Cambridge: Cambridge University Press, 1980.

Macky, Peter W. *The Centrality of Metaphors to Biblical Thought: A Method for Interpreting the Bible*. Studies in Bible and Early Christianity 19. Lewiston, NY: Mellen, 1990.

Magdalene, F. Rachel. *On the Scales of Righteousness: Neo-Babylonian Trial Law and the Book of Job*. BJS 348. Providence: BJS, 2007.

Maier, Christl M. *Daughter Zion, Mother Zion: Gender Space and the Sacred in Ancient Israel*. Minneapolis: Fortress, 2008.

Malamat, Abraham. "Conquest of Canaan: Israelite Conduct of War According to the Biblical Tradition." In *History of Biblical Israel*, 68–96. Culture and History of the Ancient Near East 7. Leiden: Brill, 2001.

———. "King Lists of the Old Babylonian Period and Biblical Genealogies." *JAOS* 88 (1968) 163–73.

Mandolfo, Carleen. *Daughter Zion Talks Back to the Prophets: A Dialogic Theology of the Book of Lamentations*. Semeia Studies 58. Atlanta: SBL, 2007.

———. "Dialogic Form Criticism: An Intertextual Reading of Lamentations and Psalms of Lament." In *Bakhtin and Genre Theory in Biblical Studies*, edited by Roland Boer, 69–90. Semeia Studies 63. Atlanta: SBL, 2007.

Mann, Steven T. "Performative Prayers of a Prophet: Investigating the Payers of Jonah as Speech Acts." *CBQ* 79 (2017) 20–40.

———. *Run, David, Run!: An Investigation of the Theological Speech Acts of David's Departure and Return (2 Samuel 14–20)*. Siphrut 10. Winona Lake, IN: Eisenbrauns, 2011.

Mann, Thomas. *Joseph and His Brothers*. New York: Knopf, 1948.

Manniche, Lise. *Sacred Luxuries: Fragrance, Aromatherapy and Cosmetics in Ancient Egypt*. Ithaca: Cornell University Press, 1999.

Marquis, Liane M. "The Composition of Numbers 32: A New Proposal." *VT* 63 (2013) 408–32.

Martens, Elmer A. "Narrative Parallelism and Message in Jeremiah 34–38." In *Early Jewish and Christian Exegesis: Studies in Memory of William Hugh Brownlee*, edited by Craig A. Evans and William F. Stinespring, 33–49. Homage Series 10. Atlanta: Scholars, 1987.

Martin, Lee Roy. "Delighting in the Torah: The Affective Dimension of Psalm 1." *OTE* 23 (2010) 708–27.

Martin, Michael W. "Betrothal Journey Narratives." *CBQ* 70 (2008) 505–23.

Martin, Troy W. "Concluding the Book of Job and YHWH: Reading Job from the End to the Beginning." *JBL* 137 (2018) 299–318.

Marx, Alfred. *The Theology of the Sacrifice According to Leviticus 1–7*. VTSup 93. Leiden: Brill, 2003.

Masenya, Madipoane J. "Parental Instruction in Differing Contexts: Using Hermeneutical Phenomenology to Understand Selected Biblical and African Proverbs." *OTE* 23 (2010) 728–51.

Mastnjak, Nathan. "Jeremiah as Collection: Scrolls, Sheets, and the Problem of Textual Arrangement." *CBQ* 80 (2018) 25–44.

Matter, E. Ann. *The Voice of My Beloved: The Song of Songs in Western Medieval Christianity*. Philadelphia: University of Pennsylvania Press, 1990.

Matthews, Victor H., Bernard Levinson, and Tikva Frymer-Kensky, eds. *Gender and Law in the Hebrew Bible and Ancient Near East*. JSOTSup 262. Sheffield: Academic, 1998.

Matties, Gordon H. *Ezekiel 18 and the Rhetoric of Moral Discourse*. SBLDS 126. Atlanta: Scholars, 1990.

May, Gerhard. *Creatio ex Nihilo: The Doctrine of 'Creation out of Nothing' in Early Christian Thought*. Translated by A. S. Worrall. Edinburgh: T. & T. Clark, 1994.

Mayfield, Tyler D. *Literary Structure and Setting in Ezekiel*. FAT 2/43. Tübingen: Mohr Siebeck, 2010.

———. "Literary Structure in Ezekiel 25: Addressee, Formulas, and Genres." In *Partners with God: Theological and Critical Readings of the Bible in Honor of Marvin A. Sweeney*, edited by Shelley L. Birdsong and Serge Frolov, 225–36. Claremont Studies in Hebrew Bible & Septuagint 2. Claremont: Claremont Press, 2017.

Mays, James Luther. "The David of the Psalms." *Int* 40 (1986) 143–55.

———. "'In a Vision': The Portrayal of the Messiah in the Psalms." *Ex Auditu* 7 (1993) 1–8.

———. *The Lord Reigns: A Theological Handbook to the Psalms*. Louisville: Westminster John Knox, 1994.

———. "The Place of the Torah-Psalms in the Psalter." *JBL* 106 (1987) 3–12.

Mazar, Benjamin. "The Military Elite of King David." *VT* 13 (1963) 310–20.

———. "The Cities of the Priests and Levites." *VTSup* 7 (1960) 193–205.

McCann, J. Clinton, ed. *The Shape and Shaping of the Psalter*. JSOTSup 159. Sheffield: JSOT Press, 1993.

McCarter, P. Kyle. "The Apology of David." *JBL* 99 (1980) 489–504.

McCarthy, Dennis J. *Treaty and Covenant: A Study in Form in the Ancient Oriental Documents and in the Old Testament*. 2nd ed. AnBib 21. Rome: Pontifical Institute, 1978.

McConville, J. Gordon. *Law and Theology in Deuteronomy*. JSOTSup 33. Sheffield: JSOT Press, 1984.

McCreesh, Thomas Patrick. *Biblical Sound and Sense: Poetic Sound Patterns in Proverbs 10–29*. JSOTSup 128. Sheffield: JSOT, 1991.

———. "Wisdom as Wife: Proverbs 31:10–31." *RB* 92 (1985) 25–46.

McKane, William. "Jeremiah and the Rechabites." *ZAW* 100 (1988) 106–23.

McKeating, Henry. "The Development of the Law on Homicide in Ancient Israel." *VT* 26 (1975) 46–68.

McShane, Marjorie J. *A Theory of Ellipsis*. Oxford: Oxford University Press, 2005.

Meier, Samuel A. *Speaking of Speaking: Marking Direct Discourse in the Hebrew Bible*. VTSup 46. Leiden: Brill, 1992.

Meinhold, Arndt. "Die Gattung der Josephgeschichte und des Estherbuches: Diasparonelle I." *ZAW* 87 (1975) 306–24.

Meinhold, Arndt. "Die Gattung der Josephgeschichte und des Estherbuches: Diasporanovelle II." *ZAW* 88 (1976) 72–93.

Melugin, Roy F. *The Formation of Isaiah 40–55*. New York: de Gruyter, 1976.

Mendelsohn, Isaac. *Slavery in the Ancient Near East: A Comparative Study of Slavery in Babylonia, Assyria, Syria, and Palestine from the Middle of the Third Millennium to the End of the First Millennium*. Westport: Greenwood, 1978.

Mendenhall, George. "Covenant Forms in Israelite Tradition." *BA* 17 (1954) 50–76.

Messmer, Andrew. "A Possible Chiastic Center for Primary History (Genesis—2 Kings)." *VT* 69 (2019) 232–40.

Mettinger, T. N. D. *A Farewell to the Servant Songs: A Critical Examination of an Exegetical Axiom*. Lund: Gleerup, 1983.

———. *King and Messiah*. ConBOT 8. Lund: Gleerup, 1976.

———. *Solomonic State Officials: A Study of the Civil Government of the Israelite Monarchy*. ConBOT 5. Lund: Gleerup, 1971.

Meyer, Esias. "Ritual Innovation in Numbers 18?" *Scriptura* 116 (2017) 133–47.

Meyers, Carol A. "Gender Imagery in the Song of Songs." *HAR* 10 (1987) 209–23.

Meyers, Eric M. "The Theological Implications of an Ancient Jewish Burial Custom." *JQR* 62 (1971) 95–119.

Middleton, J. Richard. *The Liberating Image: The Imago Dei in Genesis 1*. Grand Rapids: Brazos Press, 2005.

Mieder, Wolfgang. *The Prentice-Hall Encyclopedia of World Proverbs*. New York: Prentice-Hall, 1986.

———. *Wise Words: Essays on the Proverb*. New York: Garland, 1994.

Milgrom, Jacob. "The Chieftains' Gifts: Numbers, Chapter 7." *HAR* 9 (1985) 221–25.

———. "Does H Advocate the Centralization of Worship?" *JSOT* 25 (2000) 59–76.

———. "Ethics and Ritual: The Foundations of the Biblical Dietary Laws." In *Religion and Law: Biblical-Judaic and Islamic Perspectives*, edited by Edwin Firmage, Bernard Weiss and John Welch, 159–91. Winona Lake, IN: Eisenbrauns, 1990.

———. *Leviticus: A Book of Ritual and Ethics*. Continental Commentaries. Minneapolis: Fortress, 2004.

———. *Numbers*. JPS Torah Commentary Philadelphia: Jewish Publication Society, 1990.

———. "Priestly Terminology and the Political and Social Structure of Pre-Monarchic Israel." *JQR* 69 (1978) 65–81.

Millar, Suzanna R. *Genre and Openness in Proverbs 10:1–22:16*. AIL 39. Atlanta: SBL, 2020.

———. "The Path Metaphor and the Construction of a Schicksalwirkende Tatsphäre in Proverbs 10:1–22:16." *VT* 69 (2019) 95–108.

Millard, Alan R. "In Praise of Ancient Scribes." *BA* 45 (1982) 143–53.

Millard, Matthias. *Die Komposition des Psalters: Ein formgeschichtlicher Ansatz*. FAT 9. Tübingen: Mohr Siebeck, 1994.

Miller, Charles William. "Reading Voices: Personification, Diaologism, and the Reader of Lamentations 1." *BibInt* 9 (2001) 393–408.

Miller, Cynthia L. "A Linguistic Approach to Ellipsis in Biblical Poetry: Or, What to Do When Exegesis of What Is There Depends on What Isn't." *BBR* 13 (2003) 251–70.

———. "The Pragmatics of *waw* as a Discourse Marker in Biblical Hebrew Dialogue." *ZAH* 12 (1999) 165–91.

———. *The Representation of Speech in Biblical Hebrew Narrative: A Linguistic Analysis*. HSM 55. Atlanta: Scholars, 2003.

———. "Vocative Syntax in Biblical Hebrew Prose and Poetry: A Preliminary Analysis." *JSS* 55 (2010) 347–64.

Miller, J. Maxwell. "The Israelite Journey through (around) Moab and Moabite Toponymy." *JBL* 108 (1989) 577–99.

Miller, J. Maxwell, and John H. Hayes. *A History of Ancient Israel and Judah*. Philadelphia: Westminster, 1986.

Miller, James E. "Structure and Meaning of the Animal Discourse in the Theophany of Job (38:39—39:30)." *ZAW* 103 (1991) 418–21.

Miller, Patrick D., Jr. "The End of the Psalter." *JSOT* 80 (1998) 103–10.

———."The Place of the *Decalogue* in the Old Testament and its Law." *Int* 43 (1989) 229–42.

———. *They Cried to the Lord: The Form and Theology of Biblical Prayer*. Minneapolis: Fortress, 1995.

———. *Sin and Judgment in the Prophets*. SBLMS 27. Chico, CA: Scholars, 1982.

Mindiola, Cristian Daniel Cardozo. "Reception History of Leviticus 11: Dietary Laws in Early Christianity." *DavarLogos* 18 (2019) 39–60.
Mitchell, Christopher Wright. *The Meaning of BRK "To Bless" in the Old Testament*. SBLDS 95. Atlanta: Scholars, 1987.
Mitchell, David C. "'God Will Redeem My Soul from Sheol': The Psalms of the Sons of Korah." *JSOT* 30 (2006) 365–84.
———. *The Message of the Psalter: An Eschatological Programme in the Book of Psalms*. JSOTSup 252. Sheffield: Academic, 1996.
Mitchell, Matthew W. "Genre Disputes and Communal Accusatory Laments: Reflections on the Genre of Psalm LXXXIX." *VT* 55 (2005) 511–27.
Mobley, Gregory. *The Empty Men: The Heroic Tradition of Ancient Israel*. ABRL. New York: Doubleday, 2005.
Molnar-Hidvegi, Nora. "The Paths Not Taken: Novel Insights on the Function and the Use of *Mashal* in the Old Testament." *BN* 169 (2016) 83–109.
Moore, Megan Bishop, and Brad E. Kelle. *Biblical History and Israel's Past: The Changing Study of the Bible and History*. Grand Rapids: Eerdmans, 2011.
Moore, Michael S. *The Balaam Traditions: Their Character and Development*. SBLDS 113. Atlanta: Scholars, 1990.
———. "Jehu's Coronation and Purge of Israel." *VT* 53 (2003) 97–114.
Moore, Ricky Dale. *God Saves: Lessons from the Elisha Stories*. JSOTSup 95. Sheffield: Academic, 1990.
Morgenstern, Julian. "The Ark, the Ephod, and the 'Tent of Meeting.'" *HUCA* 17 (1942–43) 153–265.
———. *The Book of the Covenant*. 1928. Reprint, Eugene: Wipf & Stock, 2007.
———. "Isaiah 63:7–14." *HUCA* 23 (1950/51) 187–203.
———. "The Oldest Document of the Hexateuch." *HUCA* 4 (1927) 1–138.
Moriarty, Michael G. *The Perfect Ten: The Blessings of Following God's Commandments in a Postmodern World*. Grand Rapids: Zondervan, 1999.
Morrow, William S. "Consolation, Rejection and Repentance in Job 42:6." *JBL* 105 (1986) 211–25.
Moskala, Jiri. "Categorization and Evaluation of Different Kinds of Interpretation of the Laws of Clean and Unclean Animlas in Leviticus 11." *BR* 66 (2001) 5–41.
Moss, Alan. "Wisdom as Parental Teaching in Proverbs 1–9." *HeyJ* 38 (1997) 426–39.
Moscicke, Hans M. *Goat for YHWH, Goat for Azazel: The Impact of Yom Kippur on the Gospels*. Lanham, MD: Lexington, 2021.
Mowinckel, Sigmund. *Psalm Studies*. Vol. 1. Translated by Mark E. Biddle. History of Biblical Studies 2. Atlanta: SBL, 2014.
———. *Psalm Studies*. Vol. 2. Translated by Mark E. Biddle. History of Biblical Studies 3. Atlanta: SBL, 2014.
———. *Psalmenstudien II: Das Thronbesteigungsfest JHWH und der Ursprung der Eschatologie*. Kristiana: Dybwad, 1922.
———. *The Psalms in Israel's Worship I*. Translated by D. R. Ap-Thomas. Nashville: Abingdon, 1967.
———. *The Psalms in Israel's Worship II*. Translated by D. R. Ap-Thomas. Nashville: Abingdon, 1967.
———. "Zum Psalm des Habakuk." *TZ* 9 (1953) 1–21.
———. *Zur Composition des Buches Jeremia*. Kristiania: Dybwad, 1914.
Mueller, E. Aydeet. *The Micah Story: A Morality Tale in the Book of Judges*. Studies in Biblical Literature 34. New York: Lang, 2001.

Muenchow, Charles. "Dust and Dirt in Job 42:6." *JBL* 108 (1989) 597–611.

Muilenberg, James. "Form Criticism and Beyond." *JBL* 88 (1969) 1–18.

Mullen, Theodore, Jr. "Judges 1:1–36: The Deuteronomistic Reintroduction of the Book of Judges." *HTR* 77 (1984) 33–54.

———. "The 'Minor Judges': Some Literary and Historical Considerations." *CBQ* 44 (1982) 185–201.

Munro, Jill M. *Spikenard and Saffron: A Study in the Poetic Language of the Song of Songs*. JSOTSup 203. Sheffield: Sheffield Academic, 1995.

Murphy, Roland E. *Ecclesiastes*. WBC 23A. Dallas: Word, 1992.

———. *The Song of Songs: A Commentary on the Book of Canticles or the Song of Songs*. Hermeneia. Minneapolis: Fortress, 1990.

———. *The Tree of Life: An Exploration of Biblical Wisdom Literature*. Grand Rapids: Eerdmans, 1990.

———. *Wisdom Literature: Job, Proverbs, Ruth, Canticles, Ecclesiastes, and Esther*. FOTL 13. Grand Rapids: Eerdmans, 1981.

Murray, Donald F. "The Rhetoric of Disputation: Re-examination of a Prophetic Genre." *JSOT* 38 (1987) 95–121.

Na'aman, Nadav. *Borders and Districts in Biblical Historiography*. Jerusalem: Simor, 1986.

———. "David's Sojourn in Keilah in Light of the Amarna Letters." *VT* 60 (2010) 87–97.

———. "Death Formulae and the Burial Place of the Kings of the House of David." *Bib* 85 (2004) 245–54.

———. "The Historical Background to the Conquest of Samaria (720 BC)." *Bib* 71 (1990) 206–25.

———. "The Inheritance of the Sons of Simeon." *ZDPV* 96 (1980) 136–52.

———. "The Kingdom of Judah under Josiah." *TA* 18 (1981) 3–71.

———. "Notes on the Temple 'Restorations' of Jehoash and Josiah." *VT* 63 (2013) 640–51.

Nam, Duck-Woo. *Talking about God: Job 42.7–9 and the Nature of God in the Book of Job*. StBibLit 49. New York: Lang, 2003.

Namiki, Koichi. "Reconsideration of the Twelve-Tribe System of Israel." *AJBI* 2 (1976) 29–60.

Nasuti, Harry P. *Defining the Sacred Songs: Genre, Tradition and the Post-Critical Interpretation of the Psalms*. JSOTSup 218. Sheffield: Sheffield Academic, 1999.

———. *Tradition History and the Psalms of Asaph*. Atlanta: SBL, 1988.

Neff, Robert W. *The Announcement in Old Testament Birth Stories*. New Haven: Yale University Press, 1969.

Nehrbass, Daniel. *Praying Curses: The Therapeutic and Preaching Value of the Imprecatory Psalms*. Eugene, OR: Pickwick Publications, 2013.

Nel, Philip Johannes. *The Structure and Ethos of the Wisdom Admonitions in Proverbs*. BZAW 158. Berlin: de Gruyter, 1982.

Nelson, Richard D. "Ideology, Geography, and the List of Minor Judges." *JSOT* 31 (2007) 347–64.

Neufeld, Edward. *Ancient Hebrew Marriage Laws: With Special References to General Semitic Laws and Customs*. London: Green, 1944.

———. "The Prohibition against Loans at Interest in Ancient Hebrew Laws." *HUCA* 26 (1955) 355–412.

Neville, Richard W. "A Reassessment of the Radical Nature of Job's Ethic in Job xxxi 13–15." *VT* 53 (2003) 181–200.

Newell, Lynne. "Job: Repentant or Rebellious?" *WTJ* 46 (1984) 298–316.

Newsome, Carol A. "A Maker of Metaphors—Ezekiel's Oracles against Tyre." *Int* 38 (1984) 151–64.

Nguyen, Kim Lan. *Chorus in the Dark: The Voices of the Book of Lamentations.* Hebrew Bible Monographs 54. Sheffield: Sheffield Phoenix, 2013.

Ngwa, Kenneth N. *The Dynamics of Job's Intercession.* AnBib 161. Rome: Pontifical Biblical Institute, 2006.

Nicholson, Ernest W. *God and His People: Covenant and Theology in the Old Testament.* Oxford: Clarendon, 1986.

———. *Preaching to the Exiles: A Study of the Prose Tradition in the Book of Jeremiah.* Oxford: Blackwell, 1970.

Niditch, Susan. "'Better X Than Y': Context and Meaning in Proverbs, Qohelet, and Midrashic Collections." In *Reading Proverbs Intertextually*, edited by Katherine J. Dell and Will Kynes, 191–202. LHBOTS 629. London: T. & T. Clark, 2019.

———. "Ezekiel 40–48 in a Visionary Context." *CBQ* 48 (1986) 208–34.

———. *Folklore and the Hebrew Bible.* Guides to Biblical Scholarship: Old Testament. 1993. Reprint, Eugene, OR: Wipf & Stock, 2004.

———. *Oral World and Written Word: Ancient Israelite Literature.* LAI. Louisville: Westminster John Knox, 1996.

———. *The Symbolic Vision in Biblical Tradition.* HSM 30. Chico, CA: Scholars, 1983.

———. *War in the Hebrew Bible: A Study in the Ethics of Violence.* Oxford: Oxford University Press, 1993.

Niditch, Susan, and Robert Doran. "Success Story of the Wise Courtier: A Formal Approach." *JBL* 96 (1977) 179–93.

Niehaus, J. J. *God at Sinai: Covenant and Theophany in the Bible and Ancient Near East.* Studies in Old Testament Biblical Theology. Grand Rapids: Zondervan, 1995.

Niehoff. Maren R. "*Creatio ex nihilo* Theology in Genesis Rabbah in Light of Christian Exegesis." *HTR* 99 (2006) 37–64.

Nielsen, Kirsten. *YHWH as Prosecutor and Judge.* JSOTSup 9. Sheffield: JSOT Press, 1978.

Nihan, Christophe. "Rewriting Kingship in Samuel: 1 Samuel 8 and 12 and the Law of the King." *Hebrew Bible and Ancient Israel* 2 (2013) 315–50.

Noegel, Scott, and Gary Rendsburg. *Solomon's Vineyard: Literary and Linguistic Studies in the Song of Songs.* AIL 1. Atlanta: SBL, 2009.

Nogalski, James. "The Day(s) of YHWH in the Book of the Twelve." In *Thematic Threads in the Book of the Twelve*, edited by Paul L. Reddit and Aaron Schart, 192–213. BZAW 325. Berlin: de Gruyter, 2003.

North, C. R. *The Suffering Servant in Deutero-Isaiah: An Historical and Critical Study.* London: Oxford University Press, 1956.

Notarius, Tania. "Poetic Discourse and the Problem of Verbal Tenses in the Oracles of Balaam." *HS* 49 (2008) 55–86.

Noth, Martin. *The Chronicler's History.* Translated by H. G. M. Williamson. 1967. Reprint, JSOTSup 50. Sheffield: Sheffield Academic, 1987.

———. *The Deuteronomistic History.* Sheffield: JSOT, 1991.

———. *The Laws in the Pentateuch and Other Studies.* Translated by D. R. Ap-Thomas. Edinburgh: Oliver & Boyd, 1967.

———. *Das System der Zwölf Stämme Israels*. BWANT 4/1. Darmstadt: Wissenschaftliche Buchgesellschaft, 1966.

Notley, R. Steven and Zeev Safrai. *Onomasticon: The Place Names of Divine Scripture*. Jewish and Christian Perspective Series 9. Leiden: Brill, 2004.

Novak, David. *Jewish Justice: The Contested Limits of Nature, Law, and Covenant*. Waco: Baylor University Press, 2017.

———. *Natural Law in Judaism*. Cambridge: Cambridge University Press, 2008.

Oblath, Michael D. "Job's Advocate: A Tempting Suggestion." *BBR* 9 (1999) 189–201.

O'Connor, Kathleen M. *The Confessions of Jeremiah: Their Interpretation and Role in Jeremiah 1–25*. SBLDS 94. Atlanta: Scholars, 1987.

———. *Lamentations and the Tears of the World*. Maryknoll, NY: Orbis, 2000.

O'Connor, Michael Patrick. "The Ammonite Onomasticon: Semantic Problems." *AUSS* 25 (1987) 51–64.

———. *Hebrew Verse Structure*. Winona Lake, IN: Eisenbrauns, 1980.

Oderberg, David. *Real Essentialism*. London: Routledge, 2008.

Oeming, Manfred. *Das Wahre Israel: Die "genealogische Vorhalle" 1 Chronik 1–9*. BWANT 128. Stuttgart: Kohlhammer, 1990.

Ogden, Graham S. "Moses and Cyrus." *VT* 28 (1978) 195–203.

———. "Prophetic Oracles Against Foreign Nations and Psalms of Communal Lament: The Relationship of Psalm 137 to Jeremiah 49:7–22 and Obadiah." *JSOT* 24 (1982) 89–97.

———. "Qoheleth's Use of the 'Nothing Is Better'-Form." *JBL* 98 (1979) 339–50.

Okyere, Kojo. "The Rhetoric of Work in Proverbs 24:30–34." *Theoforum* 44 (2013) 157–71.

Ollenburger, Ben C. *Zion: The City of the Great King*. JSOTSup 41. Sheffield: Sheffield Academic, 1987.

Olley, John W. "YHWH and His Zealous Prophet: The Presentation of Elijah in 1 and 2 Kings." *JSOT* 80 (1998) 25–51.

Olojede, Funlola. "Sapiential Elements in the Joseph and Daniel Narratives vis-à-vis Woman Wisdom—Conjuctions and Disjunctions." *OTE* 25/2 (2012) 351–68.

Olyan, Saul M. *Biblical Mourning: Ritual and Social Dimensions*. Oxford: Oxford University Press, 2004.

———. "What Do Shaving Rites Accomplish and What Do They Signal in Biblical Ritual Contexts?" *JBL* 117 (1994) 611–22.

Olyan, Saul M., and Gary A. Anderson, eds. *Priesthood and Cult in Ancient Israel*. JSOTSup 125. Sheffield: Academic, 2009.

Orian, Matan. "Numbers 20:14–21 as a Reply to Deuteronomy 23:4–9." *VT* 69 (2019) 109–116.

Orlinsky, H. M. *The So-Called "Suffering Servant" in Isaiah 53*. VTSup 14. Leiden: Brill, 1977.

Otto, Eckart. *Deuteronomium 1,1—4,43*. Vol. 1. HThKAT Freiburg: Herder, 2012.

———. *Das Mazzotfest in Gilgal*. BWANT 107. Stuttgart: Kohlhammer, 1975.

Pardee, Dennis. "Acrostics and Parallelism: The Parallelistic Structure of Psalm 111." *Maarav* 8 (1992) 117–38.

Park, Sejin. *Pentecost and Sinai: The Festival of Weeks as a Celebration of the Sinai Event*. LHBOTS 342. New York: T. & T. Clark, 2008.

Parker, Simon B. "Official Attitudes toward Prophecy at Mari and in Israel." *VT* 43 (1993) 50–68.

———. *The Pre-Biblical Narrative Tradition: Essays on the Ugaritic Poems Keret and Aqhat*. Resources for Biblical Study 24. Atlanta: Scholars, 1989.

———, ed. *Ugaritic Narrative Poetry*. WAW 9. Atlanta: Scholars, 1997.

———. "The Vow in Ugaritic and Israelite Narrative Literature." *UF* 11 (1979) 693–700.

Parry, Robin A. *Lamentations*. Two Horizons Old Testament Commentary. Grand Rapids: Eerdmans, 2010.

Partlow, Jonathan A. "Amos's Use of Rhetorical Entrapment as a Means for Climactic Preaching in Amos 1:3—2:16." *ResQ* 49 (2007) 23–32.

Patai, Raphael. "The 'Control of Rain' in Ancient Palestine." *HUCA* 14 (1939) 251–86.

Paterson, Robert M. "Repentance or Judgment: The Construction and Purpose of Jeremiah 2–6." *Expository Times* 7 (1985) 199–203.

Patrick, Dale. *Old Testament Law*. 1985. Reprint, Eugene, OR: Wipf & Stock, 2011.

Patterson, Richard D. "Joseph in Pharaoh's Court." *BSac* 164 (2007) 148–64.

———. "Singing the New Song: An Examination of Psalms 93, 96, 98, and 149." *BSac* 164 (2007) 416–34.

Paul, Shalom M. *Amos: A Commentary on the Book of Amos*. Hermeneia. Minneapolis: Fortress, 1991.

———. *Studies in the Book of the Covenant in the Light of Cuneiform and Biblical Law*. VTSup 18. Leiden: Brill, 1970.

Pehike, Helmuth. "Observations on the Historical Reliablilty of the Old Testament." *Southwestern Journal Of Theology* 56 (2013) 65–85.

Pelham, Abigail. "Job's Crisis of Language: Power and Powerlessness in Job's Oaths." *JSOT* 36 (2012) 333–54.

Pelt, Miles V. Van. "Exegetical Evidence for Non-Solar and Non-Sequential Interpretations of the Genesis 1 and 2 Creation Days." In *The Genre of Biblical Commentary: Essays in Honor of John E. Hartley on the Occasion of His 75th Birthday*, edited by Timothy D. Finlay & William Yarchin, 199–216. Eugene: Pickwick, 2015.

Pemberton, Glen D. "The Rhetoric of the Father in Proverbs 1–9." *JSOT* 30 (2005) 63–82.

Perdue, Leo G. "The Riddles of Psalm 49." *JBL* 93 (1974) 533–42.

———. *Wisdom and Cult: A Critical Analysis of the Views of Cult in the Wisdom Literatures of Israel and the Ancient Near East*. SBLDS 30. Missoula: Scholars, 1977.

———. *Wisdom in Revolt: Metaphorical Theology in the Book of Job*. JSOTSup 112. BLS 29. Sheffield: Almond, 1991.

Perry, T. A. *The Honeymoon Is Over—Jonah's Argument with God*. Grand Rapids: Baker Academic, 2006.

Person, Raymond F. *The Kings–Isaiah and Kings–Jeremiah Recensions*. BZAW 252. Berlin: de Gruyter, 2001.

Petersen, David L. *The Prophetic Literature: An Introduction*. Philadelphia: Westminster John Knox, 2002.

———. *The Roles of Israel's Prophets*. JSOTSup 17. Sheffield: JSOT, 1981.

Pietersma, Albert. "David in the Greek Psalms." *VT* 30 (1980) 213–26.

Pfeiffer, Egon. "Die Disputationsworte im Buche Maleachi." *EvT* 19 (1959) 546–88.

Pham, Xuan Huong Thi. *Mourning in the Ancient Near East and the Hebrew Bible*. LHBOTS 302. Sheffield: Sheffield Academic, 2000.

Philips, Anthony. *Ancient Israel's Criminal Law: A New Approach to the Decalogue*. Oxford: Basil Blackwell, 1970.

Pikor, Wojciech. "A Prophet as a Witness to His Call: A Narrative Key to the Reading of Prophetic Call Narratives." *ScrTh* 52 (2020) 73–95.

Pinker, Aron. "Bildad's Contribution to the Debate—A New Interpretation of Job 8:17–19." *VT* 66 (2016) 406–32.

———. "The Fate of Undesirables (Job 24:5–12)." *OTE* 27 (2014) 960–91.

———. "A Goat to Go to Azazel." *JHebS* 7 (2007) 1–25.

———. "Job's Enemies in 30, 17–18." *SJOT* 31 (2017) 161–84.

Pirson, Ron. *The Lord of the Dreams: A Semantic and Literary Analysis of Genesis 37–50*. JSOTSup 355. Sheffield: Sheffield Academic, 2002.

Pohl, William C. IV. "Arresting God's Attention: The Rhetorical Intent and Strategies of Job 3." *BBR* 28 (2018) 1–19.

Polan, Gregory J. *In the Ways of Justice toward Salvation: A Rhetorical Analysis of Isaiah 55–56*. American University Studies. Series VII, Theology and Religion 13. New York: Lang, 1986.

Polzin, Robert. *David and the Deuteronomist: A Literary Study of the Deuteronomistic History. Part Three: 2 Samuel*. Bloomington: Indiana University Press, 1993.

———. "The Framework of the Book of Job." *Int* 28 (1974) 182–200.

———. *Samuel and the Deuteronomist: A Literary History of the Deuteronomistic History Part Two*, 205–15. Bloomington: Indiana University Press, 1993.

Pomykala, Kenneth E. *The Davidic Dynasty Tradition in Early Judaism: Its History and Significance for Messianism*. SBL Early Judaism and Its Literature 7. Atlanta: Scholars, 1995.

Pope, Marvin H. "A Mare in Pharaoh's Chariotry." *BASOR* 200 (1970) 56–61.

———. *Song of Songs: A New Translation with Introduction and Commentary*. Anchor Bible 7C. Garden City, NY: Doubleday, 1977.

Porter, Stanley E. "The Message of the Book of Job: Job 42:7b as Key to Interpretation?" *EvQ* 63 (1991) 291–304.

Porter, Stanley E., ed. *The Messiah in the Old and New Testaments*. Grand Rapids: Eerdmans, 2007.

Potter, H. D. "The New Covenant in Jeremiah XXXI 31–34." *VT* 33 (1983) 347–57.

Pracht, Erich B. "The Tragic Death of John the Baptist: Reading Mark 6:17–29 with Other Banquet Travesties." *CBQ* 83 (2021) 241–56.

Pressler, Carolyn. *The View of Women Found in the Deuteronomic Family Laws*. BZAW 216. Berlin: de Gruyter, 1993.

Prewitt, Terry J. "Kinship Structures and the Genesis Genealogies." *JNES* 40 (1981) 87–98.

Prideaux, Andrew. "The YHWH Speeches in the Book of Job: Sublime Irrelevance or Right to the Point?" *RTR* 69 (2010) 75–87.

Propp, V. *The Morphology of the Folktale*. Translated by Laurence Scott. 2nd ed. Publications of the American Folklore Society: Bibliographical and Special Series 9. Austin: University of Texas Press, 1968.

Propp, William H. "The Bloody Bridegroom (Exodus 4:24–26)." *VT* 43 (1993) 495–518.

Prosic, Tamara. *The Development and Symbolism of Passover Until AD 70*. New York: T. & T. Clark, 2004.

Provan, Iain, V. Philips Long, and Tremper Longman III. *A Biblical History of Israel*. Louisville: Westminster John Knox, 2015.

Provan, Iain W. *Hezekiah and the Book of Kings*. BZAW 172. Berlin: de Gruyter, 1988.

Punt, Jeremy. "The Aqedah in the New Testament: Sacrifice, Violence and Human Dignity." *Scriptura* 102 (2009) 430–45.

Pury, Albert de. *Promesse divine et légende cultuelle dans le cycle de Jacob: Genèse 28 et les traditions patriarcales*. 2 vols. EBib. Paris: Gabalda, 1975.

Quick, Laura. "Averting Curses in the Law of War (Deuteronomy 20)." *ZAW* 132 (2020) 209–23.

Quiroga, Raul A. "El conjuro, arma no convencional de Balaam contra Israel: Numeros 23:7–10." *Theologika* 27 (2012) 192–241.

Raabe, Paul R. *Psalm Structures: A Study of Psalms with Refrains*. JSOTSup 104. Sheffield: JSOT Press, 1990.

Rabin, Chaim. "Song of Songs and Tamil Poetry." *Studies in Religion* 3 (1973/74) 205–19.

Rad, Gerhard von. *Deuteronomium-Studien*. FRLANT 58. Göttingen: Vandenhoeck & Ruprecht, 1947.

———. "Du texte au sermon: Nombres 22:36,41; 23;7–12; 24:1–7." *ETR* 46 (1971) 217–30.

———. "Erwägungen zu den Königpsalmen." *ZAW* 58 (1940/41) 216–22.

———. *From Genesis to Chronicles*. Translated by E. W. Trueman Dicken. Edited by K. C. Hanson. Fortress Classics in Biblical Studies. Minneapolis: Fortress, 2005.

———. *Genesis*, translated by John H. Marks. OTL. Philadephia: Westminster, 1961.

———. *Holy War in Ancient Israel*. Translated and edited by Marva J. Dawn. Grand Rapids: Eerdmans, 1991.

———. "The Joseph Narrative and Ancient Wisdom." In *Studies in Ancient Israelite Wisdom*, edited by James L. Crenshaw, 439–447. New York: KTAV, 1976.

———. *Old Testament Theology, Volume II*. OTL. Philadelphia: Westminster John Knox, 2001.

———. *Die Priesterschrift im Hexateuch*. BWANT 13. Stuttgart: W. Kohlhammer, 1934.

———. *The Problem of the Hexateuch and Other Essays*. Edinburgh: Oliver & Boyd, 1966.

———. *Studies in Deuteronomy*. Translated by David Stalker. SBT 1/9. London: SCM, 1953.

———. *Wisdom in Israel*. Translated by James D. Martin. Nashville: Abingdon, 1972.

Rainey, Anson F., and R. Steven Notley. *Carta's New Century Handbook and Atlas of the Bible*. Jerusalem: Carta, 2007.

Raitt, Thomas M. "The Prophetic Summons to Repentance." *ZAW* 83 (1971) 30–49.

Rashkow, Ilona. "The Scapegoat in the Bible and Ancient Near East." *JBQ* 51 (2023) 85–90.

Rasmussen, Josh. *Who Are You, Really?: A Philosopher's Inquiry into the Nature and Origin of Persons*. Westmont: IVP Academic, 2023.

Ratheiser, Gershom M. H. *Mitzvoth Ethics and the Jewish Bible*. London: T. & T. Clark, 2007.

Redford, Donald B. *Egypt, Canaan, and Israel in Ancient Times*. Princeton: Princeton University Press, 1992.

Redditt, Paul L. "The Census List in Ezra 2 and Nehemiah 7: A Suggestion." In *New Perspectives on Ezra-Nehemiah: History and Historiography, Text, Literature and Interpretation*, edited by I. Kalimi, pages 223–40. Winona Lake: Eisenbrauns, 2012.

———. "Israel's Shepherds: Hope and Pessimism in Zechariah 9–14." *CBQ* 55 (1993) 631–42.

———. "Reading the Speech Cycles in the Book of Job." *HAR* 14 (1994) 205–14.

Redford, Donald B. *A Study of the Biblical Story of Joseph (Genesis 37–50)*. VTSup 20. Leiden: Brill, 1970.

Rendsburg, Gary A. "The Internal Consistency and Historical Reliability of the Biblical Genealogies." *VT* 40 (1990) 185–206.

Rendtorff, Rolf. *Canon and Theology: Overtures to an Old Testament Theology*, translated by Margaret Kohl. Minneapolis: Fortress, 1993.

———. *The Canonical Hebrew Bible: A Theology of the Old Testament*. Leiden: Brill, 2006.

———. *The Covenant Formula: An Exegetical and Theological Investigation*, translated by Margaret Kohl. Edinburgh: T. & T. Clark, 1998.

———. *Die Gesetze in der Priesterschrift: eine gattungsgeschichtliche Untersuchung*. FRLANT 44. Gottingen: Vandenhoeck & Ruprecht, 1953.

———. "Leviticus 16 als Mitte der Tora." *BibInt* 11 (2003) 252–58.

———. "The Psalms of David: David in the Psalms." In *The Book of Psalms: Composition and Reception*, edited by Peter W. Flint and Patrick D. Miller. VTSup 99. Leiden: Brill, 2005.

Renkema, Johan. "The Literary Structure of Lamentations (I–IV)." In *The Structural Analysis of Biblical and Canaanite Poetry*, edited by Willem van der Meer, 294–396. JSOTSup 74. Sheffield: Sheffield Academic, 1988.

———. "The Meaning of the Parallel Acrostics in Lamentations." *VT* 45 (1995) 379–83.

Reno, R. R. *Genesis*. Brazos Theological Commentary on the Bible. Grand Rapids: Brazos, 2010.

Renz, Thomas. "Proclaiming the Future: History and Theology in Prophecies against Tyre." *TynBul* 51 (2000) 17–58.

Reventlow, Henning. "Sein Blut komme über sein Haupt." *VT* 10 (1960) 311–27.

Reynolds, Edwin E. "The Feast of Tabernacles and the Book of Revelation." *AUSS* 38 (2000) 245–68.

Rhyder, Julia. "Gates and Entrances in Ezekiel 40–48: The Social Utopia of the Temple Vision." *VT* 73 (2023) 752–65.

Richter, Heinz. "Die Naturweisheit des Alten Testaments in Buche Hiob." *ZAW* 70 (1958) 1–20.

Richter, Wolfgang. *Recht und Ethos: Versuch einer Ortung des weisheitlichen Mahnspruches*. SANT 15. Munich: Kosel, 1991.

Rickett, Dan. "Rethinking the Place and Purpose of Genesis 13." *JSOT* 36 (2011) 31–53.

Rindge, Matthew S. "Mortality and Enjoyment: The Interplay of Death and Possessions in Qoheleth." *CBQ* 73 (2011) 265–80.

Ritzema, John. "After Zedekiah: Who and What Was Gedaliah ben Ahikam." *JSOT* 42 (2017) 73–91.

Robert, André. "Les Appendices du Cantiques des Cantiques." *RB* 55 (1948) 161–83.

Roberts, J. J. M. "The Hand of YHWH." *VT* 21 (1971) 244–51.

Robertson, O. Palmer. "The Alphabetic Acrostic in Book I of the Psalms: An Overlooked Element of Psalm Structure." *JSOT* 40 (2015) 225–38.

———. "Current Critical Questions Concerning the 'Curse of Ham.'" *JETS* 41 (1998) 177–88.

Roche, Michael de. "YHWH's *Rîb* against Israel: A Reassessment of the So-Called 'Prophetic Lawsuit' in the Preexilic Prophets." *JBL* 102 (1983) 563–74.

Rofé, Alexander. "Family and Sex Laws in Deuteronomy and the Book of the Covenant." *Hen* 9 (1987) 131–59.

———. "The Laws of Warfare in the Book of Deuteronomy: Their Origins, Intent and Positivity." *JSOT* 32 (1985) 23–44.

———. *The Prophetical Stories: The Narratives about the Prophets in the Hebrew Bible, Their Literary Types and History*. Jerusalem: Magnes, 1988.

Roi, Mika. "Conditional Vows—Where They are Made and Paid." *BN* 167 (2015) 3–24.

Rom-Shiloni, Dalit. "'On the day I took them out of the land of Egypt': A Non-Deuteronomic Phrase within Jeremiah's Concept of Covenant." *VT* 65 (2015) 621–47.

Rooker, Mark F. *Ten Commandments: Ethics for the Twenty-First Century*. Nashville: B & H, 2010.

Rösel, Christoph. *Die messianische Redaktion des Psalters: Studien zu Entstehung und Theologie der Sammlung Psalm 2–89**. Calwer Theologishe Monographien 19. Stuttgart: Calwer, 1999.

Rösel, Martin. "Jakob, Bileam und der Messias: Messianische Erwartungen in Gen 49 und Num 22–24." In *The Septuagint and Messianism*, edited by Michael A. Knibb, 151–75. BETL 195. Leuven: Peeters, 2006.

Rost, Leonard. *Studien zum Opfer im Alten Israel*. BWANT 113. Stuttgart: Kohlhammer, 1981.

Roth, Wolfgang M. W. "For Life, He Appeals to Death (Wis 13:18): A Study of Old Testament Idol Parodies." *CBQ* 37 (1975) 21–47.

———. *Numerical Sayings in the Old Testament*. VTSup 13. Leiden: Brill, 1965.

Rousseau, Francois. "Structure de Qohélet I 4–11 et plan du livre." *VT* 31 (1981) 200–17.

Routledge, Robin. "Did God Create Chaos?: Unresolved Tension in Genesis 1:1–2." *TynBul* 61 (2010) 69–88.

Rubenstein, Jeffrey L. *The History of Sukkot in the Second Temple and Rabbinic Periods*. BJS 302. Atlanta: Scholars, 1995.

Rudman, Dominic. *Determinism in the Book of Ecclesiastes*. JSOTSup 316. Sheffield: Sheffield Academic, 2001.

Runge, Steven E., and Joshua R. Westbury, eds. *The Lexham Discourse Hebrew Bible: Introduction*. Bellingham, WA: Lexham, 2012.

Rushdoony, Rousas John. *The Institutes of Biblical Law*. Phillipsburg: Presbyterian & Reformed, 1973.

Saebø, Magne. "Who Is 'the Man' in Lamentations 3? A Fresh Approach to the Interpretation of the Book of Lamentations." In *Understanding Poets and Prophets: Essays in Honour of George Wishart Anderson*, edited by A. Graheme Auld, 294–306. JSOTSup 152. Sheffield: JSOT Press, 1993.

Sailhammer, John H. "The Messiah and the Hebrew Bible." *JETS* 44 (2001) 5–23.

———. *The New Covenant in Jeremiah 31:31–34 and Its Place in the Covenant-Treaty Tradition of Israel and the Ancient Near East*. Springfield: New World, 1976.

Salonen, Erkki. *Die Gruss- und Höflichkeitsformeln in babylonisch-assyrischen Briefen*. Helsinki: Societas Orientalis Fennica, 1967.

Samet, Nili. "Qohelet 1,4 and the Structure of the Book's Prologue." *ZAW* 126 (2014) 92–100.

Sanders, James A. *Canon and Community: A Guide to Canonical Criticism*. Guides to Biblical Scholarship: Old Testament. 1984. Reprint, Eugene, OR: Wipf & Stock, 2000.

———. *The Dead Sea Psalms Scroll*. Ithaca: Cornell University Press, 1967.

Sandoval, Timothy J. "Revisiting the Prologue of Proverbs." *JBL* 126 (2007) 455–73.
Sarna, Nahum. *Genesis*. JPS Torah Commentary. Philadelphia: JPS, 1989.
———. *On the Book of Psalms: Exploring the Prayers of Ancient Israel*. New York: Schocken, 1993.
Sasson, Jack M. "A Genealogical 'Convention' in Biblical Chronography." *ZAW* 90 (1978) 171–85.
Sasson, Victor. "The Book of the Oracular Visions of Balaam from Deir 'Alla." *UF* 17 (1986) 283–309.
Satterthwaite, Philip E. "Zion in the Songs of Ascent." In *Zion: City of Our God*, edited by Richard Hess and Gordon Wenham, 129–69. Grand Rapids: Eerdmans, 1999.
Satterthwaite, Philip E., Richard S. Hess, and Gordon J. Wenham, eds. *The Lord's Anointed: Interpretation of Old Testament Messianic Texts*. Grand Rapids: Baker, 1995.
Savran, George W. *Encountering the Divine: Theophany in Biblical Narrative*. JSOTSup 420. London: T. & T. Clark, 2005.
Sawyer, John F. A. "An Analysis of the Context and Meaning of the Psalm-Headings." *TGUOS* 22 (1967–68) 26–38.
———. "Hebrew Words for the Resurrection of the Dead." *VT* 13 (1973) 218–34.
Scalise, Pamela J. "An Exegesis of Zechariah 7:4–14 in Its Canonical Context." *Faith and Mission* 3 (1986) 56–65.
Schaefer, Konrad R. "The Ending of the Book of Zechariah: A Commentary." *RB* 100 (1993) 165–238.
Schaeffer, Jean-Marie. "Literary Genre and Textual Genericity." In *The Future of Literary Theory*, edited by Ralph Cohen, 67–87. New York: Routledge, 1989.
Schifferdecker, Kathryn M. *Out of the Whirlwind: Creation Theology in the Book of Job*. Harvard Theological Studies 61. Cambridge: Harvard University Press, 2008.
Schiffman, Lawrence H. "The Law of Vows and Oaths (Num 30, 3–16) in the Zadokite Fragments and the Temple Scroll." *RevQ* 57 (1991) 199–214.
Schneider, Tammi J. "Achsah, the Raped Pilegeš, and the Book of Judges." In *Women in the Biblical World: A Survey of Old and New Testament Perspectives*, edited by E. A. McCabe, 43–57. Lanham, MD: University Press of America, 2009.
———. *Judges*. Berit Olam. Collegeville: Liturgical, 2000.
———. *Mothers of Promise*. Grand Rapids: Baker Academic, 2008.
———. *Sarah: Mother of Nations*. New York: Continuum, 2004.
Schnittjer, Gary Edward. "The Bad Ending of Ezra-Nehemiah." *BSac* 173 (2016) 32–56.
Scholz, Susanne. *Sacred Witness: Rape in the Hebrew Bible*. Minneapolis: Fortress, 2010.
———. "Women on the Biblical Road: Ruth, Naomi, and the Female Journey." *HS* 39 (1998) 243–46.
Schoors, Anton. *I Am God Your Saviour: A Form-Critical Study of the Main Genres in Is. XL–LV*. VTSup 24. Leiden: Brill, 1973.
———. *The Teacher Sought to Find Pleasant Words: A Study of the Language of Qohelet*. OLA 41. Leuven: Peeters, 1992.
———, ed. *Qohelet in the Context of Wisdom*. BETL 136. Leuven: Leuven University Press, 1998.
Schroer, Silvia. *Wisdom Has Built Her House: Studies on the Figure of Sophia in the Bible*. Collegeville, MN: Liturgical, 2000.
Schulz, Hermann. *Das Todesrecht im Alten Testament*. BZAW 114. Berlin: Töpelmann, 1969.

Schwarz, Baruch J. *The Holiness Legislation: Studies in the Priestly Code*. Jerusalem: Magnes, 1999.

Schwesig, Paul-Gerhard. *Die Rolle des Tag-JHWHs-Dichtungen im Dodekapropheton*. BZAW 366. Berlin: de Gruyter, 2006.

Scolnic, Benjamin Edidin. *Theme and Context in Biblical Lists*. South Florida Studies in the History of Judaism 119. Atlanta: Scholars, 1995.

Scott, R. B. Y. "Wise and Foolish, Righteous and Wicked." In *Studies in Religion of Ancient Israel*, edited by G. W. Anderson, G. R. Castellino and John Emerton, 146–65. VTSup 23. Leiden: Brill, 1972.

Searle, John. *Expression and Meaning: Studies in the Theory of Speech Acts*. Cambridge: Cambridge University Press, 1985.

———. *Speech Acts*. Cambridge: Cambridge University Press, 1969.

Segal, Ben-Zion. *The Ten Commandments in History and Tradition*. Jerusalem: Magnes, 1990.

Segal, J. B. *The Hebrew Passover from Earliest Times to 70 A.D.* Oxford: Oxford University Press, 1963.

Segal, Michael. "Numerical Discrepancies in the List of Vessels in Ezra I 9–11." *VT* 52 (2002) 122–29.

Seidler, Ayelet. "'Fasting,' 'Sackcloth' and 'Ashes'—From Nineveh to Shushan." *VT* 69 (2019) 117–34.

Seitz, Christopher R. "The Divine Council: Temporal Transition and New Prophecy in the Book of Isaiah." *JBL* 109 (1990) 229–47.

———. "How is the Prophet Isaiah Present in the Latter Half of the Book? The Logic of Chapters 40–66 within the Book of Isaiah." *JBL* 115 (1996) 219–40.

———. *Zion's Final Destiny: The Development of the Book of Isaiah, a Reassessment of Isaiah 36–39*. Minneapolis: Fortress, 1991.

Sefati, Yitzhak. *Love Songs in Sumerian Literature: Critical Edition of the Dumuzi-Inanna Songs*. Ramat Gan: Bar-Ilan University Press, 1978.

Seok, J. "The Rhetorical Function of the Witness Motif in Isaiah 43:8–13." *Journal of Christian Education in Korea* 113 (2019) 65–95.

Seow, Choon Leong. "Poetic Closure in Job: The First Cycle." *JSOT* 34 (2010) 433–46.

Seters, John Van. "The Law of the Hebrew Slave." *ZAW* 108 (1996) 534–46.

———. "Two Stories of David Sparing Saul's Life in 1 Samuel 24 and 26: A Question of Priority." *SJOT* 25 (2011) 93–104.

Seybold, Klaus. *Das Gebet des Kranken im Alten Testament*. BWANT 99. Stuttgart: Kohlhammer, 1973.

———. "Psalmen im Buch Hiob." In *Studien zur Psalmenauslegung: Buch gebraucht Kaufen*, 270–87. Stuttgart: Kohlhammer, 1998.

———. *Die Wallfahrtspsalmen: Studien zur Entstehunsgeschichte von Psalm 120–34*. Biblisch-theologische Studien 3. Neukirchen-Vluyn: Neukirchener, 1978.

Sharp, Carolyn J. *Prophecy and Ideology in Jeremiah: Struggles for Authority in the Deutero-Jeremianic Prose*. OTS. New York: T. & T. Clark, 2003.

Shea, William H. "The Chiastic Structure of the Song of Songs." *ZAW* 92 (1980) 378–96.

Shemesh, Yael. "David in the Service of King Achish of Gath: Renegade to His People or a Fifth Column in the Philistine Army?" *VT* 57 (2007) 73–90.

———. "Rape Is Rape Is Rape: The Story of Dinah and Shechem (Genesis 34)." *ZAW* 119 (2007) 2–21.

Sherwood, Aaron. "A Leader's Misleading and a Prostitute's Profession: A Re-examination of Joshua 2." *JSOT* 31 (2006) 43–61.

Shields, Mary E. "Circumcision of the Prostitute: Gender, Sexuality, and the Call to Repentance in Jeremiah 3:1—4:4." *BibInt* 3 (1995) 61–74.

Shupak, Nili. *Where Can Wisdom Be Found? The Sage's Language in the Bible and in Ancient Egyptian Literature.* OBO 130. Göttingen: Vandenhoeck & Ruprecht, 1993.

Simian-Yofre, Horacio. "Ez 17,1–10 como enigma y parabola." *Bib* 65 (1984) 27–43.

Simon, Bennett. "Ezekiel's Geometric Vision of the Restored Temple: From the Rod of His Wrath to the Reed of His Measuring." *HTR* 102 (2009) 411–38.

Simons, Jan J. *The Geographical and Topographical Texts of the Old Testament.* Studia Francisci Scholten Memoriae Dicata 2. Leiden: Brill, 1959.

Skehan, Patrick W. "Broken Acrostic and Psalm 9." *CBQ* 27 (1965) 1–5.

———. "The Seven Columns of Wisdom's House in Proverbs 1–9." *CBQ* 9 (1947) 190–98.

———. "The Structure of the Song of Moses in Deuteronomy (Dt 32:1–43)." *CBQ* 13 (1951) 153–63.

———. *Studies in Israelite Poetry and Wisdom.* CBQMS 1. Washington: Catholic University of America Press, 1971.

Sklar, Jay. *Sin, Impurity, Sacrifice, Atonement: The Priestly Conceptions.* HBM 2. Sheffield: Sheffield Phoenix, 2005.

Slomovich, Elieser. "Toward an Understanding of the Formation of Historic Titles in the Book of Psalms." *ZAW* 91 (1979) 35–81.

Smelik, Klaas A. D. *Converting the Past: Studies in Ancient Israelite and Moabite Historiography.* OTS 28. Leiden: Brill, 1992.

———. "Letters to the Exiles: Jeremiah 29 in Context." *SJOT* 10 (1996) 282–95.

Smith, D. Charles. *The Role of the Mothers in the Genealogical Lists of Jacob's Sons.* Contributions to Biblical Exegesis & Theology 90. Leuven: Peeters, 2018.

Smith, Mark S. *The Laments of Jeremiah and Their Contexts: A Literary and Redactional Study of Jeremiah 11–20.* SBLMS 42. Atlanta: Scholars, 1990.

Smith, Sidonie and Julia Watson. *Reading Autobiography: A Guide for Interpreting Life Narratives, Second Edition.* Minneapolis: University of Minnesota Press, 2010.

Snaith, Norman H. "Selah." *VT* 2 (1952) 43–56.

Snell, Daniel C. *Twice-Told Proverbs and the Composition of the Book of Proverbs.* Winona Lake, IN: Eisenbrauns, 1993.

Sohn, Seock-Tae. "I Will Be Your God and You Will Be My People." In *Ki Baruch Hu: Ancient Near Eastern, Biblical and Judaic Studies in Honor of Baruch A. Levine,* edited by Robert Chazan, William H. Hallo, and Lawrence H. Schiffman, 355–72. Winona Lake, IN: Eisenbrauns, 1999.

Soll, William M. "Babylonian and Biblical Acrostics." *Bib* 69 (1988) 305–23.

———. *Psalm 119: Matrix, Form, and Setting.* CBQMS 23. Washington, D.C.: Catholic Biblical Association, 1991.

Sonsino, Rifat. *Motive Clauses in the Hebrew Law.* SBLDS 45. Atlanta: SBL, 1980.

Sparks, James T. *The Chronicler's Genealogies: Towards an Understanding of 1 Chronicles 1–9.* Academia Biblica 28. Atlanta: SBL, 2008.

Sparks, Kenton L. *Ancient Texts for the Study of the Hebrew Bible: A Guide to the Background Literature.* Peabody: Hendrickson, 2005.

———. "Genesis 49 and the Tribal List Tradition in Ancient Israel." *ZAW* 115 (2003) 327–47.

Spaulding, Mary B. and Christopher Keith. *Commemorative Identities: Jewish Social Memory and the Johannine Feast of Booths*. Library of New Testament Studies 396. London: T. & T. Clark, 2009.

Speiser, Ephraim A. "The Wife-Sister Motif in the Patriarchal Narratives." In *Oriental and Biblical Studies*, 62–82. Philadelphia: University of Philadelphia Press, 1967.

Spieckermann, Hermann. "Jugend-Alter-Tod: Kohelets abschliessende Reflexion: Koh 11:7—12:8." *VT* 70 (2020) 193–208.

Sprinkle, Joe M. *"The Book of the Covenant": A Literary Approach*. JSOTSup 174. Sheffield: JSOT Press, 1994.

———. "The Interpretation of Exodus 21:22–25 (Lex Talionis) and Abortion." *WTJ* 55 (1993) 233–53.

Stacey, David W. *Prophetic Drama in the Old Testament*. London: Epworth, 1990.

Starbuck, Scott R. A. *Court Oracles in the Psalms: The So-Called Royal Psalms in their Ancient Near Eastern Context*. SBLDS 172. Atlanta: SBL, 1999.

Stavrakopoulou, Francesca. "Gog's Grave and the Use and Abuse of Corpses in Ezekiel 39:11–20." *JBL* 129 (2010) 67–84.

Steinberg, Naomi. "The Genealogical Framework of the Family Stories in Genesis." *Semeia* 46 (1989) 41–50.

Steiner, Richard C. "Contradictions, Culture Gaps, and Narrative Gaps in the Joseph Story." *JBL* 139 (2020) 439–58.

Steinmann, Andrew E. "Gaps in the Genealogies in Genesis 5 and 11?" *BSac* 174 (2017) 141–58.

———. "Information in the Gospels that Cannot Be Used To Determine the Date of Jesus's Birth." *JETS* 67 (2024) 493–504.

Steinmetz, Devora. *Punishment and Freedom: The Rabbinic Construction of Criminal Law*. Pennsylvania: University of Pennsylvania Press, 2008.

Sterman, Judy Taubes. "Themes in the Deborah Narrative (Judges 4–5)." *JBQ* 39 (2011) 15–24.

Stern, Philip. *The Biblical Ḥerem: A Window on Israel's Religious Experience*. BJS 211. Atlanta: Scholars, 1991.

Sternberg, Meir. *The Poetics of Biblical Narrative: Ideological Literature and the Drama of Reading*. Indiana Literary Biblical Studies. Bloomington: Indiana University Press, 1987.

Sternberg, Meir, and Menachem Perry. "The King through Ironic Eyes: The Narrator's Devices in the Story of David and Bathsheba and Two Excurses on the Theory of Narrative Text." *Hasifrut* 1 (1968) 262–91.

Steuernagel, Gert, and Ulrike Schulze. "Zur Aussage in den Büchern der Könige sowie in II Chronik." *ZAW* 120 (2008) 267–75.

Strawn, Brent A. "What Is It Like to Be a Psalmist? Unintentional Sin and Moral Agency in the Psalter." *JSOT* 40 (2015) 61–78.

Strawson, P. F. "Austin and Locutionary Meaning." In *Essays on J. L. Austin*, 47–49. Oxford: Oxford University Press, 1973.

Strine, Casey A. "The Famine in the Land Was Severe: Environmentally Induced Migration and the Joseph Narrative." *HS* 60 (2019) 55–69.

———. "The Role of Repentance in the Book of Ezekiel: A Second Chance for the Second Generation." *JTS* 63 (2012) 467–91.

Stulman, Louis. *The Prose Sermons of Jeremiah: A Redescription of the Correspondences with the Deuteronomistic Literature in the Light of Recent Text-Critical Research*. SBLDS 83. Atlanta: Scholars, 1986.

Sturrock, John. *The Language of Autobiography: Studies in the First Person Singular*. Cambridge: Cambridge University Press, 1993.

Sulzberger, Mayer. *The Ancient Hebrew Law of Homicide. 1915*. Reprint, Clark: The Lawbook Exchange, 2004.

Süssenbach, Claudia. *Der elohistische Psalter*. FAT 2/7. Tübingen: Mohr Siebeck, 2005.

Sweeney, Deborah. "Intercessory Prayer in Egypt and the Bible." In *Pharaonic Egypt: The Bible and Christianity*, 213–30. Jerusalem: Magnes, 1985.

Sweeney, Marvin. "The Book of Isaiah as Prophetic Torah." In *New Visions of Isaiah*, edited by Roy F. Melugin and Marvin A. Sweeney, 50–67. JSOTSup 214. Sheffield: Sheffield Academic, 1996.

———. "Form Criticism: The Question of the Endangered Matriarchs in Genesis." In *Method Matters: Essays on the Interpretation of the Hebrew Bible in Honor of David L. Peterson*, edited by Joel M. LeMon and Kent Harold Richards, 17–38. SBLRBS 56. Atlanta: SBL, 2009.

———. *Isaiah 1–39: With an Introduction to Prophetic Literature*. FOTL 16. Grand Rapids: Eerdmans, 1996.

———. *Isaiah 40–66*. FOTL 17. Grand Rapids: Eerdmans, 2016.

———. "The Jacob Narratives: An Ephraimitic Text." *CBQ* 78 (2016) 236–55.

———. "Jeremiah's Reflection on the Isaian Royal Promise: Jeremiah 23:1–8 in Context." In *Uprooting and Planting: Essays on Jeremiah for Leslie Allen*, edited by John Goldingay, 308–21. LHBOTS 459. New York: T. & T. Clark, 2007.

———. *King Josiah of Judah: The Lost Messiah of Israel*. Oxford: Oxford University Press, 2001.

———. *Zephaniah*. Hermeneia. Minneapolis: Fortress, 2003.

Smend, Rudolf. *Die Budesformel*. ThSt 68. Zürich: EVZ, 1963.

Smoak, Jeremy D. "'Prayers of Petition' in the Psalms and West Semitic Inscribed Amulets: Efficacious Words in Metal and Prayers for Protection in Biblical Literature." *JSOT* 36 (2011) 75–92.

Smith, Mark S. *The Pilgrimage Pattern in Exodus*. JSOTSup 239. Sheffield: Sheffield Academic, 1997.

Steiner, Richard C. "Contradictions, Culture Gaps, and Narrative Gaps in the Joseph Story." *JBL* 139 (2020) 439–58.

Stewart, Anne W. *Poetic Ethics in Proverbs: Wisdom Literature and the Shaping of the Moral Self*. Cambridge: Cambridge University Press, 2016.

Sun, Henry T. C. "An Investigation into the Compositional Integrity of the Holiness Code (Leviticus 17–26)." PhD diss., Claremont Graduate School, 1984.

Sweeney, Marvin A. *Form and Intertextuality in Prophetic and Apocalyptic Literature*. FAT 45. Tübingen: Mohr Siebeck, 2005.

Swindell, Anthony. "Gog and Magog in Literary Reception History: The Persistence of the Fantastic." *Journal of the Bible and Its Reception* 3 (2016) 27–53.

Talmon, S. "The Gezer Calendar and the Seasonal Cycle of Ancient Canaan." *JAOS* 83 (1963) 177–87.

Terrien, Samuel. *The Psalms: Strophic Structure and Theological Commentary*. Grand Rapids: Eerdmans, 2003.

Teubal, Sara J. *Hagar the Egyptian: The Lost Tradition of the Matriarchs*. San Francisco: Harper & Row, 1990.

Teugels, Lieve. "'A Strong Woman, Who Can Find?' A Study of Characterization in Genesis 24 with Some Perspectives on the General Presentation of Isaac and Rebekah in the Genesis Narratives." *JSOT* 63 (1994) 89–104.

Thiele, Edwin R. *The Mysterious Numbers of the Hebrew Kings*. Grand Rapids: Kregel, 1983.

Thiessen, Matthew. "The Legislation of Leviticus 12 in Light of Ancient Embryology." *VT* 68 (2018) 297–319.

Thomas, Matthew A. *These are the Generations: Identity, Covenant, and the 'Toledoth' Formula*. New York: T. & T. Clark, 2011.

Throntveit, Mark A. *When Kings Speak: Royal Speech and Royal Prayer in Chronicles*. SBLDS 93. Atlanta: Scholars, 1987.

Tigay, Jeffrey H. *Deuteronomy*. JPS Torah Commentary. Philadelphia: Jewish Publication Society, 1996.

———. *You Shall Have No other Gods Before Me: Israelite Religion in the Light of Hebrew Inscriptions*. HHS 31. Atlanta: Scholars, 1986.

Timmer, Daniel. "God's Speeches, Job's Responses, and the Problem of Coherence in the Book of Job: Sapiential Pedagogy Revisited." *CBQ* 71 (2009) 286–305.

Toblowsky, Andrew. "The 'Samuel the Judge' narrative in 1 Samuel 1–7." *ZAW* 129 (2017) 376–98.

Toews, Wesley I. *Monarchy and Religious Institutions under Jeroboam I*. SBLMS 47. Atlanta: Scholars, 1993.

Tomasino, A. J. "Isaiah 1.1—2.4 and 63–66 and the Composition of the Isaianic Corpus." *JSOT* 57 (1993) 81–98.

Toorn, Karel van der, ed. *The Image and the Book: Iconic Cults, Aniconism, and the Rise of Book Religion in Israel and the Ancient Near East*. Contributions to Biblical Exegesis and Theology 21. Leuven: Peeters, 1997.

Torcszyner, Harry. "The Riddle in the Bible." *HUCA* 1 (1924) 125–49.

Toretta, Gabriel. "Rediscovering the Imprecatory Psalms." *The Thomist* 80 (2016) 23–48.

Tov, Emmanuel. *Scribal Practices and Approaches Reflected in the Texts Found in the Judean Desert*. STDJ 54. Leiden: Brill, 1998.

Towner, W. Sibley. "'Blessed Be YHWH' and 'Blessed Art Thou, YHWH.'" *CBQ* 30 (1968) 386–99.

Trevaskis, Leigh M. *Holiness, Ethics, and Ritual in Leviticus*. HBM 29. Sheffield: Sheffield Phoenix, 2011.

———. "The Purpose of Leviticus 24 within its Literary Context." *VT* 59 (2009) 295–312.

Trible, Phyllis. *God and the Rhetoric of Sexuality*. OBT 2. Philadelphia: Fortress, 1978.

———. *Texts of Terror: Literary-Feminist Readings of Biblical Narratives*. OBT. Philadelphia: Fortress, 1984.

Troyer, Kristin De. "'Sounding Trumpets with Loud Shouts': Emotional Responses to Temple Building: Ezra and Esdras." In *Ancient Jewish Prayers and Emotions: Emotions Associated with Jewish Prayers in and Around the Second Temple*, edited by Stefan C. Reif and Renate Egger-Wenzel, 41–58. Deuterocanonical and Cognate Literature Series 26. Berlin: de Gruyter, 2015.

Trublet, Jacques. "Approche Canonique des Psaumes du Hallel." In *The Composition of the Book of Psalms*, edited by Erich Zenger, 339–76. BETL 238. Leuven: Peeters, 2010.

Trudinger, Paul. "To Whom Will You then Liken God?" *VT* 17 (1967) 220–25.

Tsumura, David Toshio. *Creation and Destruction—A Reappraisal of the Chaoskampf Theory in the Old Testament*. Winona Lake, IN: Eisenbrauns, 2005.

———. *The Earth and the Waters in Genesis 1 and 2: A Linguistic Investigation.* JSOTSup 83. Sheffield: Academic, 1989.

———. *Vertical Grammar of Parallelism in Biblical Hebrew.* AIL 47. Atlanta: SBL, 2023.

Tucker, Gene M. "Prophetic Speech." *Int* 32 (1978) 31–45.

———. "Prophetic Superscriptions and the Growth of a Canon." In *Canon and Authority: Essays in Old Testament Religion and Theology*, edited by George M. Coats and Burke O. Long, 56–70. Philadelphia: Fortress, 1977.

Tuell, Steven Shawn. *The Law of the Temple in Ezekiel 40–48.* HSM 49. Atlanta: Scholars, 1992.

Ulfgard, Hakan. *The Setting, Shaping and Sequel of the Biblical Feast of Tabernacles.* BGBE 34. Tübingen: Mohr Siebeck, 1998.

Udoekpo, Michael Ufok. *Re-thinking the Day of YHWH and the Restoration of Fortunes in the Prophet Zephaniah: An Exegetical and Theological Study of 1:14–18; 3:14–20.* An Outline of an Old Testament Dialogue 2. Bern: Lang, 2010.

Vanderkam, James C. *Calendars in the Dead Sea Scrolls: Measuring Time.* Abingdon: Routledge, 2002.

VanDrunen, David. *A Biblical Case for Natural Law.* Grand Rapids: Acton Institute, 2006.

VanGemeren, Willem A. *Interpreting the Prophetic Word: An Introduction to the Prophetic Literature of the Old Testament.* Grand Rapids: Zondervan, 1996.

Van Pelt, Miles V. "Exegetical Evidence for Non-Solar and Non-Sequential Interpretations of the Genesis 1 and Genesis 2 Creation Days." In *The Genre of Biblical Commentary: Essays in Honor of John E. Hartley on the Occasion of His 75th Birthday*, edited by Timothy D. Finlay and William Yarchin, 199–216. Eugene, OR: Pickwick Publications, 2015.

Van Seters, John. "The Law of the Hebrew Slave." *ZAW* 108 (1996) 534–46.

———. "Two Stories of David Sparing Saul's Life in 1 Samuel 24 and 26: A Question of Priority." *SJOT* 25 (2011) 93–104.

Vaux, Roland de. *Ancient Israel: Its Life and Institutions.* New York: McGraw-Hill, 1961.

———. "Single Combat in the Old Testament." In *The Bible and the Ancient Near East*, 122–35. Translated by Damian McHugh. Garden City: Doubleday, 1971.

Vayntrub, Jacqueline. "The Book of Proverbs and the Idea of Ancient Israelite Education." *ZAW* 128 (2016) 96–114.

———. "'To Take Up a Parable': The History of Translating a Biblical Idiom." *VT* 66 (2016) 627–45.

Via, Dan O. "Parable and Example Story." *Semeia* 1 (1974) 105–33.

Viljoen, Anneke. "An Exploration of the Symbolic World of Proverbs 10:1—15:33 with Specific Reference to 'the Fear of the Lord.'" PhD diss., University of Pretoria, 2013.

Viviers, Hendrik. "The Coherence of the *ma'alot* Psalms (Pss 120–134)." *ZAW* 106 (1994) 275–89.

Wagenar, Jan A. *Origin and Transformation of the Ancient Israelite Festival Calendar.* Beihefte zur Zeitschrift für altorientalische und biblische Rechtsgeschichte 6. Wiesbaden: Harrassowitz, 2005.

———. "Passover and the First Day of the Festival of Unleavened Bread in the Priestly Festival Calendar." *VT* 54 (2004) 250–68.

Wagner, Andreas, ed. *Parallelismus Membrorum.* Göttingen: Vandenhoeck & Ruprecht, 2007.

Wagner, Thomas. "Die Schuld der Väter (er-)tragen: Thr 5 im Kontext exilischer Theologie." *VT* 62 (2012) 622–35.

Wallace, Robert E. "The Narrative Effect of Psalms 84–89." *JHebS* 11 (2011) 283–98.

Walsh, Jerome T. "Summons to Judgment: A Close Reading of Isaiah li 1–20." *VT* 43 (1993) 351–71.

Waltke, Bruce K. "Does Proverbs Promise Too Much." *AUSS* 34 (1996) 319–36.

———. "Superscripts, Postscripts, or Both." *JBL* 110 (1991) 583–96.

Walton, John H. "Creation in Genesis 1:1—2:3 and the Ancient Near East: Order out of Disorder after Chaoskampf." *CTJ* 43 (2008) 48–63.

———. *The Lost World of Genesis One: Ancient Cosmology and the Origins Debate.* Downers Grove, IL: InterVarsity, 2009.

———. "The Mesopotamian Background of the Tower of Babel Account and Its Implications." *BBR* 5 (1995) 155–75.

———. "Psalms: A Cantata about the Davidic Covenant." *JETS* 34 (1991) 21–31.

Wardlow, Terrance Randall. *Elohim within the Psalms: Petitioning the Creator to Order Chaos in Oral-Derived Literature.* LHBOTS 602. London: T. & T. Clark, 2016.

Warren, Nathaniel J. "Tenure and Grant in Ezekiel's Paradise (47:13—48:29)." *VT* 63 (2013) 323–34.

Watson, Rebecca S. *Chaos Uncreated: A Reassessment of the Theme of 'Chaos' in the Hebrew Bible.* BZAW 341. Berlin: de Gruyter, 2005.

Watson, Wilfred G. E. *Classical Hebrew Poetry: A Guide to Its Techniques.* JSOTSup 26. Sheffield: Sheffield Academic, 1995.

Watts, James W. *Reading Law: The Rhetorical Shaping of the Pentateuch.* BibSem 9. Sheffield: Sheffield Academic, 1999.

———. "Psalms of Trust, Thanksgiving and Praise." *RevExp* 81 (1984) 395–406.

———. *Ritual and Rhetoric in Leviticus: From Sacrifice to Scripture.* Cambridge: Cambridge University Press, 2007.

Wazana, Nili. "Amos against Amaziah (Amos 7:10–17): A Case of Mutual Exclusion." *VT* 70 (2020) 209–28.

Wearne, Gareth James. "Reading Samuel as Folklore: 1 Sam 23.19—24.22 and 26.1–25, a Case Study." *JSOT* 41 (2017) 337–54.

Webb, Barry G. *Five Festal Garments: Christian Reflections on The Song of Songs, Ruth, Lamentations, Ecclesiastes, Esther.* Downers Grove: IVP, 2000.

Weber, Béai. "Akrostische Muster in der Asaph-Psalmen." *BN* 113 (2002) 79–94.

———. "Mose-Lied (Dtn 32,1–43) und Asaph-Psalmen (Ps 50; 73–83) Untersuchungen zu ihrem Verhältnis." *ZABR* 27 (2021) 257–309.

Webster, Edwin C. "Pattern in the Song of Songs." *JSOT* 22 (1982) 73–93.

Weeks, Stuart. *An Introduction to the Study of Wisdom Literature.* T & T Clark Approaches to Biblical Studies. New York: T. & T. Clark, 2010.

Weijola, Timo. "Wahrheit und Intoleranz nach Deuteronomium 13." *ZTK* 92 (1995) 287–314.

Weinfeld, Moshe. "Jeremiah and the Spiritual Metamorphosis of Israel." *ZAW* 88 (1976) 17–56.

———. "Pentecost as Festival of the Giving of the Law." *Immanuel* 8 (1978) 7–18.

———. "Sabbatical Year and Jubilee in the Pentateuchal Laws and Their Ancient Near Eastern Background." In *The Law in the Bible and Its Environment*, edited by Timo Veijola, 39–62. Göttingen: Vandenhoeck & Ruprecht, 1990.

———. *Social Justice in Ancient Israel and in the Ancient Near East*. Philadelphia: Fortress, 1995.

———. "The Uniqueness of the Decalogue and Its Place in Jewish Tradition." In *The Ten Commandments in History and Tradition*, edited by Ben-Zion Segal, translated by G. Levi, 21–27. Jerusalem: Hebrew University, 1987.

Weippert, Helge. "Das geographische System der Stämme Israels." *VT* 23 (1973) 76–89.

———. *Die Prosareden des Jeremiabuches*. BZAW 132. Berlin: de Gruyter, 1973.

———. "Schöpfung und Heil in Jer 45." In *Schöpfung und Befreiung: Für Claus Westermann zum 80 Geburtstag*, edited by Rainer Albertz et al., 92–103. Stuttgart: Calwer Verlag, 1989.

———. "Das Wort vom neuen Bund in Jeremia xxxi 31–34." *VT* 29 (1979) 336–51.

Weis, Richard D. "Patterns of Mutual Influence in the Textual Transmission of the Oracles concerning Moab in Isaiah and Jeremiah." In *Isaiah in Context: Studies in Honor of Arie van der Kooij on the Occasion of his Sixty-Fifth Birthday*, edited by M. N. van der Meer et al., 161–84. Leiden: Brill, 2010.

Weiss, Meir. "The Origin of the 'Day of the Lord.'" *HUCA* 37 (1966) 29–60.

———. "The Pattern of Numerical Sequence in Amos 1–2: A Re-Examination." *JBL* 86 (1967) 416–23.

Weis, Richard. "A Definition of the Genre Maśśa' in the Hebrew Bible." PhD diss., Claremont Graduate School, 1986.

Weitzman, Steven. "David's Lament and the Poetic of Grief in 2 Samuel." *JQR* 85 (1995) 341–60.

Wellhausen, Julius. *Prolegomena to the History of Israel*. Translated by J. Sutherland and Allan Menzies. Edinburgh: A & C Black, 1885.

Wenger, Paul D. "How Many Virgin Births Are in the Bible? (Isaiah 7:14): A Prophetic Pattern Approach." *JETS* 54 (2011) 467–84.

Wenham, Gordon J. *Psalms as Torah: Reading Biblical Song Ethically*. STI. Grand Rapids: Baker, 2012.

Weyde, Karl Wilhelm. *The Appointed Festivals of YHWH: The Festival Calendar in Leviticus 23 and the Sukkôt Festival in Other Biblical Texts*. FAT 2/4. Tübingen: Mohr Siebeck, 2004.

Wessels, Wilhelm J. "Connected Leadership: Jeremiah 8:18–9:3: A Case Study." *Koers* 75 (2010) 483–501.

———. "The Metaphorical Depiction of Nineveh's Demise: The Use of Locust 'Marked Metaphor' in Nahum 3:15–17." *Scriptura* 116 (2017) 246–59.

Westbrook, Raymond. *Studies in Biblical and Cuneiform Law*. CahRB 26. Paris: Gabalda, 1988.

Westermann, Claus. *Basic Forms of Prophetic Speech*. Translated by H. C. White. Philadelphia: Westminster, 1967.

———. "The Complaint against God." In *God in the Fray: A Tribute to Walter Brueggemann*, edited by Tod Linafelt and Timothy K. Beal, 233–41. Minneapolis: Fortress, 1998.

———. *Genesis 12–36*. Translated by John J. Scullion. Continental Commentaries. Minneapolis: Augsburg, 1985.

———. *Genesis 37–50*. Translated by John J. Scullion. Continental Commentaries. Minneapolis: Augsburg, 1986.

———. "Das Heilswort bei Deutrojesaja." *EvT* 24 (1964) 355–73.

———. *Praise and Lament in the Psalms*. Translated by Keith R. Crim and Richard N. Soulen. Atlanta: John Knox, 1981.

———. *Prophetic Oracles of Salvation in the Old Testament*. Translated by Keith Crim. Louisville: Westminster John Knox, 1991.

———. *The Structure of the Book of Job: A Form-Critical Analysis*. Translated by Charles A. Muenchow. Philadelphia: Fortress, 1981.

Wevers, John William. "Study in the Form Criticism of Individual Complaint Psalms." *VT* 6 (1956) 80–96.

Weyde, Karl Willem. *The Appointed Festivals of YHWH*. FAT 2/4. Tübingen: Mohr Siebeck, 2004.

Wheaton, Gerry. *The Role of Jewish Feasts in John's Gospel*. SNTSMS 162. Cambridge: Cambridge University Press, 2015.

White, John B. *A Study of the Language of Love in the Song of Songs and Ancient Egyptian Poetry*. SBLDS 38. Missoula: Scholars, 1978.

White, Thomas Joseph. *Exodus*. Grand Rapids: BrazosPress, 2016.

Whitekettle, Richard. "Leviticus 12 and the Israelite Woman: Ritual Process, Liminality and the Womb." *ZAW* 107 (1995) 393–408.

———. "A Study in Scarlet: The Physiology and Treatment of Blood, Breath, and Fish in Ancient Israel." *JBL* 135 (2016) 685–704.

Whitwell, Christopher. "The Variation of Nature in Ecclesiastes 11." *JSOT* 34 (2009) 481–97.

Whybray, R. Norman. "Ecclesiastes 1,5–7 and the Wonders of Nature." *JSOT* 41 (1988) 105–112.

———. "The Identification and Use of Quotations in Ecclesiastes." In *Congress Volume: Vienna, 1980*, edited by J. A. Emerton, 435–51. VTSup 32. Leiden: Brill, 1981.

———. "Qoheleth, Preacher of Joy." *JSOT* 23 (1982) 87–98.

———. *Reading the Psalms as a Book*. JSOTSup 222. Sheffield: Sheffield Academic, 1996.

———. *Wealth and Poverty in the Book of Proverbs*. JSOTSup 99. Sheffield: JSOT Press, 1990.

———. "The Wisdom Psalms." In *Wisdom in Ancient Israel: Essays in Honour of J. A. Emerton*, edited by John Day, R. P. Gordon and H. G. M. Williamson, 152–60. Cambridge: Cambridge University Press, 1995.

Wiele, Tarah van de. "What Rights Get Wrong about Justice for Orphans: An Old Testament Challenge to a Modern Ideology." *Studies in Christian Ethics* 29 (2016) 69–83.

Wildberger, Hans. *Isaiah 1–12*. Translated by Thomas H. Trapp. Continental Commentaries. Minneapolis: Fortress, 1991.

———. *Isaiah 13–27*. Translated by Thomas H. Trapp. Continental Commentaries. Minneapolis: Fortress, 1997.

———. *Isaiah 28–39*. Translated by Thomas H. Trapp. Continental Commentaries. Minneapolis: Fortress, 2001.

Wiley, Henrietta L., and Christian Eberhart, eds. *Sacrifice, Cult, and Atonement in Early Judaism and Christianity: Constituents and Critique*. Resources for Biblical Study 85. Atlanta: SBL, 2017.

Wilf, Steven. *The Law before the Law*. Lanham, MD: Lexington, 2008.

Willey, Patricia T. "The Importunate Woman of Tekoa and How She Got Her Way." In *Reading between Texts: Intertextuality and the Hebrew Bible*, edited by Danna Nolan Fewell, 115–31. Louisville: Westminster John Knox, 1992.

Willgren, David. *The Formation of the 'Book; of Psalms.* FAT 2/88. Tübingen: Mohr Siebeck, 2016.

———. "Ps 72:20—A Frozen Colophon?" *JBL* 135 (2016) 49–60.

Williams, David S. "Once Again: The Structure of the Narrative of Solomon's Reign." *JSOT* 86 (1999) 49–66.

Williams, James G. "The Alas-Oracles of the Eighth Century Prophets." *HUCA* 38 (1967) 75–91.

———. "Deciphering the Unspoken: The Theophany of Job." *HUCA* 49 (1978) 59–72.

———. "The Power of Form: A Study of Biblical Proverbs." *Semeia* 17 (1980) 35–58.

Williams, Michael J. "An Investigation of the Legitimacy of Source Distinctions for the Prose Material in Jeremiah." *JBL* 112 (1993) 193–210.

Williamson, H. G. M. "The Origins of the Twenty-Four Priestly Courses: A Study of I Chronicles XXIII–XXIV." In *Studies in the Historical Books of the Old Testament*, edited by John Emerton, 251–68.

———. "The Sure Mercies of David." *Journal of Semitic Studies* 23 (1978) 31–49.

———. "'We Are Yours, O David.' The Setting and Purpose of 1 Chronicles 12:1–23." OTS 21 (1981) 164–76.

Williamson, Paul R. *Abraham, Israel and the Nations: The Patriarchal Promise and Its Covenantal Development in Genesis.* JSOTSup 315. Sheffield: Sheffield Academic, 2000.

Willis, John T. "A Cry of Defiance—Psalm 2." *ZAW* 91 (1979) 381–401.

———. "The Song of Hannah and Psalm 113." *CBQ* 34 (1973) 139–54.

———. "The Juxtaposition of Synonymous and Chiastic Parallelism in Tricola in Old Testament Hebrew Psalm Prosody." *VT* 29 (1979) 465–80.

———. "'They Did Not Listen to the Voice of the Lord': A Literary Analysis of Jeremiah 37–45." *ResQ* 42 (2000) 65–84.

Willis, Timothy M. "Blasphemy, Talion, and Chiasmus: The Marriage of Form and Content in Lev 24, 13–23." *Bib* 90 (2009) 68–74.

———. *The Elders of the City: A Study of the Elder-Laws in Deuteronomy.* SBLMS 55. Atlanta: SBL, 2001.

Wills, Lawrence M. *The Jew in the Court of the Foreign King: Ancient Jewish Court Legends.* HDR. Minneapolis: Fortress, 1990.

Wilkens, Steve. *What's So Funny About God?: A Theological Look at Humor.* Downers Grove, IL: IVP Academic, 2019.

Wilson, Gerald H. *The Editing of the Hebrew Psalter.* SBLDS 76. Chico, CA: Scholars, 1985.

———. "King, Messiah, and the Reign of God: Revisiting the Royal Psalms and the Shape of the Psalter." In *The Book of Psalms: Composition and Reception*, edited by Peter W. Flint and Patrick D. Miller, 391–406. VTSup 99. Leiden: Brill, 2005.

———. "The Qumran Psalms Scroll (11QPsa) and the Canonical Psalter: Comparison of Canonical Shaping." *CBQ* 59 (1997) 448–64.

———. "The Use of Royal Psalms at the 'Seams' of the Hebrew Psalter." *JSOT* 35 (1986) 85–94.

Wilson, Ian Douglas. "Tyre, a Ship: The Metaphorical World of Ezekiel 27 in Ancient Judah." *ZAW* 125 (2013) 249–62.

Wilson, Lindsay B. "Job 38–39 and Biblical Theology." *RTR* 62 (2003) 121–38.

———. "The Role of the Elihu Speeches in the Book of Job." *RTR* 55 (1996) 81–94.

Wilson, Robert R. *Genealogy and History in the Biblical World*. Yale Near Eastern Researches 7. New Haven: Yale University Press, 1977.

Wilson-Wright, Aren. "Love Conquers All: Song of Songs 8:6b–7a as a Reflex of the Northwest Semitic Combat Myth." *JBL* 134 (2015) 334–45.

Winkler, Matthias. "Haupt und Haare des Nasiräers/der Nasiräerin in Num 6." *BN* (2021) 33–57.

Winslow, Karen Strand. *Early Jewish and Christian Memories of Moses' Wives: Exogamist Marriage and Ethnic Identity*. Studies in the Bible and Early Christianity 66. Lewiston, NY: Mellen, 2005.

Wold, Donald J. "The Kareth Penalty in P: Rationale and Cases." SBLSP (1979) 1–45.

Wolde, Ellen van. "Job 42:1–6: The Reversal of Job." In *The Book of Job*, edited by W. A. M. Beuken, 223–50. BETL 114. Leuven: Leuven University Press, 1994.

———. "A Leader Led by a Lady: David and Abigail in 1 Samuel 25." *ZAW* 114 (2002) 355–75.

Wolde, Ellen van, ed. *Job 28: Cognition in Context*. Biblical Interpretation Series 66. Leiden: Brill, 2003.

———. *Narrative Syntax and the Hebrew Bible: Papers of the Tilburg Conference 1996*. Biblical Interpretation Series 29. Leiden: Brill, 1997.

Wolfers, David. "The Lord's Second Speech in the Book of Job." *VT* 40 (1990) 474–99.

———. "The Speech-Cycles in the Book of Job." *VT* 43 (1993) 385–402.

Wolff, Hans Walter. "Die Begründungen der prophetischen Heils-und Unheilssprüche." *ZAW* 52 (1934)1–22.

———. *Obadiah and Jonah: A Commentary*. Translated by Margaret Kohl. Continental Commentaries. Minneapolis: Augsburg, 1986.

Wolters, Al. "Proverbs XXXI 10–31 as Heroic Hymn: A Form-Critical Analysis." *VT* 38 (1988) 446–57.

———. *The Song of the Valiant Woman: Studies in the Interpretation of Proverbs 31:10–31*. Carlisle, UK: Paternoster, 2001.

Wong, Gordon C. I. "Faith in the Present Form of Isaiah vii 1–17." *VT* 51 (2001) 535–47.

Woolcock, Collin. *The Lost Illumination: Acrostic Biblical Compositions*. Truro: Playing Place, 2013.

Wright, Addison G. "Ecclesiastes 9:1–12: An Emphatic Statement of Themes." *CBQ* 77 (2015) 250–62.

———. "'For Everything There is a Season.' The Structure and Meaning of the Fourteen Opposites (Ecclesiastes 3,2–8)." In *De la Torah au Messie: Études d'exégèse et d'herméneutique bibliques offertes à Henri Cazelles pour ses 25 années d'enseignement à l'Institut Catholique de Paris (Octobre 1979)*, edited by J. Doréet et al, 321–28. Paris: Gabalda, 1981.

———. "The Riddle of the Sphinx: The Structure of the Book of Qohelet." *CBQ* 30 (1968) 313–34.

———. "The Riddle of the Sphinx Revisited: Numerical Patterns in the Book of Qohelet." *CBQ* 42 (1980) 38–51.

Wright, Christopher J. H. *Old Testament Ethics for the People of God*. Downers Grove, IL: InterVarsity, 2004.

———. "The Israelite Household and the Decalogue: The Social Background and Significance of Some Commandments." *TynBul* 30 (1979) 101–24.

Wright, David P. *The Disposal of Impurity: The Disposal of Impurity: Elimination Rites in the Bible and in Hittite and Mesopotamian Literature.* SBLDS 101. Atlanta: Scholars, 1987.

———. Inventing God's Law: *How the Covenant Code of the Bible Used and Revised the Laws of Hammurabi.* Oxford: Oxford University Press, 2009.

———. "Observations on the Ethical Foundations of the Biblical Dietary Laws: A Response to Jacob Milgrom." In *Religion and Law: Biblical-Judaic and Islamic Perspectives*, edited by Edwin Firmage et al., 193–98. Winona Lake, IN: Eisenbrauns, 1990.

Wright, Jacob L. and Michael J. Chan. "Isaiah 56:1–8 in Light of Honorific Royal Burial Practices." *JBL* 131 (2012) 99–119.

Wright, John W. "The Legacy of David in Chronicles: The Narrative Function of 1 Chronicles 23–27." *JBL* 110 (1991) 229–42.

Würthwein, Ernst, Kurt Galling and Otto Plöger. *Die Fünf Megilloth.* HAT 18. Tübingen: Mohr Siebeck, 1969.

Yaakov, Ariel. "Still Ransoming the First-born Sons?: Pidyon Habben and Its Survival in the Jewish Tradition." In *Human Sacrifice in Jewish and Christian Tradition*, edited by Karin Finsterbusch et al., 305–19. Studies in the History of Religions 112. Leiden: Brill, 2006.

Yamada, Frank M. *Configurations of Rape in the Hebrew Bible: A Literary Analysis of Three Rape Narratives.* Studies in Biblical Literature 109. New York: Lang, 2008.

Yamuchi, Edwin M., and Donald Wiseman. *Persia in the Bible.* Grand Rapids: Baker Academic, 1997.

Yap, Timothy. "The Purpose and Function of the Feast of Tabernacles in Ezra 3." *JETS* 64 (2021) 253–64.

Yarchin, William. "Is There an Authoritative Shape for the Book of Psalms? Profiling the Manuscripts of the Hebrew Psalter." *RB* 122 (2015) 355–70.

———. "Were the Psalms Collections at Qumran True Psalters?" *JBL* 134 (2015) 775–89.

Yaron, Reuven. "On Divorce in Old Testament Times." *RIDA* 4 (1957) 117–28.

Yee, Gale A. "The Anatomy of Biblical Parody: The Dirge Form in 2 Samuel 1 and Isaiah 14." *CBQ* 50 (1988) 565–86.

———. "By the Hand of a Woman: The Metaphor of the Woman Warrior in Judges 4." *Semeia* 61 (1993) 99–132.

———. "'I Have Perfumed My Bed with Myrrh': The Foreign Woman (*'iššâ Zârâ*) in Proverbs 1–9." *JSOT* 43 (1989) 53–68.

Yeivin, Israel. "The Division into Sections in the Book of Psalms." *Textus* 7 (1969) 76–102.

Yoder, Christine Roy. "On the Threshold of Kingship: A Study of Agur (Proverbs 30)." *Int* 63 (2009) 254–63.

———. "The Woman of Substance: A Socio-Economic Reading of Proverbs 31:10–31." *JBL* 122 (2003) 427–47.

Younger, K. Lawson. *Ancient Conquest Accounts: A Study in Ancient Near Eastern and Biblical History Writing.* JSOTSup 98. Sheffield: Sheffield Academic, 1990.

———. "The Deportations of the Israelites." *JBL* 117 (1998) 201–27.

———. "The Fall of Samaria in Light of Recent Research." *CBQ* 61 (1999) 461–82.

Zabán, Bálint Károly. *The Pillar Function of the Speeches of Wisdom: Proverbs 1:20–33, 8:1–36, and 9:1–6 in the Structural Framework of Proverbs 1–9*. BZAW 429. Berlin: de Gruyter, 2012.

Zadok, Ran. "Notes on the Biblical and Extra-Biblical Onomasticon." *JQR* 71 (1980) 107–17.

———. "On the Reliability of the Genealogical and Prosopographical Lists of the Israelites in the Old Testament." *TA* 25 (1998) 228–54.

Zakovitch, Yair. "The Woman's Rights in the Biblical Law of Divorce." *JLA* 4 (1981) 28–46.

Zenger, Erich. "The Composition and Theology of the Fifth Book of the Psalms: Psalms 107–45." *JSOT* 80 (1998) 77–102.

———. *A God of Vengeance? Understanding the Psalms of Divine Wrath*. Translated by Linda M. Maloney. Louisville: Westminster John Knox, 1996.

Zenger, Erich, ed. *The Composition of the Book of the Psalms*. BETL 238. Leuven: Peeters, 2010.

———, ed. *Der Psalter in Judentum und Christentum*. Herder's Biblical Studies 18. Freiburg: Herder, 1998.

Zerafa, P. "Retribution in the Old Testament." *Angelicum* 50 (1973) 464–94.

Zevit, Ziony. "Converging Lines of Evidence Bearing on the Date of P." *ZAW* 94 (1982) 481–511.

Zimmerli, Walther. *Ezekiel 1: A Commentary on the Book of the Prophet Ezekiel, Chapters 1–24*, Translated by Ronald E. Clements. Hermeneia. Philadelphia: Fortress, 1979.

———. *Ezekiel 2: A Commentary on the Book of the Prophet Ezekiel, Chapters 25–48*, Translated by James D. Martin. Hermeneia. Philadelphia: Fortress, 1983.

———. *I am YHWH*. Edited by Walter Brueggemann. Translated by Douglas W. Stott. Atlanta: John Knox, 1982.

———. "Zur Struktur der alttestamentliche Weisheit." *ZAW* 51 (1933) 177–204.

Zucker, David J. "The Prophet Micaiah in Kings and Chronicles." *JBQ* 41 (2013) 156–62.

Zvi, Ehud Ben. "The Account of the Reign of Manasseh in II Reg 21, 1–18 and the Redactional History of the Books of Kings." *ZAW* 103 (1991) 351–74.

———. *Hosea*. FOTL 21A/1. Grand Rapids: Eerdmans, 2005.

———. *Micah*. FOTL 21B. Grand Rapids: Eerdmans, 2000.

www.ingramcontent.com/pod-product-compliance
Lightning Source LLC
LaVergne TN
LVHW100510110826
845146LV00002B/579

* 9 7 9 8 3 8 5 2 4 9 6 2 6 *